MW00628080

We Remember Pearl Harbor

DESTINATION: PEARL HARBOR -- Aboard the carrier Akagi, flagship of Vice Admiral Chuichi Nagumo, a crewman rests in the shade under the wing of a Mitsubishi Zero fighter somewhere in the north Pacific, on the way to Hawaii. (Abel L. Dolim photo collection)

We Remember Pearl Harbor

Honolulu civilians recall the war years
1941 - 1945

Lawrence Reginald Rodriggs

Communications Concepts
Newark, California

Copyright, 1991, by Lawrence R. Rodriggs

All rights reserved. No part of this book
may be used or reproduced without written
permission of the publisher.

Library of Congress Catalog Card Number:
91-73254

Published by
Communications Concepts
35111 Newark Blvd., Suite 19
Newark, California 94560

Printed in the United States of America

Design: Robert Cox
                     Robert Cox and Associates
                     Oakland, California

Type: James B. (Brad) Canutt
                     BGC Enterprises
                     Newark, California

Production: Earl W. Swaney
                     EWS Enterprises
                     Bradenton, Florida

Printed on acid-free paper and meets the
guidelines for permanence and durability
of the Council on Library Resources

ISBN 0-9663739-0-1

This book is dedicated
to my father

Reginald Kaleilani Rodrigues
(1906-1976)

Reginald K. Rodrigues
(Circa 1927)

7:55 a.m.

December 7, 1941

That moment,

when Pearl Harbor

became a time,

not merely a place . . .

TARGET: U.S. FLEET -- In the photo opposite page, two Nakajima torpedo bombers leave death and destruction behind on Ford Island as they return to their ship. The map shows the mooring location of many of the ships on Sunday morning, December 7, 1941. (Photo courtesy of Abel L. Dolim -- Map courtesy of Stan Cohen, taken from his book, "East Wind Rain")

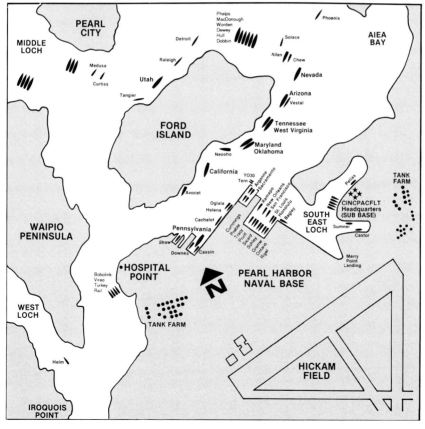

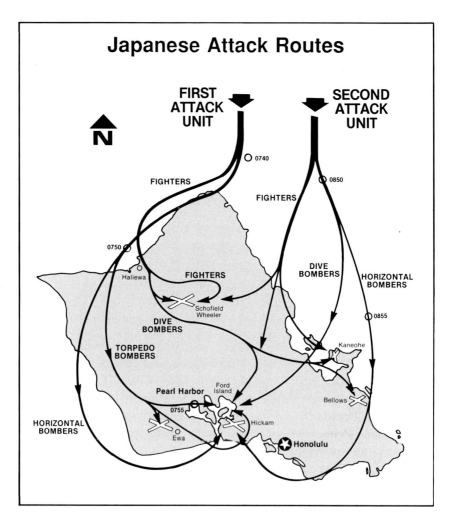

TWO WAVES OF ATTACK — The first attack, at 7:55 a.m., approached Oahu from the northwest side of the island. The second wave, an hour later, came in from the northeast. (Map courtesy of Stan Cohen, taken from his book "East Wind Rain.")

Table of Contents

Pictorial History - *Wartime Topics*

Acknowledgments

This book could not have been possible without the assistance and support of many of my relatives and friends. I am indebted to so many people that it would be impossible to list them all on this page. I apologize to anyone I may inadvertently miss, but I feel I must give it a try, anyway. First, and most importantly, I thank all those individuals who allowed me to use their stories. Their patience and cooperation is very much appreciated. I am particularly thankful to those who helped me find subjects for this book, especially *Dick* and *Joan Rodby* of Honolulu. Others include *Dr. Carol Ann Hall, Virginia Leach, Nettie Boucher*, and *Joe* and *Betty Wrixon*.

Helping me dot the "i's" and cross the "t's" is an effective proofreading team that I also count as special friends: *Bill Hunter, Frank Del Greco, Tom Herbert*, and *Jane Tom*. The patience, understanding, and computer expertise of typesetter *Brad Canutt* helped to get the job done efficiently. In Honolulu, I received especially helpful assistance and cooperation from *Violet* and *Kum Pui Lai, DeSoto Brown, Jeanette Campbell, David Shapiro, Eleanor Au, James Cartwright, Bea Kretschmann*, and *Margaret Souza*. In California, encouragement, interest and help also came from *Sam King, Wil Tom, Marilyn Baggett*, and *Bryant King*.

I am indebted to my son, *Steven Rodriggs*, for offering his photographic skills to my project; and to *Bob Cox*, who contributed many hours of his artistic talents in the overall design of the book and its cover.

I am also very fortunate to count among my friends, *Earl Swaney*--a long-time colleague--who suffered with me through hours, days, and months of planning, brainstorming, and editorializing in the formation of this book. Earl contributed his talents as a production artist, writer, and photographer in helping to make this idea a reality, and I am thankful.

Finally, I am indeed blessed to have a very special companion who gave me not only her love, understanding and encouragement on this project, but also her expertise in research and interview assistance. To my wife and best friend, *Jean*, I am eternally grateful.

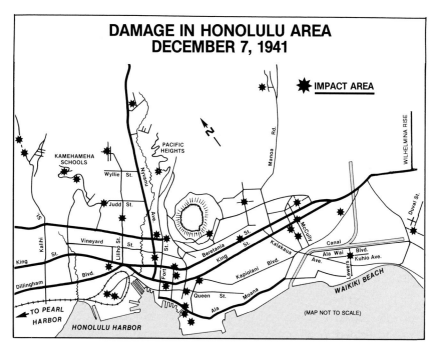

DAMAGE IN HONOLULU AREA
DECEMBER 7, 1941

★ IMPACT AREA

WILHELMINA RISE

Manoa Rd.

PACIFIC
HEIGHTS

Duval St.

KAMEHAMEHA
SCHOOLS

Wyllie St.

Nuuanu Ave.

Judd St.

McCully

Vineyard St.

Liliha St.

Beretania St.

Kalakaua

Canal

Ala Wai Blvd.

Kalihi St.

King St.

King St.

Ave.

Kuhio Ave.

Fort St.

Kapiolani Blvd.

Lewers

Dillingham Blvd.

Queen St.

Moana

WAIKIKI BEACH

TO PEARL
HARBOR

Ala

(MAP NOT TO SCALE)

HONOLULU HARBOR

ACCIDENTS OF WAR -- *Perhaps the most notable of the impact areas on December 7, 1941 was the corner of King and McCully streets, pictured above. The entire block of stores and dwellings were struck by U.S. projectiles that missed their targets and fell on the civilian site. The fires that followed completely destroyed the complex.* (**Star Bulletin** *Dec. 9, 1941; War Depository Collection, University of Hawaii. Map above, courtesy of Stan Cohen, taken from his book, "East Wind Rain.")*

Preface

On Sunday, December 7, 1986, I listened to San Francisco radio station KCBS broadcast a tribute to the servicemen who were killed when Pearl Harbor was attacked forty-five years earlier. As a native-born Hawaiian of Portuguese ancestry, and resident of Honolulu through my high school years, I had vivid childhood memories of that Sunday in 1941, so I listened with great interest. I thought of my father, who experienced firsthand the death and destruction at Hickam Field, that morning, as a civilian volunteer ambulance driver. Even up to 1976, when he died, he had never talked about the experience that left him shell-shocked and terrified. My father was a "Pearl Harbor survivor" who would never share his story.

I had often talked about my recollection of December seventh and the war years with friends and relatives. I probably became more intrigued by the subject because of my father's refusal to discuss it. My fascination was galvanized by the 1986 KCBS commemorative broadcast. That's when I decided to write this book. I enjoyed reading "The Good War," by Studs Terkel, particularly because he wrote an oral history that used an interesting conversational style. That was the conceptual stage for this book.

I bought all the Pearl Harbor books I could get my hands on, and there are many. The most complete documentation of the events in Honolulu beginning with the Japanese attack came from Gwenfread Allen's "Hawaii's War Years," published in 1950. An autographed copy is my prized possession. Until recent years, most of the books written on the subject focused on the military side of the story. I concluded there was another important story to be told, from the civilian point of view. At no time in American history has a group of citizens been subjected to such drastic loss of personal freedom and such stringent military control. I started talking to some of my relatives about what happened to them during the war years in Honolulu, and the book took off from there. While it's true that the passage of time may cloud one's memory, the events that took place beginning at 7:55 that morning are so significant--dramatically affecting the lives of everyone in Honolulu--that most of the people I interviewed had clear, detailed recollections of the incidents.

Many of the stories report somewhat similar situations at the outset of the attack. Most interpreted the early-morning explosions as maneuvers, since military war games were frequently conducted at the time. With the exception of those who were actually at Pearl Harbor at 7:55 a.m., most turned to the radio to learn what was happening. Announcer Webley Edwards used the now-famous phrase, "This is the real McCoy," to alert people to the reality of the report. I was fortunate to be able to include a few of the radio scripts written by Mr. Edwards, which were used when he served as a war correspondent during the war.

Similarly an attitude, expressed by many in this book, is the belief that the Japanese could have occupied the islands, following the attack, if they had landed troops. The fear of imminent invasion was very real during the first few months of the war.

Of the issues raised by people interviewed, perhaps the most prominent is the question of the loyalty of the Japanese civilians in Honolulu. Despite repeated reports that not one case of espionage by locals was ever documented, the rumors that proliferated at the outset of the war furthered the myth. Some people still hold a sincere belief that many local Japanese--even the nisei (second generation Japanese American)--were collaborators or, at least, were in communication with Japan. A case was often built on the fact that many Americans of Japanese ancestry (AJAs) had short-wave radios, without regard to the fact that short-wave radios were commonly used by many in Hawaii to receive programs over long distances.

Plans were discussed to incarcerate the Japanese residing in the islands. These were not carried out--not because the idea was morally questionable--but because the logistics of transporting nearly forty percent of the Hawaiian population were prohibitive. Additionally, the result of such an act would cripple the productive workforce of the islands at a crucial time.

While it may not have been considered an issue early on, the fact that the islands were immediately turned over to the military became a hot political question as time went on. Every facet of civilian life was placed under martial law and civil liberties were abruptly tossed aside under the guise of military necessity to resist the threatened invasion. If that were the case, however, it would seem logical that the civilian government would be reinstated following the Battle of Midway in June 1942, when the threat of invasion was significantly lessened. It lasted in some form, however, until October 1944.

Most civilians in Honolulu dutifully accepted martial law, some out of fear of reprisal, and others in agreement--at least initially--that it was the right thing to do. The media supported the restrictions and encouraged public cooperation. What the Japanese attack did, however, was to mobilize civilians in a common cause to sacrifice whatever possible--including their basic civil rights--to win the war.

A popular misconception of the events that morning resulted in the belief that the attacking airplanes actually dropped bombs on key utility buildings and other civilian facilities. While one accidental incident was considered the result of an enemy bomb, the thirty or so impact areas in Honolulu were the result of our own anti-aircraft shells missing their targets and falling throughout the city, causing death and destruction. To this day, people sincerely believe that the destruction resulted from Japanese bombs. The Japanese accomplished their objective that morning--not to bomb Honolulu--but to cripple the U.S. fleet at Pearl Harbor.

The mass evacuation to the mainland (by ship to California, primarily) following the attack also became an issue. The military regime encouraged such an exodus of women and children, to make available badly needed housing and to ease the food shortage problem. Military dependents were shipped out almost immediately, but civilians were also encouraged to leave the islands if they had relatives on the mainland who would take them in. In most cases, these were "haoles" (white people, residents, but not native to the islands) but they also included many "kamaainas" (native-born). Some of the locals resented the fact that "the haoles ran away" while others took advantage of the situation by purchasing homes, inexpensively, from the haoles.

The stories contained in this book are those of the people featured. I did not attempt to correct any attitude or belief, even when I identified misconceptions. They lived through difficult times, enduring them in different ways. Some ended up in the military. Others served the war effort working in the shipyards, tending the victory gardens, harvesting pineapple and sugar cane, rolling bandages for the Red Cross, donating blood, and obeying their military rulers. This side of the Pearl Harbor story needs to be told. Here it is.

Lawrence R. Rodriggs

September 1991

Civilian Deaths by "Friendly Fire"

The following information is taken from the Fingerprint Cards of deceased war casualties on December 7, 1941, at the Division of Registration, Office of Civil Defense, at the Kawaihao Church basement. These are just a few of the many civilians who were killed that day, not by Japanese bombs, but by shrapnel bursts and projectiles from U.S. shells which missed their intended targets, and by the paranoiac accidents of war. Information shown here is **exactly** as typed on the cards. *(War Depository Collection, University of Hawaii)*

WHITE, Mrs. Willard D. - Age 35, 44 Dowsett Ave., Shrapnel wounds and shock (body intact)

NAGAMINE, Masayoshi - Age 19, from Hilo, employee of Honolulu Rapid Transit, 19 Peleula Lane

ORNELLAS, Gertrude - Age 16, 2707 Kamanaiki (identified by father)

THREE DIE IN PACKARD -- This 1937 Packard sedan was riddled with shrapnel on Judd Street near Nuuanu, where its three passengers were killed on Sunday morning, December seventh. All three, from Heeia, were Pearl Harbor workers answering the call to duty. Driver John Adams, 25, his father Joseph, 50, and passenger Joe McCabe, 43, were all killed by a projectile determined to be "friendly fire." (Star Bulletin Dec. 7, 1941; War Depository Collection, University of Hawaii)

KOBA, James Takao - Age 25, 2209 Young St., both legs amputated; admitted to hospital, died at 2:40 p.m. December 7

KAHOOKELE, David - Age 27, from Kaneohe, Pearl Harbor Badge 01876

ARAKAKI, Nancy Masako - Age 9, 1220 College Walk, killed in air raid

OHTA, Kiyoko (female) - Age 21, King & McCully

CHONG, Patrick - Age 30, 135 N. Kukui St. (Chinese/Hawaiian), laborer at Fort Armstrong

ADAMS, John - Age 25, Heeia, Oahu, (Chi/Hwn) Nuuanu & Judd

ADAMS, Joseph - Age 50, Heeia, Oahu (Pt Hwn), killed at 802 Judd St.

PAIVA, Manuel - Age 55, Kakaako, found off Ft. Armstrong on row boat with gun shot in right chest. Case of US Army

KIDA, Kushi - Age 25, 55 Cunha Lane. Right index finger fresh amputation from bullet -- brot to Sampan Wharf by Navy

OKOJI, Riyoro - Age 56, 1349 River St. - Brought to sampan wharf by US Navy

OGAWA, Mataichi - Age 35, 519 Ohui Ln. - machine-gunned on sampan on high seas - disemboweled also by machine gun

AKANA, James Lum - Age 60? - Chi-Hwn - Fatally assaulted as a suspected parachutist at about 11 p.m. December 7 in vicinity of Jack Lane, Nuuanu - while he was patrolling as a CD volunteer by other CD volunteers -- Died December 8

The Attack:
Its Effect on the People of Hawaii
by George W. Bicknell

The following is an excerpt from a report written by Col. George W. Bicknell, taken from the microfilm files of the Hawaii War Records Depository at the University of Hawaii, Manoa Campus. It was not dated. The full report was entitled "Security Measures in Hawaii During World War II." Col. Bicknell served as director of counter-intelligence for the army when the war broke out. While the stories in this book are accounts by Honolulu civilians, this report is included as it gives an excellent overview of the events that took place prior to and beginning on December 7, 1941, and the weeks that followed, including the general reaction by the civilian population. It is reprinted here by the kind permission of the Colonel's widow, Mrs. Dorothy Bicknell.

The attack upon Pearl Harbor created no widespread hysteria or great fear in its early stages. The people of Hawaii were dazed and bewildered. They moved in a state of shock.

Practically every person on the island of Oahu had been lulled into a sense of false security through the constant reiteration of the belief that the defense of the island made it practically impregnable. Our system of military and naval defenses had long been the subject of various newspaper and magazine articles, with photographs of various installations and many types of late model equipment, and each concluded with the fact that such defenses existed elsewhere only on the Rock of Gibraltar. Frequent military and naval maneuvers, carried out in full view of the public and with the attendant publicity, had brought a sense of pride, security, and might to the people.

In addition, it had been constantly stated that Japan, as a military and naval power, amounted to nothing when pitted against the superior equipment and personnel, and tactics of our own army and navy. Many times it had been stated that the Japanese fleet would be simply and easily annihilated if we started an offensive against them. The marksmanship and maneuvers of Japanese naval units had been observed by many United States naval officers who had actually seen displays of poor judgment, ridiculously inadequate fire power and marksmanship, and had assumed that our apparent superiority gave us tremendous advantages. Little thought was given to the possibility of such displays being provided solely for the purpose of deception.

Little was actually known about Japanese air power although, again, there were many stories of the poor quality of Japanese aircraft, the lack of proper equipment, and the alleged fact that the Japanese made poor aviators and would never be as good as occidentals in this field. Stories of Japanese having such poor vision that their flying ability was hampered, and tales of other physical characteristics which prevented them from ever becoming truly proficient in handling aircraft, were common and many times retold.

While potential dangers had been brought to public attention for months preceding the attack, they still had not registered seriously on the public mind. The Commanding General had repeatedly urged all persons to buy excess staple food necessities in the islands. He had pointed out that should hostilities break out in the Pacific, it was quite possible that supply lines from the mainland would be severed, hence food must be stored against such a crisis. The territorial legislature had been called back into extraordinary session to pass legislation giving emergency powers to the Governor in case of war or threatened attack. All plans were made for air raid protection, necessary police expansion, auxiliary first aid and medical organizations and other emergency procedures.

In spite of all this activity, there were many who felt that the Hawaiian Islands could be adequately and easily defended and, consequently, there was no immediate danger. After all, they reasoned, the islands were invincible even if the extremely unlikely occurred–a Japanese attack on the islands.

The mental groundwork had been laid for consternation, surprise, and bewilderment.

Had the attack occurred on a week-day morning, rather than Sunday morning, the situation would have been more critical. Under normal conditions, the majority of families would have been separated, with husbands at work or enroute to their places of business, children at or near schools with transportation and traffic congestion at its peak. Uncertainty, worry, panic, and hysteria would have made an immediate appearance. Similarly, it would have been more difficult to congregate immediately emergency workers and personnel; the trucks and vehicles which became instantly available as emergency ambulances would have been on their daily routines and employment; and the word of excessive damage and loss of life would have spread much more rapidly.

Another fortunate coincidence would not have occurred on a week-day. On this Sunday morning, all doctors and surgeons of the city had congregated in an auditorium to listen to a lecture on the modern methods of treating war wounds and thus were all available to answer the call for assistance at military and naval hospitals. As it happened, the time of the attack was largely responsible for the expeditious and highly efficient operation of all emergency activities as well as being one of the greatest factors in maintaining order and comparative calm in the community as a whole. The element of surprise, from a military and strategic point of view, was well accomplished but, as far as breaking public morale and spreading confusion and chaos throughout the islands, the timing was distinctly in error.

Because of these factors it is easy to understand that the immediate reaction to the attack was one of incredulous bewilderment. The radio announcer, in making the first announcement of the raid on Pearl Harbor, felt it necessary to include the words, "This is the real McCoy." Even then few believed what they heard. Innumerable individuals, both civilian and military, actually witnessed the attack, heard the explosions,

---

" I saw the civilian population standing in the roads and fields calmly watching this terrific spectacle with no more show of emotion than would be found at a Fourth of July display. "

---

saw the bursts of anti-aircraft shells, and the attacking planes, only to dismiss the subject with the expressed belief that it was simply another very realistic military maneuver. Much difficulty was experienced in calling some military personnel to their stations. They did not believe that they were being correctly informed. Such a thing simply could not happen, and they were extremely hesitant in accepting the reports being given to them.

Watching the attack from the heights behind Pearl Harbor, the writer himself experienced a few seconds of absolute unbelief. It was only the terrific explosion aboard the *Arizona*--the clearly marked Japanese plane wheeling about and dropping a string of bombs on the runway of Hickam Field and again circling back toward the battleships to meet a burst of machine gun fire and fall flaming into the harbor--which finally forced the realization that war had come. Rushing to the telephone, I called headquarters and experienced some difficulty in convincing the officer-of-the-day that we were actually under enemy attack.

Leaving the house and driving to Fort Shafter under a canopy of anti-aircraft fire, I saw the civilian population standing in the roads and fields, calmly watching this terrific spectacle, with no more show of emotion than would be found at a Fourth of July display. While the police radio in my car bellowed forth orders and warnings such as "All regular and auxiliary police report immediately for duty; All firemen proceed immediately to Hickam Field; Explosion in Lewers and Cooke Building." I passed Japanese, Portuguese, Hawaiians, Caucasians; defense workers, gardeners, yard boys, and bankers, all in the same condition--gazing, spellbound by what they saw but unable to realize what it really meant. In town, realism became apparent--fire engines dashing toward Hickam Field and Pearl Harbor and, most indicative of all, the constant stream of regular and emergency ambulances, answering their calls to the duty for which they had long practiced and prepared.

Even among the officers grimly assembled at Fort Shafter, some could not fully realize the meaning and the magnitude of this action. When I informed them that I had seen three battleships apparently sunk by enemy air action, their immediate reaction was absolute unbelief. Such a thing could not happen to Hawaii. Along my return route to Honolulu, the stark disaster became more apparent. Ambulances were emptying capacity loads of wounded who were being ranged on the grass because the receiving rooms of the hospital were already overtaxed. Nurses, doctors, and orderlies filed between the rows of victims, giving emergency aid, entirely disregarding anti-aircraft fire, shell fragments, speeding airplanes, and the sound of bursting bombs. They were performing the duty for which they had been trained for months and years. The realization that the island was under enemy attack had not yet permeated their busy minds.

Within the city, the police, auxiliary police, firemen, emergency committees, first aid organizations, and other such groups were taking up their duties in a quiet, calm, and matter-of-fact manner. It might well have been a gigantic maneuver for many. They handled themselves without fear, hysteria or panic--efficient even in their bewildered state of mind.

Another reason why fear was so noticeably absent during these early hours was that only those who had work to do were in the areas under attack. These included military and naval personnel, emergency crews, defense workers, and others who had been summoned to duty. Action is the best antidote to fear, and many of these people carried on and

---

" . . . much un-evaluated and erroneous information became available to those who listened to the police radio. "

---

performed outstanding services, utterly devoid of any sense of fear. Some of these same people became fearful in later stages when their activities slackened and the full realization of the situation became apparent.

Among the civilian population, relatively few fully realized what was going on. The bombing activities took place in the vicinity of Pearl Harbor, Hickam Field, and Kaneohe Bay, all of which were several miles distance from residential areas and from the city of Honolulu itself. No attacks were actually directed against the city, its waterfront or public utility installations. True, there were a few scattered and highly localized explosions in widely separated areas of Honolulu, but the widespread residential sections were not acutely aware of the seriousness of the situation. There were many individuals and families who did not learn of the attack until the following morning.

During the initial stages, reports and alarms were widely reported by local radio broadcasting stations but within a few hours, the control of these transmitters was taken over by the military, and the announcements curtailed to bulletins directing public action and behavior. Police radio systems were, of course, greatly overloaded with both military and police instructions and many persons soon learned that the material being broadcast on this system was more informative than anything carried by commercial stations. As a result, much un-evaluated and erroneous information became available to those who listened to the police radio.

Another factor which would normally have assisted in dissemination of news was the press. However, one of the two local papers had torn down its presses for repairs after printing the Sunday edition late Saturday night. When the attack came, its plant was entirely out of action, all mechanical manpower had been summoned for emergency duty at Pearl Harbor and Hickam Field, and it was impossible to restore the machines to operating condition. Hence, all news was carried by the one paper, which ran a series of extra editions, but the material contained in these issues was of necessity fragmentary.

As a result of all of these circumstances, the general attitude of Hawaii during the daylight hours of December 7 was largely one of incredulity, bewilderment, and shock. This greatly simplified the handling of the situation. Had conditions been otherwise, organized authorities would have been forced to divert large portions of their personnel to quieting the population and controlling panic rather than devoting their energies to more important and pressing requirements.

At 4:30 p.m., a state of martial law was declared and extremely restrictive measures imposed on all phases of civilian life. Control was established over traffic, press and radio, and all other types of communication. The sale of all alcoholic beverages was suspended and all bars closed. A complete blackout was ordered over all of the Hawaiian islands. Curfew regulations were established, with no enemy alien allowed on the streets between nightfall and dawn. No person not on authorized duty or work was allowed at large between 8:00 p.m. and 5:30 a.m. Police and police reserves were placed under command of the Provost Marshal, and military jurisdiction blanketed the entire area. Thus, Honolulu, in but a space of a few hours, changed from a civilian city to a vast military outpost.

The announcement of all these measures over the radio, as well as radio orders to police to check upon various rumors and false reports, caused fears to begin to develop in the minds of many people. Rumors were born; a trying period began for the organized authorities, which caused serious repercussions in the days, weeks, and months to come. In a period of extreme emergency, the craving for news becomes excessive; if it cannot be satiated with truthful statements. Anything available at the moment will be substituted.

For example, the order to police to investigate reports that parachutists had landed was heard by an individual who transmitted it to his neighbor not as an unconfirmed fact, but as actual occurrence. In turn, it was repeated to others until the rumor had gained such momentum that it could not be stopped, and a general alarm spread to the effect that enemy paratroops had actually landed on the island. At this point numerous people, who saw the top of a cumulus cloud over the mountain ridge, an old white cloth fluttering in a distant tree, or any other sight which stirred their imaginations, spread a new alarm to the effect that they had seen parachutists actually dropping in various localities.

It is not necessary to repeat all of the many wild rumors which originated during the daylight hours of December 7, 1941, and developed as the day wore on. The attack itself and the counter-measures did not bring about any marked degree of fear, but rumor and imagination

> " . . . military jurisdiction blanketed the entire area. Thus, Honolulu, in but a space of a few hours, changed from a civilian city to a vast military outpost. "

did, toward the close of the day. Stories spread that the water supply had been poisoned; that the Japanese fleet was offshore within shelling range of the islands; the city of Honolulu was in flames and being utterly destroyed; hundreds of gliders filled with Japanese soldiers had been seen landing in the cane fields; hills and fields were filled with snipers who were picking off police, defense workers and military personnel. These were some of the rumors which began to run through the population like a brush fire before the wind. By nightfall, fear and uncertainty pervaded Hawaii.

As minds began to work and grasp the significance of the happenings of the day, people began to imagine that perhaps this was but the prelude to a large-scale attempt to capture the islands. Such a possibility appeared real and logical. Troops were manning all defense positions, firing-points and trenches were already being dug near beaches and landing places; artillery, trucks and heavy equipment rumbled through the streets; and announcements were made at frequent periods with reference to blackout regulations to go into effect immediately. With all of these occurrences and stringent restrictions suddenly imposed upon them; confined to their blacked-out homes; under severe nervous tension with the approach of darkness and uncertainty, people began to realize their predicament, and fear and hysteria grew.

Then came flooding back all of the witches' tales of the past--the things which had been talked about at bridge tables, dinners, social gatherings, and other such occasions--namely, what would the local Japanese do should war come to Hawaii. Perhaps the maid would poison the food; the yardman probably would cut some throats; the Japanese garbage collector who had been coming to the door for many years would very likely be prepared to burn the house down over their heads--all these and many, many more ideas became real, living actualities.

As darkness fell, the police began shooting out lights which had been left burning in business establishments, inexperienced guards challenged and fired upon shadows, a machine gun outpost fired bursts at a phantom-like log which was floating in toward the shore.

Throughout the city, lights flashed, some flares were observed, and many reports of signalling to the enemy were received. It became practically impossible to run down and check each individual story. So many proved to be accidental blackout violations, tracer bullets, and other similar occurrences, that it was impossible to ascertain with any degree of certainty whether any systematic attempts were being made to communicate with the enemy. In cases where prowlers were reported, it usually developed that these were people lost in the blackout, telephone or electric power repairmen, or some other persons engaged in a legitimate occupation.

" . . . inexperienced guards challenged and fired upon shadows, a machine gun outpost fired bursts at a phantom-like log which was floating in toward the shore. "

Due to impossible driving conditions, with absolutely no lights allowed on automobiles, the narrow road to Pearl Harbor was soon hopelessly jammed so traffic was suspended until daylight, and large numbers of people slept in cars. This may have provided ground for some of the stories, related at a later day that Japanese sympathizers had blocked the road to Pearl Harbor during the attack early Sunday morning.

At 7:12 p.m. and again at 9:04 p.m., approaching friendly planes were mistaken for enemy aircraft and alarm quickly spread that the island was again under attack. The police radio warned, "All cars turn off your lights; Pearl Harbor is being bombed again." Defense measures were taken and the resultant fusillade of gunfire heightened the population's impression that the Japanese had returned, perhaps in response to the alleged signals.

Intelligence agencies devoted practically their entire manpower for several hours to an attempt to discover some concrete evidence of actual communication with the enemy. Many drastic steps were taken, under military necessity, and some time elapsed before it was ascertained that there was no attack and, as far as could be determined, no communication with hostile forces. There may quite possibly have been some attempted communication but none could be discovered at the time. Proper steps were taken to protect against this potential danger and attention was directed to other more pressing matters.

Throughout the night, reports, rumors, and wild stories came to the counter-intelligence center, each requiring evaluation and check. Many were evidently erroneous but no chances could be taken, and as many as possible were followed through and investigated. Again, nothing definite developed.

The night brought ample evidence of the necessity, from an intelligence angle, of checking, evaluating, and confirming information transmitted in the time of a great emergency. People see, or think they see, some suspicious object, movement, or person; immediately jump to conclusions; and report what they imagine to be taking place. They very rarely confine their statements to actual, basic facts and leave the evaluation to others who are more adequately prepared to draw the conclusions.

Rumor was injected into the situation by reports, made in all seriousness, to the effect that a dog had been heard "barking in code," but no explanation as to whether English or Japanese code was given. A man dropped a lighted flashlight which rolled down a steep hill, with a resulting report that a very slowly oscillating flare had been seen in the neighborhood. Radio transmitters communicating with the enemy were heard in one building. This proved to be the hum of an electrical pump.

A suspect lurking under the tree next to an electrical transformer station developed into the armed guard at that point taking shelter from a passing shower. A red flare seen rising in the sky was nothing more sinister than an uncovered tail light of an automobile climbing a steep hill behind the city. There were innumerable such instances, all based on common sights and sounds, which point out the impossibility of obtaining exact information. Each was interpreted, under the strain of events, into some subversive or enemy act.

Thus the night progressed and all of us began to wonder what tomorrow had in store. Would the Japanese attack at dawn with their fleet and a landing force? There was no sleep--so much to do in so little time--combat forces prepared to meet an attack while intelligence agencies speedily and quietly collected the enemy aliens who were considered potential saboteurs, agents, or dangers to internal security. By midnight, those persons who might act as the leaders of any latent organization of local Japanese were out of circulation. The possibility of organized sabotage or material aid to the enemy had been greatly reduced. Only sporadic or individual action might be expected.

All through the night, trenches were being dug, barbed wire entanglements were erected, while artillery and automatic weapons were emplaced to repel any possible landing attempt. The exhaust of gigantic tractors barked like gunfire and the rumble of large-caliber weapon carriers shook the foundations of homes. Occasionally, red trails of fire arched across the black sky as tracer bullets from some machine gun nest challenged an unknown object offshore. The unextinguished fires at Pearl Harbor and Hickam Field still cast aloft their baleful, dull, red glow which was visible from many parts of the island. Doctors, nurses, and first-aid workers tirelessly continued their merciful endeavors while the number of those heroes who had passed beyond the realm of any human aid continued to increase.

The first gray break of dawn on December 8, 1941 arrived with no salvos of gunfire, either from an attacking force or the defending garrison. People began to move about and traffic on the Pearl Harbor road was disentangled. Workers who had slept, or tried to sleep, in their cars now retraced their way to the navy yard and their work with no thought of going home. With the morning, confidence began to overcome the fear and hysteria of the night, and people became more nearly normal. To those who saw the sun rise and cast golden reflections from the gleaming bodies of reinforcement aircraft, arriving from the mainland, came a vast feeling of relief and the belief that although dangers still existed, we would soon be organized and able to protect the islands. There was the beginning of a satisfactory feeling that the enemy had "missed the boat" in any plan to capture Hawaii.

" All through the night, trenches were being dug, barbed wire entanglements were erected, while artillery and automatic weapons were emplaced to repel any possible landing attempt. "

They had struck a heavy body blow. Our navy and our air forces had been temporarily crippled, but the first replacements were arriving already and we knew that more would follow soon. Each day that the enemy held off would make us that much stronger.

Fortunately, port facilities, power and light generators, and water supply were unharmed, and food supplies for a reasonable period remained on hand. Hawaii had passed through the opening of hostilities, suffered frightful damage to its military and naval equipment, and experienced casualties hitherto unknown to the community, but it had survived. The first night of terror caused by doubt and uncertainty was now past and the future could be faced with more fortitude and confidence.

During the daylight hours that followed, every measure was adopted to strengthen our defenses. Rescue and salvage work was already well in hand and even some damaged equipment had been repaired and placed back in service. Workers, both military and civilian, continued their endeavors and produced results typical of Americans when such a superhuman task is thrust upon them. Traffic and transportation returned to nearly normal while the slightly damaged gas works were being rapidly restored to full operation.

Schools were closed, removing this strain on traffic and safeguarding against casualties in case of another raid. Censorship of communications was beginning to function and, consequently, it was possible for some to communicate with the mainland. Sandbags and barricades were being placed to protect buildings and installations from possible bombs.

Windows were being covered with paper, or painted black, in order that lights might be used inside during the blackout hours. Instructions were issued that all civilians should immediately construct air raid shelters for the protection of their families.

Business, however, was completely disorganized. Military authorities had commandeered trucks, automobiles, engineering and construction equipment and supplies, as well as entire buildings or portions of them for emergency use. Since it was necessary to survey, inventory, and control all foods and necessities of life, a temporary restraint was placed on practically all trade.

With the declaration of martial law, the courts had ceased to function and all violations were to be tried in provost courts which were being organized. The telephone system had been taken over by the military authorities, and all travel between the islands had been completely stopped. Every normal civilian activity that did not in some way aid in the defense of Hawaii and its population had ceased. Everyone became a member of the garrison of a gigantic fortress under siege by an enemy.

As these measures became effective and a part of the life of each individual on the island, it brought emphasis to the fact that a real danger existed and that it might become necessary for all to take part in a final struggle for survival. Many began to think of flight to the mainland. Then came word of enemy submarine activity in nearby waters. Even flight to the mainland became hazardous. Preliminary plans were announced for the prompt transfer of women, children, the sick and aged to California. Some individuals who had not considered evacuation before now became extremely anxious to leave, or to send their families away, and a small stampede to register for available space aboard departing airplanes and ships resulted. As this had been anticipated, it was soon controlled and all were assured of their priorities under proper direction and consideration.

Within a very few days, the local residents became aware of the great damage done to military and naval installations. They also learned of the large number of casualties and of the numerous mass burial services held for deceased members of the armed forces. There was no further doubt of the seriousness of the situation. It was evident that the islands were extremely vulnerable to attack and that preparations for defense were still inadequate. The fact that the Japanese military strategists had not taken immediate and full advantage of their element of surprise by attempting at least commando raids, using submarine or airborne units, afforded an interval during which practically everyone came to realize the extreme vulnerability of the islands to this type of action. As all of these factors became fully understood, a great wave of indignation and anger swept over the people. This reaction, coupled with the knowledge of their complete isolation, brought about a marked change in attitude.

" Working hours were entirely disregarded and individuals labored without rest until exhaustion overtook them. "

A spontaneous desire arose throughout the entire community to do something at once. Defense and emergency workers redoubled their efforts and efficiency. Working hours were entirely disregarded and individuals labored without rest until exhaustion overtook them. Volunteer workers appeared from all walks of life offering their services for anything to which they might be assigned. Organizations such as the Red Cross, Community Service, and blood banks were flooded with applicants for employment. Censorship bureaus, government agencies of all classes, as well as the military authorities were besieged with persons desiring to make a contribution to the task. Such services were offered without recompense and came from all races and classes of the population.

This demonstration continued over a period of several weeks until it became fairly evident that the Japanese military machine had focused its attention toward objectives other than Hawaii. During this interval, the impossible had been accomplished. Reinforcements in both men, material and equipment had flowed into the islands from the mainland, and our chances for beating off a general attack were now fairly even. It may be safely stated that such tremendous strides toward adequate defense could not have been made without such a stimulus.

The most irritating and annoying influence upon the military and civilian population during this entire period, from December seventh onward, was the uncertainty of the attitude of the local Japanese elements. Rumors of their plans and probable intentions ran wild; as a result, fear created by this potential danger reached high proportions. It must be recorded again that this hysterical panic was a result of rumors and false information, and not from any overt act on the part of the local Japanese. As has been officially stated, **there was not a single act of sabotage or subversive activity by any citizen of Japanese extraction either during or after the attack on Pearl Harbor.**

Such rumors developed during the comparatively early hours of December seventh. They continued for many months and spread to the mainland, especially after the arrival of the first evacuees from Hawaii. In the states, they reached an all-time high and presented a most distorted and untrue picture of the situation in Hawaii.

Early stories included the tale that many of the enemy pilots were graduates of local high schools, as demonstrated by their complete familiarity with local landmarks. Others included the story that one aviator who had been shot down wore a McKinley High School class ring. Later, exaggerated tales of sabotage were spread. These included the blocking of traffic on the Pearl Harbor road by Japanese trucks and passenger cars; the appearance on the runway of Hickam Field of a local milk truck with machine guns manned by Japanese who mowed down soldiers and other personnel; a Japanese man wearing his customary kimono seen walking toward Pearl Harbor at the time of the attack, who threw off his kimono, to appear in full uniform as an admiral of the Japanese navy.

Wild stories were circulated of local newspapers carrying large advertisements which contained coded messages addressed to local Japanese, warning them of the attack. There were also "eye witness" accounts of the execution of local Japanese spies by the military.

In the minds of many people, every local Japanese became an enemy agent or saboteur. The fear of this danger not only infected the civilians at large, but also took root in the minds of some military and naval personnel. Desire for revenge upon any and all individuals of Japanese blood was freely expressed. These expressions ranged from wishing to shoot each Jap on sight to devising the most lingering form of death. These false stories created a fear of the local Japanese that became greater than the fear of the armed forces of Japan. The flame was fed by reports from the mainland of severe action being taken against the Japanese on the West coast. Public hue and cry was raised for evacuation of all Japanese from Hawaii. Where they were to be sent and how they were to be transported was immaterial, but they must be evacuated immediately.

Wholesale evacuation of Japanese already had been fully considered by military authorities and found impractical. A restudy, based on the current situation, reached the same conclusion that such an action was unnecessary and incompatible with military plans and requirements. The record of handling the Japanese problem in Hawaii . . . represents an application of all the principles of democracy and common sense for which Americans live and die. The story of this accomplishment should remain a bright spot in the history of the United States, and the people of Hawaii, through their final reasonable acceptance of these solutions, are largely responsible for this achievement.

At the end of the war, Col. Bicknell was selected to head the Veterans Administration offices in Hawaii. He served in that capacity from 1945 until his retirement in 1963. He died in 1967 at the age of seventy-four.

Martial Law Declared

On December 7, 1941, Governor Joseph B. Poindexter declared martial law in the territory and turned over the governmental responsibilities to the Commanding General of the Hawaiian Department, Lt. Gen. Walter C. Short. There followed hundreds of "General Orders" that, overnight, changed the American form of government in the islands to that of a military government, providing stringent control over the civilian population. These included arrest and detention of citizens without bail, and trial without jury in criminal cases. With the force of law, these military orders imposed regulations on schools, foodstuffs, traffic, the possession of currency, the censorship of the media, the censorship of the mails, and monitoring of personal telephone conversations. Martial law in Hawaii has been called the only true fascism ever to exist on American soil. It lasted until October 1944. *(Allen, Hawaii's War Years)*

MILITARY GOVERNOR -- Lt. Gen. Delos C. Emmons became the "military governor" on December 17, 1941, after Gen. Short was dismissed. Gen. Emmons held that powerful position until June 1, 1943. He is shown here addressing civilians over radio station KGU. (Honolulu Advertiser; War Depository Collection, University of Hawaii)

Hester Adams Rego

Her family was from Molokai. Her mother was Hawaiian and her dad was Scottish, Irish and Dutch. He was a direct descendant of John Quincy Adams, and came to the islands with the Army in 1914. Hester was their second child of ten (five boys and five girls). Primary school years were spent in Haleiwa and Waipahu, Oahu and at Kaunakakai on Molokai. She attended Kamehameha School from the seventh grade and graduated in 1940. She spent a year at the University of Hawaii and six months at the Queen's Hospital School of Nursing, while working part-time for the telephone company. She was nineteen at the outbreak of war.

After high school, I went to the University of Hawaii and took a pre-nursing course. Then, in September of 1941, I went to Queen's Hospital as a student nurse. I worked part-time at the Mutual Telephone Company. On the weekends, I worked eight hours. I worked Friday evenings from four to midnight. On Sundays, I worked from six to ten in the early morning. It was quite a schedule but I didn't have anything else to do.

The telephone company was on Alakea Street, downtown between Beretania and Hotel, right next door to the Central YMCA. On December seventh, I got to work at six o'clock in the morning. The telephone company had four stories. It was one of the tallest buildings in Honolulu at the time.

I remember they were remodeling the building and we were on the third floor. And the wall back of the switchboard was gone. There was no wall there at all while they were working on it. It was very frightening, because while we were sitting at the switchboard, we looked out and could see these planes going overhead and dropping bombs at Pearl Harbor. While sitting there, they dropped two bombs in our area. One was supposed to hit us at the telephone company and one was supposed to hit the Hawaiian Electric Company. But they missed by a block.

When the bombs exploded, all of us were lifted out of our chairs. That's how close it was. It was very frightening. Very scary. I remember one little girl (an operator) wet her pants, she was so scared. It was a miracle that they didn't bomb any of the buildings.

Hester Adams Rego (continued)

The bomb directed at the electric company fell in the Iolani Palace grounds. There was this big hole there. They eventually filled it up. The one for the telephone company fell where Royal School is, up on Emma Street. But we felt the one near the Hawaiian Electric.

We even saw the red insignia on the bottom half of the planes. Except for those two bombs, they all held their bombs to drop on Pearl Harbor, Hickam Field, Fort Kamehameha, and those places.

In those days, we had what was called radio telephone service. You'd talk to the neighbor islands on a radio circuit. And we had to close down that morning, because that was how the Japanese planes were coming in--the signals from the telephone company and from the radio station. So they closed down those inter-island circuits. But the circuits to San Francisco were still open.

We worked twelve hours that day before we were relieved. And we couldn't go home. We had to stay at the telephone company. The army brought in all these cots and mattresses and blankets and what-not, and set up like a dormitory on the same floor that we were on. And we slept there.

*HALT, WHO GOES THERE? -- Armed guards, standing behind the sandbag sentry box, check all entrants to the Mutual Telephone Company building, a vital communications spot in the war effort. Note the lack of light globe covering on right pillar. The light was not used, anyway, as nights were blacked out. (**Star Bulletin** Jan. 2, 1942; War Depository Collection, University of Hawaii)*

We got up the next morning and some of us had to go back to work to relieve the other operators that were on over night. Some of us were sent home to pick up our stuff. When we went to leave the building, we had to open our purses and the MP's frisked us, to see that we weren't taking anything out that we shouldn't have. Then they put two or three of us in a jeep and they drove us home and waited outside while we went in and got our clothes and things. Then they drove us back to the telephone company.

We all had to live there. There were about sixty of us. The telephone company fed us, you know. We didn't have to worry about that. We had showers. We just went to sleep, had something to eat, and went to work. Eventually, they set up a cafeteria in the basement and we could go down there and get our meals. And it was about two weeks before they finally let us go home.

I went back to school, and they called me at Queen's Hospital and offered me a dollar-an-hour to go to work permanently at the telephone company--and I took it! And my mother--my poor mother--was so upset. She was very upset. If you knew my father, you'd understand why. My father felt that a girl with an eighth grade education was fine. My mother, being a school teacher, disagreed. She was very disappointed in me.

Most of the calls to the neighbor islands, like I say, were shut off during the attack. But we used a scrambler so that anyone listening in couldn't understand what was being said. And, most of the calls came from Fort Shafter to San Francisco and on to Washington D.C.--the trans-Pacific and the inter-island line. The local calls had no plugs, just buttons. You dialed zero and waited for an empty space. Sometimes you waited half-an-hour or so before you could get an operator.

The old plugs were on those trans-Pacific and inter-island boards. And, ours was the first telephone company in the United States to get dial phones and to use the automatic switchboard. This was even before December seventh.

My father worked for the telephone company. My oldest sister also worked for the telephone company. I have three brothers and their spouses who worked for the telephone company. At the time, the telephone company was run like a family. So most people who were employed were related.

They arranged shifts--and those of us who worked until midnight or until ten o'clock at night, were transported home in taxis. The telephone company paid for it. Each operator had a pass so that she could be out after seven o'clock at night. About a month or so later, we all had rotating shifts, so we weren't all working nights. Everybody took a turn.

And I remember working for two years before I got a day off. So it was every day that we were working--and at a dollar an hour. Oh boy! That was a lot of money in those days.

We eventually got telephone censors. The navy handled the trans-Pacific and overseas calls. And the army handled the inter-island calls. And, to begin with, the telephone operator monitored the call--she handled it. And I remember what we would say, "Your conversation must be in English. If it isn't, we'll cut you off." They couldn't talk in their native tongues. They had to talk in English. And the Japanese, especially, were so distressed. They had to speak in English and some of them had a difficult time.

" . . . the Japanese were so distressed. They couldn't talk (on the telephone) in their native tongue . . . and some of them had a difficult time. "

I was living on Spencer Street, 910 Spencer Street, up in the Punchbowl area--near Robert Louis Stevenson School and the Phillips Commercial School. I was between the two schools.

My oldest sister and I shared an apartment. My family was on Molokai, except for my sisters Marie and Jo. They were in school at Kamehameha. And it was two weeks (after the attack) before they were able to send them home to Molokai.

My brother John worked for the Hawaiian Dredging Company. He was at Midway. He was out there working for Dillingham Brothers. They were dredging the entrance to the harbor. This was on the ninth of December. And my folks were notified that he was missing. The notification came to the telephone company because my father worked there. The part of the dormitory that John lived in at Midway was blasted away when the Japanese attacked.

VICTORY POSTERS -- Winners in the school poster contest for the Honolulu Community and War Chest pictured with C. W. Turner, chairman of the publicity committee are (L to R) Pamela McCarty, first prize winner, Betty Ellis, second prize, Marcella Kaopua, Florence Akina and Marie Adams, honorable mention winners. (Marie Adams is the sister of Hester Adams Rego). (Star Bulletin Oct. 26, 1943; War Depository Collection, University of Hawaii)

And then, we didn't hear anything else for about ten days. Then John came home. He just showed up. He said that he just happened to be playing cards at the other end of the dormitory when they attacked. He was just lucky. He doesn't talk about that. I guess, like so many others, he just wiped the scene from his mind. He was seventeen, going on eighteen at the time.

We had to pack gas masks and a helmet with us every day--the kind of helmet the men wore in the first World War--olive green with a chin strap. The gas mask was one of those you put over your head. It had a canister on the bottom. You could suffocate in it, if you didn't know how to use it. It's a good thing I never had to use it. Going shopping, going downtown, whatever, we had to carry them with us.

I remember they took pictures for IDs. We had to wear these big old badges. They took our finger prints. They gave us a card, an identification card, plus this badge, and then, a special pass to be out after curfew.

About two months later, this naval ship was delivering cargo to Molokai--the *S.S. Frank*, I think it was. And as it came out of the harbor going to Maui, one of those little Japanese submarines sunk it--right off the island of Molokai. They sent these one or two-man submarines from their ships. They were called the kamikaze type. They didn't care if they died or not.

And then, one night, one of their planes dropped a bomb above Punchbowl. The air raid alarm sounded and my sister got up and ran out the door. I just turned over and faced the wall and said I'm not going to go. She got very upset at me. I finally went with her down to the shelter. That happened in February or March 1942.[1] There were several of those--that type of hit and run kind of tactic. But those little submarines--there were a lot of them in the waters off of the islands.

I remember you stood in line for everything. In fact, lines attracted people--you would wonder what they were selling--so you waited in line to find out.

My friend, Amy Jones, and I were downtown one day, on River Street. We were going to meet her brother, who was a policeman. We noticed this long line that came around the corner. Since we were early, we joined the people to see what it was we were waiting for. We were just curious. We were both about twenty years old at the time, I think. We didn't pay any attention to the giggles of the servicemen in line ahead of us. When we moved a couple hundred feet around the corner, Amy's brother came by, in his police uniform, and was very upset with us.

"What the blankety-blank are you doing here?" he yelled. We were shocked when we were told that we were in the "red light" district, and then understood the reaction of the guys waiting in line with us.

Those were interesting times. I remember my brother and sister, Dick and Irma, came down from Molokai to go to school in Honolulu. So for two years, I had a younger brother and sister to look after, too.

My mother used to send us care packages. We looked forward to those. It was hard, on Oahu, to get beef or pork. Somebody would come around and say, "Hester, Kaimuki Market is selling hamburger." And Irma and Dick would go together to see if they could get some of this hamburger, or chicken, or whatever, but somebody had to know it was

---

[1] *On Wednesday, March 4, 1942, at 2:15 a.m. two Japanese amphibious bombers unsuccessfully attacked Honolulu. Hampered by cloud conditions, the pilots dropped bombs harmlessly on Mt. Tantalus and in the ocean. The planes flew from the Marshall Islands and were refueled by submarines.*

there. When my mother sent this package, she always had a roast and some steaks in it. She never sent vegetables because we could usually get them.

> *" . . . it just felt great that I could be doing something for my country. "*

We used to have milk delivered from Hind Clarke Dairy and because we were single and didn't have any children in our house, we were asked to stop taking milk. They felt the children needed it more than the adults did.

Oh dear, I haven't talked about this for ages. I was nineteen years old and, to me, it just felt great that I could be doing something to help my country. And, you know, I think we all felt that way.

Hester Adams married Bob Rego in 1945. They had three children, all married and now living on the mainland. Hester had various jobs while raising the family in Honolulu and in Turlock, California, where they lived for twenty-seven years. She retired after ten years at Castle Air Force Base, Merced County, California. They have six grandchildren, all girls. Hester and Bob are both enjoying the slower pace of retirement life in Hilo, Hawaii.

Censorship is Imposed

Army and navy censors were on the job at telephone, radio, and cable companies within two hours after the attack. They instructed radio announcers: "All eyewitness stories are out . . . all detail of places are out . . . don't mention or speculate on size of attack." They moved into newspaper offices, and they were soon reading the mail at the post office. Experts in various fields examined mail that might be expected to have specialized or technical information in it. A heavily bonded and rigidly supervised unit handled all registered mail. Besides statements of military activities, the censors refused to pass such things as bills of lading which showed the dates and names of ships, blueprints, scribblings of children, and young love's rows of XXXs. Letters reached their destination bearing holes where offending words had been carefully cut out, the envelopes resealed with censor's tape. *(Allen, Hawaii's War Years)*

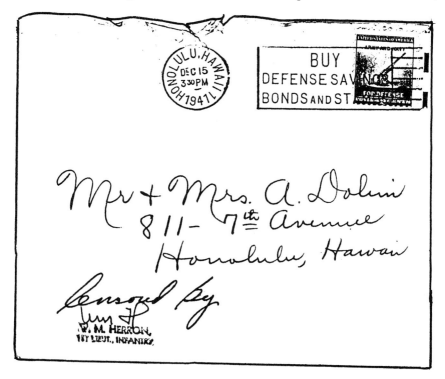

"CENSORED" — *This letter was received by Mr. and Mrs. Augustine Dolim, of Kaimuki, in the first few weeks of the war. Note the censor's stamp and signature. (Abel Dolim collection)*

Yoshiji Aoki

His father, Shosaku Aoki, was born in Japan and was a soldier in the Japanese army in Manchuria for about six months at age eighteen. The following year, 1906, he came to Hawaii as a contract laborer on the plantation. Yoshiji's mother, Kiyo Fukuda, was born in Waianae, Oahu, and worked as a maid for the plantation manager there. Because Shosaku couldn't stand plantation work, the manager hired him as a groundskeeper at his home. So Shosaku and Kiyo met, married, and had seven children, four boys and three girls. Yoshiji was the second oldest, born in 1920, in Aiea. The Aoki family lived at Fisherman's Camp, right at the edge of Pearl Harbor. Yoshiji was schooled at Aiea School and entered Farrington High School in 1936, the year the school opened. He graduated from Farrington in 1939, in the first graduating class. He had hoped to go on to college, but his family was very poor. Yoshiji went to work for Takeo Sato Reinforcing, where he became a reinforcement steel worker.

Although we were on a seven-day work week, doing reinforcement steel work at Pearl Harbor, for some reason I wasn't at work on December 7, 1941. We could hear these explosions and shells, but at first we didn't think it was any kind of conflict. Maneuvers were quite frequent in those days, so we didn't think too much about all that racket.

But, quite suddenly, a dive bomber was hit over Pearl Harbor and came toward the hills, probably flying only about two hundred feet off the ground. He came right over us, a Mitsubishi dive bomber, with a gunner in the back staring down at us. The rising sun was evident on the wings. I knew it was the real thing.

I immediately went back into the house and turned on the radio. I heard the announcer saying that this was not maneuvers, that this was the real thing and we were at war with Japan. I felt scared. Being only twenty-one, though, I didn't really realize the impact this event would eventually have on all of our lives. I thought of my father. At that time I'm sure that his allegiance was to Japan. I know it was traumatic for him.

The elders of the village came running by, asking everybody to evacuate the area, to retreat to the hills. So we all started toward the hills, while the explosions from Pearl Harbor became deafening.

Suddenly someone said, "How about Mr. Yamamoto?" We had

forgotten an elderly man, wheelchair bound, who was paralyzed from the waist down for several years. So I volunteered to leave the group and run back after him. When I got to his home, I yelled his name. I opened his door, and there he was, sitting in his wheelchair across the living room. He must have heard the bombing and maybe he knew from the radio that we were at war with Japan. His face was pale and he looked like he was in a state of shock. He didn't say anything. I told him, in Japanese, that we had to evacuate the area and that I came back to get him. With that he lunged forward, and as God is my witness, he got out of his chair and walked twenty feet across the living room, grabbed my arms with a strong grasp, and collapsed in my arms. I look at it as a miraculous event. I can still sort of feel that strong grasp as he grabbed me. He never walked again.

So we all evacuated the area and walked toward the hills. I don't recall anything significant about what we did when we got there. I know that we came back later that day, because we were home again that night.

I do recall something that seemed rather comical at the time. A few hours after the main attack was over, a flight of B-17s flew over the Pearl Harbor area toward the Schofield Barracks area, accompanied by what seemed like fighter cover. These smaller planes were Japanese, and they apparently were using the B-17s as a shield. The naval gunners were firing, but their anti-aircraft shells were exploding about half-way to the planes, their fuses way too short.

After the war was over, I read in the paper some de-classified information about this particular flight of B-17s. They were being ferried over from the mainland U.S., and to save weight, all their armament was removed, so they couldn't fire on the Japanese planes. Since this flight of B-17s was expected, when an American radar unit picked up the Japanese attacking force, they assumed it was the B-17 flight, so they shut down their radar and went for breakfast, some miles distant, because the radar unit was operating in the mountains. I have often wondered what might have been the outcome had these events not coincided.

I remember I slept very fitfully that night of December seventh. Several times during the night, we heard more firing from Pearl Harbor. I think there was another small attack that evening. There was a lot of shooting. But I didn't think about an invasion at that point.

My older brother, Robert, was drafted the year before, so he was in the Territorial Guard. They sent him out to stand guard in the

Waimanalo area. He later told me that a Japanese submarine had run aground out there when he was there.

I thought about my father. I know it was traumatic for him to know that his children were not in support of Japan. When we were born, we were all registered as citizens of Japan. So we all had dual citizenship, American as well as Japanese. At some point, though, we renounced our Japanese citizenship. I don't really remember when that was, I think it was when we were teenagers. Our Japanese priest was the one that actually helped us do that. My father was hurt by that, but, I guess in some ways, he let us do what we wanted. My mother's allegiance was to my father.

My father prized a samurai sword, a family heirloom, that had been passed down through the generations. His ancestors were samurai warriors. I guess my father figured that if he were caught with the samurai sword, it would have been confiscated. So he buried it that day, on December seventh. He didn't retrieve it until 1945, after the war was over. But by that time, it was all rusted.

Funny thing, though. My father served in the Japanese army in Manchuria, was a Japanese citizen with allegiance to Japan, but he was never called in for any kind of interrogation.

" This marine . . . pointed the rifle at me and told me if I stepped out of line again, he would shoot me. "

I had an experience the following day that I shall never forget. Monday morning, December eighth, I went back to work at Pearl Harbor. We all reported to our job site at seven in the morning, as usual, without any incident. Then, a group of armed marines came by and rounded us all up. Most of us were Japanese Americans. They had us line up and they marched us out of Pearl Harbor. About a half mile from the gate, I stepped out of line. This marine came up to me, he pointed the rifle right at me, and he told me if I stepped out of line again, he would shoot me. I think he meant it. He looked very nervous and he had a loaded gun, too. He really scared me. When we got to the gate, where our cars were parked, some of us fell out of line to go to our cars. We were ordered back in line, then we were marched about another mile past the

27

gate and parking lot. Then we were let go and told to go home and not to come back to Pearl Harbor. We didn't know what it was all about. They probably thought some of us were spies or something. Within a week, we got word that we could go back to work, because the jobs we were doing were considered vital to Pearl Harbor. I worked there until early 1943.

I remember the curfew, the rationing, the blackout, and the bomb shelters. We built a bomb shelter in our yard. We took things as they came. We obeyed orders. We didn't question authority. That's the Oriental way, I think. But I don't think we suffered much. I don't think life was so unbearable during those times.

There was a call for volunteers for the army. It was through word of mouth in Fisherman's Camp. We had a draft board in our village and they held a meeting for all those of draft age. I had resolved that I would do it, if I had the chance. So I attended the meeting. After the meeting, I came home and I told my parents that I had decided to volunteer for the 442nd, and that quite a lot of us were doing it together. My older brother was already in the 100th Infantry, and, in later years, our younger two brothers would also serve in the army--all four Aoki boys. So I volunteered, and my father didn't try to stop me.

We were sent to Camp Shelby, in Mississippi. We were in training for over a year there. I remember once, during my time at Camp Shelby, some of us went over to visit a Japanese-American relocation camp in Arkansas. Of course, we were all in uniform. But they still stopped us. They even searched us. And we were wearing the same uniforms they were. But then, again, we went along with it. We didn't question it at that time. We allowed them to search us before we entered the camp.

Although I personally didn't know anyone in camp, there were many members of the 442nd who had relatives in these relocation camps, and their visits led to visits by those without relatives. For about three days, we were treated as royally as possible, everyone sharing their rations with us. Their lot didn't seem too different from ours, living in tar-paper barracks and all. I remember that on departure, each of us received a Japanese picnic lunch since the bus ride back to camp was about eight hours.

In retrospect, I feel that this kind of visit was encouraged by the higher-ups, perhaps to allay our fears about conditions in the relocation camps, and also for the internees to receive reassuring news about the

American-Japanese soldiers.

We were sent overseas in 1944, leaving from Newport News. We stopped at Sicily, then continued on to Naples. We stayed in a place called Bagnoli, near Naples, for two or three weeks before we were put on landing ships and taken to Anzio. We had further training in a place called Civitavecchia, then we were sent into battle in June 1944.

I was on the front line and saw action. Very little action, unfortunately, because I was wounded on the second day of the battle. I was hit by a fragment of an artillery shell on my left shoulder. So I was put in a hospital in Italy for about a month. I then asked to join my outfit, but my outfit had already gone up to Marseille, in France. So I hitched a ride up on a landing craft and I joined my outfit in Marseille. We continued on and I saw more action in France.

Near the German border, in a French town called Bruyeres, I was wounded for the second time. I was behind this hill and we were preparing to move up. There was a "tree burst"[1] and one of the big fragments caught me on the head. It cracked my helmet right in the middle. I am one hundred percent sure that if it wasn't for my helmet, I'd be dead. It was that hard a blow. Another small segment caught me in the back, but I wasn't hospitalized.

" I was on the front line and saw action. . . I was wounded on the second day of the battle. "

On November 3, 1944, I was wounded for the third time just after our unit rescued the "Lost Battalion" of the Texas 34th Division. I took a bullet in the right shoulder. The doctor who operated on me said that if the bullet had been one-fourth of an inch nearer my bone, it would have shattered my right shoulder. I was very lucky. Other than being a little stiff, with some aches and pains, and a small V.A. disability compensation because of my wounds, I only have three purple hearts to show for my army service. Oh, I also have my Good Conduct Medal.

---

[1]*The shell detonated when it hit a tree, rather than the ground, spreading shrapnel over a greater area.*

29

The rescue of the Lost Battalion is my most vivid memory of my army service, and I have often relived both the good and bad memories of the rescue. I was privy to the actual rescue because I was the scout for our platoon which made first contact. I remember as I neared the first foxhole, a 34th Division soldier stood up, saw we were Americans, and ran towards me. I naturally thought he was glad to see me, and I suppose he was, but he ran past me to a dead German officer about seventy-five feet from his hole. He took a Luger pistol from the body and said to me that he had been waiting for three days and nights for the pistol. I was bitter at his selfishness because some of my buddies had been killed rescuing him, including my best friend. But my bitterness somehow disappeared when I made a trip to Texas in 1975 and met some of the 34th Division veterans. It seemed that everyone, not just the veterans, knew about the Lost Battalion and its rescue. Veterans of the 442nd Regimental Combat Team are honorary citizens of Texas.

" Suddenly, a guy from another platoon jumped out of his foxhole firing his Thompson sub-machine gun, and yelled, 'Let's go!' "

The morning after the rescue, I saw the bravest act of my lifetime. The Germans had reinforced their forces during the night, and as we started toward our next objective, they opened intense fire. I guess all the others were cowering in their foxholes, as I was, afraid to make a move. For a while it seemed like **we** were going to be the "Lost Regiment." Suddenly, a guy from another platoon jumped out of his foxhole firing his Thompson sub-machine gun, and yelled, "Let's go!" That was the spark we needed, and we drove the Germans back. It so happened that this GI and I were in the same group coming back to Hawaii, so I made a special effort to get to know him. Back in Hawaii, we became best friends.

I got out in 1945, near the end of the war. I remember it was a long way home, coming back. I started out in January and didn't really get home until June, shunted from one camp to another. I remember Marysville, California, then up to Seattle, Washington, then back to San Francisco, then finally back to Hawaii. I was in a camp by Punchbowl for several months before discharge. My younger brother served in the occupation forces in Japan. My youngest brother served briefly, in Hawaii.

I was home on VJ day, Victory over Japan in August 1945. Some of my friends and I got together and we were celebrating the end of the war. My father's allegiance was still with Japan and he got angry and ordered us out of the house.

He had always thought of going back to Japan, again, to settle. He did take a trip later, as he still had many relatives living there. But when he came back, he said he wouldn't care to see Japan again because it had changed so much. It wasn't the way he remembered it. He had many good memories of his youth in Japan, and it had changed so much. Hawaii was his home.

My older brother, who was with the 100th, was wounded also. When we were wounded in action, officers would come to our home and notify our parents, personally, that we were wounded but we were doing all right. My parents knew that that would not be the norm if we were living in Japan. The fact that we both received compensation for our wounds also impressed them. My father had said that in Japan, if you were wounded or died in the army, it was meant as a service to your country and you would not expect any compensation. He was also impressed that I had the GI Bill available to help me attend college. He died in 1978, a changed man, and I can't help but believe, an American.

When I look back now, I feel that my life took a dramatic turn beginning on that Sunday morning in 1941. I had really thought that I may be able to go on to college after high school, but of course, we were poor so I started reinforcing steel. Because of the GI Bill, I went to the University of Hawaii after the war and graduated with a teaching certificate.

There's another very positive thing the war did for me. I would not exchange my wartime experience in the 442nd for anything, because of the lifelong friendships I gained. Some of my best friends are 442nd buddies, from Seattle, San Francisco, Los Angeles, and Hawaii. I trusted my life to them and I can never forget them. Some of the people I served with went into the political arena and did very well. I know for a fact that our participation in that well-publicized fighting unit of Japanese Americans gave them that opportunity. It never would have happened otherwise.

Yoshiji Aoki married Betty Hiraoka in 1948, while he attended the University of Hawaii. They have three children, two daughters and a son. He retired from teaching at the elementary level after twenty-eight years, the last twenty-six years at Manoa School, near their home. Yoshiji and Betty's children have given them seven grandchildren, four girls and three boys. In retirement, Yoshiji volunteers his time for the Disabled American Veterans, helping out with the groundskeeping, and he delivers meals to shut-ins with the Meals on Wheels program. He serves as president of the Manoa Community Garden organization--at this writing he has held that position for nine years. And, of course, he actively participates in the 442nd veterans club events.

Violet Lai

Violet Lau Lai (Mrs. Kum Pui Lai), a fourth generation Chinese-American, was twenty-five and the mother of one-year-old Alma at the outset of the war. The family lived at 1037-C Seventh Avenue in Kaimuki. The couple agreed with the President's wife, Eleanor Roosevelt, that "The home was the first line of defense...that the war is won or lost at home." Instead of taking a defense job, Violet was a full-time housewife, tending to Alma and a "victory garden," and she did some free-lance writing. Her daily column, written for the Office of Civilian Defense, "We Women," appeared in the Honolulu Advertiser *in August 1942.*
(Photo by Barbara Bennett Peterson)

Kum Pui and I were living on Seventh Avenue, close to Pahoa and Harding. We were in the back house, down the driveway. We just had the one daughter, Alma, who was a year old at the time.

I remember that day. I just couldn't believe that we heard this radio announcer saying that we were at war, that Japan had attacked us. I remember that my sister, Marion, who was about thirteen or so then, came over on her bicycle. She came from Mokihana Street, about six or seven blocks away, to inform us that war was on. I asked her to go home--she wasn't supposed to be on the streets--according to the radio announcements.

" So we all slept in the living room. We had . . . kitchen knives . . . next to us to defend ourselves in case we were attacked. "

And I remember meeting a neighbor, June Ades, whom I had hardly spoken to before. She was a young navy wife, about eighteen. Her husband, Bill, was called to sea right away. So that night, I invited her to stay with us. She was very relieved to do that.

So we all slept in the living room. My husband and I, the baby, and our neighbor. I kept shoes on Alma in case we had to run. We had picked up all our kitchen knives and put them next to us to defend ourselves in case we were attacked. Being together, we could have moral support, I suppose, and defend ourselves with our blunt kitchen knives.

I took a piece of cloth and wrote in indelible pencil, "Alma Yuke-lin Lai," and her birth date, "born November 25, 1940, daughter of Violet and Kum Pui Lai." And I sewed it to her undershirt. She wore that throughout--I don't know how many--days and weeks. I kept taking it off and putting it back, when I washed the undershirt. I thought we might get lost in the shuffle, you know.

We expected an invasion. You expect the worst. Then we started to buy food, quickly. Run to the store and get canned goods, rice, and so on. Pretty soon there were lines for this and lines for that. Lines for fresh meat, vegetables, yardage goods, everything we had to stand in line for. Then we started growing a victory garden--that's what we called it--victory garden. I remember we had some lettuce growing because my neighbor gave me some lettuce seedlings--dry-land taro, too. I remember we also called hamburger "victory steak."

Then we were told to paint our windows black. We did. And we had to paint the headlights of our car black, except for an opening the size of a dime. Except for an emergency, we were not allowed to drive at night at all.

In fact, in 1943, when my son Morris was born, we called the police station to let them know that I had to go to the hospital. They took our number down. We had to drive at ten miles an hour at night. There were no street lights, just those dim lights from the automobile. We could hardly see anything, it was so dark. We did get to the Queen's Hospital, but the darn kid didn't come that night. Everybody else went into labor and I was just sitting there, waiting. I must have taken some prune juice, or something that gave me false labor pains.

And that night cost us--I think it was $9.50 for a semi-private room. That was a lot of money those days. So Kum Pui picked me up the next day. We came home, and the doctor told me the next time I got labor pains, "We're going to give you castor oil." Morris was born about two weeks later, fortunately without the nasty-tasting oil.

My husband was thirty-one at the time. He was executive secretary of the Tuberculosis Association in Honolulu. That was the Christmas Seal organization, located at Palama Settlement. He was in health work, so he wasn't called into the service. It was considered very important in the war effort. He organized sheltered workshops for ex-patients, and he started the use of portable X-ray machines, with buses going here and there to X-ray persons for early detection of tuberculosis.

We all carried gas masks and little Alma had this horrible smelling chemical thing they called the bunny mask which had little bunny ears. Every time I put it on her for a drill, she would tear it off. She couldn't stand the smell. It contained an awful chemical smell like formaldehyde.

Then later on, since the child wouldn't use it, I would take one of these women's sanitary napkins and put something--I forget what it was-- baking soda or something, on it. It was a little more portable. Wherever she went, she had to carry her mask in a pouch with a strap hanging

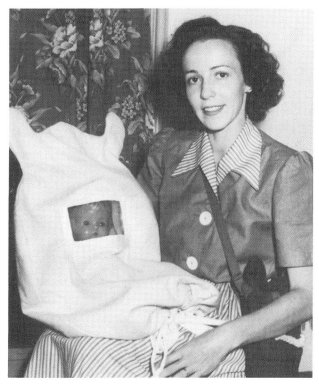

THE INFAMOUS BUNNY MASK -- This protective blanket with plastic peep hole, nicknamed the bunny mask, was devised to be used for infants in the event of gas attack. They usually caused the youngsters to rebel loudly and were frequently discarded. Perhaps this is why this publicity photo included a doll rather than a real live baby. The woman, who was not identified, has her gas mask dutifully hanging around her neck. (Hawaii State Archives photo)

over her shoulder, and I carried my military-issue mask when we went shopping or whenever we left the house.

I remember our first Christmas party. A neighbor family, the Lams, invited us to a Christmas party. It was quite exciting to go there. They had cookies, cakes, sandwiches. It was a very simple party, but oh, so nice. Every once in a while, when we couldn't stand the stuffiness in the blacked-out room, we would turn off all the lights, open the windows, and let the fresh air in.

We also worked with them on a bomb shelter--sort of a cooperative bomb shelter. Clarence Lam did most of the digging. My husband would come after work and dig a little. It was quite deep, at least six feet deep, I think. We would walk in there and sit on a wooden bench. Sand bags were on top of a sheet of corrugated iron. Every once in a while they'd ring a siren for us to practice and we'd all run in there. Then, we imagined the sirens weren't for practicing but for an alarm. With unauthorized planes overhead, we'd run to the bomb shelter.

It was a time of close living--you didn't go very far--I think we were allotted ten gallons of gas a month. Ten gallons a month, period. We had a Model-A Ford, not a fuel economy car, but we managed.

Another problem we had during the war was inadequate housing. The person who owned our home put it on the market because she had earlier bought it for $2,000, and she could get $6,000 or $7,000 for it on a re-sale. And, I thought, oh what a horrible price to pay for a house--a small three-bedroom house.

So we bought another home in St. Louis Heights, which was a little nicer home. But then there was a young girl there, living with her father. And they promised to move out but they never did. My husband said he just couldn't see kicking a young sixteen-year-old out in the street and to go through litigation while I was eight months pregnant with our son.

So, we said we would move in temporarily with my mother at 3286 Mokihana Street. And we were there four long years. Then we bought this home we're in now. By that time, houses had been going higher and higher and higher. I could have bought the other house for $7,000, but I had to pay $10,000 for this little house here.

Of course, during war time, the Orientals were able to buy into Manoa Valley. Before this, Manoa was strictly for the Caucasians. And I remember my aunty went to see a house there--a beautiful home--all interior decorated, with five bedrooms. I think she and uncle paid $12,000 for it, completely furnished. Today, you couldn't buy it for a million.

During the early days of the war, many Caucasians ran away--went to escape the islands. Many went to live on the mainland. That's why the Orientals could buy in special areas--there was no pressure to keep them out. So my aunty bought this home in Manoa around '42 or '43. A few years later, the former owner returned and wanted to buy it back from her. Aunty was too comfortable then to move.

Of course, Dr. Fred Lam had gone in there (Manoa) in the early 1930s and the whites wondered what's going to happen when you have an Oriental family in this beautiful neighborhood? So I think the war helped to cut away many of the prejudices. People were equally afraid, equally exposed.

HEALTH POSTER — Kum Pui Lai, husband of Violet Lai, is shown at left in a newspaper photograph published in 1943. The caption identifies Mr. Lai as the executive secretary of the Tuberculosis Association of Hawaii, inspecting one of the new posters that was to be put on display in Honolulu in connection with the national "Food Fights for Freedom" program. The women are identified as, from left, Marjorie Abel, Board of Health nutritionist, Erma Guntzer, Asst. Territorial Director of the Office of Community War Services, and Miriam Jackson Emery, director of Home Services Department, Hawaiian Electric Company. They were all members of the Territorial Nutrition Committee. (Star Bulletin Oct. 11, 1943; War Depository Collection, University of Hawaii)

My navy wife neighbor and I became very fast friends. In fact, we went into business together. We started to do block printing. Her husband was very artistic. He had linoleum and he carved these hibiscus and orchid pictures and different flowers, and we would block print them on scarfs and handkerchiefs. We had one called, "Remember Pearl Harbor." I remember it was red, white and blue, with a big "V" for victory. We sold these for seventy-five cents in my father-in-law's jewelry store, which added Hawaiian curios during World War II.

" Of course, during the war time, the Orientals were able to buy into Manoa Valley. Before this, Manoa was strictly for the Caucasians. "

During the war years, this store was located right on Hotel Street, where all those servicemen would come off the boat and walk up and down. And, he'd sell all our block print items. We had quite a bit of fun doing that.

I remember during the war I went into another business. You see, I was home and kind of bored. So a friend of ours, my husband's former assistant in the Tuberculosis Association, said "Why don't we go into the diaper laundry business? After all," he said, "no washing machines are being imported and babies are still being born."

And so we got into business with them--Mique Hutchinson and his wife Ann, who's a nurse. The Snowhite Diaper Service, we called it. It was quite an experience. We also had another partner, Linas Brown.

Mique bought a huge wooden drum. There were three sudsing cycles and seven rinses so that the diapers would be really clean. On the first day, Mique called me. He said, "We have a 'mell of a hess' here." I said, "what happened?"

Well, we had hired people to do these net bags so we wouldn't need to mark each diaper. So we merely put each family's diapers into one net--like a fish net, with holes about an inch and a quarter in diameter-- all hand woven and hand tied. We attached each net with a huge safety pin with the owner's name, like McAllister, Wong, Ching, and so on.

But these Curity diapers, they're narrow, not more than eighteen inches wide, and long. They were made of thin, light-weight gauze. Well these diapers, after three sudsings and seven rinses, oozed out like eels from these holes. And all the diapers were all mixed up. The only clue we had was that so-and-so had three dozen, so-and-so had two dozen, etc. And so we said, I guess this goes to this person, that to that person. The phone was ringing, "You gave me the wrong diapers. I sent you Curity diapers, I got back these Birdseye diapers!"

Most of the good workers were taken by defense programs. So I think we were paying seventy-five cents an hour to these Korean immigrant women who could hardly read, and they're trying to see who the diapers belonged to. And, we could no longer use those bags. We had to mark the diapers, and get bags with smaller holes, and it was really a chore.

Another problem was our driver--always drunk on Monday--'cause he had been drinking all weekend. I remember one day, Mique called. He was busy supervising the laundry, and somehow his wife was busy, too, and I had to go deliver and pick up the diapers.

I think I was expecting our youngest, Barbara, at the time. I'd drive over, and some dogs would chase me. I'd grab the diapers--throw in this clean batch--and run for the car.

Some women, because they were paying us $3.50 a week, thought that they didn't have to rinse the diapers. They'd give you everything, just everything. We picked up and delivered Mondays, Wednesdays, and Fridays. Can you imagine Friday's diapers sitting in the bag for three days? And when you picked up those diapers, the ammonia would just clean out your sinuses. You can't believe the fumes that came out of those diapers! Not to mention the solid stuff that came.

We were located on Hauoli Street. And every month we could barely pay our workers, and barely pay the rent. Not to mention scraping for Uncle Sam's withholding taxes every three months.

During this time, Mique, our full-time manager got paid $400 a month when we could afford it. His wife, Ann, also full-time and I--who baby-sat their two children and our two, and managed the books--each received a total of $150 for a year-and-a-half of work.

I think we were in business eighteen months. Mique later left to go to the mainland and my brother-in-law was working with us. He saw a future in the business and he bought us out.

Well, the only thing good that came out of that diaper service, besides

these funny stories, was that when I later applied to the Honolulu
Vocational School to work as an English teacher, I had to have a
minimum of eighteen months of trade experience--so I wrote "diaper
laundry." And I worked for Honolulu Vocational, later named Honolulu
Community College, for twenty-five years. So it was an entry to that job.

But the war years were frightening times. I think our child really felt
the tension. There was that fear of invasion, and you couldn't do this
and you couldn't do that under martial law.

*ON THE BEACH -- Alma Yuke-lin Lai, age two-and-a-half, daughter of Violet and Kum Pui
Lai, seems oblivious to the barbed wire surrounding her as she plays at Kuhio Beach in Waikiki
in the spring of 1943. She wears her identification bracelet. (Photo by Kum Pui Lai, courtesy of
the Lai family)*

At first, we couldn't go much to the beach. Whenever we left the house, we had to be sure there was a bomb shelter nearby. We couldn't play much or do anything; we wondered where our next good meal was coming from, because of rationing. You were always tense, fearing danger. You just didn't relax. And, you just knew--you had a sense--that your child felt that way, too.

Violet and Kum Pui Lai are both retired. Before retirement, Violet taught English, and was in charge of the library, publicity and publications for the Honolulu Vocational School, later rè-named Honolulu Community College. Violet returned to the University of Hawaii at age fifty to earn a master's degree in library studies. In 1970, she lobbied for a new library/classroom building and organized a successful college-wide march to the state capital for it. In 1974 she retired as head librarian, the same year the new library/classroom building was completed.

After retirement, Violet and Kum Pui spent almost eight years researching and writing the biography of her great grandfather. He Was a Ram: Wong Aloiau of Hawaii, was published in 1985 by the University of Hawaii Press and the Hawaii Chinese History Center, where the couple served as volunteer researchers and librarians for ten years. They also edited the Center's Researching One's Chinese Roots, published in 1988.

Their three children are Alma (Mrs. Bong Ro) a missionary in Asia; Morris, a researcher/evaluator in the College of Education, University of Hawaii; and Barbara (Mrs. John Bennett) an artist in Los Angeles. The three have given the Lais seven grandchildren.

Food Supply Crisis

$\mathbf{A}$ few days after the attack, Oahu stores were ordered closed and not to open until they had filed an inventory of nine types of food. Most stores accomplished this in only a day or so. The inventory showed that Oahu had a thirty-seven day supply of most staple foods and smoked meats, but only enough potatoes and onions for eighteen days, and enough rice for only thirteen days. In view of submarine-infested waters and the fact that available shipping space was inadequate even for top priority defense materials, these figures were cause for considerable alarm. Part of the solution was the encouragement of civilians to start victory gardens. *(Allen, Hawaii's War Years)*

VEGGIES FOR VICTORY — The community victory garden in Kaimuki was supervised by the two men identified as Mr. Johnson and Mr. Souza. Community cooperative gardens were used by civilians who didn't have garden space at home. At the peak of enthusiasm for victory gardens, one thousand Honolulans were working in the community gardens and another fifteen thousand in home gardens, producing twelve tons of vegetables monthly. (War Depository Collection, University of Hawaii)

Ernest V. Pacheco

Ernest Pacheco was born on June 23, 1914, in California. His father was from Lihue, Kauai and his mother was from Lemoore, California. Following the death of his mother in 1921, his father moved back to Hawaii with Ernest and his younger brother Bill. They lived in Kaimuki and Ernest attended Liliuokalani School, completing eighth grade. After several jobs, he went to work at Pearl Harbor as a pipefitter's helper in 1934. He married Philomia Gouveia on January 1, 1938. On December 7, 1941, he was living in Kailua with his wife and his son Richard, who was almost three-years-old.

When I think of Pearl Harbor, I think of the people I met there--people who became good friends--people who really gave me my start in life.

I remember, in 1939, I was looking for a home to buy. I saw an ad in the paper on Thanksgiving Day. There was this little house in Kailua at 409 Maluniu Street, on the corner of Keaniani. It was for sale for $1,500. So my wife and I, we get in the car and we go down to Kailua and look at this place. I fell in love with it. Nobody was living in Kailua at that time. It was country.

So we gave them a $25 deposit. My wife took the $25 from her purse and that was all the money we had. This was a cottage, completely furnished, and two lots, right on the corner of the main drag, for $25 down. The ironic thing was that we didn't have any money to pay for it. And I said to myself, "So what the hell are we going to do for food tomorrow? Well," I thought, "something will come up."

I belonged to the credit union at Pearl Harbor. I was one of the directors when the credit union first started. So I went to Eddie Lund, who was the secretary-treasurer. I asked him, I said, "There's a house in Kailua I want to buy, but I have to put down at least $500." He says, "Yeah, but you gotta resign from the board." That was all right with me. They could get somebody else to take my place. He said I had to have two co-signers to borrow the money--to back up the loan.

So I went to see my two buddies, both of them were riveters. Caesar Paishon was a big, strapping man. I told him what I wanted to do and he said, "Ah Pacheco, you're a galloot. You can't settle down. You're still wandering around--a loose link."

I talked to him for about a half hour before work, and he kept shaking his head, "No, no." So finally he says, "Tell you what. You go see Johnny Mendonca. If Johnny Mendonca signs it, I'll sign it."

So I go see Johnny and right away, he says, "No way you gonna do this." So I said, "You know, Johnny, I'm married now. I got responsibilities. What I need is a start. I need guys like you to give me a start." He saw that I was sincere. So he says, "You go see Caesar. If Caesar signs it, I'll sign it." They were both giving me the run-around. So I said, "I seen Caesar already. Caesar says if you sign it, he'll sign it." So Johnny said, "Give me that paper." He had a wife and seven kids and here he was, co-signing a big loan for me. That must have given him something to think about for a long time.

So I took the signed slip and I went to see Caesar. He said, "I don't know how the hell you did it, but if Johnny got enough nerve to sign it, I'll sign it." That was the start of my life. Two guys from Pearl Harbor gave me my start.

When we moved to Kailua, there were five other people who worked at Pearl Harbor that I already knew. So we formed car pools. We commuted every day from Kailua to Pearl Harbor--on the old, winding, two-lane, Pali Road. I was driving a 1935 Chevy sedan at the time. I remember Manual Quintel and his son Manual junior, were in the car pool--and Tommy Clark, too.

One night I will never forget. This happened later, during the war. I got stuck on the job maybe an hour or so later than quitting time, so the guys took off without me. I was a supervisor at that time. And information about the job had to be carried over to the next shift. We were always on an emergency, where the ship had to get out the next day or something. So you had to explain what you were doing--to the next shift--and I missed my ride.

It just so happened that my next door neighbor was working late, too, that night. So I went to Moses "Moke" Haia's shop and asked if I could have a ride home with him. He was a shipwright. He said "Sure, but I'll be held up here for a while yet." So I waited.

When we got to his car, he said he was tired and asked me to drive. So everybody piled in, me and five other guys. They all went to sleep. I was driving his 1938 Packard.

When we got up to the top of the Pali, the wind was blowing like crazy. As we started down the other side, I down-shifted. I put on the brakes to slow it down but when I hit them, there was no brakes. I didn't panic. I shifted that thing right down to compound low and I held it there so that it wouldn't jump out on me. Halfway down we got to the hairpin turn and it was really picking up speed. Jesus, boy, I tell you, it was scary. I hugged the left side of the two lane road at the hairpin. Lucky no cars were coming up the other way. It was about 8:30 at night and it was dark. Oh my God, talk about stress. I came all the way down that winding road in low gear, with the engine screaming. All five guys slept through it all and I never said a thing to them. Finally, I got them home and everything was all right. I drove Moke's car into the driveway. His wife came out and told him, in Hawaiian, that she needed him to go to the store.

So I went into my house and told my wife what happened--that I drove all the way down the Pali with no brakes. Well, Moke came over about fifteen minutes later, and he tells me, "Pacheco, what happened?" He said, "I backed up the car to go to the store, and I hit the coconut tree." He said all the coconuts fell down and made big dents on the top of his car. When I told him how we got home--all the way down the Pali with no brakes--he said, "Oh, my God." That was one hair-raising experience.

Well, anyway, the night before December seventh, we had gone to a party at Joe Pau's house in Puunui. That Saturday was a free day for me, but I had to go in on Sunday. The navy never paid you overtime--they had a way of bleeding you. Joe Pau was a big developer in Kailua. He built that Enchanted Lakes area. Joe and I were buddies. We ran around together when we were single. His house was near the Oahu Country Club, right in back of it. So we came home late that night.

The next morning, Sunday December seventh, I rode in to the yard with Tom Yoeman. He was working that day too. We started work at eight o'clock, so we were there earlier. I went down to the shop and got my tools. I ran into Lyman Wilson—we called him Lymie. He and I were teamed up that day on the work order--to go to the destroyer *Shaw*. We were gonna test the forward compartments on the *Shaw* for leaks--to make it seaworthy.

Joe Bulgo was to work on the rudder, getting the rudder fixed--there were lots of cracks on it. He was at the head of the dock--at the big grinder where you would grind your tools. We stopped at the tool room and it must have taken us ten minutes or so to get the service we needed. From there we started walking across the docks--Docks One and Two-- and over to the *Shaw*--which was on a floating drydock.

Just about the time we got to the floating drydock--I had tools in my hands and a hose on my shoulder. Lymie had a gauge that we used, a pressure gauge, and he stopped at the head of the dock. He didn't come on the dock. I continued walking. So he looks up and he sees these planes up there, and he yells to me. I'm about, oh, thirty or forty feet onto the dock already. "Pacheco, come back, take a look at this." I couldn't see what he was talking about because the pontoons were thirty or forty feet in the air and they were blocking my view from that angle. I said, "What's going on?" He says, "Look at these airplanes. We're going to have trouble with the Japanese because our boys are up there early already."

Remember, it was early Sunday morning. Those military guys usually had a big party on Saturday night--that's what the guys used to say around there. And then they'd sleep in on Sunday morning. This is eight o'clock Sunday morning and they're up there already; so that means they had to be up at least by 5:30, 6:00 o'clock, to get in the air that early.

I kept walking towards the ladder and Lymie says, "Pacheco, you gotta see this--this is really spectacular. Come on and look at this. Those boys can really fly." I yelled back, "Shit I'm not interested. Let's go do our job." He insisted, "No, no, you gotta see this, please, come on back and look at it." So I'm about seventy-five, eighty feet away by now and getting close to the ladder to climb up on the *Shaw*. There's no gangway to get on--you had to climb up a ladder.

I threw everything down in disgust and walked off of the dock. Well, when I got over there and looked up, it really was spectacular. They were way the hell up there--about 10,000 feet. They looked like little bugs running around up there. They were circling around, coming from different areas. When I got there, they were just about finished forming and then they started peeling off. I stood there with Lymie and watched these planes come down. The floating drydock is just about three hundred yards from the hangar on Ford Island. That's just at the entrance of the harbor--a narrow strip to the harbor.

And that plane came down--you could see him coming--nose down, just like that. We followed him all the way down. Just before he gets to the hangar, I told Lymie, "My God, he's really going to do some bombing maneuvers." All of a sudden he leveled off. Just about a hundred feet before he hit the hangar, he dropped what I thought was a sack of cement. "Boy, they're doing it for keeps, look at that," I said, "they're dropping a sack of cement." All of a sudden that thing went up in a ball of fire. Incendiary bomb. We were shocked. When that guy peeled off of that dive, he banked over where we were, and we could see that rising sun underneath the wing. That's the first time we realized that it was the Japanese that was attacking us.

Lymie was an athlete, I wasn't. I was just carrying my own--but boy did I move. We went in different directions, fast. I didn't realize it then but if I had stayed on the floating drydock a little longer--if Lymie didn't insist that I look at the planes--I would have blown up with the *Shaw* and the drydock. A short time later, a bomb set off the magazine storage of the *Shaw* and blew off its bow, and the drydock sunk along with it.

They were leveling off the land where the hospital used to be, at the head of the drydocks. They were going to build shops, workshops, and there were materials ready to build there. So everything was leveled off-- there were no holes in the ground--nowhere you could duck under cover.

So I ran into the roundhouse building--where they keep the locomotives. And that wasn't safe, either, because there were other planes coming behind, machine-gunning the round house. And I was between an I-beam, just wide enough to hold my body, protecting me from a bullet that came whizzing by. I was scared as hell.

" . . . if I had stayed on the floating drydock a little longer . . . I would have blown up with the Shaw and the drydock. "

Then I seen that that was no place to hide 'cause they were coming back, punching everywhere they could, using machine guns. So I peeled out of that area and I ran like hell towards Drydock Number One--which was a bad thing to do, I found out. They had a big mound of dirt at the head of Drydock Number One, 'cause they were excavating the land, leveling off, and they were piling all the dirt in one spot.

47

SPECTACULAR FIREWORKS – The destroyer USS Shaw explodes in floating Drydock No. Two during Pearl Harbor attack. A bomb blast forward touched off the ship's magazines and the explosion tore off the ship's bow and sunk the drydock. (Official U.S. Navy photograph; War Depository Collection, University of Hawaii)

SMOLDERING SHAW -- The destroyer USS Shaw, blown in two pieces, smolders hours after the attack. Months later, she will rejoin the fleet with a refitted bow. (Official U.S. Navy photograph; War Depository Collection, University of Hawaii)

So where did I land? Right at the top of that mound. And I'm looking down at Drydock Number One at the two destroyers, the *Cassin* and the *Downes*, and the battleship *Pennsylvania*. And a plane flew right over my head. I mean I thought he would take my head off, he was that low. And he dropped a torpedo right there. It looked like it just missed the *Cassin*. If it had hit the *Cassin*, the *Pennsylvania* and the other ships would be right on my lap. The force of the water had picked them right out of the drydock.

I seen the *Oglala* take that torpedo--the *Helena* was right alongside--she developed a big leak. And I'm looking over to the *Arizona* and the *Oklahoma* and they're having Mass on the fantail. And I'm saying to myself, "What's the matter with those guys, can't they hear these bombs?" I could see them plain as day. They were having Sunday services. And they stayed there until a torpedo plane came down and hit the water. I'm frozen, too. I couldn't move. I couldn't yell. I couldn't do a damned thing. I saw the *Nevada* pulling out. They got it underway and it was trying to make its way out of the harbor. It passed by where I was while all hell was still breaking loose.

The thing that was really scaring the hell out of me, at that time, was those fuel tanks around Pearl Harbor. I said to myself, "My God, where can I go to keep from getting that oil on me if they blow it up?" So I started running over to the Shipwright Shop--towards the Ad Building. That was still a dangerous place 'cause bombs and bullets were falling everywhere. I kept hoping they don't hit those oil tanks while I'm still there. We would all be goners. Nowhere to hide from that.

I had a bird's eye view. I seen the planes coming down, hitting those battleships. If I could have only taken a picture of everything that went on. It would have been history if I had a camera. But the picture is in my mind and will always be there. It is so real, so detailed, so clear. It will always be there, in my head.

Then a guy drove by--I don't know who the guy is--and he hollers to me, "Want a ride out?" And I says, "Yeah, let's get outta here." So I jumped in his car--dived in his car—and he's still going about five miles an hour when I dived in. We went out the main gate. The marines weren't stopping us--they were too busy shooting at the planes--with rifles, even pistols. We drove right under these airplanes attacking Hickam. Everything was just in an uproar. So this guy lived up in Nuuanu someplace, so I told him to drop me at my brother's in Nuuanu.

Ernest V. Pacheco (continued)

I knocked at the door--this was still very early--maybe 8:30 in the morning, and everyone was still sleeping. Mr. Franks came out, that's my brother's father-in-law. Frankie Franks. He used to be a vice president of Hawaiian Trust Company. He came out and said, "What's the matter, Ernie?" I said, "Japanese are attacking Pearl Harbor."

"Oh, you're crazy," he said. My brother, Bill, jumped out of bed, "What's up, Ernie?" I said again, "The Japanese are attacking Pearl Harbor right now." He says, "Oh, no." I said, "No? Look at the smoke up there--see that black smoke?"

He picked up the phone and he called the police station--he was a police officer. They didn't answer any of his questions. They just said, "You get down here as soon as you can."

So Bill knew, right away, that something big was wrong. And KGMB radio was playing symphony music--sweet symphony music in the morning, you know. I thought, what in the hell are they playing that God-damned music for instead of warning the people? They're crazy.

Well, my brother Bill went out. He later told me he had a hard time, too. He had to go to Pearl Harbor, and there was only a two-lane highway down there at that time. He had to get out of his car too--the planes were strafing the road. And he ended up in the cane fields.

Finally the radio music went off. "All Pearl Harbor employees, report to your shops." Then five minutes later, "All Pearl Harbor employees, stay away from the shops." I'm standing there thinking, I'll be a son-of-a-bitch if I'm going back down there. It's suicide.

I told my sister-in-law, "They're crazy, the bastards." Then the announcement came back, "All Pearl Harbor employees return to your shops." So I told my sister-in-law, "I better go in. They need me down there. I'd better go back." I had calmed down a bit by that time. So I walked out to the corner, and lo and behold a guy comes by with a station wagon, going to Pearl Harbor.

And, you know, that's the first time I realized I still had my lunch pail under my arm. Imagine carrying my lunch pail through all of that? When I went out to look at the planes, I threw my tools down, but I guess I kept my lunch pail with me. I didn't want the ants to get to it, I guess--the ants and the cockroaches. Can you imagine carrying that thing after all the running and diving under cover I did?

So the guy with the station wagon drove me in. By that time the road was packed with cars. When we got to the gate, there was planes still coming down, strafing the front gate--RAT-TAT-TAT-TAT-TAT. We jumped out of the car, parked it right at the gate, and ran for cover. "Oh no," I thought, "here I go again."

Those planes dove, strafing with machine guns, shooting down at the marines, at us, at anybody that was walking by. So I got down on the ground with the guy that drove me in, dodging bullets again. Then I ran for the gate. About that time, another plane came down--RAT-TAT-TAT-TAT-TAT. I don't know whether it was the same one that made a U-turn and come around again or another plane.

I was right in line with the bullets and boy I made a dive. There were these two pillars on either side of the gate--stone walls. And I dived behind that son-of-a-gun and hit my head. I had a hole in my head and I don't know whether I was knocked out or how long I stayed there, but I lost track of time for a while. I do remember that I had a headache for quite some time after that.

Well, I finally got into the yard, watching for planes--a whole hour since I first went in. At that time, there were no high buildings, so you could see the battleships all on fire, many of them sinking, some with just the main deck and gun turrets above the water.

I finally got to my shop. My supervisor looked up at me and he thought he saw a ghost. "Pacheco, you're alive," he said. "How did you make it? How did you get out?" I said "Lymie saved my life. He called me away from the *Shaw* or I would have blown up with it. Where's Lymie?" I asked. He said, "Oh, he's okay. He's around here somewhere." He says, "Boy you guys had a hell-of-an experience." I asked him how's Joe Bulgo doing, and he said he made it, too.

" My supervisor thought he saw a ghost.
"Pacheco, you're alive," he said. "

He told me the *Oklahoma* tipped over and there were people still alive in compartments in the bottom of the ship. They were getting "knocks" on the hull from inside, so they knew some sailors were still alive but they had to get to them in a hurry, before the air runs out. In fact, my supervisor said they accidentally killed some of them they were trying to

51

Ernest V. Pacheco (continued)

save. The torches they used, cutting a hole in the hull, ate up all the oxygen and they suffocated to death. I think he said they lost eighteen men that way.

They were picking up a crew to try another rescue. Julio "Lefty" DeCastro was the supervisor of the operation, and he picked out the guys he wanted to take with him to the *Oklahoma*. He picked Bulgo, and he picked me, and a bunch of others. Lefty DeCastro was a real hero that day.

Anyway, I got my tools and got on the launch to go out to the *Oklahoma*, and my chief quarterman came by and he yelled to me to get off the launch. He said, "No, Pacheco, you don't go, I got a job for you." So he took me off of the launch. When I got off, he said, "You had enough for one morning." The job he had for me was the *Helena*. It had a bad oil leak when they hit the *Oglala*. The concussion from the shell made a big oil leak on that side of the ship. So he told me, he says, "I want you to go over there and stop those oil leaks." That's the reason why I didn't go with Joe and Lefty on the *Oklahoma*. They saved those guys. They did a wonderful piece of work. You can imagine saving

RESCUE LEADER AND FAMILY -- *Julio DeCastro, who lead the group of twenty civilian workers at Pearl Harbor who rescued thirty-two navy men trapped in the hull of the overturned USS Oklahoma during December 7th attack, is shown with his family (front row, left to right) Rose Marie, Mr. DeCastro, Loretta May, Mrs. Lydia DeCastro, and Richard. (back row, left to right) Harold and Julio Jr.* (**Star Bulletin** *March 24, 1942; War Depository Collection, University of Hawaii*)

those guys locked in a compartment and slowly losing all their air. They were going to suffocate if you didn't get in there fast enough.

So they cut open a hole in the hull and crawled inside, from compartment to compartment, trying to find the sailors. Imagine that the ship is turned over on its side and you're climbing on the walls and ceilings, trying to find the guys knocking on the hull. What a hazard that was. One slip and you'd fall sixty, seventy feet down the other side. Julio and those guys did a great piece of work.

That night we had a lot of trigger-happy people around. You couldn't leave the ship without meeting someone with a gun. You couldn't use a flashlight outside--everything was blacked out. The trigger-happy marines were going crazy. Anything that moved, they'd shoot at. So I was safer staying on that ship all night. It was daylight when I got on that ship, and I didn't get off that ship until daylight the next day.

During the night, while I was working on the oil leaks way down in the hole on the *Helena*, we heard planes flying back over again. Blackout went back on again and "secure the ship" order was announced. They cut my pneumatic air hose (they didn't take the time to run up and turn the air off, they just cut the hose.) They dropped the hatch over me and secured it. There I am, down in that hole there, way down at the bottom of the ship--just above the water line--corking leaks with a pneumatic caulking gun and everything goes pitch black. The siren on the ship sounds general quarters--WHEEE, WHEEE, WHEEE.

I was still shaking from all the excitement from the day, and here I am, scared as hell, one more time. "My God," I said to myself all alone in that dark hole, "what the hell's going to happen to me now?"

Well, planes did come back. We didn't know it then, but they were our own planes. But they didn't identify themselves, or something, and they got shot down by our own trigger-happy, frightened military. I stayed in the dark all night, expecting to be bombed again and maybe even go down with the *Helena*. You couldn't sleep. You were just wondering when that thing was going to let go. You wanted to be awake when they dropped the bomb.

So I didn't leave that damned ship until the next day. Matter of fact, I had breakfast on the *Helena*. I didn't have no dinner the night before. I must have eaten that lunch that I was carrying around with me--I really don't remember. I only remember it was a long time since I ate anything.

53

I don't know what happened to that lunch pail. I must have ate the lunch but I don't know where the hell the lunch pail went. All I know is that I didn't have it no more. Nuthin' important to worry about, though. We had the Japs to worry about now. The hell with the lunch pail.

Anyway, the next morning, DeCastro and Joe Bulgo and that crew were still over there working on the *Oklahoma*. They worked all around the clock. I understand when the planes came over that evening, they had to turn the lights out. But they kept working. They had to do the best they could in the dark--drilling and getting that hull open so they could drop down inside the ship. They would keep tapping and the sound would come back--tapping to each other to find out where the survivors were. That's what Joe told me. They were in the storeroom somewhere. They knew that that was the only place they could be. Anywhere else, and they'd have been dead--they'd have drowned already. But in the storeroom they could latch the hatch and save some of that air down there. They knew that. They finally went through three or four compartments before they got down to where the sailors were. When it was over, Julio and his crew of Pearl Harbor workers saved thirty-two navy men. What a heroic thing they did.

The next morning, I was relieved from my post. I tried to call my wife, but couldn't get through. We lived near the Kaneohe Air Station–only about a mile and a half from there. I didn't know, at the time, that the Japs bombed there, too. I found out later that two or three shells hit close to my house.

When I got home, I found that my wife wasn't there. I knew where she would be, though. Just as I thought, she took the car and went with our three-year-old son, Dick, over to her sister's place in Kaneohe. I was real worried about her. She was six months pregnant at the time.

Well, when we went back to our house to get clothes to stay at her sister's, there was navy people at our house. They asked us if they could use our home for people who were being evacuated from the barracks at the naval station. They said they had our home perused for about two months, to use in case of war. So we gave up our home to them and stayed with my wife's sister and her husband, Joe Texeira, who had a dairy in Kaneohe. We stayed there about a month.

I remember, about two months later they brought the *Nevada* up. She had grounded and sunk near the entrance to the harbor, trying to get out that morning. I was asked to take over the pneumatic tools section, testing for leaks on the *Nevada*. They brought her up, put her on pontoons and put her in the drydock. There was a lot of damage to her-- a lot of bombs or torpedoes hit her. One side of the ship was a mess. I was in control of the air testing--testing her seaworthiness.

I worked on that job for two years. It was a big job. And, I seen a lot of guys die working on that ship. Some awful sights. And the smell. Oh my God, no matter what you did, you couldn't get rid of that awful dead body smell. It stuck in your nostrils.

We had to go down and check different compartments for things for the navy and clean out stuff like the foul weather gear--jackets, raincoats, boots--stuff like that. We didn't know at the time that the chemicals in the raincoats and the boots, when mixed with salt water for a long time, made a gas. And I saw nine sailors and the chief die that morning because of the toxic gas. They were on the cleanup crew. I had gone down there too, but I didn't stay very long. I was just down there to see the condition of the area before assigning the workers. I was just lucky. I had an angel on my shoulder. But those poor guys were down there to work--to clean up--to get all that garbage out of there. They were down there for a long time. They didn't realize what was happening to them. They never came back up.

That was a long-time job. I stayed with it until we got the *Nevada* out of drydock. Then they towed her to the west coast--Hunter's Point or Bremerton--to get her ship-shape to go out and fight again.

In the meantime, we had all these other battleships, carriers, coming in for work. We worked long hours--ten-hour shifts, sometimes twelve hours--getting the work done.

Then I became supervisor of the drydock area. I had all the underwater work--testing, inspecting, assigning the men to different jobs. The carrier *Yorktown* came in. She was all loaded down with troops, ammunition, gasoline, you name it. She was ready to sail. She had to get off the next morning, no ifs ands or buts. The Japanese were sending an armada to Wake Island.

The *Yorktown* had a bad oil leak, and I had Jim Kramer down there working on it--stopping that leak. An oil leak is just like a flare tipping off your location. The glitter of that oil on the water forms a streak. That's very dangerous--submarines can pick that up. So we got the leak stopped. Then, next morning the carrier went out. That was the last time we saw her. She never came back. That was the sad part--seeing all those young kids on there. They had everything--gasoline, ammunition--everything that they needed for combat, for landing. And they never came back.

I remember the *Indiana* and the *Carolina* collided. Almost sunk the *Carolina*. Ripped the whole side of the ship out. They had a training exercise going on somewhere in the Pacific and the accident happened. The *Carolina* was a super battleship. She came in for repairs. That was another fast, around-the-clock job with twelve-hour shifts. I didn't know what an eight-hour day was anymore until we finally started losing so many men. They were stressed, fatigued, even dying. Then they made it compulsory that you take one day off every eight days. That kind of eased the stress a little bit.

We got a lot of help from the mainland. Shipyard workers came from Mare Island, California, and Brooklyn, New York. We had to train those guys.

The *Indiana* and the *Carolina* repairs got to be one of my biggest projects. But we got them out on time--according to our schedule. But our shopmaster lost his job during that project. He went berserk under

---

" I had a lot of near misses . . . Somebody up there must have been really looking after me--a real guardian angel. "

---

the stress. And he wasn't the only top guy that caved in under the pressure. Many did. They weren't kids, you know. Many of them were in their fifties when the war broke out.

I had a lot of near misses during those days. Somebody up there must have been really looking after me--a real guardian angel. I remember one morning in 1942 some of my mechanics told me that I had to go down to look at a job. So I was walking out of the shop, about thirty or forty feet from the shop door, when one of the guys yelled at me to come back so he could talk to me about troubles he was having on the job. I was going to get into a small tractor--we called it the Leaping Tuna--that pulled little cars around the base. You'd go in it, sit down, and it would take you where you wanted to go. So I walked back to the shop door and he told me what was troubling him. At that time, they had an airplane maneuver going on and two planes were going through the motions of a dogfight up there--and they collided--tipped each other's wings over the base. One of the planes went down towards the drydocks and landed in the harbor, and the other one came down right where I was going to get into the Leaping Tuna. Seventeen people, plus the driver of the tractor and the pilot were all killed--burned to death. That was a close call. It was only a matter of split seconds and I would have been right where the plane had hit if I didn't go back towards the shop. I remember Nick Akana was down at the drydock area when that happened and he swam out and brought the other pilot in. He saved that guy's life.

Another time I was standing under a cruiser, the *New Orleans*, in drydock. I was inspecting the hull, the props, the rudders, to see if there's any oil leaks or any kind of electrolysis damage to the hull. That was my job. If the problem had to do with my area, I would assign a man to get the job done. If it didn't, I'd get the trade that's involved with that particular problem to work on it. So I'm standing there inspecting the prop, seeing if there's anything visible I could spot, and all of a sudden I saw something that didn't look right to me. So I took one step in to get a closer look and then I hear a loud bump--like a thud. I turn around and there was a sailor that fell off the main deck laying there all crumpled. He was killed instantly. And he landed just where I had been standing a few seconds earlier. Life at Pearl Harbor during the war was rough.

I remember at home, in Kailua, there was an epidemic of infantile paralysis going around. That worried us. Our second son, Kenneth, was born in March 1942. A lot of kids around there developed infantile paralysis--some of them lost their lives and some were crippled. As if we didn't have enough to worry about.

We didn't have any problems with blackout, though. In fact, I only blacked out one room in the house, the bathroom. That was my dining room, my living room, that was my "everything" room. All the rest of the rooms were left wide open--no blackout paper--breeze running through all the time at night.

Jimmy Marciel wanted to know how come I never had any problems with my children during blackout. I told him, no problem. Only got one blacked-out room. My wife cooks during the day and when I come home all she has to do is warm up the food--you don't need a light for that. So my table is set on the dresser in the bathroom. I take my shower, I shit, I eat, right there in the same place. Everything is done right there in one room. In case the kids got sick during the night, usually that's where you end up with the child--in the bathroom--in the medicine cabinet. When Jimmy heard that, he pulled out all his blackout paper at his house.

Well, those were interesting times. I will never forget the guys I worked with, especially Ed Welch (quarterman), Tom Curry (supervisor), and Lt. (jg) Henry Rumbble, who was superintendent of one of the projects. Their help and support will always be appreciated.

And, I can't forget that mound of dirt where I had a bird's-eye view of the destruction. I didn't talk about it for a long time. Years. I think it was my granddaughter that asked me about it--that got me talking about it. The thing that sticks in my mind are all those sailors at Sunday service and all that noise and bombing going on. Everyone of them got killed. Those that didn't get blown off the ship got burned in the oil in the water. That's the picture that really gets to me. And it will until I die.

Ernie and Philomia had four children, three boys and a girl. Richard was born three years before Pearl Harbor; Kenneth just three months after the attack; Anthony in 1944; and Phyllis in 1946. Ernie transferred to Hunter's Point in California following the war and he retired from shipyard work in September, 1965, after more than 30 years of service. Their children have given them eleven grandchildren, although one of them was killed in an accident. They live in retirement in Sunnyvale, California.

Rose Mary Souza Baptiste

Her father, Manual Souza, came to Hawaii in 1878 at five years of age. He and his family sailed aboard the first ship from Portugal (San Miguel) with contract laborers to work the cane fields. Her mother, Isabella Borges, was born on Kauai. Rose Mary (Mona), was born in Honolulu in 1925. She was the last of ten children born to Manual and Isabella, six boys and four girls. The Souza family lived at 1119 8th Avenue in Kaimuki. Mona attended St. Patrick's grade school, Liliuokalani junior high, and McKinley High School. She was sixteen years of age and a junior at McKinley in December 1941.

I was a tomboy as a teenager, always getting into things. One of our favorite sports--my brother Val and I--was to wave at airplanes that would fly low over our house. We knew a lot of the pilots from Bellows Field out in Waimanalo. So when they came by, they would buzz our house and we'd climb up on the roof and wave to them. It was a thrill seeing them tip their wings at us, as in a salute.

That morning my father had gone to church early and had already come home. We were getting ready to go to a later Mass, when we heard all these planes flying over. They were always having maneuvers and it sounded like they were having a big one this time. We would watch them have dogfights in the sky above our house. They sure sounded like they were flying low this time, so Val and I ran out the back porch and climbed up the vines and the wires that they grew on, up the side of the house to the roof.

We perched on the peak of the roof and saw more of them coming over. Boy, was it exciting. We waved our arms at them, and a few of them tipped their wings. We saw the rising sun insignia on the planes, but just thought they painted the planes that way for this maneuver. Anyway, they tipped their wings at us, so they must have been our friends from Bellows Field, right?

Just then, my mother started yelling at us, in Portuguese, to get off the roof. She really sounded hysterical, saying something about an enemy attack. We didn't pay too much attention--we knew that she was anxious that we hurry off to church--but this was too exciting to miss. There were a lot of airplanes up there, more than we were used to seeing.

Val was nineteen. He had graduated, already, from St. Louis, and he was working at Pearl Harbor. He was just a kid at heart, like me. Mother became very insistent. She said that the radio announcer was saying that this was war--the real thing--the Japanese were attacking us at Pearl Harbor. Stubbornly, I answered, "No, mother, it's the men from Bellows Field. We know them all and they're tipping their wings at us."

" . . . this was too exciting to miss. There were a lot of airplanes up there, more than we were used to seeing . . . "

It took a while before what my mother had said really sunk in. But then the radio announcer was calling for all Pearl Harbor workers to report to the base. Valentine had a little putt-putt, kind of a motor scooter. He drove off on that thing with our other brother, Richard, hanging on the back. It wasn't too long before they were back. They said that they got half way down there, but that the roads were blocked and they were sending everybody back home. They couldn't get through.

But, I couldn't believe what they were telling us. They said that they saw a car that was riddled with bullets, with people hanging out of the car, dead. They were really shook up about it.

Our front porch was pretty high and we could look down toward Pearl Harbor and we could see smoke and fire, from where they bombed. The next day, we discovered the spot where they bombed was on McCully. I guess they were trying to hit Fort DeRussy and missed. It was a mess. Apartment houses and stores were all in shambles.

That night, we were told that everything had to be blacked out. No lights at all. We were all in the house, together, and you would bump into somebody, yelling, "Who is it?" I had horrible visions of Japanese soldiers coming up our front steps or sneaking into our house in the dark.

Then we heard that there were parachutists that landed up near Wilhelmina Rise. You would hear soldiers outside in the dark yelling,

"Halt." And then you would hear shots. We just imagined everybody out there was getting killed. It was frightening.

It was so scary that night. I remember that all of a sudden the guns at Fort Ruger started firing in the dark. Our house just rattled and shook. My sister, Bea, was holding her son, Butch, on her lap and when the guns went off, she ran over in the dark and jumped on my lap, scared to death. So there I was, with my sister on my lap, and her baby on **her** lap--the three of us--piled up and trembling. We thought for sure that the Japanese were back.

I understand that some of our own planes were coming in that night and they did not identify themselves, or something, so they got shot at by the big guns at Fort Ruger. Ruger was only about a mile from us and when those guns went off, you knew it. We were so frightened, but I bet we looked silly stacked up on the couch like that. But it was so dark, nobody could see us.

It took a few days, but we finally got blackout material and covered

FOOD LINEUP -- Despite announcements that food would still be available during the emergency, women lined up early to await the opening of Central Market in Kaimuki, right around the corner from the Souza family home. The woman at right (with white shoes) is believed to be Isabella Souza, Rose Mary Souza's mother. (Star Bulletin Dec. 8, 1941; War Depository Collection, University of Hawaii)

61

the windows so that we could have some light at night. That helped us to calm down a bit. Your imagination kind of runs away from you when you're in pitch black darkness, you know.

Immediately there was the call out for blood. Queens Hospital was running a blood drive and we all went down there to do our part for the war effort. My sister, Bea, took me down to give blood. It was a nerve-wracking experience. I had never done anything like that before. I told Bea how nervous I was.

Standing in front of us in line, was this great big man, listening in to our conversation. He told me not to worry--that giving blood was easy to do--that there was nothing to it. It was one of the funniest things I can remember, but when it was his turn to give blood, he turned pale white and passed out on the table while they were taking his blood. Anyway, I managed to get through it with no problem, but I'll never forget that big guy telling me there was nothing to it, then passing out himself. He sure was embarrassed about it.

WARTIME SNAPS — In the photo at left, Mona Souza, eighteen years of age, dons a soldier's cap in a popular pinup pose of the day. In the right snapshot, Mona and sister, Margaret, pose with gas masks and helmets, ready and alert for any emergency. (Photos courtesy of Souza family photo collection)

My blood type was in demand--I guess I was considered a universal giver. So I did it every chance I could and was proud to belong to the "Gallon Club."

School was out for quite a while there right after December seventh, and they were looking for people to take jobs that were formerly handled by men. I really felt that the future didn't look too bright, what with the war and the possibility of a Japanese invasion that would put us under their control. I thought about it, then decided that I wanted to quit school, go to work, and live a little before I die. I really felt that way.

". . . what with a war and the possibility of a Japanese invasion . . . I wanted to quit school, go to work, and live a little before I die."

So I hopped on the street car, hanging on the outside, and went downtown to look for a job. I was hired right away at Liberty House on Fort Street. I did a number of things, including wrapping gifts and running the elevator. My sister, Margaret, also ran an elevator at Liberty House during those years.

So I was sixteen, almost seventeen, and a junior in high school, and I quit school and got a job. I did it because I wanted to experience more of life, while I had the chance. I never went back to school. I worked at Liberty house for two years. I then went over to Hawaiian Electric Company and did a variety of things for them for four years. I ran the elevator, ran errands for the company, and filled in as the telephone operator.

Wartime life in the islands--particularly when you're in your late teens--includes loads of servicemen. My folks had a beach house out in Hauula, and they were always entertaining a bunch of servicemen. They came from all over--from Fort Shafter, Schofield, and some from Bellows Field--and my mother cooked for all of these servicemen. Often they would be there all weekend. At one time, I remember, I counted twenty-five soldiers in the basement of our beach home. I didn't mind being the center of attention. It was fun, but very innocent in those days, of course.

I remember, towards the end of the war, there was a big camp of soldiers right across the road from our beach house, where the Sacred

Falls parking lot is now. I would have fun meeting the guys, and flirting with them. I would wear their caps.

In the evenings, after dark, they would have first-run movies outdoors on the lawns. This was after blackout restrictions were lifted. We would go over there and sit on the lawns and watch these great movies. It was a time I won't forget.

> **" There were five of these servicemen . . . that I got to know . . . killed in action. That was difficult to take. "**

There were five of these servicemen—navy men--that I got to know real well. It was always hard when they would be shipped out. I would hear from them from time to time and would write back to them. Then, after that, we would hear of a tremendous battle in the South Pacific, and then we would never hear from them again. Five of them that I had known were killed in action. That was difficult to take. But the memories of the good times we had can never be taken away from me. I'll remember those times for the rest of my life.

After the war, Mona moved to California and married. After thirteen years, the marriage ended in divorce and Mona returned to Hawaii. She married her childhood sweetheart, Melville H. "Buddy" Baptiste in 1965. She worked for First Hawaiian Bank, as a research analyst and retired after more than eighteen years of service in 1985. She and Buddy live in Honolulu and enjoy travelling, particularly on cruises. They are members of the Outrigger Canoe Club and may frequently be seen using its facilities.

Robert M. Gibson, D.D.S.

His father, Dr. Henry L. Gibson, was a dentist who came from San Francisco, California to do an internship at the Strong Carter Dental Clinic at the Palama Settlement in 1926. His mother, Helen Black, also from San Francisco, came over to Honolulu a short time later to marry Dr. Gibson. They had two children. Robert was born in 1927 and his sister, Nancy, came along four years later. The Gibson family lived in Manoa Valley, on Oahu Road, at the outset of the war. Robert was fourteen years old and in the ninth grade at Punahou School.

You know, as I think back now, I recall that it was a week before December seventh when we were having a training drill in Honolulu and the troops were on the beaches, downtown, everywhere. They had troop trucks in convoys and soldiers running around in the outlying areas. They were having maneuvers--a rehearsal in case of some kind of emergency--in case we were attacked. There was even notice of it in the papers, I remember. And that was just a week before the real thing occurred.

I was asleep in bed, the morning of December seventh, when I was awakened by these explosions. I thought to myself, "Oh, they're still having those maneuvers out there." I didn't think too much about it for a few minutes, then I began hearing all these planes and more explosions.

Just then, my dad yelled out to us, he says, "Get out of bed, everybody, this is war." I bolted out of bed in disbelief. "It's the Japs," he said. He had seen the action and had turned on the radio and learned what was going on. Just then a bunch of planes came flying overhead and I ran outside. I could see a whole fleet of planes with the rising sun insignia on them. I also saw one lonely P-40 chasing them.

My father grabbed his guns to see if he could shoot one. He loaded his .30-06 and began peppering away at them. I couldn't believe what I was witnessing. It was scary. But, just then, there suddenly was a huge explosion on the hillside above us, only a few hundred yards in the back of us. Right away we thought they were dropping bombs on us. We dove for the cover of the garage. My heart was pounding. Talk about a rude awakening. Anyway, that blast was the closest we came to being hurt.

Later we found out, however, that we weren't being bombed by Japanese planes at all. It turned out to be our own anti-aircraft shells that were falling back down on us. And I guess that happened all around Honolulu that morning.

The McCorristons, our neighbors right next door to us, on the makai[1] side of us, had a daughter who was engaged to a young naval officer stationed on one of the destroyers at Pearl Harbor. One of his fellow officers brought his family, his wife and children, to stay with the McCorristons. They had lived on the base and were told to evacuate to the hills. So they gave us a detailed account, from their own perspective, as to what happened during the first wave of Japanese attackers. This was still early in the morning while the devastation continued at Pearl Harbor and Hickam. We could still see the planes flying around and see the smoke and hear the explosions.

> *" We started planning for our possible evacuation to the hills behind us. . . gathering up canned goods, canteens . . . rifles and ammunition. "*

We started planning for our possible evacuation to the hills behind us. While we had no previous plan for doing this, we just started gathering up canned goods, canteens, and such under my father's directions. We also packed rifles and ammunition. My father had it pretty well organized in no time.

My dad was part of a medical alert team through the Territorial Guard, and they set up a hospital facility at Castle Hall on the Punahou campus. So they called him right away and asked him to help run it. Before he left, he looked at me and said, "In case we have to head for the hills, this is what you should do," and he explained what he wanted me

[1]*Hawaiian word, a direction, meaning toward the ocean.*

to do. "In case I don't come back," Dad said, "you take your mother and sister and go up to the mountains." I was familiar with all the caves and places behind us where I knew we could survive for quite a while.

We heard rumors of an invasion of paratroopers and thought sure that we were going to have to move to the hills. We never had to do that, thank God, but I felt ready if we did.

An interesting and ironic story about that morning was that at the Mabel Smyth auditorium, there was a large group of physicians who were hearing lectures from medical experts on how to provide medical care in case of an attack. During the middle of the presentation, someone ran into the auditorium and yelled, "Doctors, report to your medical stations. I think we've got a real one going on right now." They all reported to their hospitals and clinics and started a marathon of patient care. There were quite a few casualties that day--three thousand dead, so many more wounded--and these doctors worked around the clock for seventy-two hours, saving lives and mending limbs. And they were prepared, too. It was quite a heroic thing they did.

Our neighbors on the other side were also close to the military, which helped keep us informed on what was going on. In fact, one of their close friends was Col. Kendall J. Fielder, who was head of the G-2 (intelligence) unit in Hawaii. We would visit when he was there and he would talk about what great souvenir hunters Americans were. He recalled that when Japanese airplanes would crash in the area that morning, they would report to their intelligence units on the army radio, "Another Jap plane just went down in the Aiea area. Get up there quick before those damned souvenir hunters strip the thing." Then, invariably, they would dash to the crash site and find just a smoldering engine. The intelligence guys, see, wanted to study the aircraft for intelligence purposes, and here they would find civilians sawing away at what was left of the plane.

That night was scary. My father didn't come home, so we were alone--my mother, me, and my sister. We would hear shots outside. Someone would light a cigarette and a nervous civil defense guy would shoot at the light, even from across the valley.

My father was able to call home, though, and tell us that he had to stay at the make-shift hospital. He said they were going to stay there until they were sure that the crisis was over. He was gone for about three days, I think, and slept right there in one of the hospital beds.

Robert M. Gibson, D.D.S. (continued)

My mother was very concerned, but no one was really panicky. There were rumors going wild, but no invasion had taken place. So we kept the radio going. It was our only contact to the outside world.

I remember we were listening to the Bob Hope show from the mainland that night. He said something on his show about Sweet Leilani, a pineapple field, being attacked by a bunch of hornets. I guess he was trying to send out a message and be funny at the same time. If he was trying to be funny, it was "serious" funny, you know, referring to the Japanese attack that morning. It was very dark out and we were all blacked out.

Then, all hell broke loose. It was about nine o'clock, I'd say, when we heard all these terrific explosions again. It sounded like all the anti-aircraft guns on the island opened up, again, against the attacking aircraft. Of course, we found out later that those weren't Japanese airplanes, but our own.

My school, Punahou, was taken over that day by the U.S. Engineers. So we lost our school. We were out of school for some time then, but when we started up again, we would go to private homes in the valley. I went down to the Cooke home, and then to another one, on Oahu Avenue. There were about thirty in our class--an entire class--and we had the same teacher. Eventually, we attended classes at the University High School campus next to the University of Hawaii.

My dad immediately became involved in the Businessmen's Military Training Corp (BMTC).[2] He was the captain for the Manoa Valley area and his prime responsibility was to organize and protect the valley. He had a lot of men from the First World War under his command. They issued guns, equipment, pot helmets, and they did guard duty. They would be assigned to intersections to check on people out after curfew and also to watch for blackout violations.

We had a very close neighborhood and were always running next door to visit our neighbors, back and forth. The neighbors on the mauka[3] side of our house were the Whitemans. Chauncy Whiteman was

---

[2]*Organized in Jan. 1942 limited to Caucasians and part-Hawaiians. The average age was 42, mostly WWI veterans. Allen, **Hawaii's War Years**, Honolulu, 1950, p. 96.*

[3]*Hawaiian word meaning the direction toward the mountains.*

the executive secretary of the Sugar Planters Association, and they knew how to entertain the military brass. He had a special expense account, I am sure, so that they may have some influence over the military (like where they would place an airfield, or something).

So, anyway, there was always a line-up of military staff cars out in front of the Whitemans' house. The cars would have flags with one, two, or three stars on them, so you knew that very important military people were visiting. And Mrs. Whiteman's sister was married to an admiral from Washington D.C., so they really knew the Washington style of entertaining.

Our place was always busy with military, too. I remember as the war went on, we had regular visits from the soldiers from the Seventh Infantry Division (California National Guard), and sailors from the submarine, the *USS Silverside*. The *Silverside* had quite a reputation as a fighting boat in the Pacific. After some of the sailors had a few drinks under their belts at our house, they would go next door and tell the admirals how to run the war. It was hilarious.

THE BMTC STANDS GUARD -- An anti-tank gun is manned by members of the Businessmen's Military Training Corps somewhere on an Oahu outpost. They are identified as (from left) R. H. Corbett, John F. Stone, H. C. Smith, and D. N. Shephard. (Signal Corps Photo, U.S.Army; War Depository Collection, University of Hawaii)

Then, on the other side, the McCorristons' daughter was marrying this young officer from a destroyer, so they would frequently have guests from the destroyer fleet over there. Robert McCorriston was vice president of the Bank of Hawaii. I remember once they even had the famous banjo player, Eddie Peabody, over there to entertain their guests. This would go on in the middle of a blackout, and everyone would be running back and forth from one house to the next. Hard to believe there was a war going on.

I was very patriotic and wanted to do my part for the war effort too, even though I was only fourteen years old. I begged my dad to let me join his BMTC unit and help patrol the streets at night. I was almost fifteen years old then and thought I needed to do something to help. He didn't think it would look too good to have his own son under his command. "I might be accused of favoritism," he said. But then, he said, "Why don't you join the Chinese army?" That was the nickname for a group of men, mostly Chinese, that banned together to help support the military in defense of the islands. The actual name of the group was the Hawaii Defense Volunteers. While they mostly had Chinese members in the group, they also had Filipinos, Hawaiians, Puerto Ricans, and Caucasians.

The Japanese students from the University of Hawaii had already organized their own unit. They started as an ROTC group and they were willing to go out on the beaches and clear the kiawe trees from around the beaches for gun emplacements. Later, they formed the famous 442nd Regimental Combat team and their accomplishments made history during the war.

Anyway, the Hawaii Defense Volunteers (HDV) were formed under the direction of Richard C. Tong, a member of a very well-known Chinese family in the islands. They had four companies. There were enough younger guys like me willing to join, so they put together a company--Company D--under Walter Chuck as our company commander (a prominent attorney in Honolulu today).

So we would go every weekend and drill and they would train us in the use of guns and equipment. We were given guard duty assignments at places like the electric substations and the water pumping stations. And we would ride around with the military patrols. It was very exciting. But the best thing was, we were given passes that allowed us out at night. That gave us adult status, that not too many adults had.

I'll never forget that summer they sent us to the Kahana Valley Jungle Warfare School, way up in the valley behind Kahana Bay. They trained us in the use of Japanese weapons during that training session. I guess they did this in case the Japanese invaded and we fought them as guerrillas in the hills. We needed to know how to use their weapons if we captured any. They even set up little Japanese villages that we could use for our war games.

> *" . . . we would go every weekend and drill and they would train us in the use of guns and equipment. . . And we would ride around with the military patrols. It was very exciting. "*

There were about forty or fifty of us in that summer war school. I remember they taught us how to make "shave" charges, explosives, using big blocks of TNT. You'd shave out a cone from the block of TNT and when it exploded, it had a much greater force. So we were being taught about the use of explosives and how to make all kinds of devices. Survival skills were taught, too.

We would go out on maneuvers at night and sleep out on the ground. We had to go across these ridges, way back in that valley. We had our compass, trying to get to a certain vantage point. Guys slipped off those ridges--"Yaaaaahh"--sliding down the side of the mountain. Nobody really got hurt, though. We all survived.

We didn't have any accidents with the guns, either, because we were trained really well. The army issued us shotguns at first, but later, we were toting around with tommy guns. The squad leaders were the ones that got the tommy guns.

The Jungle Warfare School was real interesting and though it was certainly serious business, we were young and had a lot of fun. They would have some Medal of Honor winner who would just be back from a major battle—like Guadalcanal—tell us all about it and take us through various exercises in the valley.

One time they told our group that they were going to teach us how to use bangalore torpedoes. These were the devices you use to stick under barbed wire fences to blow them up. The instructor asked for a volunteer, and we all raised our hands. "What's the matter with you guys?" he said, "Where the hell did you guys come from?" We were just a bunch of eager, gung-ho kids, you know. He just couldn't believe it, 'cause most army men never volunteered for anything.

Another time the instructor was teaching us how to camouflage ourselves. In the middle of the instruction, he said, "By the way, I want my group to stand up right now." And, all of a sudden, all these people who were camouflaged stood up right in front of us. We couldn't believe it. We didn't even see them. "My God," we said. It just blew us away. They were so well hidden, but that's how we were learning.

Then there was the time when an engineer unit in front of us was making a grenade out of TNT. I remember this guy came up there and lit it, but got excited and dropped it and ran. Everybody started to scramble when the sergeant ran up and pulled out the fuse real quick. Damned near blew us all up.

Those were exciting times. I guess the youngest guys were about fourteen. When they turned eighteen, they'd usually go into the service. They had a PX and everything out there. And we got to drink beer. Talk about feeling big.

The best thing about the HDV for me, though, was I got the night passes. We could travel at night. And during that period when there was a strict curfew, we were allowed to go out with the MPs and assist them. I remember going down to Kau Kau Korner, that drive-in restaurant on Kalakaua and Kapiolani. That was where all the action was during the war. It was wild in those days. All blacked out, but they were operating after dark. They were serving food, drinks, and poker games were going on. It was really wild. I think there were other things going on, too, in that building in the back.

I also worked at a summer job during the war, at Schubert's Cyclery down off of Nuuanu Street one block up from Beretania. I helped out as a bicycle mechanic and I remember there was this flight of stairs in the back of the cyclery that went upstairs to a "call" house. These guys, in uniform, would be lined up all around the block. Whoever owned the building rented the upstairs quarters, it had nothing to do with the Schubert business. Anyway, one day I was asked to help out with the sales up on the mezzanine. This very nice lady from a well-to-do Nuuanu family wanted to buy a bicycle for her child. So I was doing my sales pitch on this bike when you could hear these squeaking sounds coming from someplace nearby. "What is that noise?" the lady asked. And I replied, trying my damndest to keep a straight face, "Oh, that must be the rats making noises in the roof."

Those are some of my memories of the war years. I guess the HDV had the greatest impact on me. Not just the instruction on warfare and the freedoms I felt as a teenager, but also the interesting associations I gained from membership in the group. One of my fellow squad members, Alexis Lum, is now the head of the National Guard in Hawaii. (We used to call him "pretty boy Lum" because he always slicked his hair back). I made a lot of good friends in the HDV that I still know to this day. It brought me closer to my community, to a better appreciation of all the different ethnic groups that make up Hawaii. I am a richer person, I think, for having the experience.

Bob Gibson graduated from Punahou in 1945, just a few months before the end of the war. In fact, he missed his graduation exercises because transportation services was still operating under wartime conditions. No advance notification was given for any ship movement until just a few hours before departure. So he left for school in California in the middle of the night, the day before the graduation ceremonies. Bob attended Menlo College for two years, transferring to the University of California in Berkeley. He followed in his father's footsteps and became a dentist, graduating from the University of California at San Francisco's School of Dentistry. He returned to Honolulu and set up his practice in 1952. Dr. Gibson is married to Dr. Gina Whest, a chiropractor, and is the father of three, two girls and a boy, from a previous marriage; stepfather to Gina's daughter from a previous marriage; and he has one granddaughter. Dr. Gibson has been active on the Hawaii Board of Dental Examiners, the Pacific Oral Cancer Conference and Clinic, the American Cancer Society, and the Hawaii State Board of Health. He co-authored a historical novel about a nineteenth century dentist, Dr. John Mott-Smith, who was the first royal dentist and last royal ambassador for the Kingdom of Hawaii. It was published in 1989. He continues his dental practice in Honolulu.

Evacuation to the Mainland

 T he evacuation to the mainland of as many persons as possible was urged to lessen defense problems and relieve crowded conditions. About 20,000 army and navy dependents and 10,000 island women and children left Hawaii, most of them during the first months of the war. Conditions on crowded ships were trying. Public rooms were converted into dormitories and some decks were strung with hammocks. Pandemoniun reigned as babies bawled and shouting children slid down bannisters and played tag in the crowded passageways. Persons evacuating sometimes waited weeks, expecting at any moment, telephone summons to report to their ship within the next few hours. Then they would scurry around making last-minute preparations. They were warned to say goodbye to no one, but their relatives and neighbors could not help to know of their impending departure. *(Allen, Hawaii's War Years)*

WANTED: TRANSPORTATION OUT -- Civilians crowd the steamship offices seeking passage to the mainland. As the Japanese invasion was feared imminent, women were encouraged to take their children and leave the islands. Transportation was made available only to those who had a place to go to on the mainland. (**Star Bulletin** Dec. 31, 1941; *War Depository Collection, University of Hawaii*)

Dennis and Katherine Rodrigues

Born in Honolulu in 1908, Dennis Rodrigues was the second of five children of Frank and Jessie Rodrigues. He graduated from St. Louis College (high school) in 1928, and married Katherine (Kate) Robello in June 1933. On December 7, 1941, Dennis had been working at Pearl Harbor for one year. Katherine Robello was born in Pahalo, Hawaii. She was one of seven children, four girls and three boys. She graduated from McKinley High School in 1928 and attended Normal Training School in Honolulu. At the outset of the war, Kate was thirty-three and living with her husband, Dennis, at her parents' home at 243 Huna Lane, off Kuakini Street. She was a teacher.

Dennis: Kate and I were living with her folks on Hunu Lane at the time. I was working for Fritz Hoddick, the Chief Clerk in the Accounting Division at Pearl Harbor. I worked in the Administration Building, handling the orders for maintenance for the District Public Works.

I remember on December seventh, I was playing golf at the Ala Wai Golf Course with Louie Moniz, Johnny Moniz, and a chief petty officer from the navy yard. We started early in the morning--about 7:00-7:10, somewhere around there. And we were on the fourth or fifth hole when I noticed planes flying in formation--I mean real good formation. They were flying from the Diamond Head side, flying right over Diamond Head--coming over the golf course. They were high, but you could see them flying in formation.

I looked up and I said to Louie--"What the hell are those planes doing up there?" I said, "Jesus, we went off maneuvers last night at midnight. What are they doing?" And he said, "Oh, those are carrier-based planes." Well they certainly were carrier-based planes, but we didn't know at the time that they weren't American. We let it go at that.

A few minutes later we were surprised when one of those big bombers (B-17s) came flying low from the Diamond Head side--dangerously low. Then I realized he was trying to land on the golf course. I said, "What the hell's the damned fool trying to do, land here?" We didn't know what the hell was happening.

He found out real soon, though, that he couldn't make it down on the golf course--so he headed towards the ocean, out to sea.

I found out later that there were a number of those bombers coming in from the mainland that morning. They were ferrying them in from the mainland to Honolulu. They must have been attacked and they had no guns or anything to defend themselves. We all couldn't believe what we just saw.

Those planes were supposed to go out to Midway, Guam, the Marshall Islands--all through there where we were building these bases, building up our defenses. We really figured something was going to happen soon, but we didn't know when.

Well, anyway, about a few minutes later, a report came from the club house loud speaker system. "All navy yard workers report to the navy yard immediately. Very important." They said the navy yard was being attacked. They didn't say by whom, or what.

So we got in our cars, and like darn fools, we went down to the navy yard. We went in my car, Louie Moniz, and the rest of them. We drove down Kamehameha Highway. There were several accidents along the way. People were all rushing to get down to Pearl Harbor. It was terrible.

At Hickam Field, they had already set up anti-aircraft guns and they were firing them as we passed--right close to us. I yelled at them, "Hey, watch out what you're doing," I said. They were so close to us.

So when we got to the main gate at Pearl Harbor, we were told to park in the housing area--Housing Area No. 1, at that time. So we had to walk in. The planes were still attacking at that time, you know. I didn't know what the hell was going on yet, really. In fact I remember making a comment--I told Louie Moniz--I said, "Look at that damned fool running and throwing himself on the ground." He was being strafed and I didn't know that.

I was amazed to see marines flat on their bellies, you know, with rifles shooting at the planes. Shooting with rifles. I did see those planes diving, but we still didn't know what was going on. In fact, I remember this admiral was in the Ad Building and he runs out and says, "What are those damned fools doing shooting at our own planes?" And he was right. Some of our own planes got off the ground and the confused marines were shooting at them too. It was mass confusion.

They assigned us duties--we had to carry buckets of sand to fight fires. I saw one last Japanese plane leave the area. I think it's the one that landed on Kauai.

I remember seeing another one of our planes that took off from Wheeler Field and tried to help. But we were shooting at it, too. He flew out to sea. I don't know what happened to him, whether he was hit or not. I know he flew out to sea. He was flying very low.

Later, when we were pretty tired carrying the damned sand, we thought we'd go down to the marine barracks and pick up some sodas and lunch. There was a hospital, a navy hospital, inside the yard there, close to the marine barracks. That's when we saw these bodies they were collecting from the battlewagons. White men with flesh turned black with burns and oil. They must have jumped overboard and the oil burned them. They had picked them up with the tugs.

"... we saw these bodies they were collecting from the battlewagons. White men with flesh turned black with burns and oil ... I heard one doctor say, 'Leave this one out, he has no chance. Take this one in.'"

I heard one doctor say, "Leave this one out, he has no chance. Take this one in." In other words, he was just picking out the ones that had a chance. They were actually doing that. Some of the bodies were still moving, but I guess they were brain dead. Then we went back and worked all afternoon.

Later I walked down to the drydock to take a look at the damage. The *Pennsylvania* was at the end of 1010 drydock. And there were two other ships in there, that's how big the drydock is. The *Pennsylvania* wasn't hit at all, they just missed it. But what a big hole in the drydock. One of the other ships was hit.

Then I looked out and I saw the battlewagons all burning, one tipped over. Spilled oil was everywhere--fire still in the water.

Later on, when we were all through working, we wanted to go home.

It was now dark. There was no more firing. The Japs had dispersed. And we wanted to go home.

So when we got by the main gate, I was almost killed by a marine with a bayonet. He jumped at me. Good thing I could duck and jump back. So I had to call Mr. Hoddick and have him tell these sentries that we want to go home. He called certain people and they finally let us go.

Then we had to drive home in the dark. It was very dark that night of the seventh. And sometimes I didn't know whether I was on the road or off of it. Half of the time I was on the road--only half of the time. I had to take Pappy DeMello home, one fellow lived up at Punchbowl. Then Louie. That was crazy. I was the last one to get home.

I remember on the way home I stopped at the service station because my tires were low. It was closed and the lights were all off. I was filling the tires, but I didn't hear anything. I figured the air pump wasn't working. But it sure was. So I over-inflated them, but I didn't know it at the time. Good thing I stopped doing it, because I could have blown myself up with the darn thing. If they would have burst, it would have killed us. Driving home I noticed how hard riding the tires were.

As it was, I ruined four tires. I had to get four brand new tires. I had to get a special permit from Pearl Harbor to buy them because tires were immediately rationed.

For several nights after that we were on alert. Our homes had to be blacked out. I remember a Japanese sub had fired from off shore. One time, it was a false alarm. One of our own planes had dropped a bomb, I think, in Tantalus someplace. They thought it was a Japanese plane. It wasn't. It was one of our own planes, I heard later.

Louie Moniz and I were exempt from being drafted, but we volunteered to go in as naval officers. At that time, they were sending all these supply officers on ships to the Solomons. If our admiral hadn't said that we were more important in the jobs we held, we'd have joined the navy. And if we had gone, I'm sure we'd have lost our lives. All of those ships--the supply ships--were sunk by the Japanese. And we were supposed to be stationed on supply ships, providing the navy with materials.

I joined the Businessmen's Military Training Corps, the BMTC. We patrolled the streets at night. We were actually drafted into the army. Actually, I could say I belonged to the army at the time. But later on, they didn't recognize that service for vets privileges. Many nights I patrolled the streets, and put in a full day's work the next day.

" One thing I remember, we never did hire Japanese in the navy yard. . . There were Chinese, but no Japanese. "

One thing I remember--we never did hire Japanese in the navy yard. There were no Japanese working there. There were Chinese, but no Japanese. And I remember there were a lot of stories, a lot of rumors, about local Japanese helping the enemy--about cutting arrows in the cane fields, supposedly helping the enemy pilots flying overhead by pointing the way to Pearl Harbor, and things like that.

The battle of Midway was the turning point. Because if the Japs had taken Midway, at that time, the islands would have been taken by them for sure. But I'll tell you one thing. If the Japs had an invasion going on here in the islands on December seventh, they would have taken us. We were so disorganized. They would have controlled the islands at that time.

They accomplished their goals, though. They crippled the U.S. Navy. The battlewagons were all here--they were all docked. It's a darn good thing that our carriers were still out.

They (the Japanese) thought they hit a carrier, but they didn't. That was the *Utah* that was being used as a target ship. It resembled a carrier from the air with a large flat deck. But they accomplished their goals. And if they wanted to, they could have controlled the islands. How lucky we are that they didn't do it.

Kate: I remember the night before the attack. Dennis and I went to a dance. One of the girls got married and we went to the party. It was funny--kind of strange. I don't know what it was, but you could feel it in the air. A weird, strange feeling.

The dance was close by so we walked. I remember it was late at night when we walked home. The Japanese Embassy was on the corner of Kuakini and Nuuanu. There was a whole Japanese complex there. When we passed by, we heard noises and we saw smoke. We peeked through the fence and saw this guy burning papers in the back of the embassy. There was an opening in the fence and we could see through. We thought it was funny for them to be burning papers so late at night.

The next morning, Dennis was playing golf early, and I can remember hearing these loud sounds, you know, bombs, guns, and things like that.

I had my car already packed up with Christmas things, a Christmas tree and everything. I was going to go to school to decorate my classroom for Christmas. I taught fifth grade at the civilian housing area school at Pearl Harbor.

I heard all this noise. So we all went outside and looked up, wondering what was going on. My mother and dad said something like, "Oh, they're only going through maneuvers. They said they would be doing something like that."

But it wasn't so. All that smoke. Those things--shells were whizzing by--I didn't know where they were coming from or where they were shooting. Somewhere up on the hill, I thought. You would hear these things going--WHEEEE--just whistling by, and then--BOOOOM!--right in front of the Japanese store where we would buy sushi. There was a big hole there. Something fell in there.

My dad had just come home from work. He was working for Dairymen's where he had a job washing bottles at night. He was already retired from the plantation--he was a supervisor out in the cane fields-- but he was working for the dairy because we needed more money.

He was born in Portugal. He came to Honolulu when he was only three years old. And my dad learned to read and to write, even though he only went to the first grade.

Anyway, we didn't know what was going on. Then they announced it over the radio. I forget what they said, something like Japan has declared war against us, or something like that. They asked us to keep away from Pearl Harbor. And you know, these people were climbing up the coconut trees, watching all those planes fighting up in the air. I guess it's the only way they could see.

So I said, "Gee whiz, I can't go to school." So I didn't go to Pearl Harbor. I left everything in the car. When things quieted down later, I brought the stuff back in. Good thing I didn't go earlier. If I was on my way there it would have been terrible. I would have been so frightened. I probably would have driven off the road someplace and gotten hurt.

My dad was sitting at the table there, and he just cried like a baby. I'll never forget that. He knew something was badly wrong. He said, "We'll never see that flag again." And that man just cried and cried like a baby, sitting at the kitchen table there.

" My dad . . . just cried like a baby. . . He knew something was badly wrong. He said, 'We'll never see that flag again.' And that man just cried like a baby . . . "

My sister, Angie, wasn't too far away from us. She was living up at Pahoa. She had Patrick and he was just a baby. Her husband was at work that day--or was called to work--I'm not sure. So she was alone. I called and she was crying and crying. And I said, "Hang on, Angie, I'll come to get you." I had to get her and the baby and bring her over.

It was scary. I drove through the shooting, you know. It was horrible driving there. You heard all those doggone airplanes firing away, and what-not. It was awful.

That was the only time I really took a chance. I said, I'm going to take that chance. Dennis wasn't home, so I had to do it. So I went and got her. She never saw her husband for four days. We all thought he must be dead or something. No phone calls, nothing at all from him. But he was working all that time. And when he came home, he was a wreck.

The nights were terrible. For four years, we just stayed in the house at night. You couldn't go out. We had to black out everything.

I never did go back to that school in Pearl Harbor. They closed it down. But all schools were closed, you know--for quite a while--until things settled down. I went to this school in Damon Tract when we went back.

While school was out--I'll never forget--teachers were assigned to take names of people who lived in homes, apartments, like a census. I guess because we had to be paid and school was closed, so they had to give teachers something to do. Our district was the Kapalama area--that's where our school teachers were. Every school had their own section of the city to do.

We had to go door to door and explain to the people what it was all about. Just take the names down, so they could figure out how many were killed, or something. I didn't like it, but I had to do it.

> " *We'll never forget those times. Nobody knew what the Japanese would have done to us if they had landed. Rape us? Kill us? Who knows?* "

Every time the siren went off--every time there was an air raid--we had to go into these ditches. They had men making these ditches for shelter. Later we had covered shelters, down in the ground, with roofs. All day long we'd hear those damned sirens, then we had to go down into the shelters, under the ground. We had to train the children what to do. I'd get so nervous. Every time we had to go into the shelter--oh boy, I don't know--I couldn't go. I'd stay in the lavatory--that's where I'd stay--until the all clear signal.

And the gas masks. I hated them. I don't like anything on my face, anyway. I think when you have certain fears, things like that make it difficult for you. It was horrible. I never even tried to use it.

We'll never forget those times. Nobody knew what the Japanese would have done to us if they had landed--rape us? Kill us? Who knows? But it didn't happen. They had their chance, catching us so unprepared. I guess the Lord was with us. Thank God.

Kate and Dennis have a daughter, Linda, born during the war. Linda is married, and living in Florida with her husband, Jim Jackson and three children, Todd, Jamie, and Staci. Dennis retired in 1967 after twenty-eight years of service at Pearl Harbor. Kate taught school for close to thirty-five years before retiring. They lived in Waikiki, where Kate passed away in October, 1990.

Joan Martin Rodby

Her paternal grandfather had jumped ship in the 1890s to begin a life in Honolulu. He raised cattle and pigs and trained horses for Prince Kuhio, on the slopes of Diamond Head. Her father, Charles Martin, was born in Honolulu and graduated from McKinley High School and the University of Hawaii. He joined the merchant marine and, on one of his visits to Australia, married seventeen-year-old Fredrica Sleeman and brought her back to live in Honolulu in about 1925. They lived in a house his father built for them on Wela Street, on the family Diamond Head property. The four Martin children were born there. Joan Martin has an older brother and sister, and a younger sister. She attended Thomas Jefferson School and was in the fifth grade and ten-and-a-half years old when war broke out.

We went to Australia in the summer of 1941. I remember we went by ship--the whole family--and we were gone for six weeks. It was my mother's first trip home since she had left, sixteen or so years before. It was a lovely trip, but now that I think of it, on our way back--we sailed on the P & O Line--and they were painting it in camouflage colors. I mean there were fellows actually hanging over the sides on little seats with ropes and they were camouflaging the ship. It was a British ship and England was at war already. I also remember we zig-zagged through the water all the way back. I guess it was a defensive move in case of torpedo attack or something. I don't recall being concerned at all, though. But it's interesting, isn't it, that they were taking those kinds of precautions that long before December 7, 1941.

The Salvation Army sunday school was held right across the street from my grandparent's home, right there on the corner of Hinano and Campbell avenues. I remember my grandparents had leased the land to the Salvation Army for one dollar a year. All the grandchildren would attend Sunday School at 7:30 in the morning. We walked from home (it was probably only a block-and-a-half). That's where we were on December seventh.

I remember in the middle of the service, someone came running in to the church yelling that we were being bombed, that the Japanese had attacked Pearl Harbor. We all went scurrying across the street to grandmother's house--my two sisters, my brother, my cousins, and I. We were very frightened.

My grandmother and grandfather had a two-story house. All the kids ran upstairs where there is a very wide hallway on the second floor, a good six to eight feet across. In the very center of the hallway there was a wooden ladder. We climbed up the ladder and went into the widow's peak, which was a little room right on the top that's all glass enclosed. It was sort of small, though, so not many of us could be in there at the same time. Our purpose was, of course, to see the action at Pearl Harbor. At that time, there were very few buildings in Waikiki and Pearl Harbor was easy to see from this third floor vantage point. I remember seeing the fire and smoke at Pearl Harbor. It was very scary. What was really frightening, however, were the fires and smoke over in the McCully area. We could see that clearly--it seemed so close--I guess it's actually only one or two miles from where we were.

> *" In a short period of time, there were fifteen of us there at my grandparents' house. . . We all slept in the living room. "*

In a short period of time, there were fifteen of us there at my grandparents' house. My dad was working for the Honolulu Iron Works at the time. He was head of the government section, but he was home on that Sunday. So we all congregated there at the grandparents' place. Besides Grandma and Grandpa, there were my mom and dad and us four kids; my dad's sister, Alice, her husband and their two boys; and my dad's other sister, Edna, her husband and their one son. Fifteen of us, and we all just moved in.

The shock of it all was that I don't recall the adults, or my parents, talking about war or anything before that. If they knew anything might have happened, they never did discuss it in front of us kids. So it really was a complete surprise that we could be in any danger.

So we all stayed there as a family for, I think, a couple of weeks, even though we all lived just a few blocks away. I guess the important thing at that time was that we were all together. We all slept in the living room. The kids slept on the floor. Some of us had mattresses.

It was fun being together, being a child, but it also was frightening because the adults kept saying that the Japanese were going to come back. And the air raids we would have at night, with all those searchlights in the sky looking for enemy planes, and the sirens, and the blackout, was really a scary time. We went back to our homes during the day, but returned to our grandparents' at night. I really can't remember just how long we stayed at my grandparents' at night, but it was quite a while. We spent a lot of time sitting outside after dark, talking, chatting. We were feeling very bad for those people who were killed or injured that day. I remember my parents talked about that a lot.

When we returned to our house to sleep, I remember we were very cautious in the blackout. My dad would go around the house, checking every corner for a light leak. And there were wardens who would come by and check us out. We used to dread the evenings, the nights. Sometimes we would have two air raids in the same night. We'd have to get out of our beds and go into the air raid shelter. We had one in our back yard. I remember my knees just shaking and not being able to stop them.

And rumors were running rampant. My cousin, Charles Porter, recalls that they were talking about the water being poisoned. I barely remember that. We were afraid to do much, afraid to go too far away from our home.

I remember, we were all issued gas masks. We had to carry our gas masks at all times. I don't know how long we were out of school, but it seemed like a long time. Anyway, we had to have our gas masks with us in school, too. And we'd have air raid tests during the school day and kids would have to run for the shelter. Because our grandparents lived close to the school, we were allowed to go over there. There was a bomb shelter there. But, oh, I remember the cockroaches in it. Gosh, I couldn't go in there with all those cockroaches. It always had roaches in it. We kept food down there. We had a trap door that we had to lift up to go in. But no matter how careful we were trying to keep them out, the roaches kept getting in. I'll never forget that.

It was a relatively quiet, secure, life for a child as time went on. It was school, then home again. Mother was always home. Dad worked and was home before dark. I know they tried not to talk about the war too much in front of us, but they were always listening to the radio. But you couldn't help feeling scared. It was just the times.

WAIKIKI IS WIRED -- Popular Kuhio Beach in Waikiki is framed with barbed wire in this picture taken early in the war. Looking Ewa,[1] this photo shows the Royal Hawaiian and Moana hotels. The barricade remained until 1943. (Bishop Museum photo)

I remember how we worked on victory gardens at Thomas Jefferson School. We all planted these lovely vegetables. We'd go out and check them every morning. That was all part of the school program. We had a victory garden at our Wela Street home, too. And my grandparents had one, too, that their Japanese friends took care of, on either side of their big home. One garden was on the corner of Makini and Campbell, and the other was on the corner of Hinano and Campbell. And my grandparent's home was in the center. We used to get wonderful, fresh produce from that garden. The Kiyabus were a wonderful Japanese family that worked the garden. They lived close by and I have fond memories of their New Years Eve parties that they used to have with all that wonderful Japanese food--particularly that Japanese gelatin--the green and red dessert. Even now, when I see that food in the market, I think of the good food and wonderful times at the Kiyabu house.

---

[1]*Hawaiian word used as a direction, toward the district of Ewa, west of Waikiki.*

We didn't have to pay too much attention to the curfews in those days, since we were too young. We were always home before dark, anyway. My parents didn't socialize much. They were more family oriented. We did go to Hanauma Bay for picnics as a family, though, mostly on Sundays. We didn't go to Waikiki beach much, though. I remember the barbed wire at Waikiki and all the sailors in their uniforms, walking the streets. I especially remember the barbed wire so vividly.

We had Japanese neighbors on one side of us. They raised chickens and we used to buy the fresh eggs from them. They were wonderful people, even though they had one son in Japan who I think was in the Japanese army. That son stayed in Japan and never really came back. They also had one son here. It must have been tough on them.

" We had Japanese neighbors on one side of us. . . They were wonderful people, even though they had one son in Japan who I think was in the Japanese army. "

Then they began evacuating families to the mainland. They wanted women and children to leave, to escape the dangers of living in Hawaii at that time. So we signed up for it, knowing that my dad couldn't go with us. We expected to go to Oakland, California, where my dad's brother, Bill, lived. Bill was in school when the war broke out. Our name came up twice and each time my mother decided that she couldn't do it. So we stayed here. You do what you have to do. My mother felt that it was better to stay right here. Of course, later, as the war progressed, it no longer became as dangerous to be in Hawaii.

It was quite an experience growing up in those years. We have always been so thankful that no one in our family was really hit by the war--nobody was killed or injured. Our dad and uncles were too old to go into the service at the time and, of course, we were all too young. How lucky we were.

And how lucky, too, that the attack occurred on a Sunday. I'm sure there would have been a lot more deaths and injuries if it had happened on a Monday, with a lot more people at Pearl Harbor.

Those were very impressionable days when I was young. Even today, when I hear the sirens which go off on the first day of every month, no matter where I am or what I am doing, for that one second, I remember those war years. You never forget.

Joan Martin graduated from Roosevelt High School in 1949. She went to a private secretarial school in Waikiki for a year-and-a-half, then worked at the Hawaiian Electric Company for two years. In 1952, she married Clinton Sherman Ballentyne. They had a three-year-old son, Scott, and Joan was four months pregnant with their second child, Nancy, when Clinton was accidentally killed while serving as a jet pilot in exercises with the Air National Guard. Joan married Dick Rodby in 1958 and they had one daughter, Robyn. Dick manages Kemoo Farms in Wahiawa. Son Scott Ballentyne is married, living in Boise, Idaho, and has two sons. Daughter Nancy is married and living in Maui. She has one daughter. Joan and Dick's daughter, Robyn, is married and lives in Honolulu.

Richard and Leo Rodby

Their father, Leo, arrived in the islands as a first sergeant in the army at Schofield Barracks in 1920. A short time later, he began working at nearby Kemoo Farm and in the 1930s, he purchased controlling interest in the corporation. Leo B. Rodby married Carita Fisher in 1924. Carita's father was in the army and her family was one of the first to arrive at the newly opened training facility, Schofield Barracks, in 1909. They were transported out to Schofield from Honolulu by train and they built their house out of the packing crates their household goods were shipped in. Leo and Carita had five children, Leo, Byron, Jayne, Richard, and Linnea. Richard "Dick" (above, left), who was ten at the time war broke out, was in the sixth grade at Leilehua school. Leo was fifteen and in the eleventh grade at the same school. They lived in a big, old, house, right across from Schofield Barracks, a short distance from Wheeler Air Field.

Dick: For some reason, our father was home that morning on December seventh. He hadn't gone fishing as he usually did on Sundays.

Leo: No, he didn't go fishing. As I recall, he was home that morning because he had gone over to Wheeler Field the night before for a big party at the officer's club. So he probably wanted to sleep in.

Dick: Every Friday and Saturday nights were special occasions for the military at that time. Those were very social times for people in the military.

The first recollection I had that morning that anything was happening was hearing the airplanes and the blasts of the bombs. They must have been bombing Wheeler at the time.

Leo: We ran in to try and wake up our father. His first words when he woke up were, "Oh, boy, those sure are realistic maneuvers going on out there." I know that he felt, just like everybody else did, that this could never happen to us. Not to the United States.

Dick: Then they flew by this area so low that we could see the pilots clearly. We even waved to them, and they waved back. We still didn't know what was going on. But they were practically tree-top high when they flew past here. That was when they started strafing the barracks at Schofield.

<u>Leo</u>: And, you know, when they flew by we could see the red circles on the planes. And then we started noticing all these machine gun clips on our front yard. You know, the machine gun bullets are locked together with these metal clips. When the bullets go through the machine gun, the base of the cartridge and the clips would go sailing out and falling to the ground below. And they were all over our front yard. So we went running here and there, busy picking them up. Then, somebody turned on the radio in the house and we heard, "The islands are under attack." We finally realized what was going on.

Then we could hear the sirens at Schofield and see ambulances dashing in and out. Schofield wasn't bombed, only strafed. The explosions in Schofield were from anti-aircraft shells--our own.

<u>Dick</u>: But they sure did bomb Wheeler, of course. They destroyed the planes and hangars at Wheeler. And I think the reason the planes were strafing the barracks at Schofield was just to keep our soldiers down. They were shooting at the planes with their rifles--BARs--Browning automatic rifles.

<u>Leo</u>: The planes used this reservoir back here as a landmark, they've told me. You can see the Wilson reservoir from almost anywhere around here and Schofield and Wheeler are right next to it. Some people call it the Wahiawa reservoir. It is the water that is used to irrigate the sugar fields down below at the Waialua plantation. It was built back in 1906, I understand. And Wilson used to be the head of the water company out here so they called it the Wilson reservoir. Anyway, this was the landmark the Japanese planes used to find Schofield and Wheeler.

<u>Dick</u>: At first, I remember, we were going to get away from the danger of the area by going to our beach house at Mokuleia. We were told to get away from here. But they didn't want us to go to the beach because they expected an invasion. So we all drove to our other home in Wahiawa heights. I remember the drive up there. At that time, the road was straight and there were eucalyptus trees on both sides of the road. As we turned by the school, I looked under the tree branches and I could see guys running away from the barracks--some with clothes on and some without clothes on. We could also see the smoke and fires from Wheeler Field. I remember people started to come in from Pearl Harbor later in the day, telling of all the death and devastation that happened there. I just couldn't believe it.

<u>Leo</u>: The electric plant--the transformer station--the only line that

WHEELER FIELD BURNS -- *This photo, taken by one of the Japanese pilots, is believed to be the only aerial photo of Wheeler Field under attack on December 7, 1941. (War Depository Collection, University of Hawaii)*

PLANE DESTROYED -- *A P-40 fighter plane was destroyed by the Japanese air attackers at Wheeler Field on Sunday morning, December 7, 1941. (War Depository Collection, University of Hawaii)*

brought electric power to Schofield, was right here in the area. They set up security around that place right away.

I remember we moved in with the Wiley family. They were here because the father was a member of the California National Guard and he was training at Schofield. They were renting our family home at the time. And we just moved right in with them because we were evacuated from the lower area near the bases. I got a big kick out of it, because Mrs. Wiley had all girls--three daughters--and she used to keep her daughters under close surveillance. She was always concerned that us guys were going to be too close to her daughters. And yet, we were all sleeping in the same back bedroom.

<u>Dick</u>: I remember I had to sleep in the house next door. People just opened up their homes to whoever needed it.

<u>Leo</u>: During the course of the evening, there were people shooting at each other--shooting at cows--anything that moved, they'd shoot at it. You'd hear the shots but you don't know where it's coming from, what's happening. It made us kind of nervous.

I remember there was a large estate about a half mile from our home. That evening, they were bringing some families up from Wheeler Field to stay at this place. I was over there with a group of older men. I remember there was a lot of disorganization. It was dark and planes were flying overhead. This Japanese guy, someone I knew, was kind of the unofficial custodian of this estate and he didn't want the military to

---

" . . . there were people shooting at each other--shooting at cows--anything that moved. . . "

---

move these people in. Anyway, in the course of mulling around with all this, the Japanese guy takes out his flashlight and turns it on. Remember, this is supposed to be blackout time and there are planes flying overhead. Well the GIs got all excited, thinking he was trying to signal the enemy so they grabbed him and wanted to shoot him right there on the spot. The tension was running very high. The guy who had the gun was a guy I knew from the DeMolay's organization--we were in it together--so I told him, "You can't shoot this guy."

He shouted back, "I seen my friend shot at Wheeler this morning and, yes, I **can** shoot him."

And I yelled back, "No you can't, he's my friend." So he put his gun down and they took him down to Civil Defense headquarters, which was in the old court house in Wahiawa. My father was down there when they got there. He was active in the Civil Defense. My father knew him too--as a matter of fact, this Japanese guy had bought my grandfather's place from us many years before, so my father knew him well. "What are you doing here?" my father asked him. He told my father what had happened and my father said to the soldiers, "Lock him up." About an hour later, after all the GIs had left, my father got him an escort to take him to his home. Believe me, he never left the house after dark after that night. He was a man in his forties, I'd say, and I guess I was somewhat responsible for saving his life.

And there were a lot of rumors going around. We heard rumors about people being taken away because they were Japanese. All of the folks who had anything to do with Japanese schools were suspects. I remember there was a story about a fellow who used to run a beer hall up in Schofield, a guy by the name of Charlie Hasabe. There were stories that Charlie had a radio and he was talking to Tokyo. And the story went that they took Charlie out and shot him. I don't think any of that was true, but that was the kind of stuff that was going around there.

<u>Dick</u>: I remember we used to hear shots at night. It was frightening. You didn't know what was going on outside. Maybe you'd have a crack in your blacked out window and someone would come by and yell for you to seal it up or turn off the lights.

I remember we didn't go to school for a while. Since the military took over the school here, we used the Japanese school in Wahiawa when we went back. We only had a half day of school, too, I recall.

<u>Leo</u>: Yes, the military took over many schools for their own use. The school in Wahiawa was taken over by a hospital. But I never went back to school--at least here in Hawaii. After about a month or so, we had a snack bar or a coffee shop up by Leilehua High School, or where it was located in those days, now it's Wheeler School. And so dad put me to work in the coffee shop, helping out up there. By the next September, when school started, we had evacuated to the mainland and I attended school again, in Minnesota.

In June 1942, my mother and us five kids left Hawaii for the mainland. My dad wasn't allowed to leave. My brother, Byron, and I-- we were the older ones--had to sleep down in the hold of the ship, the cargo deck. I remember there were a lot of men down there--a bunch of them were Pearl Harbor workers--and they used to have big crap games down there, but I never got involved with them. There were bunks on the wall. And we ate in some kind of a mess hall.

" It changed our lives so much. We never lived as a family, together, again. "

<u>Dick</u>: I remember it was on the *USS Grant*. It was an army troop transport ship. Think of what it took for my mother to do that. A mother, travelling with five children. I was young enough to stay in the room with my mother.

<u>Leo</u>: And mother was so seasick. She would just have to look at a boat to get seasick. What a sight it was. My mother so sick, so sick, and little Jayne was jumping all over the place--climbing on everything-- having a grand old time.

<u>Dick</u>: And when we landed in San Francisco, the Red Cross was there to help us. I remember we stayed a night in a hotel. Then the next day we caught a train to go across the country. We went to Omaha, then changed trains and then went to Minneapolis. And then we had to take a bus up to Virginia, Minnesota, which was a horrible eight-hour bus ride. We stopped in every little hick town there was along the way.

<u>Leo</u>: When we were in San Francisco, I remember there were a number of stores with signs in the window, "We are not Japanese." They were run by Chinese people and at that time emotions were quite strong. They were probably moving the Japanese people into the relocation camps about then, although we didn't know it.

Our family was never the same after that. It changed our lives so much. We never lived as a family, together again. I joined the navy at 17. I came back to Hawaii during the war, in 1944, while still in the navy. My dad was here the whole time. My mother came back in August of 1945, after the war was over. The war separated our family and life wasn't the same, ever.

Leo was discharged from the Navy in 1945 and moved back to Hawaii. He returned to Minnesota in 1946 to continue his education in Virginia, Minnesota. He married Kuulei Directo in 1954 and they had five children. They later divorced. Leo, now retired, lives in Wahiawa. He has four grandchildren.

Dick graduated from Schofield High School in 1948. He attended Woodbury College in Los Angeles and earned a bachelor's degree in business administration. In 1958, Dick married Joan Ballentyne. He has directed the operation of Kemoo Farm since 1958. They have three children and three grandchildren. Dick's future includes history writing--primarily the interesting history of Kemoo Farm, which is 75 years old in 1991.

Immunizations Ordered

Immediately after the war began, the biggest compulsory vaccination program in island history was undertaken. All civilians in the islands, except infants and the aged, were immunized against typhoid, paratyphoid, and smallpox. Immunization against tetanus was recommended but not required. Vaccinating teams composed of service and civilian doctors, nurses, clerks, and assistants, immunized 200,000 persons at the registration centers; and private physicians immunized 163,000 others. In June 1943, diphtheria immunication for all children became mandatory. *(Allen, Hawaii's War Years)*

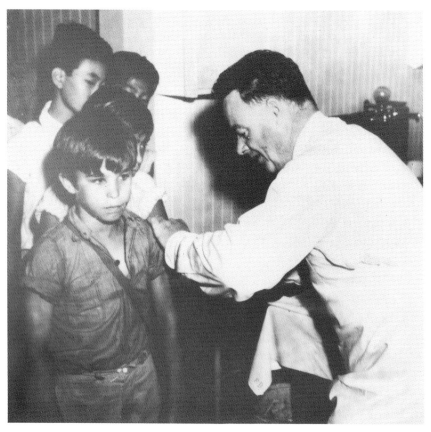

OUCH, THAT HURTS -- This youngster appeared not to be too happy to get his vaccination in a March 1942 newspaper photograph. The boy, identified as Richard Mariera, is shown being treated by Dr. Enright during the territorial-wide program to vaccinate all children. (Star Bulletin Mar. 18, 1942; War Depository Collection, University of Hawaii)

Donald Y. Keliinoi

His paternal grandparents, both half-Hawaiians, were born in Maui. His father, Samuel Keliinoi, born in Honolulu, married Emily Rapoza. They were farmers and had five children, three boys and two girls. Donald was the fourth child, the third son in a row. Goldie, the oldest, was seventeen and a boarder at Kamehameha School in December 1941. Gordon was sixteen; Tom was fourteen; and Donald was a nine-year-old fourth grader, at the outbreak of war. Annette was two.

$\mathbf{W}$e were living at Puuloa Farms, in Ewa Beach, which would be at the tip of the West Loch of Pearl Harbor. We had a big, ten-acre farm out there. There was no address to the farm, we were just described as living at the Keliinoi house in the Puuloa farming area.

I lived with my parents and brothers and sisters. One sister was away at Kam School. My little sister was just a few years old. We had two cousins, Al and Edward, living with us, too. We were going to Ewa Elementary School in Ewa Beach. I remember it had a statue of Lincoln out in front of the school.

We had this big farm with vegetables and a few livestock. Tomatoes were the big product, our main product. We also had lima beans, string beans, carrots. The chickens and ducks were mostly for the family to eat.

Farm life was so lonely. You just had each other--brothers, sisters, cousins. We were all alone out there, isolated, like you're at the end of the earth. And so when a car would come up the dirt road, everyone would rush out to the front and hope that the car coming would be a visitor to your farm. Then the car would go--WHOOSH--right by. And you wouldn't see another car for the rest of the day.

And, boy, did we work on that farm. My father was kind of a hard guy. My mother was a slave to the farm. We all worked like slaves. My mother hated the farm. She used to wash clothes with brackish water that would never suds up. She had to pound it, wash it by hand. And then when we had to have drinking water, it was a matter of catching the rain. When it didn't rain, you had to go down to the plantation with your truck and fill big barrels of water for drinking. We dug a well to get the brackish water, but you couldn't drink that. That's how we lived. A real farm life. My father was a real farmer. I hated that farm.

The only enjoyment we got out of the farm life was when we would clear the land, we would cut these kiawe trees. We cut a lot of them so that we could plant crops. At the end of the day, we'd have a big pile of kiawe wood and we'd build a big bonfire. Then at night we'd sit around the fire and play music and sing. That was our big farm-life entertainment, and it was fun.

On Saturdays and Sundays, when there was no school, we just slept in because there was nothing to do. It wasn't farm day. So we would sleep in and my mother used to call us, "Would you kids get up? Come on, get out of bed." Nobody would move. I'll never forget one day she said, loud enough for us to hear, "Oh, hi, come on in. Gee, how nice of you to come. How are you?" Everybody jumped out of bed and rushed to the front door to see who was there. My mother said, with a grin, "Now that you're all up, get in that kitchen for breakfast."

That was so funny, I'll never forget it. But that's how lonely it was out there. Day in and day out, you just saw each other. A visitor was a major event.

On December seventh, we were sleeping in when we were awakened with a lot of banging going on outside. The windows were rattling--the old fashioned slide-down windows--were constantly rattling. My dad came in the room yelling, "Hey, we got something going on out there. There's a lot of planes flying around, a lot of action." So we all ran out the front door and there were all these planes coming over us. You could see the pilot's head--flying low as heck right over us--over our house.

My dad said, "Look at that big red mark on the plane. That must be the red army plane. They must be having a maneuver game going on." We saw another plane with a blue mark and we said, "They must have the red and the blue armies battling it out." Pretty soon it was too real to believe.

We were out on the front porch looking up in great excitement when we saw one of our planes go straight up in the air--a two-seater job--a Douglas Dauntless, I later found out. And it burst into flames, when this Japanese plane came around, shooting at it. The pilot bailed out and the plane caught the parachute, fell back, and both pilot and plane came crashing down pretty close to our farm, maybe about a mile away. We were standing there, in shock, when another plane came by and it was as if someone took a pick and dug up our front yard--bullets or something started to hit our yard--the dirt was bouncing up. Dad grabbed us and pushed us in the house. That's when we turned on the radio and heard for the first time what actually was happening just a few miles or so away from our back yard.

" . . . we saw one of our planes . . . burst into flames . . . The pilot bailed out and the plane caught the parachute, fell back, and both pilot and plane came crashing down close to our farm. "

We were sitting around, shocked at what was going on outside, when someone started pounding at our door. This guy was all shook up--pounding at our door. "The Japanese are attacking Pearl Harbor," he yelled, "and my wife is in town." My father tried to cool him down, but he was really panicked. He didn't help us feel any calmer. My father poured whiskey in a water glass, half-full, and the guy just swished it down. So my father filled it up again. He kept saying something about his wife being in town and that they were strafing his house, down on the waterfront. After several shots of liquor, my father finally said, "Tell you what, we'll get in the car and go back down to your house and see what we can do."

So we jumped in the car--my two brothers, my cousin and me--and went with them down to this guy's house. He lived on the waterfront, looking right into the West Loch of Pearl Harbor.

My dad said for us to stay in the car while he went in the house with the guy. When they went in, we all jumped out and ran the twenty or thirty yards to the bushes near the water's edge. Then we saw something we will never forget. We saw ships burning, fire everywhere. We saw these planes dropping bombs. Some missed--the water would explode in the air--but one hit on the deck of this ship that blew up everything, sailors and everything went flying off the deck. Then one exploded in the water, about two hundred yards away from where we were standing, and we got scared and ran back to the car. We thought the next bomb would fall in our laps. Then the plane went right over us, but nothing happened--he didn't drop anything.

When we were running, my brother let out a muffled yell. I said, "What happened?" He said, "Nothin'." My father was the kind of a guy that you don't say anything if you're hurt, because he'd beat you. So my brother just grabbed his side and kept running to the car before our father got back.

Dad got back to the car and said that we were going back to our house. I don't know what he said to the guy, or what happened to him, but I guess he stayed there at his house because we never saw him again. Driving up the dirt road, my brother pulled up his shirt to see what happened to him and there was a big red mark on his stomach. Something hit him but it didn't penetrate the skin, or anything. We figured it was a piece of shrapnel from the bombings. We went back to the house.

We were all nervous and scared. We just hovered in the house, watching for things to happen. We had no telephone way out there. The only connection to the outside world was the radio. And then, after a while, everything kind of quieted down, cooled off. That night we didn't get evacuated or anything, like many people who lived near Pearl Harbor were. I guess, at that point in time, we were so far out in the boonies that nobody even knew we existed.

" *. . . we saw something we will never forget. . . ships burning, fire everywhere . . . planes dropping bombs . . . one hit this ship that blew up and sailors and everything went flying. . .* "

I'm afraid I lost track of the exact time frame, but I do remember my uncle came over to our house to tell us that his house was bombed, but the bomb didn't go off. It didn't explode. This might have been the next day. So we went up to his house, in the hills above Waipahu, to see this thing. It came right down through the roof and broke through the shower and landed under the house. It was a missile of some sort. The military people were sent up to inspect it and they looked at it and dug it out. They found that it was a live shell--an American missile--that missed its target and landed on my uncle's house. It landed right near their bedrooms. If it would have exploded, they would have all been killed. And his was an isolated house, out in the middle of nowhere, but it got hit. It's located where Makakilo is now, on the side of the slopes above Waipahu. That's the closest any of our family got to being hurt that day. They were lucky.

A short time later, it may have been a few days, my two brothers, my cousin, and I went looking for that airplane that crashed not far from our house. We also remembered seeing a Japanese plane crash in the area, too, so we wanted to see if there was anything left of them. There was no school and we weren't busy on the farm since everything was in chaos at that point. We were so excited at what we were going to do.

We walked toward the area that we thought they had come down. Less than a mile from the farm, but in a remote area--there were no houses around—we found the Douglas Dauntless. The plane was pretty much intact. Nothing was hot. When you touched the plane, it was cool. One piece of the wing was hanging on a kiawe tree and the rest of it was smashed on the ground. We found pieces of the parachute, but the guy's body was not there. They must have found the body and took it away or something.

But, wow, talk about excitement. We found the plane. We climbed on it and took everything we could take off that plane and carry. We found the guy's cigarettes. They were in a tin can that was still intact. So we took those. This machine gun was still in the back of the plane and there were just rows and rows of bullets, fifty calibre--those long jobbies--about eight inches long. The barrel on the machine gun was crooked, but otherwise it looked all right. The guys worked at taking it off the plane. I was the small guy, so I was just the observer while they did all the work. They got the machine gun and bullets out. There was also an American flag and we took it too. We took all the bullets out. And we took all that stuff home. Oh, yes, we even cut the wing, where the star was--the emblem--and took that home too. Boy were we excited at our secret.

We took the stuff and put it in the shed we had out back. My mother was home, but she was busy all the time cooking, sewing, a real farmer's wife. So she didn't see us with the stuff.

Then, we went out for more. We wanted to find the Japanese plane, too, and get some souvenirs off of it. We found that one, too. It wasn't too far away from where the American plane crashed. It was burnt, but you could still get in it. No pilot around. We found a Japanese flag, half burnt, but we took it. We found some bullets, too. And we cut the rising sun emblem off the wing. You could slice right through that thing—it was like balsa wood. The Douglas was real tough, we needed a chisel. But the Japanese plane cut right through with a knife.

So we took that stuff home, too, and went to the shed in the back and tacked the flags up on the wall. My brothers had lots of bullets and figured that when school started again, they were going to sell some souvenirs.

Later, they took the bullets and took the powder out and melted the lead with a blow torch. They put a little hook on the end and inserted a chain and sold these things, as key chains, later when school started. They sold a lot of them when we were back in school. The kids bought them, too. They were really attractive because you could shine them up a lot. Again, I was the observer. I watched them do it. I don't remember what they sold it for. I only know I reaped some of the profits, myself. I guess it was a dangerous thing to do. And, I guess we could have probably got arrested if we were caught.

" We found the plane . . . took everything we could carry off that plane . . . rows and rows of bullets . . . machine gun . . . Boy were we excited . . . "

Speaking of getting caught, right after December seventh, just after we had gathered these things, the military started coming around. The MPs came by and would break into your house looking for stuff that might be used by suspected spies. This one day, they came by with a bunch of guys in the back of a truck. They were local guys, mostly Japanese kids, and they were blindfolded with their hands tied behind their backs.

The MPs came into our house, looked at our radio, and ripped all the wires out. They were looking for shortwave stuff, I guess. They probably considered anybody with a shortwave radio set was a spy. Then they started searching around the yard.

My brother ran back to the shed and threw a bunch of bullets out the back into the bushes. Then the MPs came into the shed and found all our stuff. They took everything out--the flags, some bullets, and the big machine gun. We were only able to save some bullets, which were the ones we used later to make souvenir key chains. So, anyway, we were in trouble. They took my brother, Gordon, away with the other guys in the back of the truck, tied and blindfolded. My father wasn't there. He was in town, I think. My mother was so upset--she was hysterical. They drove away with all the stuff they confiscated as evidence that these people were spies, I guess.

My guess is they were picking up everybody close to Pearl Harbor who may have shortwave radios, or who they thought may have been spies who were giving messages to Japan through the shortwave radios. They were picking up everyone near Pearl Harbor who looked suspicious. And now my brother was one of them. I saw that one of our Chinese neighbors was also on the truck.

When my dad came home, we told him what happened. I don't exactly know how he did it, but he called somebody and then he went and got my brother. By that evening, he was home again. I guess my father explained that his kids had found the plane and took the stuff as souvenirs. I really don't think my father knew about the stuff we collected until he had to go and get my brother. I don't know where he had to go to pick up my brother. But that was scary. Everything turned out all right, though. I don't remember us getting punished or anything.

Then, some months later, we were kicked off our farm. They just confiscated the whole thing. "This is war," they said, "so you're out." So we had to move out of there in a hurry. They paid my father something for it, the fair market value at the time, I think. But, we had been farmers for years, and now, overnight, they threw us out. We were out of there. They made some sort of an airport out of it--for small aircraft, I think. So we moved to Ewa town, not near the beach, more towards town. We were living in a place called Tenny Village--something like plantation workers' homes. I remember it was a crummy place to live. There was no water in the bathroom. You had to wash with a pan of water. We would have to bring in water every day.

I also remember they set up a fifty-calibre gun emplacement right near our house--right in front of us. There were sand bags and bunkers all over the place. The army guys were all around there. They set up kind

103

of a defensive mechanism there. We used to watch these guys fire tracers in the sky. We always had these army guys around the place, you know. My sister, Goldie, was beautiful, and so they would come around to get to know her.

We were there for a short time then we moved to Pearl City. Then in a year or so, we moved to Alewa Heights. I went to Ewa Elementary, August Ahrens, Pearl City Elementary, (that was at the navy base down there) and finally St. Patrick's in Kaimuki, when we lived at Alewa Heights. So I attended a lot of schools from 1942 to 1944.

I couldn't get into St. Teresa's when we moved up to Alewa Heights, so I went in to Kaimuki to attend St. Patrick's until the eighth grade, in 1946. Then I went to St. Louis for high school.

I guess, looking back now, the war years were more exciting to me than they were scary. My father used to talk about rumors and things, and he would tell us not to worry about those things. I will never forget, though, what we saw on December seventh. There are certain things that I remember so vividly, like bombs blowing up and airplanes crashing. Those memories scared the hell out of me for years. In fact, I had a lot of dreams about it, nightmares, really. I used to get up at night screaming. So it may have affected me more than I realized.

" I will never forget . . . what we saw on December seventh . . . bombs blowing up and airplanes crashing. Those memories scared the hell out of me for years. "

I know that having older brothers at that time was helpful. My oldest brother was always the most responsible guy. So he had it harder, covering up things from my father. I used to ask my brothers about those events, but they never used to talk about it much. I don't know why.

Well, one thing's certain. If the war hadn't happened, we probably would have stayed on that farm for years. We probably would have been there until we got out on our own. That would have been at least seven more years for me, maybe even longer.

The property would be worth a fortune today. I remember trying to reclaim our family property from the government some years ago and was told that they paid my father the market value for it at the time--something like $3,000--for ten acres of prime land. It was agricultural in value at the time, but through the years it changed to a suburban, residential area, probably worth a lot today. We lost it because of the war. We might have been millionaires today if we still had that land. Who knows?

Donald graduated from St. Louis College (high school) in 1950. He attended the University of Hawaii for a couple of years, then continued his studies at night, receiving a degree in accounting. He married Geraldine Medeiros in 1952. They had three children. Don went to work for the Hawaii Medical Service Association in 1957 and is vice president of marketing. He and Geraldine, divorced in 1987, have nine grandchildren. Son, Donald Jr., is the father of two girls. Daughter, Avis, has four children, three girls and one boy. Denise, the youngest of the Keliinois, is the mother of two boys and one girl. While most of Donald's time is taken in job activities, he does enjoy golfing and sports. He has served on many community health activities and enjoys traveling, both for work and pleasure. He lives in Kailua, Oahu.

Youth Organizations Help

Children in the Scouts, YMCA, YWCA, and Young Buddhist clubs helped with war work during out-of-school hours. When long lines of families formed for gas mask distribution, finger printing, or vaccination, Girl Scouts helped care for small children. They typed, filed, rolled bandages, made cookies, and served as junior aides at hospitals. Boy Scouts tilled victory gardens, collected scrap, helped at the blood banks, draft boards, and Red Cross headquarters, and distributed posters and leaflets. *(Allen, Hawaii's War Years)*

FOR THE WAR EFFORT -- *Two Boy Scouts and a Cub Scout participate in the rubber drive, turning in old tires at a gas station collection point at Beretania and Keeaumoku Streets. (War Depository Collection, University of Hawaii)*

Tai Sing Loo

Tai Sing Loo was born in Honolulu in 1886. He had to leave school at the age of twelve (7th grade) to help support his family. He learned to be a sign painter and calligrapher from his father, lettering beautiful ornamental scrolls in gold leaf. At age 25, he hand-printed the names of all the Punahou School graduates on their class diplomas. He also designed the diplomas for the Kamehameha Boys School. He went to work at Pearl Harbor in 1918 as a woodworker helper. The following year, after climbing up a 760-foot radio tower to take an aerial photograph of the newly completed Drydock No. One, Loo earned the respect of his colleagues and became the official navy yard photographer. In 1928, at age 42, Loo met and married Florence Chang, 28, a match promoted by his mother and sister. On December 7, 1941, they were living near the University of Hawaii and were the parents of four children, two girls and two boys. The following is Mr. Loo's personal account, unedited, of his experiences on that day. It appeared in the CHA-3 Pearl Harbor Banner publication on the second anniversary of the event, December 7, 1943. It is reprinted here with the permission of the Commandant, Pearl Harbor Naval Ship Yard, and Mr. Loo's daughter, Mrs. Evelyn L. Lee, who also provided the photographs of her father.

How Happen I Were at Pearl Harbor, on the Morning of Sunday, 7th of December

On the 6th of December, Saturday Afternoon, I had made arrangement with Tech. Sergeant Christen to have all his Guard be at the Main Gate between 8:30 to 9:30 o'clock Sunday morning to have a group of pictures taken in front of the new concrete entrance as a setting with the "Pearl Harbor" for Christmas card to send home to their family.

Sunday morning I left my home for Pearl Harbor after 7:00 o'clock. I was waiting for my bus at corner Wilder Avenue and Metcalf Street. Saw sky full of anti-aircraft gun firing up in the air, I call my friend to look up in sky, explain them how the Navy used their anti-aircraft gun firing in practising, at that time I didn't realize we were in actual war. Our bus stop at Bishop and King Streets. We heard the alarm ringing from the third story building of the Lewer's & Cooke, Ltd. Saw the window shattered. I walk up to Young Hotel corner and cross the street. Stop for a cup of coffee at Swinky & Franky. Suddenly all excitement arouse the Honolulu Fire Engine rush down Bishop Street all directions. Taxi full load of sailor and marine dashing toward Pearl Harbor. I'm very much surprise what's all this excitement. I wave the taxi to stop and get on it to go back to Pearl Harbor. When I approach to Pearl Harbor surprise with great shock. Thought one of oil tanks caught in fire, showing black velum of thick smoke in the air. I got off at the Main Gate of Pearl Harbor, met all the guards with arms and Machine Gun in placed. I was great shock with surprise the war are on. Watching many Japanese war planes attacked Pearl Harbor, dropping bombs right and left on dry docks and Ford Island. Suddenly terrific explosion. Fire broke out. I was very calm and waiting for the opportunity to get a ride to the Studio to get my camera. I was at the Main Gates standby with Marines. Guards at the Main Gates were bravery and cool headed to keep the by standing away for safety and clear traffic. There were the young, fighting Marines. We were under fire. The Japanese painted in aluminum, Red Ball under each wing, flew around very low toward the Main Gates.

Japs Bomb Hickam Field

I wish my Graflex with me. I would had a wonderful close up shot of the Japese (sic). Again the Japese flew around the Navy Housing Area and turn back, head direct to Hickam Field, very low to drop a bomb to the Hangars, with terrific explosion, set fire the buildings. More planes flew direct the dry dock. Suddenly, I saw one plane had a hit. It flew direct toward West Locke stream of smoke screen. Now this my opportunity to get in the Yard, one of the Leadingman of Machine Shop drove in his automobile. I hop in, he take me to the Studio and pick up my Graflex Camera to take some picture second thought I change my mind, reason is because first place I didn't had no order second place I didn't had my Famous Trade-Mark helmet on. I had a new English Helmet from Singapore, given by Admiral Murfin a year ago, so I'm afraid some one will make a mistake me as a Jap and shot me down.

I went up to the Administration Building everything O.K. I met Mr. William McIlhenny and Mr. W. C. Bohley at the stairway. We talk and both went toward the dry dock. I went to the Supply Dept. and saw many boy had a Steel Helmet on, so I went to see Lt. Comdr. Supply Officer for permission to had one, the size are too large and heavy for me so I select one smaller size, painted green and white stripe. I went direct to the dry dock to help put out the fire on *USS Cassin* had the depth charges on her stern, the *USS Pennsylvania*, bow between *Cassin* and *Downes*, I knew it was very dangerous it may exploded damaged the dry docks and the *USS Pennsylvania*. We put our hoses directed the depth charges keeping wet. An Officer came near by said keep up the good work we had our hose right at it all the time, and I turn around and saw Lt. Spear, order all men stand back, somethings may happen, so I obey his order and ran back toward *USS Pennsylvania*, sudden really happen the terrific explosion came from the Destroyer few people were hurt and some fell down. I notice some large pieces of Steel Plates blew over the dry dock when I turn around and look, afterward I notice two extra hoses without nozzles, so I went to the Fire Station and brought back 2 volunteers pointed direct, the depth charges, I call for more volunteers to help me clear and straighten up the hose around the First Street to clear for traffic at the same time purpose to gave the fire fighter a chance to extended the hose across over the bow of *USS Pennsylvania* to fight the fire at the *Downes* on Starboard side. Here comes an other Fire Engine from Submarine Base, I direct them to place their engine and connect this Hydrant No. 151 and direct them to the depth charges, so everything are well done and successful accomplishment their service. A few words of my appreciation see the depth charges were wet and kept away the fire. The Marines of the Fire Dept. of the Navy Yard, are the heroes of the day of Dec. 7, 1941 and that save the *Cassin* and *Downes* and *USS Pennsylvania* and thanks and successful credit to Lieut. Spear, in charge with his gallant spirit to kept his staff and volunteers calms right at the job to Dry Dock No. 1.

Anti-aircraft Crews in Action

I saw the crew threw out empty 5" shell on the dock I gether up in piles with some sailors, so I met Chief A. LeTendre, to help me order some hose from Supply Dept. to place in this Hydrant No. 151, corner Avenue D and First Street. I also request Lt. Foster to order me more hoses, with in half and hour the Chief brought back 6 new more hoses, with and other load from Lt. Foster and other Chief which I have about 12 lengths of hose to stand by. Why I order this hoses for? The Answer--for emergency something may happen I will be there with readiness, reason why, the magazines were taking out from the *USS Pennsylvania*, and many casing and empty shell, at the same time were under fired the Jap Airplanes flew over head where up in the cloud. The

USS Pennsylvania, Anti-aircraft crews were in full action, I wasn't excited and very calm about Street to protect the 2 new hoses, I were little worry because I have no nails and lumber to nail between, the two planks separated while the heavy traffic going by with Emergency Cases to the Navy Hospital without crushing the hoses. I met Captain Swain passing by I had his permission to have the Carpenter of the Boat Shop to help me nail this planks together. He went to telephone, within few minutes four men marching down with nails and lumber. I were very happy, here comes the Carpenters ready to started nailing suddenly the roaring Anti-aircraft guns in action, I call my men to dodging for safety, after the Enemy Planes disappear we all returns to our duty, the four men didn't come back at all left the hammers nails, and lumber, so I was very fortunely for two of our local boys passing by and helping me to finish the job, it were very thankful to volunteers and their service to stand by with me during the Emergency I had two men standing by the Hydrant No. 119 located Corner Avenue E and First Street near the head of Dry Dock No. 1, had four men guarding the two hoses in emergency for readiness in case of fire broke out from the Magazine Casing.

Volunteer Traffic Policeman

I was self volunteer to be Traffic Police and directing the Traffic during the rushing hours of Emergency, I get a big pieces of Maroon cloth to signaling the ambulance to look at those planks, easily passing over, to have my hose and other word to give the wounded patients rest easily from rough crossing on the heavy planks. I direct all four hours to deep the First Street clear of right away to the Naval Hospital. Many heavy Contractor Trucks passing by with all Defenders and Emergency Call Employees, to report to the Shop of Standby. I directed all this group of trucks turn up to Avenue E and unloaded the Employees. Everythings were successfully executing, I enjoyed my duty and a word of appreciation to my volunteers friends of their bravery and courageous to their service, during and Under Fired. Everythings were under control and we all secure and roll up the hoses and returns to the Supply Dept. We were hungry no lunch so I brought each one a Box Ice Cream for lunch and we all dismissed about 3:30 p.m.

One of the Marine Patrol approaching toward me, if I will do the boys a great service of the Marine Guards and Sailor, which their have no lunch and some without breakfast, so I went to the garage to take my red Put Put to the 3rd Defense Fleet Marine Mess Hall to see my friend Tech.

Sergt. Newland for help. I told the story regards the Post Guard have been neglected to release for lunch. Tech. Sergt. Newland were very kind and his Cook to prepares some sandwiches ham and chicken fruit all I can delivery to the Post. You should hear what were their saying. Charles you are one life saver. I have been riding around I have the driver to take back to Garage night force. I left the Navy Yard at 7:30 p.m. at Main Gates. I was very fortunely and automobile pass by. Lady invited me to take me back to town, she just drive off the Ferry boat from Ford Island. She left me off the Hawaiian Electric Co. It was black out night, I walk across to Army and Navy YMCA to the Beretania Street to walk direct to the Thomas Square and stopped for a rest.

I ask the soldier guard on patrol, with appreciated very kindly if he will halt an automobel to take me home, if convenience on their way home. I told him I came back from Pearl Harbor, I'm Chinese. He shake my hand and glad to be of service, to the Chinese Friend. An automobile approach and stop the soldier request the owner if he will help to take me home to the University. Happening the driver knew me very well,

PUTT PUTT -- Tai Sing Loo, his camera, his elephant hat, and his three-wheeled motor scooter were familiar scenes for much of thirty years at the Pearl Harbor Naval Shipyard. Getting around the yard for photo assignments was no problem with this vehicle. (Photo courtesy of Evelyn Lee and the Loo family photo files)

111

he heard my voice, so he invited me in his car and drove me to my home at the front door, I extend my appreciation and thanks him very kindly to see safely home. My wife and four children were happy and thankful I were safely at home.

AS THE CONFUCIUS SAY, "EVERY KIND DEEDS ITS RETURN MANY, MANY TIMES FOLDS."

Tai Sing Loo, his camera and elephant hat, became as much a part of Pearl Harbor as the drydocks. The list of people he recorded on film reads like a page of Who's Who, including Franklin Roosevelt, the Prince of Wales, King Gustaf of Sweden, Vice President John Garner, and Adm. Chester Nimitz, who Mr. Loo knew when the future chief of naval operations was a young lieutenant. Celebrities he photographed included Douglas Fairbanks, Mary Pickford, Shirley Temple, Babe Ruth, Gene Tunney, and Bob Hope.

He was one of the best known and liked employees at Pearl Harbor. In 1949, after 31 years of service, Tai Sing Loo retired. Among his many prized possessions and photographs is a citation he received from the Commandant, 14th Naval District, which states: "For outstanding loyalty, efficient action, and disregard of personal safety during the attack on the Fleet in Pearl Harbor, Territory of Hawaii, by Japanese forces on December 7, 1941, in assisting in fighting fires in Drydock No. 1 and floating Drydock No. 2 in the Navy Yard despite the danger from explosions as well as enemy strafing and bombing." Mr. Loo died in 1971.

His philosophy for life will be remembered by all who knew him. In his memoirs, written in 1962, he states..."I am very grateful and happy in my life, enjoy all friendships. Thank the Good Lord, blessing me for the years of my happiness and health."

Joan Padgett Chalmers

*She was born in Honolulu in 1931. Her
parents were John and Mac (Elsie) Padgett.
They both moved to Hawaii in the 1920's as
young professionals. John was from California,
with a degree in electrical engineering; Mac
was a registered nurse from Canada. Joan
lived with her parents on Wilhelmina Rise and
attended Aliiolani Elementary School in
Kaimuki. She was in the fifth grade on
December 7, 1941. (Photo by Luther Greer, St.
Paul, Minnesota)*

The onset of World War II brought irreversible changes to all our
lives. I was a child when it began and an adolescent when it ended.
However, I was too young to be frightened by the ramifications of war
and invasion. Instead, I became an innocent participant in an adventure.
My life was disrupted but I was never a victim; opportunities to grow
and learn were everywhere.

During 1940-1941, my mother, an avid anglophile, knitted for the
British War Relief. She picked up the skeins of wool at the British
Legation in Honolulu and knit beautiful socks, sweaters and watch caps
for members of the British army and navy.

There were military maneuvers off the Hawaiian Islands during the
first week in December 1941.

On December the sixth, my dance class with others performed for
servicemen at Fort Armstrong, Honolulu. I have no idea why little kids
were selected to entertain servicemen as they celebrated the end of their
military maneuvers. But, they were. And there we were, in our sateen
Pierrot costumes with pink ruffs. Drunken servicemen worked back
stage as stagehands and made leering comments; others proffered
whistles and cat calls from out front. The juvenile dancers stumbled
along. And, I saw the level of relief and celebration the military feel at
the conclusion of maneuvers.

December 7, 1941 we awoke and turned on the radio. All we heard was the repetitive radio message--"This is the real McCoy. We are under military attack. This is the real McCoy. We are under military attack."

With a beautiful view of Diamond Head, Honolulu and Pearl Harbor from our family home, it was easy for us to look out and see air force activity and exploding bombs. Our neighbors, Myrtle and Newton May, lived on the rim of Palolo Valley. That morning they stepped to their wall of windows overlooking the valley to ponder all this activity. What they saw brought the Japanese offensive very close to home. A Japanese fighter plane was flying down the length of the valley. The pilot looked out at them and they stared at each other, their gazes interlocking. Other friends lived in Waikiki where a bomb landed near their home. Pearl Harbor was a disaster.

I overheard my parents discussing whether my mother and I should go to church as usual. My mother said if we really were under attack, it seemed like the most appropriate thing to do. My father argued against the risk when we could pray at home. We didn't go.

We expected the Japanese to return again that day for a second attack and invasion. We spent the whole day preparing ourselves. That night, I was put to bed in my brother's room in the basement because my parents thought I would be safer there. My father and the neighbors Ed Char, Hal Ross, Herman Kuhlman served as unofficial air raid wardens. My mother, a nurse, boiled water, assembled medical supplies and prepared for any emergency. In the middle of a quiet night, I crept out and asked if I could return to my own bed. Permission granted. There was no second attack.

In the days immediately following December seventh, the Territory of Hawaii was declared under martial law. Barbed wire was strung across all our beaches.

My parents accepted civil defense responsibilities. My mother was asked to set up a First Aid Substation in our home. She took over my father's workshop and capably converted it into a suitable place for first aid care. Neighbors Molly Castle, Kay Ross, Alice Kuhlman and others came regularly to make 2 X 2's and 4 X 4's (gauze swabs for wounds) and to roll bandages. My mother designed a compact, portable medical kit. By December the eighth, good quality consumer goods were virtually unavailable but mother just happened to have on hand a supply of stout fabric yardage which she cut up for the medical kits. She and her helpers made three of them. The economical and innovative design had inserts in which to store splints and room to store bandages, medicines, hypodermics and other essentials.

My father and neighbors organized into a team of Air Raid wardens. They pooled a few dollars and built an air raid shelter/bunker in a cave, over the edge of the valley rim, accessible through our neighbor's garden.

Blackout was instantly required. My father got rolls of tar paper and meticulously cut pieces to fit each pane of glass. The windows of each upstairs room were adapted except for my bedroom which remained light and airy, night and day. I was miffed because I could no longer read in bed at night.

My mother loved to tell of our standard, trusting response when someone knocked at our door after dark. We unquestioningly turned off all the lights, opened the door and invited the individual to enter. Then we closed the door, turned on the lights and identified our friend--or stranger.

Food stuffs that had to be shipped in were in short supply. My mother recalled going to the butcher. He would whisper, "I saved you something," and slip her a wrapped package over the counter. She accepted it and paid for it. It was only when she got home that she could find out what cut of meat she had bought.

" Since our travel opportunities were limited by the war, it was a big treat to drive around the island on Mother's Day. "

We did have gas rationing--ten gallons a month. Since our travel opportunities were limited by the war, it was a big treat to drive around the island on Mother's Day. We'd save up our coupons and take any guests with us who happened to be hanging around or appeared to need an outing. A Sunday drive was a big event.

My brother was in his senior year at Roosevelt High School and had taken classes in drafting and related skills. There was an immediate need for these fledgling engineer types and he was allowed to graduate early to go to work at Pearl Harbor in January 1942; shortly thereafter, he moved out of our home to live in an apartment in Waikiki.

The infusion of military and civilian workers into the Pacific wartime offensive created a housing shortage in Hawaii. With my brother gone, mother converted his basement bedroom area into an apartment which we rented to a navy couple, a chief petty officer and his wife. Many of the basement apartments in our neighborhood were rented. Other neighbors, the Kings and Mays, had young, single women secretaries as tenants; they added a bright touch to our staid street.

Many island families with family ties on the mainland saw mothers and children depart for the continental U.S. They began their evacuation in early 1942 and returned two years later when further attacks seemed unlikely. The husbands/fathers stayed home alone. Many of our friends' families were separated and some were never reunited.

The early days of the war were not all bad for our family. My father had new opportunities to practice his wealth of problem-solving skills. There was lots of coming and going of friends and neighbors as the air raid wardens determined how best to protect their families; the bomb shelter builders hiked off to assure the security of the neighborhood; the bandage rollers met to build up and maintain the sterile fields and medical supplies of a first aid substation; the victory gardeners planned their plots.

Everyone was inoculated for tetanus, typhus, typhoid and smallpox. We were issued identity cards to be carried at all times. School was suspended until late January 1942. Our school grounds were dug up for trenches and bomb shelters. When it rained, the trenches filled with water. One day the air raid sirens blew and we had no place to go but to the wet, muddy trenches where we clustered and ate our lunchtime sandwiches. We went to school for half days on Saturdays for much of the rest of the school year to make up the two months we missed.

We were issued gas masks. I have a very small head. Fitting a standard, vintage 1940 gas mask to my small face was not an easy task. Masks with ever-increasing amounts of contour padding were ordered for me in hopes of finding one with sufficient padding to protect me in the event of a gas attack. It was mandatory that gas masks be with us at all times. Government issue required that they be worn suspended from one shoulder, with the strap diagonally crossing the chest and the gas mask delicately supported on the opposing hip. Adults and children developed playful or stylish ways to embellish the ugly, olive drab, canvas cases: some were decorated wildly and colorfully with colored pencils, paint or inks. Some exhibited decorative string weaving techniques on the lanyard that was supposed to fasten the gas mask closely around the body. Boys used them as weapons against their playmates and some wore them jauntily over one shoulder.

In late 1942, my day of reckoning arrived. A gas mask check was scheduled for all students at Aliiolani Elementary School. By this time I had been issued the most heavily padded gas mask available. We lined up in an orderly fashion in a school room that had been prepared for such an occasion with all windows and possible air leaks closed and sealed. An officious army officer commanded us to put on our gas masks. We did. He explained that he would be releasing tear gas to

---

" In late 1942, my day of reckoning arrived.
A gas mask check was scheduled for all
students at Aliiolani Elementary School. "

---

check the protective capacity of our gas masks. We nodded. He released the tear gas. Immediately, my eyes filled with tears. He asked if anyone had any reaction to the still releasing gas. I raised my hand. With some consternation, he hustled me out, trying to minimize the impact of my exit on the "purity" of the tear gas in the test chamber. It was now official: there was no satisfactory protection from a gas attack for this eleven-year-old girl.

Victory gardens were common on the mainland and in Hawaii too. My father and neighbors Hal Ross and Herman Kuhlman developed a victory garden that beat all. They took over an undeveloped lot that lay between the Ross and Kuhlman homes. Breaks in the property line hedges were made to allow the men and their families quick access to their garden. The men cleared the city-sized lot of dense hoalekoa and weeds and began creating large planting beds for a wide variety of vegetables.

My father was ordinarily resistant to the introduction of any fresh vegetable into his diet, yet in the course of their development of this garden, he paid frequent visits to the agricultural departments at the University of Hawaii and the Territory. He brought home exotic strains of vegetables for planting. I remember the "calico bean" that is now commonly available in grocery stores. They planted small groves of bananas and papayas; they grew exotic strains of tomatoes, herbs, lettuces, cabbage, corn, potatoes. My father made soups, hotly seasoned chili, Portuguese beans, wondrous salads dressed with heavily herbed oils and vinegar. The men kept this lavish exercise going for several years. With the decline of the garden, my father's kitchen creativity diminished and once again he rudely complained about what he called "rabbit food."

During the war, most island families enjoyed an influx of military visitors. Our extended military family included Lt. Bill Goodman from New York City, Chief Petty Officer Andy Anderson. There was Stoney from New York state; Edgar Poole and George H(?), English sailors who we picked up at the downtown YWCA in Honolulu, prewar. Also, young men from my father's hometown, Sanger, California. And a crew of SeaBees who were assigned by the military to work for my father

---

" Both my mother and father were proud of me when I was invited to 'christen' a rowboat . . . of the submarine tender USS Griffin on July 31, 1943. "

---

developing emergency access roads for the Department of Public Works, Territory of Hawaii. All of these men and more remained our friends throughout the war and after. They would appear at our door unannounced when they got a short leave. We fed them, entertained them and gave them a home in the middle of the Pacific. None of them were killed during the war. They added richness and humor to our lives at a time when everybody needed it. They gave us affection and loyalty. Once, navy cook Barr Olsen of the Sanger, California Barr family stole a whole ham for us in appreciation of our hospitality. He smuggled it out, wrapped in blue dungarees.

Both my mother and father were very proud of me when I was invited to "christen" a rowboat in celebration of the second anniversary of the commissioning of the submarine tender *USS Griffin* on July 31, 1943. One of our extended military family members, Chief Andy Anderson was on the crew of the *USS Griffin* and offered my services when this event was suggested as a bit of in-house R & R for the crew.

There was great fussing and polishing at our house. My mother was concerned that my clothing be as appropriate to the occasion as possible.

"I CHRISTEN THEE JUNIOR" -- said twelve-year-old Joan Padgett as she does the honors on a rowboat aboard the USS Griffin at Pearl Harbor, July 31, 1943. (*Official U.S. Navy photograph; courtesy of Joan Padgett Chalmers private photo collection*)

SMILE AT THE CAMERA -- Cutting the six-foot long cake in the ship's mess brought smiles to little Joan Padgett, shown before the cake was served with Captain W. B. Thorpe, and K. R. Shaw, baker first class (left), and J. L. Magowan, baker first class. (*Official U.S. Navy photograph; courtesy of Joan Padgett Chalmers private photo collection*)

I was outgrowing my prewar clothes. New shoes were difficult to obtain and my old ones were badly worn. For the occasion, it was eventually decided that I should wear a hand-me-down dress from Patty Ross. My old shoes were polished several times. My father stayed home from work to watch my departure.

A naval jeep with driver and Andy Anderson were sent to escort me to Pearl Harbor for the days' events. When we arrived at the *USS Griffin*, I was met by Captain Thorp, the executive officer, Commander Prosser and Commander Tambling who escorted me to his quarters and left me alone there for a little while. I was confused by this until I realized that the kindly officers were delicately offering me the use of a toilet. I did.

It was a trying day. I felt shy in this exclusively male environment with all these important appearing officers and busy crew members. I was also aware of my own lack of female glamour. But, it was a busy day: I was given tours of the submarine and tender. Captain Thorp and I cut one of the huge sheet cakes baked and decorated by ship's bakers Shaw and Magowan. I broke a tough bottle of champagne and "christened" a modest rowboat. I was photographed and smiled a lot.

When the navy escort returned me to my home, my mother wisely insisted that I record my memories and I did:

> July 31, 1943
>
> Today at 10:30 a USN car drove up and I said good by (sic) to Mom and Dad and got into the car with Chief Petty Officer Anderson, Commander Hood and a fellow by the name of Brooks.
>
> Chief Anderson had given me a corsage of orchids for me to wear in my hair.
>
> We had a half hours (sic) drive to Pearl Harbour and there I met a lot of nice officers. At 11:30 I went out on the pier about even with the bow. There was a little band there and they played some music. After that I was handed a champiengn (sic) bottle and then with a whack I knocked it against the ship and said thus, "I christian (sic) thee Junior."
>
> I then went down to the enlisted mens mess where a

cake was (sic) it was 6' x 3' with two candles on it for this was the ships (sic) birthday. After that I went to see a submarine. It was all swell fun.

I was given three gifts. A pretty gold locket from the officers and a hanky and little gadget to wear on my dress from Anderson. In all I had a super time (sic)

Joan Padgett

My parents received the following note:

July 31, 1943

My dear Mr and Mrs Padgett--

Please accept the thanks of the officers and men for loaning us Joan. She did a wonderful job and has quite won the hearts of all hands.

Albert L. Prosser

Commander, U S Navy

Executive Officer

A touch of glamour entered my life early in the war when an ordinary house behind ours was bought by Tony and Peaches Guerrerro. Suddenly, in wartime, extravagant remodelling projects were underway there: a paddle tennis court was built in their backyard with the standard high wire fence; kitchen, living and bedroom areas were remodelled, sliding glass doors, new drapes, furnishings, landscaping were installed.

Patty Ross and I used to challenge each other to walk along the top two-by-fours of the Guerrerro's tennis fence and that must be how we met Tony and Peaches.

Peaches was gorgeous, in her late thirties, a brunette with beautiful white skin. She told us she'd been in the movies and had movie stills to prove it, probably from Hollywood's polynesian extravaganzas of the 1930s. She certainly did not resemble our mothers. Tony was tall, heavy set, swarthy with a world-weary air about him. I think he worked in the wartime Office of Price Administration (OPA). Obviously, he had access

121

to precious building materials--cement, wood, wire, glass windows and doors as well as civilian nonessentials.

They invited Patty and me to use the paddle tennis court anytime we wanted and showed us how to get in when they were absent.

We took them at their word and simply moved our play into their yard when it suited us. We played for hours in the newly landscaped Japanese garden off their bedroom--draping scarves about, planning and acting out exotic bits of make believe. Sometimes, we'd just drop by to visit them and no matter when, they'd invite us in, entertain us graciously, listen to our gossip and show us their show biz photos.

As I neared my teens, friends began to return to our neighborhood, back from the WWII exodus. Bev Hicks had boxes of clothes the likes of which I'd never seen before: heavy wool coats, boots, scarves, mittens, wool suits.

Donna LeGoullon's father was in the army Special Services and had ready access to a wealth of entertainment. He brought home dog-eared armed forces editions for us to read. He also brought home current movies that we watched, as we sat on the floor of the LeGoullon living room. We had a movie theatre and library at our command, free of the limitations of gas rationing and blackout.

> " . . . as part of the war effort, junior and senior high school students were asked to work for the sugar cane and pineapple industry . . . "

In 1944 and 1945, as part of the war effort, junior and senior high school students were asked to work for the sugar cane and pineapple industry to help "hoe hana"[1] the fields. We were offered a small wage for two days work per school year. Disabled students were not expected to participate and any student could decline to work. My father made that decision for me. He flatly declared that no daughter of his was going to work in the cane or pineapple fields. It was hard, hot, dirty, painful work. On those two days of each school year, my father dropped

[1]*Hawaiian term meaning to do your share of the work.*

my friends, Patty Ross, Donna LeGoullon, Bev Hicks and me off at Robert Louis Stevenson Junior High School as usual. My friends were dressed in heavy duty work clothes and hats and in a holiday mood. They hopped out, climbed aboard the workers trucks and roared off. I felt very lonely. I went to an assigned room and spent the days doing meaningless make-work as specified by the overseeing teacher. One time I was given the loathsome job of converting the values of monthly sales of Victory Bonds per student per homeroom into graphs. Grim!

A new friend arrived. Her father was in the army and stationed in the Pacific. Her family were Methodists and she enlisted us all into the Methodist Youth Fellowship (MYF) at their church on Beretania Street, diagonally across from Thomas' Square. The church is long since torn down.

One of the highlights of that experience was the staging of a "Gay 90's" show. Our group leader was a hyperkinetic, overworked, family man, Bill Green. He was with the USO in Hawaii, preparing entertainment for the military. He had plenty of moxie and with this highly mixed bag of amateur talent, he formed it and his material into an entertaining whole. He had some ringers to work with--one, Katherine Martin, had a mature figure, a beautiful face and a superb soprano voice. He could stick her into any skit and it came alive. Some of the more senior members of our youthful group, Richard and Dave Vanderberg and one or two from the U. S. Army, added an important maturity to our undertaking.

This was a "Hey kids, let's put on a show" that would have done Judy Garland and Mickey Rooney proud. All success was due to the redoubtable Bill Green who played ALL the music on the piano and dashed in to add just the right piece of business to a number. He was impresario and director. Music, choreography, sets, costuming--all were dependent on him. He accomplished all of this over and above his USO duties.

We gave several performances at the church and then, were "booked" into performances at schools and military bases. This was wartime and people were desperate for fresh entertainment. We were fresh all right.

We also sang Christmas carols at nursing homes and military bases. Bill Green had us doing and going everywhere. MYF offered us heady, wonderful experiences.

Joan Padgett Chalmers (continued)

Some of my friends and I were members of a Girl Scout troop. We walked to the meeting site from school and usually got there early with time to stroll down Beretania Street to buy an afternoon snack. We sang songs . . .

"Pardon me boy, is this the Chattanooga Choo Choo?
Track 29, oh won't you give me a shine..."

and thought we were sophisticated. Along our route, we passed a mortuary that held a morbid fascination for us. One afternoon, we got up the courage and peeked in the windows. Between a narrow crack in the window draperies we saw the corpse of a soldier, laid out, in full uniform, ready for his funeral. We were awestruck and silent.

The war ended in 1945, at the onset of my ninth grade year. The innocence of prewar Hawaii no longer existed. We had grown up.

Joan Padgett was a sophomore at Roosevelt High School in 1947. Richard Chalmers, from Hilo, transferred to Roosevelt midway through the school year and joined her Albegra II class. She moved to Hilo with her family when her father accepted a job there as Chief County Engineer the next school year. Dick returned to Hilo for his senior year at Hilo High School at the same time. She graduated from Hilo High in 1949. Joan married Dick Chalmers in 1952 in California at the end of her junior year at San Jose State College. They raised two children in California and Wisconsin and now live in the Twin Cities, Minnesota. During winters, they wonder what two little kamaainas[2] are doing, living in the country's icebox. But they maintain their Hawaii roots by returning to the islands at least once every three years...during winter.

[2]*Hawaiian word meaning native-born; child of the land.*

Alfredo P. Fernandez

Al Fernandez was the last of four children. His parents, Evaristo and Vicenta Fernandez, were both born in the Philippines. They met and married while living in Alameda, California, in 1927. Their first son, Eddie, was born there. Daughter Lolita was born in Hong Kong while the family was travelling in search of warmer climate for health reasons. Hawaii became the final choice and Bobby and Al were born there. At the start of the war, the Fernandez family was living in Damon Tract, adjacent to the airport and near Hickam Field and Pearl Harbor. Al's brother, Eddie, was fifteen at the time. Sister Lolita was thirteen; brother Bobby was eleven; and Al was nine. He was a fourth grader at St. Theresa's School.

I remember the night before December seventh. It was Saturday and Pop was going to really treat us. He said, "I'm gonna take you kids to the movies tonight." So we all jumped in his '36 Studebaker--a four-door, black job as I remember--and we went all the way downtown to the Princess Theater. And would you believe the movie playing? It was "The Great Dictator" with Charlie Chaplin. I tell you I laughed so much. This little guy with his moustache and his cane, and he portrayed, of course, Adolph Hitler. He was the great dictator. We really enjoyed ourselves. I laughed and laughed.

The next morning, Mom and Pop got up early and went into town to meet some friends and play golf at the Oahu Country Club. Brother Eddie got us up early, too, and the four of us kids went to the eight o'clock Mass at St. Philomena on T Road, about a quarter of a mile from home. We walked.

As soon as we got out of the house, we heard a loud BOOM here and a BOOM there, you know, and then we heard RAT-TAT-TAT-TAT-TAT. I remember we were walking down the middle of Kalauloa Road towards church as there was no traffic at that time. In fact, Kalauloa Road split Damon Tract in half. The lower half was makai,[1] where we lived; and

---

[1] *Hawaiian word meaning a direction, toward the sea.*

the upper half was mauka.[2] So we lived closer to the ocean and down the road a little ways was John Rodgers Airport (now we know it as Honolulu International Airport).

Anyway, a plane flew right over us and we could see the pilot. We could see the big red circle on the fuselage. We waved at the pilot and he flew towards the airport and started shooting his machine gun. We thought, "Oh, that's the red army. They're having maneuvers." We thought it was aerial maneuvers at that time. He was flying so low, if anything, about a hundred feet above us.

When we got to the church, we saw this huge billow of black smoke in the distance. So we went in and the priest started Mass, although he looked a little apprehensive. We all knelt down together in our same pew, about in the third row. The noise continued outside while Mass went on.

Then a man came running in the back of the church--down the aisle--hysterical. He yelled, "We're at war with Japan. We're being attacked by the Japanese." He had run from the airport and he was drenched with oil and his clothes were torn. "Everybody get out of Damon Tract," he screamed.

The priest tried to calm him down. I got excited. I thought, "Wow, what is war?"

The priest said to the man, "Now take it easy, take it easy. What do you want us to do?"

"They're telling us--the police and the military--to get everybody out of the area and get them towards town," the man said, calming down a bit.

Very few people had automobiles in those days. My dad had taken our car. So Eddie said, "Let's go home first and see what we should do." So we ran very fast towards home.

The police came by in their 1940 Fords and olive brown uniforms trying to get people out of their homes. Some of the people didn't want to leave. So the police went up and down the streets escorting people out of the area. They allowed people with cars to drive, but only in one direction--towards downtown--on Kamehameha Highway.

---

[2]*Hawaiian word meaning a direction, toward the mountains.*

Then we began hearing these strange sounds and things started falling around us. SHOONG, SHOONG, WHEE, SHOONG. Guns were firing at the airplanes and shells and shrapnel were coming down where we were. When we went in the house, it really started coming down, hitting the roof. We were lucky we didn't get hit. The corrugated roofs of the chicken coops really got it.

We actually saw planes dive bombing. We saw them go down out of sight, then shoot up again. Then a few seconds later we would hear this loud BOOM. Then we'd see this billowing, black smoke. I guess they were hitting the battleships at Pearl Harbor at that time. We probably heard the *Arizona* blow at that time.

" We walked along the railroad tracks . . . like a bunch of refugees . . . Everybody was walking towards town . . . carrying whatever possessions they could. "

We waited a little while and when we thought the stuff stopped falling, we started walking towards town. We walked along the railroad tracks, with a lot of other people. Some of them had pillow cases filled with stuff, handbags over their shoulders. I guess we looked like a bunch of refugees. It was very crowded. A thousand people, maybe. The whole population of Damon Tract, I suppose. Those who didn't have cars, anyway. Everybody was walking towards town, carrying whatever possessions they could. We weren't carrying anything. What would we have to carry, anyway?

Eddie was the mother hen, walking along the tracks, and the three of us followed him. The excitement was still there. We were doing things that we don't normally do.

We looked up and saw planes chasing each other in the air. I mean there were real dogfights going on. We didn't see any planes crash. But the realization hit me at that time--what the man had said about being at war--and the shrapnel and bullets in our yard. This was for real, not fake, not maneuvers. Everything--boom--came into focus and I got real scared.

As we were going towards town, my dad and mom tried to drive back to Damon Tract to find us. They stopped cars at Middle Street and Kamehameha Highway, at the Flying A gasoline station there. They wouldn't let civilian cars go beyond that point. That was about two miles away from Damon Tract. So Dad left Mom waiting in the car and started walking.

He was practically running, in the opposite direction of all the people, looking for us. He was so worried about us. Anyway, he finally found us, on the railroad tracks. He spotted us and yelled out to us. He was so glad to see us, he grabbed everybody, the four of us, hugging. "Okay, okay," he said. "Let's go. Mom's waiting for us in the car." By the time we walked the half mile to the car, Mom was biting her fingernails. She was so relieved to see us. She kissed us all. Thank God, the whole family was united again.

So, where do we go from here? The police were trying to move all the cars away from that barricade point. There were a lot of people there. And a lot of chaos. The police asked people to clear out and go to friends' or relatives' houses.

Finally, Pop said, "We're going to the Gorospes'." Constantino Gorospe and his family were our good friends. They lived in lower Alewa Heights on Makanani Drive. Mr. Gorospe worked as a manager for the Palama Theater. So we drove to the Gorospes'. They were happy to see us. They welcomed us. They also had some other friends there, too.

I remember they had a balcony that overlooked the airport, towards Pearl Harbor. That night, shots were still being fired. We could see these tracer bullets going this way and that way, shooting at planes in the air. Bullets were going like crazy. It was complete chaos.

So, anyway, we stayed at the Gorospes' for two nights--Sunday and Monday nights--before they let us return to Damon Tract. It was like living in a big Filipino family. The Gorospes had three boys and two girls. With the four of us kids, and the other people who were also staying there, there sure was a whole bunch of Filipinos in one house, boy.

They put on a big pot of stew and rice to feed this small army. I remember there were four or five of us in one bed. Space was so limited. But it was a big house. We played games. We played cards. The adults were very concerned about what was going on. They had the radios going all day and night. Everything was done in the house; nobody was allowed outside in the yard. They were very strict about that.

I don't think I was scared at all. But I do remember that the adults were really concerned about us being invaded; that the Japanese would be coming in swarms and kill us all.

" That night, shots were still being fired. . .
Bullets were going like crazy. It was
complete chaos. "

All of a sudden, there was a block warden at the door. Where he came from, I don't know. They must have been prepared or something. They were volunteers. They came around with the arm bands and they told us to put the lights out. We were in blackout. They also had the Territorial Guard people out patrolling. They wore the khaki uniforms and the wide brim helmets.

Mom was a nurse for the sugar plantation in Waipahu. She wasn't called--that is, if she was, she didn't go. I guess she wanted to stay with her family.

Pop was a federal worker. He worked for the post office at Hickam Field. He would normally work every other Sunday. But on December seventh, that was his Sunday off. So I would say he was very fortunate that he wasn't there at Hickam that morning or he might have been killed. In fact, when he went back to the post office later, he said there were bullet holes all over the wooden building at Hickam. It was just full of puka's.[3]

On Tuesday they let us go back to Damon Tract. We started to inspect our property to see if there were any puka's in the house, or in the garage. Brother Eddie, you know, he was so smart. He went out to check the chicken coops. We raised chickens and turkeys and he remembered hearing the shrapnel and bullets hitting the corrugated roofs during the attack, so he wanted to see if there were any souvenirs around. We saw bullet holes in the roof. It was like a string in a row. (We found out later that they were shooting at aircraft at John Rodgers,

---

[3]*Hawaiian word meaning a hole or an opening.*

the Hawaiian Airline's planes and civilian planes, too). Anyway, Eddie traced the angle of the bullet holes in the chicken coop roof and started digging in the dirt. And he found them! A whole bunch of 50-caliber heads. We kept them as souvenirs. I don't know what happened to them today. I think brother Ed got 'em, you know.

We had to dig bomb shelters. Everybody did. They gave you the dimensions. We covered it with wood, then put dirt on top. There was an entrance on one end. The Territorial Guard inspected it when it was done. We got our old kerosene lantern and put it down there with canned goods and water, if I remember.

Oh, and yes, we had these Red Ryder BB-guns. The three of us smaller ones had BB-guns. But brother Eddie, he had a pump gun. It shot pellets. We used the guns to shoot doves in Damon Tract. But now we were going to use them to shoot the Japanese when they came down from the sky. So we told Mom, we said, "Mama, we goin' to get you a Japanese with our BB-guns." And I was good with that gun. I remember telling Mama, "I'm gonna shoot them in the eye." I'll never forget that.

" . . . we had air raids. The sirens would go off and we would all run for our guns and dash for the shelter. "

Then we had air raids. The sirens would go off and we would all run for our guns and dash for the shelter. We'd all go down there and sit and wait...and wait... for the "all clear" siren. Then we came out again. We did that a lot. But that was fun when you're nine years old.

I don't think I was scared after that. The only time I really felt scared was years later when I was in St. Theresa School and they announced that President Roosevelt had died. Wow, I think about that moment and how scared I felt. The war was still going on and our president died. We were all sent home from school that day.

There was no school for a while after December seventh. I remember they asked all the residents of the Damon Tract area to come in to the community center as soon as possible and pick up gas masks. We had to have gas masks because they thought we were going to be gassed by the Japanese.

When we went back to school, we had to take our gas masks with us, too, every single day. I kind of cheated, you know. I used my gas mask to carry candy bars. I actually put candy in the face portion of the gas mask. That was a big "no-no" with the military, but what did I know?

Oh, and they gave us inoculations, too, I remember. Boy did it hurt. They got all these people back to the community center and everybody had to have tetanus, typhoid, maybe smallpox, too. Because they said that spies might poison the water. And they wanted to keep diseases down to the minimum with the civilian population. Any outbreak of a disease would have been double jeopardy.

In 1942, the haole[4] population was moving out of Hawaii. They were afraid of an invasion and many of them left. They sold their homes at low prices. We were interested in moving to Alewa Heights since the Gorospes were living there. So we picked up a four-bedroom home, two baths, two stories, for $11,000.

And people like Chin Ho, Hiram Fong, and some other of my good pake[5] friends made out at that time. That's why they have all this land today. Chin Ho bought out that Ilikai area, the duck ponds and all that area.

So we moved to Alewa Heights in the latter part of 1942. I remember it was close to Christmas time and we went up to Kamehameha School and cut off the top of a Norfolk pine. We brought it home, decorated it, and that was our Christmas tree in 1942. I don't think we had any in 1941, just after Pearl Harbor.

Where we lived on Alewa Heights, there's a tea house right above us, called the Natsunoya Tea House. I remember there were rumors that they were directing the planes to Pearl Harbor from that tea house. That was the rumor we heard, probably only because it was a Japanese tea house and it was up on a hill.

Later on, when I was a few years older, I joined the Boy Scouts. We heard that the military was throwing stuff away down at Makalapa dumps. So we went down there and found all kinds of things. Would you believe brand new pup tents? Canteens? It was more fun going on that scavenger hunt. We used those things in the Scouts.

[4]Hawaiian word meaning white person, formerly any foreigner.

[5]Hawaiian word for China or Chinese.

131

Oh, yes, I also remember there was a prisoner of war camp across from Lanakila Park, where the health center was. They kept prisoners from Europe--Germans and Italians--in those camps. There was another one in Kaneohe, where Benjamin Parker School is. They tell me there were more, too, in Wahiawa and Schofield. They were all barricaded, green barracks, painted with camouflage. There were barbed wire fences completely around and sentries with rifles walking around. A lot of people didn't know that. I remember that they allowed us kids to go in to the camps to watch movies, along with the prisoners. It was fun.

" We saw a lot as little kids. . . I guess that's why we felt, when we grew up, that we wanted to defend our country. "

We saw a lot as little kids. We saw what was going on. I guess that's why we felt, when we grew up, that we wanted to defend our country. Brother Eddie got drafted out of high school. He was the top man in ROTC at St. Louis. He was seventeen when he was drafted and sent to New Caledonia. Eddie later got his officer's commission from the ROTC at the University of Hawaii. Bobby was also an officer. He graduated from St. Louis in 1948 and went to West Point. He was sent to Europe and became a linguist. He also served in Viet Nam. I got my commission from Officer's Candidate School (OCS). So we all retired from the military. Sister Lolita became a nurse and still serves at Tripler Army Hospital, as a civilian.

Yes, we saw a lot when we were young. But how fortunate we were that nobody got hurt through all of it. I guess our whole lives were affected, whether we realized it or not, by those wartime experiences in Honolulu.

Alfredo graduated from St. Louis in 1950. He saw action in the army as a second lieutenant in the signal corps during the Korean War, then attended the University of San Francisco and the University of Hawaii, graduating with a degree in psychology in 1958. He retired as a major from the U.S. Army Reserve in 1981 after thirty-one years of service. In 1955, Al married Lorraine Quiniola, a McKinley High School graduate, and they had three children. Teresa was born in 1955; Alfredo Junior in 1956; and Steven in 1960. Teresa, a flight attendant with Hawaiian Air Lines, is married and has a son, Paul Kainoa Reyes. Al Junior died in an automobile accident in 1978 at the age of twenty-one. Steven is single and also works as a flight attendant for Hawaiian Air Lines. Al retired from the Hawaiian Telephone Company in 1987 after 30 years of service. He was a senior marketing consultant. He works part-time as a termite inspector and estimator but still finds time for active memberships in the Veterans of Foreign Wars, the Special Forces Association (Green Berets), the 100th Battalion-442nd Group Association, the Lions Club, the Elks Club, and the Filipino Chamber of Commerce. He also is a member of the St. Louis School and University of Hawaii alumni associations. He lists his favorite pastimes, however, as supporting and assisting his grandson in soccer, baseball, football and basketball activities; and travelling, especially to Las Vegas.

They Lined up for Gas

Gasoline posed the biggest rationing problem throughout the war in Honolulu. At the time of the Pearl Harbor attack, there was only a forty-seven day supply of gasoline on hand. Most islanders, fearing rationing, rushed to their service stations to fill up their tanks. Restrictions were immediately placed on the amounts of gas civilians could purchase. Then, on December fourteenth, all service stations were ordered closed, by military order, to prepare for gasoline rationing beginning the following day. Under the rationing system established, automobile owners were given coupons entitling them to purchase ten gallons of gasoline per month. *(Allen, Hawaii's War Years)*

HALF-A-MILE LONG -- Probably the longest of all the long lines of the war in Honolulu formed at City Hall to obtain gas ration cards. At times, it extended a half-a-mile to Thomas Square. The Office of Civil Defense recreation and morale committee sponsored musical troupes which entertained the throngs while they were waiting. (**Star Bulletin** *December 17, 1941; War Depository Collection, University of Hawaii)*

Isabel Joseph

Isabel was born in Wailuku, Maui, in 1911, one of seventeen children born to Isabella and Ricardo Silva. She attended St. Anthony's grade school in Wailuku. Isabel married Alfred Joseph in 1934. At the outbreak of war, she lived with her husband and two daughters, Yvonne, six, and Mary Louise, three, on Keeaumoku Street in Honolulu. Alfred worked at Pearl Harbor.

I remember we got up early that Sunday morning, December seventh, and we were having breakfast when we could hear these airplanes droning on and on. I recall saying that the noises sounded different, unusual. I know there were a lot of them, and they weren't flying very high. That's what I remember from the noises they were making. "That's an unusual sound," I said to myself.

We didn't think too much of it for a while and continued eating breakfast. Suddenly, we heard a loud knock at the door. Someone was yelling, "Al, Al, open up. We're at war." We were startled for a moment, but Alfred jumped up and ran to the door. It was our neighbor. He was going around waking the neighborhood up with the news that the Japanese were bombing Pearl Harbor. "Put on your radio, " he said, "and you'll hear what I'm saying."

Then we heard it. "It was the real McCoy," the announcer kept saying. We could still hear the planes and I started thinking that they were going to drop bombs on us. I became real frightened for all of us, for our little girls.

They started asking for volunteers to report to various places and they mentioned that all Pearl Harbor workers should go down to the navy yard. Al was a patternmaker in the pattern shop down there. If there was a part of the ship that was needed, they would use drawings and patterns and the part would be manufactured to their specifications. So they were calling all navy yard workers and Alfred had to go. I was so scared and hated to see him go. I had no idea, at that time, that I wouldn't see him again for three days.

We were told to stay off the streets and not to use the phones. I worried about my parents up in Kaimuki. But I didn't try to phone.

One of my neighbors came over--her husband was an ammunition inspector at Pearl Harbor--and she was alone too and wanted company. A little later, another neighbor came by. Before we knew it, there were four of us neighbors, with our children, all at my house, consoling each other. We were frightened. We were worried about our husbands.

Someone talked about the Japanese taking over the islands. That worried us all the more. My mind went wild. "Oh, my God," I thought, "what will they do to us? Would they shoot the older people? Put the younger people to work for them?" I looked at my little ones, Yvonne and Mary Louise. I would just die if we were separated. And what was happening to Alfred? He was in great danger. Will he come home again?

" We all slept in the living room, on the floor
. . . We talked, we cried . . . Then there would
be silence and you knew that some of us
were praying. "

All the neighbors thought it would be better for all of us if we just stayed together that night. So we did. We all slept in the living room, on the floor, and listened to the radio in the dark, all night. I don't know how much sleep we were able to get that night. But, anyway, we weren't alone. We had each other. We stuck together. We talked, we cried, we even laughed at times. Then there would be silence and you knew that some of us were praying. And we did a lot of praying. That's when you really turn to God, isn't it? When you need something, when you're frightened.

While listening to the radio, I thought, "Gee, all the Japanese had to do to get control of us was to take over KGMB." And the other stations.

They could have moved right in. And everybody in the islands was listening to the radio that night.

I was waiting for Al to come home. I was worried about him. When he didn't, I thought for sure he must have got killed. It was an empty feeling, like I was sick to my stomach.

And I think they came back that night. I know there was an air raid and guns were shooting. We kept down, in the dark. We were all so frightened.

What a surprise that day brought. We were all in a state of shock. We didn't know what to expect, what was going to happen. I think that was the difficult part. And, there was nothing we could do about it. We were so helpless.

When the fear subsided, and the bombing didn't come back, the neighbors went back home and we tried to get back to our normal lives. We didn't feel like eating. We didn't feel like doing anything. Everything was so tense.

" We were all in a state of shock. We didn't know what to expect, what was going to happen. . . And, there was nothing we could do about it. We were so helpless. "

Then, Al came home the following Wednesday. He was tired. He looked sick, drained. He couldn't eat. I was so happy to see him--to know that he was still alive. "Oh, Lord," he said, "you have no idea what I've been through--what I've seen." He said that his knees were wobbly whenever those planes would come over. He thought sure they were going to bomb his shop. He said he could still smell that burnt flesh and see all those dead bodies that they were bringing in from the ships. "They were throwing them like lumber into these trucks," he said. "It's hard to believe that anything like that could happen. It's a nightmare," he said.

Thank God the worst was over. We didn't have to put up with all that killing any more. But then, of course, we did have to abide by the rules, under martial law. No lights at night. We had to be ready for an emergency evacuation if and when the order came. We all had to carry gas masks everywhere we went.

And the bomb shelters. They started digging one right in our front yard, right away. It was a neighborhood project. It had a little entrance to come in and out. You were all enclosed with sand bags on the sides and the top. Then the sirens would sound and we would have to run in there. I remember doing that many times.

Everywhere you went, there were shelters. I remember I was on my way to town on the bus one day and the air raid sirens went off. The bus driver pulled the bus over and stopped and everybody had to run to the nearest community shelter. There was one at the nearby school. So we all went in there, sat, and waited for twenty minutes or so until the "all clear" alarm sounded. The bus driver was there with us, too. Then we all got back on the bus and went on our way.

Those were the years that I did a lot of worrying. You worried about your children, your parents. You had to be more on the alert. And you

SHELTER ENTRANCE -- *A no smoking sign marks the entrance to an underground air raid shelter for area office workers in downtown Honolulu. Note Territorial Office Building and Kamehameha statue in background. (Advertiser; War Depository Collection, University of Hawaii)*

138

listened to the radio all the time. You never knew what to expect. And you kept thinking of all sort of things happening. The worst things, of course. But we lived through it all. We managed to survive.

Alfred retired in 1963 after more than thirty years service at Pearl Harbor. He died in 1978. Isabel lives in Kaneohe, at the foot of the Koolau mountain range, and keeps herself fit with a daily regimen of gardening work. She lives close to her daughter, Mary Louise, and frequently travels to Los Angeles to visit her first-born daughter, Yvonne. Her daughters have given her seven grandchildren, and she is the great-grandmother of four.

Speak American Campaign

Every effort was made to convince the local Japanese, particularly the elderly aliens, that their best interest lay with the United States. To be sure, the great majority needed no convincing. Japanese schools, clubs, and societies of all kinds were closed down. Japanese language newspapers and radio stations were censored. Telephone conversations were monitored and callers warned to speak English or they would be disconnected. The use of kimonos and Japanese sandals became a rarity. The "Americanization through Language" program, sponsored by the University of Hawaii Adult Education department, launched English language classes for older people. They were primarily attended by local Japanese. *(Allen, Hawaii's War Years)*

CLASSES IN ENGLISH — Many English centers were established in Honolulu for non-English speaking residents immediately after the war began. Shown at Pohukaina School is teacher May Wedemeyer, a librarian who turned tutor for the program. The Friends Society, the YWCA, and the Palama Settlement helped to sponsor the campaign. (**Star Bulletin** *December 31, 1942; War Depository Collection, University of Hawaii)*

Herbert Y. S. Foo

Herb Foo was born in Honolulu in 1920. His father, Wa Sang Foo, was born in Guangdong, China, and came to Honolulu in 1896. Herb's mother, Ho Shee, was born in Waikiki, Honolulu. Herb's parents were married in 1904 and lived in what was considered the country area of Kaimuki. There were just a few houses in the Ocean View tract area where they lived on 17th Avenue. His mother passed away when he was just three years old and Herb and his two sisters and two brothers lived with relatives until his father got the family back together, at the family homestead in Kaimuki, in 1938. That was the year Herb graduated from McKinley High School. He attended the University of Hawaii, majoring in business. He worked at Pearl Harbor when the war began.

I know a lot of people are not aware of it, but a national emergency was declared by Congress or President Franklin Roosevelt, long before the attack on Pearl Harbor. This was due to the fact that the war in Europe was heating up and the fact that Japan was moving into China and other parts of Asia. War clouds seemed to be on the horizon and different government jobs were being created as a result. They were building up the navy yard and military installations, hiring people. So I decided I was going to leave school after my sophomore year at the University and join the navy. I'm the type who always wanted to travel and see the world.

I was very disappointed when the navy wouldn't take me because of my weight. I remember I weighed one-hundred-sixteen pounds then and I guess that wasn't enough, so they rejected me. So I went to work at the Pearl Harbor Navy Yard--in the Transportation shop--shop 02, they called it.

This shop was in charge of all of the transportation needs, including maintenance of all the locomotives, cranes, the travelling cranes, all the trucks--things of that sort--that were used at Pearl Harbor. So that's what I was doing when the war broke out, still living at home with my dad and sister.

141

Herbert Y. S. Foo (continued)

I do remember December the seventh very well. I remember it was early in the morning and I was home and I heard heavy artillery fire. At first I didn't pay any attention to it. We had heard that sound before. But it persisted, so I went outside, and I could see planes in the sky and black puffs of smoke all around the planes. I thought they were having practice maneuvers, but I didn't recall that they would shoot so close to the planes when practicing. We are only about two miles away from Fort Ruger, which was built as a defensive unit, with big guns located in Diamond Head pointing towards the ocean to repel any ships that might come to attack the Hawaiian Islands.

But, of course, that didn't help because the attack came from above. Anyway, my dad and I went over to my aunt's home on Keanu Street-- near 6th Avenue--to help install a light fixture.

It was while we were there that we heard the announcement over the radio that Pearl Harbor had been attacked. They warned people to stay off the street. They also asked all Pearl Harbor employees to report to work. So I immediately got hold of my carpool driver and he picked me up at my aunt's house, and, along with other passengers, we drove to Pearl Harbor.

We drove down through the old Dillingham Road area, which led directly to the main gate of Pearl Harbor, passing by Hickam Air Field. I noticed, on the way down, that people were just driving like crazy. There just wasn't any speed limit at all. And we got into several very close encounters with other cars. Everyone was in a big rush to get there. Of course, we didn't know what we were supposed to do when we got there, we were just following orders to get there in a hurry.

When we got to the front of the main gate to Pearl Harbor, traffic was backed up. Normally the guards would just look at your badge and we would go right through. But this particular day they were paying close attention to identification, so traffic was backed up.

While waiting in line there, the seriousness of the situation hit me personally. I saw this Japanese plane just dive right over the telephone post, strafing Hickam Field. And, I could see the pilot's helmet and his face. And he strafed the field and he went on. The first sight of that airplane strafing Hickam and the face of that pilot really made a big impact on me. I realized that this was war. This was the first direct contact I had with the war. From that point on, I was very fearful. "Gee," I thought, "this is not something to be taken lightly." I thought

142

that lives would surely be lost. Of course, I had no idea at that very moment in time that many lives had already been lost.

So we finally got into the yard and to the Transportation Department. We did our jobs, as usual, not really knowing the extent of the devastation so close by. When the drivers would come back for relief or

---

" The first sight of that airplane strafing Hickam and the face of that pilot really made a big impact on me. I realized that this was war. "

---

to get off their shifts, we would hear these stories about how many people were killed and that they had to haul the injured and the dead from the drydock area. They used any kind of transportation that was available to do the job. I remember, most vividly, those stories about all the people who were killed and wounded.

We were all fearful of the Japanese invading these islands at that time. Just from our first experience in the Navy Yard, we could sense the feeling of this total, chaotic situation. We felt that they could have come in at any time and taken over the islands. In fact, it became public knowledge that they could have easily walked right into the Hawaiian Islands. We were in a demoralized situation because of the surprise attack and the damage they had done to our naval forces, as well as practically wiping out our air force.

There was no official quitting time that day. But, as it was getting to be dusk, our shop master, E. Miller, advised us to leave. He was a hapa haole,[1] a gentleman who was really respected in the whole yard for his knowledge of heavy equipment. He suggested that we leave because he didn't know what conditions we were going to encounter outside the yard.

We had to walk from our office to the main gate, about a quarter of a mile, to get transportation home. But it seemed that every few steps we took, we'd be challenged by sentries. It was dark already--which made us really afraid--because we heard that the Marines were in so much

---

[1]*Hawaiian words meaning part-Hawaiian and part-Caucasian.*

turmoil that they were trigger-happy.

So we finally made it to the gate, but there was no public transportation available because the island was completely blacked out. People had to drive in the dark. Because our driver was nowhere to be found, we started walking. We walked almost all the way home, about ten miles, when a ride came along and we rode the last two miles home. What a relief to get home to my dad and sister.

A few days later, they had salvaged a Japanese plane that had been shot down in the harbor. I remember one of the drivers asked me if I wanted to go with him to see the airplane. So we went over there and I saw the plane wreck. It was completely damaged. I even picked up a bolt from the wreckage as a souvenir.

Then we heard the rumors. One of the drivers said that paratroopers landed in Palolo Valley and then it spread all over the navy yard.

And we were under martial law. One of the most strict of rules the military leaders issued, I believe, was the fact that cars could not use their headlights. You had to paint out most of the lights, leaving a tiny strip--a tiny rectangular beam of light--showing. Just so that you could barely see the street. You couldn't see another car at all.

I remember coming back from work in the dark. But because traffic moved very slowly at night, we didn't encounter too many accidents. You could not see oncoming cars until they were very close to you. You could see a very tiny beam of light in the distance, but you really couldn't see the car unless it was a bright, moonlight night. The beam of light was just enough for you to see the center of the road so you could stay on your side of the highway. I think most people who drove under those blackout conditions would certainly remember that experience.

Blacking out our homes was something else we will never forget. We had to cover windows with heavy material so that light would not seep out. Some people would build like a fence on the outside of the window whereby the light would not shine directly out and you would have a tiny space on the bottom of this vent where you could let air into the house. But everybody seemed to get along fine, even under these restrictions. We sat in the dark a lot, with windows and doors open to enjoy the fresh air. We certainly had meals on time, usually before dark.

We got to work on time, too. The navy yard was very, very busy during the early months of the war. At first, there were hardly any days off. In fact, many people were working double shifts. They were trying to repair the damaged ships as soon as possible, to get them out to sea again.

The Oahu Railway and Land Company played an important transportation role at that time. It ran from Honolulu, across from Aala Park, down to Pearl Harbor. We would take the bus to the depot, and the train down to work. That would help alleviate the traffic load.

Gasoline was rationed, I remember. You were given just enough gas to get you to and from work, and they also took into consideration the fact that you were in a carpool. So, they didn't give you much gas for recreational purposes. I guess some of us--I'd say most of us--would cheat a little by taking the train and saving gas for one or two days to go on trips of a personal nature. But that railroad served the navy yard well, because it was always packed with navy yard people.

Oh, and we had a bomb shelter, too. That was the first project we did, as soon as they recommended it. We decided we wanted to be on the safe side, so we built it right away. It was built for the whole family. I remember taking a picture of myself with my gas mask on, right at the entrance to the bomb shelter. It held six of us very comfortably. At least ten feet long, by five feet wide. And the gas masks were something else. It seems so far-fetched that we would have to use gas masks, but I guess

FROM DOWN UNDER -- Herb emerges from his underground bomb shelter, wearing his gas mask in this family scrapbook photo taken during the early war years. (Courtesy Foo family photo collection)

145

from the military viewpoint at the time, we needed it. I don't think there was any need for gas masks in any battle during all of World War II. I still have my gas mask stashed somewhere.

Another thing I remember while living under military rule is the fact that if you did something wrong, many times your sentence was to give a pint of blood for the war effort. That's true. And, you know, for some people, that was a very hard sentence. So I continued to work at Pearl Harbor all through the war. We were restricted to our jobs. We were aware of how the war was going, by the ships that would come in for repairs. We heard from the military people what was going on, and we were much impressed with how it was progressing. After a while, we were reasonably comfortable that we were not going to be occupied by the Japanese. It was really a very fast recovery, only eight or nine months after Pearl Harbor. We bounced back from a real low point.

After the major fighting, ships were repaired and put back to sea. We employees were given an "E" pin by the United States Navy for "excellence." At that time, I thought it was insignificant because we did what we were supposed to do. However, today I really treasure the pin because I realize now--after so many years--that we contributed a lot to getting our ships back to the offensive in record time.

We were under martial law until sometime in 1945, I think. After that period of time, we started to enjoy some form of recreational activities. That took the pressure off the constant working that we had been through. So we would gather in people's homes and have a few beers and something to eat. But of course, that was only on the weekends. For a long period of time, we still worked six days a week.

The month the war ended, though, a funny thing happened. I was drafted into the army. So, I thought this would finally be my ticket to travel. I was hoping that they would send me to Japan as part of the occupational troops, or even to New Caledonia, where they had military stations.

So, wouldn't you know, I was sent to Schofield--only an hour's drive from home at that time--for my basic training, and then to the 13th Detachment Depot at Wahiawa, thanks to my clerical experience. I became in charge of the separation center, where all the local soldiers coming back from Europe and Japan would be discharged from the army. So we did all the separation clerical work.

It was a good assignment, though, because you got to hear a lot about what the guys did during the war. And many of them were my friends who were being discharged. They all had to come through us.

The war years were not unhappy times for me. In fact, I met my future wife while working at Pearl Harbor. And, the GI bill gave me a college education I probably wouldn't have had.

When I look back, though, I realize that I lived through such an important part of U.S. history. In fact, this was such a big event in world history--the first time a huge, powerful American fleet was damaged so severely, by a sneak attack at the hands of an Asiatic military air force so many thousands of miles away from their homeland.

And I was there when it happened. I actually saw combat planes in the air and saw those planes being shot at. And we were indirectly involved in taking care of the dying and wounded, through the transportation services we provided that morning.

I'll always remember the words of President Franklin Roosevelt the next day. He said that December 7, 1941, will go down in history as a day of infamy. That's really imprinted on my mind--a day of infamy. And it happened right here, only a few miles from where we live.

Herb married Laura Mock in 1948 after being discharged from the service. He continued his education following his marriage and received a BS in business from the University of Southern California in 1951, and a master's in education from the University of Hawaii in 1977. He owned and operated a bakery in Honolulu for many years before beginning a teaching career at the Honolulu Community College. He retired in 1985, after close to fifteen years of service with the college. Herb and Laura had two children, Marcella and Matthew. Marcella is married to Peter Yee and they have given the Foos two grandsons, Christopher and Andrew. Matthew died in 1989 at the age of 28.

Hawaiian Hospitality

Dear Lady Next Door: August 5, 1942

It is written that the way to a man's heart is through his stomach. That being so, you have earned your way into the hearts of this entire outfit by your kindness and thoughtfulness during the past few weeks. To say that your delicacies were appreciated is putting it mildly, the cookies and cakes remind us of the kind our mothers used to make, and what hit the spot just as well, was the idea that someone in Hawaii was actually going out of her way to be extra nice to a group of lads she didn't know. If that's a sample of Hawaiian hospitality, we say bravo--but we think it more a sample of the kindness and generosity of a fellow American who is Remembering Pearl Harbor by not forgetting the servicemen. As for the thanks we'd like to extend--we'd like to express it in a much stronger manner than this note could ever do. If you'll just let us know the next time any Jap planes come over your home, we'll do our best to keep the big bad wolf away. Thanks again for the cakes and cookies, and until the time comes when we can write "Thank You" across the skies, we remain a few of the lads across the street.

(Signed by thirty-five men from one of the military posts in Honolulu)

(War Depository Collection, University of Hawaii)

*REST AND RECREATION -- The world famous Royal Hawaiian Hotel became the site of R & R for the submarine service of the U. S. Navy. Civilian women, pictured on the outdoor dance floor along Waikiki Beach, were invited by the military to act as hostesses. (**Star Bulletin** April 8, 1942; War Depository Collection, University of Hawaii)*

Bette Ballentyne

Her father, Gustave (Gus) Ballentyne, born in Victoria, B.C., was just a few years old when he came to Honolulu with his family in the 1890s. He later helped to organize the newly created rail transportation system, the Honolulu Rapid Transit Company, commonly called the HRT. Her mother, Hazel Sherman, came to Hawaii from Cambridge, Mass. to visit a married sister whose husband was with the Army Medical Corps at Schofield during World War I. She later decided to stay and make Hawaii her home, and was married. They raised three children; Bette, born in Honolulu in 1921; Barbara, born a few years later, and Sherman, the youngest, born eight years later. Bette graduated from Punahou High School in 1939 and from Colby Junior College in New London, New Hampshire. Her family home, at that time, was located in Manoa Valley. She came home in June 1941 for summer break, but her father didn't want her to return to college in the fall. He was afraid that there would be a war and wanted her home. When World War II began, Bette was twenty, and a student at the University of Hawaii. Her sister was a junior at Punahou, and her brother, ten, was in elementary school.

I well remember Saturday night, December the sixth. The fleet was in and there were many parties. I was with a group of girls and officers from the *USS Arizona*, and dancing at Lau Yee Chai's in Waikiki. It was one of the favorite night spots at the time. We had fun. We weren't thinking about war.

The next morning, our family was abruptly awakened by a neighbor, a boy friend of my brother, whose father was an officer on the *USS Arizona*. He came in yelling that his father was called to Pearl Harbor and had to rush out there because his ship was on fire! He said that they were being bombed! My father shouted, "What are you talking about?"

Right then my cousin called, who lived in Palolo Valley. He said, "Something's happening here in the valley. There's been a great big blast." That's when we turned on the radio and realized that we were at war.

In the lower, left corner of our lot, my father had built a small, one-bedroom apartment over an existing garage. The couple renting the apartment were Scots, and had experienced World War I in England. They told us to hurry and get under their apartment that morning. The apartment foundation was made of hollow tile, and was a safer bomb shelter than the dirt one we had dug in our front yard. We were there three or four times during the morning of December seventh.

My father owned a freight forwarding company, the Hawaiian Freight Forwarders. He immediately called his company in Chicago, to tell them to hold all shipments, etc., as we were at war and presently under attack. I think he also called his mother and sister on the mainland, as many people did. He was a quick thinker and so luckily his calls went through before the telephone company stopped and censored phone calls out and into the islands. Almost at once, the radio stations began requesting volunteers for hospital duty, guard duty, etc. As my father used to be a member of the American Legion, he resurrected his overseas cap from the toy-box and jumped in the car to go to his office. He took my sister Barbara with him so she could bring the car back in case he had to stay there for a long time. He thought he should guard his papers and his office. My mother, brother, and I stayed home.

My sister returned a few hours later, without my father, and full of wild tales. She claimed she saw two Japanese flyers that had been picked up. They had on aloha shirts and swimming trunks and they were being ushered into the Dillingham Building, where the FBI office was.

We had three radios going all the time; one on KGU; another on the second station, KGMB; and the third on the police radio band. We could hear what was going on at all times, plus the many telephone calls from friends.

Although Manoa Valley was out of the direct line of action, about mid-morning we did see a Japanese plane flying overhead.

Friends of my sister kept coming by and instructing us on what we should do. They said we should fill up all bottles with water, then told us to fill up the tub, too, as we might need the water later to survive. Later they told us that the water had been poisoned and to dump it all out! Rumors were rampant and we didn't know who or what to believe.

Our Japanese maid didn't come back that night. She was a live-in maid, with her own quarters. She usually had Sundays off but would come back Sunday night to be there Monday morning. She did return Monday morning.

I remember some well-dressed men came by our house about mid-morning, December seventh, and asked us where the Sumitomo National

Bank house was. We told them right up at the end of the street on the right. We were told later--I certainly can't verify it--but we were told that there were several Japanese men sitting around the house talking and they had on kimonos. Under their kimonos, they had on Japanese army uniforms. They were supposedly taken away. And one of the men who came to check on these Japanese nationals became my brother-in-law, years later. But lots of stories like that were going around.

" They said we should . . . fill up the tub . . .
as we might need the water later to
survive. "

That first night, the four of us were home alone and it was dark about six o'clock. My father was a member of a local group of men, the Businessmen's Military Training Corp. So, as we later found out, he was on patrol that night down by the waterfront, near his office, and under their command.

We were scared. We four stayed downstairs in the living room. My mother slept on the couch and the three of us on the floor. We had a flashlight and candles. We didn't know at that time what my father was doing. We were, of course, also very worried that the Japanese might come back. We just stayed together, listened to the radios, until we finally went off to sleep. My father did come home during the night and we were very relieved.

The next day we were busy preparing for the night time blackouts. We had to shop for blackout material, for food, canned goods, and other necessities. We, of course, didn't know when the next shipment of supplies would arrive from the mainland, and everything came by ship. No air shipments then. Everybody started stocking up as much as they could. We were encouraged to do so. People shopped for rice by the ten-pound bag, and cartons of toilet paper. A lot of people even made arrangements for the storage of larger amounts of supplies.

At home, we painted some windows in the bedrooms and covered others with paper. We painted my windows because I had windows that were smaller and we could more easily shut off my room. My brother slept in a screened room, so no problem there. We blacked out my sister's room and that's where we spent most evenings. And it was

151

hotter than Billy-be-darned! We used her room in the evenings until we blacked out more of the house.

All the schools as well as the university were closed and, of course, we didn't know when any of them would open. Punahou was taken over by the U.S. Army Engineers, and as it was a private school, they shouldn't have. They were aiming for the University of Hawaii but took over Punahou. So Punahou kids were farmed out to different private residences when school started. Barbara went to someone's house in Nuuanu Valley. Many high school students were working too. They were sent to the pineapple fields to help, as there was a shortage of workers. Many adults went to Pearl Harbor, as soon as they could, to assist military and civilian workers.

I was at the University of Hawaii studying chemistry and finishing my studies to be a medical technician. I remember later being told that someone had thrown away all the experiments we had been working on in class. They had emptied everything down the drain. And so I thought, "That's the end of my education." And I never went back.

Just a few days following December seventh, a friend called to invite me to a special meeting. She said that a very secret organization was starting and that although she couldn't tell me about it, (military secret), she thought I might like to join. I didn't go to the first meeting, but I did go later when the meeting was held at the Iolani Palace. That was the start of the Women's Air Raid Defense, the WARDs, a wartime organization.

The use of radar as an aircraft warning device was just starting and very new to Hawaii and the Pacific. There were six mobile radar stations on the island of Oahu at the time of the Japanese attack. Soldiers were actually being trained on December seventh to operate this equipment and the information control center. These men were sent later to forward military bases, and we, as WARDs, replaced them.

When the United States Army decided to use our services, one hundred women from local families, as well as wives of servicemen stationed in Hawaii, formed the nucleus. The women could be no younger than twenty and no older than thirty-four years of age. They could have no dependents and they must be willing to work on a twenty-four hour basis and to live at army quarters at Fort Shafter. And, we had to go through physical examinations and army intelligence review.

152

Remember, the WACS and the WAVES were not in existence then, so this became the first uniformed, all-women's organization to serve the country during World War II. We worked at a large plotting board at the Information and Control Center for the Hawaiian Department, United States Army. I was a plotter. Basically, we'd receive a direct call from "Oscar" (the code name for the caller at the radar installation). He'd advise us that the airplane or target was at a specific location in code. We would indicate that position on the plotting board with a small plastic arrow. The activities and location of the center were top secret, at the time.

We were hired by the army--the Signal Corps--but we, with some officers' privileges, were under the Civil Service system. Even though we were uniformed, we were still civilians. We were paid $125 a month, as a base pay.

WARDs ON DUTY -- In a top secret tunnel location near Fort Shafter, members of the WARDs receive information from radar operators and plot aircraft locations. This form of data interpretation became a major part of the defense system of Hawaii. (Advertiser; War Depository Collection, University of Hawaii)

As mentioned, we all had a thorough FBI check and gave references which the FBI checked. I know they checked all of my references. They told me! There were more wives of servicemen hired than local girls. Although we hired Chinese, Korean, Filipinos, every nationality represented locally, there were no Japanese. We couldn't hire them, which was certainly silly from our local point of view. We recruited, then, women from the mainland, and in February 1943 the first group started to arrive.

We had two types of uniforms--a plain shirt-waist type dress called a fatigue, and a dress-jacket and skirt. Also, we had overseas hats. All very simple and good looking in blue with red piping, and brass wings pinned over our breast pocket.

They started evacuating civilians from the islands almost at once. Those, first of all, who weren't well were put on ships for the mainland. My parents decided to leave too, mostly because of business. My father was asked by the government to help regulate shipments, especially because food and luxury items would be limited due to wartime priorities. So they packed up, rented our house, and left with my sister and brother for California in May 1942. I stayed here in Honolulu to work at my new job with the WARDs.

My aunt and uncle also remained in Hawaii. He was a physician--an X-ray diagnostician--and when I had time off from the WARDs, I stayed at their home in Dowsett Tract. In fact, my uncle came to my rescue once when I got in trouble with the martial law.

I was stopped one night for being out after curfew during a blackout. My ticket was for not having the right address on my identification card. My legal address was our home on Ferdinand Avenue. So I had to go to court and my uncle came with me. There must have been one-hundred-fifty people lined up for the same offense. They all pleaded, "Guilty," "Guilty." I stood up and said, "Not guilty." When my uncle spoke for me, I got off without a fine. But, all the money civilians had to pay for various fines--to this day, they have no record of where it went.

Our workplace was located at Fort Shafter, the far end of the valley in a newly built, very large, tunnel. We had six-hour shifts, around the clock. Representatives from all of the military branches worked with us in a small plotting room in the middle of the tunnel.

I remember General Charles Lindbergh there one day, looking over our operation. There were a lot of very famous people there frequently to see the operation. Half of the time we didn't even know they were there. They could look down at us from the balcony areas.

" . . . we had to learn how to operate a gun. They said if anything happened, we were on our own . . . "

We were given special training in radio work and in other duties. We even had a teacher come in and teach us physics. I don't know why. Some of us enjoyed it and some of us didn't. And, we had to learn how to operate a gun. I can't really say if I ever learned how. They said if anything happened, we were on our own and wouldn't have any special attention. The military would have to defend the islands and we couldn't be singled out. So they proceeded to teach us to fire a gun. I don't know where we'd get a gun if we ever needed one; they didn't issue us any.

One night in early January, our shift was walking down a short hill on a wooden walk to the station we called Little Robert. As we approached, the guard yelled, "Halt!" The first girl in line said, matter-of-factly, "What for?"

He yelled louder, again, "Halt!" We then heard the click of his gun and saw the gleam of his bayonet. So one of the girls said, "You'd better stop right now. He's serious."

We were all so busy talking about what social event we were going to attend, we hadn't paid any attention to the guard. We were very cocky. We knew where we were going and we knew what we were going to do. Doesn't he know about us working here? Why should this person question us? No one had told us about this possibility.

The guard stepped forward and said, "Now listen, ladies. From now on you better learn that this is war. When we say halt, you better do just that." Well, that made everybody wake up and look alive. We followed orders after that.

We had many bomb shelters at Shafter, large, long and dark ones. There were many times during an air raid when we had to go to the shelter, and a lot of the girls just refused. Because there were other animals in there before us. Cats! We had a lot of rain in early 1942, so it was very wet and very cold, particularly at night. And for some reason when there was an air raid, it was usually at night and raining. We'd have to go down a few steps into the shelters. There were two entrances, one at each end, and you could go all the way through to come out the other end. I didn't go back very far--in all that mud--and as it was pitch black.

One of my roommates was a Catholic and often had to get up early to go to church. The church was at the Fort Shafter theater, a good twenty-minute walk from our quarters. As we couldn't be out alone, I went with her. It was about five o'clock in the morning, one time, and very dark. We had a flashlight that had been painted black with a blue dot in the center, consequently very hard to see where you were walking. We would finally arrive and enter this large room then sit in the back. It was a large theater and usually filled with people. "Cathy, you can't see or hear anything from way back here. There's no point in coming."

WOMEN AT WORK -- Members of the WARDs, the Women's Air Raid Defense organization, became the first uniformed, all-women's unit to serve the country during World War II. (Photo courtesy of Bette Ballentyne and the WARDs)

She'd answer, "Oh yes, I can hear just fine." We did that only a few times. But since we weren't allowed to be out alone, she found earlier or later Masses–in daylight hours.

We asked once if we could be transferred "down under" and to go where the action was. Admiral Montgomery firmly said, "No, you're doing a very good job for us right here." We think we felt pleased.

While off duty, we volunteered for organizations, hospitals, and time helping patients. We were also asked by different groups to go to parties at the officers' clubs for social affairs. We would be picked up and brought home by an escort, and we had many good times. We got home early, and because of the blackout, parties would start at three o'clock in the afternoon. We were told that as WARDs, we should associate mostly with the officers. Of course, we all had friends who were enlisted men, but all were treated well and nobody made a big issue of it.

Almost all the civilians in town entertained the military. They just opened their houses to the servicemen. My uncle and aunt had a beach house in Lanikai, and ten feet away there was a twenty-foot machine gun nest of solid concrete. The whole beach was fortified like Fort Knox. The Massachusetts Battalion was camped in that area and at the Kailua Beach Park. So every Sunday, four of the fellows were always asked for dinner. And most of them were quite nice. My uncle and aunt heard from some of them for many years after the war.

We had very nice living quarters at Shafter. The row of houses, all connected, were mostly two-bedroom, two-story units. We had three girls to a unit, and all units were blacked out.

On a few occasions we did have problems with prowlers. One night a girl came home and went upstairs to bed. She opened her closet door and said, "What are these boots doing in my closet?" She looked up and there was a man standing there, in back of her clothes. She let out a hoot and a holler and came running downstairs.

We had what we called the OD button, an alarm that called the "officer of the day." But it was in the living room, opposite the stairs. By the time we ran to ring the bell, the man would unlock the other door and run out and away. That only happened a few times.

We had most of our meals at the Fort Shafter Officers' Mess. We had Filipino waiters who took good care of the three of us. The WARDs ate in one large room most of the time. When the waiters saw us, however, they would say, "Right over here, mum." Especially when it was crowded, they would choose our meal and bring it to us. We never argued!

One night, in the Officers' Mess, a public relations army officer I knew arrived with Jack Benny and some friends, who had just flown in for a show for the troops. We were sitting next to them. Phil told us later that whoever Jack Benny met on his trips, he would jot down their name and home address. Then, when he returned to the mainland, he would write or call the parents and say, "I saw your son and he looked fine." That was something I shall never forget.

We also went to a USO show early in January 1942 at Fort Shafter and the star was Joe E. Brown. Sadly, he'd heard that very day that his son had been killed in action. Terribly shocked, he gave an excellent show.

There was a fairly steady turnover in the WARDs. Some women would join then find out they didn't like it, and leave. Some of the military wives, who joined when their husbands were stationed in Hawaii, decided to go back home when their husbands were shipped out to combat. A lot of girls from the mainland had signed up for a tour of duty for one year. They were given transportation over and when their tour was up, they were given transportation back. Others would meet a fellow, get married and then they would resign. A sad part, though, was when the military wives would lose their husbands in military action and so have to return to their mainland homes.

I think that we must have had about five hundred women serve in the WARDs. They were a wonderful group of ladies and some lasting friendships were made. We still get together for reunions. Those were exciting times for us here in Hawaii, and as I think, mainly, we all felt very involved and proud to be helping our country.

Bette Ballentyne joined Matson Lines in Hawaii soon after the war. She lived and worked on the mainland and Hawaii and retired in 1985 as a library assistant from the University of Hawaii. In retirement, she enjoys her ninth floor condominium overlooking the blue Pacific at the foot of Diamond Head.

Robert Rego

Bob Rego, born in Wailuku, Maui in 1918, was the last of eleven children born to Joseph and Mary Rego. Bob attended St. Anthony's School and graduated from Maui High School in 1936. He attended the University of California at Santa Barbara in California and earned a degree in education in 1941. On December seventh, he lived at his parents' house on Kaimuki Avenue, atop the hill near 6th Avenue. He was twenty-three.

My brother, Joe, shared a room with me at the folks' house. He was a bachelor then--he was divorced a year or so before I graduated. Anyway, it seems like everybody was on the town the night before. I was, too. I had a date with a nurse from Queen's Hospital. We went to a nightclub in Waikiki. Got in about two o'clock in the morning. Feeling a little high.

Early the next morning--I was still in bed--my sister, Irene, came running up to the house. She was married and lived just a few blocks from us. And she was all excited--she says with a high voice--"Japanese are bombing Pearl Harbor." I got up and said, "What the heck is this?"

She said, "Well, look out the window." We were pretty high up on Kaimuki Avenue--you could see right down to Pearl Harbor. You could see all the black smoke down there. I guess the *Arizona* must have been already hit by that time.

She said, "Put the radio on, you'll see what I'm saying." So I put on the radio--and I think it was Web Edwards on the radio. And he was all excited. "People now, now, now, you better be calm," he says. "Ah, ah, Japanese have bombed Pearl Harbor, the *Arizona* is down . . ." He kept on rattling away. He said, "Civilian defense workers report to your jobs."

I was working for the U.S. Engineers then. I was a storekeeper. I had just gotten the job, a couple of months earlier. So I had to report to work. Policemen were on the streets directing traffic, sending all the people who don't belong on the streets back home. I had a little 1936 Willys. I remember that little Willys that Dad Rego got for me. I showed the police my badge and passed through. I had to report to Kapalama Basin, across the bay from Hickam Field.

When I got there, the bombing was still going on, it was still early in the morning. We were out in the open, we didn't know anything about warfare. There's this big open beach area there. We were out in the middle of it and Japanese planes were flying all around, right next to Fort Armstrong.

And there were all these anti-aircraft guns shooting away at the planes. They couldn't hit the broad side of a barn. I don't think they ever fired those guns before. Well anyway, something buzzed by me and I started running. I was twenty-three years old, still in good shape. But I didn't know where to run, so I ducked under this warehouse.

I got under there for awhile and I thought, "My God, you better get outta here. What if a bomb drops on this warehouse?" It held nails, roofing paper--a regular storehouse of materials.

I remember what a funny feeling it was. I thought about home. What were we supposed to do? Joe and I were the only ones at home. Should we go home to protect the folks, or what? What if the Japanese troops have landed? Where were we going to hide? Up in the hills? Would we be playing guerrilla warfare, or something? You know, it was a funny sensation. All those things came to my mind.

" . . . if the Japanese would have landed troops here, we'd have been goners. . .We weren't prepared at all. "

I remembered that my sister's husband, Frank, was on the old *Oglala*, at Pearl Harbor. The old ship was a minelayer and he was stationed on that ship. He was a warrant officer, I think.

Well, anyway, we didn't know whether he was dead or alive. We were all relieved when he came back that evening about 7:30. We learned that his ship was attacked in Pearl Harbor and it went down. He lost his clothes and almost everything he owned. It was a scary feeling, that day.

I had to report to my job the following morning. They had all these young kids as guards. They were more afraid then I was. This guy yelled, "Halt." He was about ten yards away from me and surprised me. He almost stuck that bayonet in me. I told him, "For God's sakes, give me a warning. Let me know where you are." I mean, they shouldn't have been given that duty. They didn't know what the score was.

That's the kind of shape we were in that morning. I mean, by gosh, if the Japanese would have landed troops here, we'd have been goners. Really. We didn't know beans. We weren't prepared at all.

I reported to my job and in the next few days, everything was different--our lives changed from then on. There were blackouts. We were on martial law. That was something. You had to have a special pass to be out on the streets at night.

Right after the attack, I remember the folks moved to Prince Edward Street in Waikiki, just a couple of blocks in from the ocean. And we'd have alerts. When anything was out there, we'd have an alert. There could even be a whale out there in the ocean, and we'd have an alert.

I remember Dad Rego. We used to go under the house, to the cellar--

PRIVATE REGO POSES -- Private Robert Rego struck up a pose for the camera at Fort Armstrong in Honolulu, during the latter part of 1942. (Photo courtesy of Rego family photo collection)

kind of a basement--during the air raids. We would get under there and wait for the "all clear" signal. Dad Rego got so every time they'd have an alert, he'd just turn over in bed and say, "Heck, if I'm going to die, I'm going to die right here, in bed." We slowly adjusted to the new routines.

Brother Joe got into the Businessmen's Military Training Corps. They were supposed to protect the islands. Hah! All they did was march down to the Primo Brewery and get soused. They all got their free beer there.

Our home on Prince Edward Street was just like a USO center. I'd bring my buddies home, many who went to college with me. They'd drop over to see me and we'd have a few beers, shoot the bull. I remember this one night in the kitchen there--it was blacked out--and that's where we visited. But we didn't have the window closed like we should. The wardens came by. They almost took us in.

"You gotta close that window. What are you doing, anyway?" they yelled. You know, they really questioned us. They really handled the situation. You either shaped up, or that's it. They were pretty rough. That's the way they handled things in those days.

" I was drafted . . . went right to Schofield with a bunch of local boys. . . they wouldn't issue rifles to the Japanese boys. They marched with shovels, they dug ditches. . . they wouldn't trust them with guns just because they were Japanese. "

Then I got into the army, two months after the war broke out. I was drafted. I remember it was February 7, 1942, when I went in. We went right to Schofield. I had my training out there. I was out there with a bunch of local boys. Quite a few of them were local Japanese boys. You know, they wouldn't issue rifles to the Japanese boys. They marched with shovels, they dug ditches, and they learned camouflage techniques, and things like that.

I was drafted with this little guy named Paul. I still remember him marching along with a shovel. "Hello, Bob," he would yell. He took it so good-naturedly, you know. They gave them shovels to march with, to go off there in the hills and learn how to dig trenches and camouflage equipment. Imagine, they wouldn't trust them with guns just because they were Japanese. That's how bad it was. This guy, Paul, was a more loyal American than me. But that's the way it was. And, that's the way it was for a long while. I'll never forget that.

It wasn't until later on, when the 100th Battalion and the 442nd formed their own group with Japanese of American ancestry, that they made quite a name for themselves. Paul took it so good-naturedly. He would laugh about it. He did his share. Eventually, they learned how loyal he was, I'm sure. I lost track of him. He didn't train with me. I don't know where he ended up at--whether he went in with the Japanese battalion--and went on to Italy, where many of them ended up.

I remember this one Japanese fellow lost both legs during the attack. His name was Tamanaha. He was a boxer, a good boxer. A bomb, or whatever it was, hit his car. He was one of the civilian casualties.

There were some houses that came pretty close to being hit. But, I'd say the Japanese attackers were pretty accurate. They knew just what they were after. Oh, yes. But, it was a mess, that morning. This is my own opinion, but I think about the only thing that saved us was the fact that we didn't have any aircraft carriers in Pearl Harbor at the time. They were all out at sea. I remember when I was stationed at Fort Armstrong--I was in the guard detachment--and they wouldn't tell us what was going on. But we were pulling guard duty for about a couple of weeks--six hours on duty and six hours off. I had to stay on the post. We were on alert. That was when the battle of Midway took place. We found that out later. And that was the turning point in the war. Because if the Japanese had gotten through from Midway, that would be it. They'd have attacked Hawaii again and taken us.

But we stopped them out there. We stopped them at Midway. And after that, things seemed to be going our way. It was strictly a naval warfare. And, as I said, our carriers played a big part in it. We were lucky that they didn't get caught in Pearl Harbor. And, we're lucky that the Japanese didn't land any troops on December seventh. Because if they did, it would have been something. It would have been like the Philippines. But they knew what they were going after. They knew what their objectives were and they went right after them.

But, you know, towards the end of the war, I still remember, I was stationcd then at Sand Island, pretty close to the end of the war. It was just a matter of time before it was over. We were just about at the battle of Okinawa. But I remember we had these FBI fellows talking to all of us there, at Sand Island.

And the question came up; were there any instances in the islands of any civilian Japanese spying or aiding the enemy?

He said, "Not one, documented instance." He spoke very highly of the loyalty of the Japanese in Hawaii. So if you heard anything differently, well you heard it wrong. That's what this guy said. I never forgot that.

But, the army in those days had its humor in many ways--our style of training--we didn't know what the heck we were doing, really. As the war went on, though, things started changing. But without our navy, and without those carriers, we'd have been goners. The Japanese would have come right back at us and we'd have been gone. Because we weren't prepared at all. Not at all.

I used to talk to the kids at Turlock High School when I taught in California. I told them about my experiences. I said, "A lot of you may be too young to understand what had taken place, but you better have some confidence in your defense department so that it never happens again." I would say, "Before you go around protesting, you better start thinking. It could happen again. We never want to get caught with our pants down again. That's what happened to us in 1941."

" We never want to get caught with our pants down again. That's what happened to us in 1941. "

I don't know whether this has any bearing on the story or not, but I remember when I was in high school at Maui High. The big night was always "boat night"--when the Hualalai and the Waielele (inter-island boats) would leave, on Tuesday and Thursday nights. So we'd all go down to the pier. The main thing was to meet the pretty girls, you know. But every time we were down there, they were loading scrap iron. I remember asking where the heck all that scrap iron was going? "Going to Japan," was the answer I got.

You know, that was way back before I graduated in 1936. They were preparing for war back then. Now, when you think about it, all that scrap iron was going to Japan. And that's what they used to bomb us with.

Those were unforgettable times, the war years in the islands. But it was nip and tuck there for awhile. Oh, yes. It was no laughing matter. I'll never forget those times.

Bob married Hester Adams in April 1945, just a few months before the end of the war. Two weeks after their wedding, Bob was shipped out to Kwajalein Island, where he was stationed for four months before returning to Sand Island, Honolulu. Following discharge from the service, Bob taught at Konawaena High School on the big island and at Robert Louis Stevenson School, and Roosevelt and Kaimuki High schools in Honolulu. He moved his family to California in 1957, holding various teaching positions in Turlock, including four years as principal of Osborn Elementary School. After thirty-nine years of teaching, Bob retired in 1984 and moved to Hilo. Bob and Hester have three children, two daughters in California and a son living in Montana. They have six grandchildren, all girls.

Accidents of War

Most islanders believed, and many still do, that all the damage in Honolulu was caused by Japanese bombs. It has been definitely established, however, that American anti-aircraft action caused almost all the injuries and damage in civilian areas, especially in Honolulu itself. Neither the army nor the navy ever made an official announcement concerning the cause of civilian damage, but at least two army officers testified that it had been due to navy anti-aircraft shells. One testified, "The five-inch ammunition was falling all over the island. Only one bomb hit the town of Honolulu and I think that was an accident." The number of civilian deaths by "friendly fire" was never determined. Private property destroyed was valued at $500,000. *(Allen, Hawaii's War Years)*

*HOME DAMAGED — The home of Paul Goo, located at Liliha and Kuakini Streets, was severely damaged by projectiles the morning of December 7, 1941. (**Star Bulletin** December 7, 1941; War Depository Collection, University of Hawaii)*

Joseph R. Duarte, Sr.

He was born in Kohala, Hawaii, in 1909, one of seven children born to Henry and Mary Duarte. The family moved to Honolulu when Joe was two years old. He graduated from high school in 1929, a member of the first class to graduate from St. Louis at the new campus at Kalaepohaku, in Kaimuki. He went to work at Pearl Harbor following graduation. In 1934, Joe married Vera Grihalva. At the outset of the war, Joe and Vera had one daughter, Jo-Ann, who was two years old. The family lived on Dole Street, near the University of Hawaii. Joe was a machinist in Shop 38, Pearl Harbor Naval Shipyard.

On Saturday, the sixth of December, I was working on one of the destroyers in Drydock No. One. We were working on the propeller shaft, on the bearings. I remember I worked late that night, until about midnight. So I got home late, got cleaned up, and went to bed, very tired.

I got up pretty early for a Sunday. I woke up hearing loud noises, like the sound of explosions. I got up and looked out the kitchen window. I saw some smoke in the air, and I thought that something had happened, but I didn't pay too much attention to it. I decided it was time to mow the lawn, so I got out the lawn mower and went to the front yard. My daughter, Jo-Ann, was in a stroller out there with me as I started mowing.

Just then, Vera came rushing out of the house, yelling, "Daddy, Daddy, they're announcing on the radio that Pearl Harbor is being attacked." She was very excited. She said, "They're announcing that they want all workers to report to their shops. You got to go back to work."

So I went back inside and got ready to leave. I picked up my helper, George Lindo, and we drove down to the yard. As we got near Pearl Harbor, we could see these planes swooping down from above. They weren't too high, and you could see the red markings on them, the Japanese insignia.

They wouldn't let us go through the gate. The traffic was all backed up. So we had to park the car in the officers' parking lot at the officers' quarters, and walk to the gate. So we walked towards the submarine base gate.

While we were walking, the planes came back. They were strafing with their machine guns. We had to run to get out of their line of fire. We thought for sure that they were going to shoot us. We saw some cars parked near there and so we dove under the cars to hide from the planes.

We could see sailors on the pier on Magazine Island. They were waiting for their boats to pick them up so they could get across to Ford Island to get to their ships. The planes came right down and strafed at them, where they were standing. Some of them jumped in the water and some got shot.

I was numb for a while. I don't know if I blacked out or what, but it must have been some time before I came to. In the excitement and confusion of it all, I didn't realize what we were going through. Then it hit me. We were really in a dangerous spot. This wasn't a dream. Those were really Japanese airplanes up there and they were bombing and shooting at us. We got out from under the car and ran as fast as we could to our shop. We ran for about three-quarters of a mile to get there.

---

*" Then it hit me. . . This wasn't a dream.
Those were really Japanese airplanes up
there and they were bombing and shooting
at us. "*

I couldn't believe what I was seeing when I got to the shop. They were bringing in dead bodies, into the shop. Many of them. I looked at that and I was shocked. Then we saw the ships on fire. Some of them were sunk, some were over on their sides, capsized. Fire and smoke were everywhere. Everything was in confusion. People were running all over the place trying to figure out what to do.

The *Arizona* was bombed and she was on fire. The *California* was hit, too. The *Nevada* was hit near the entrance to the bay. She was trying to get out of the harbor. The military had nets there, at the entrance to Pearl Harbor, that were hooked up to prevent the enemy submarines from coming into the bay. But the submarines got in, anyway, that morning.

We changed into our work clothes and were told to stand by at our work stations. We were told that we would have further orders to work on the ships as soon as it was safe to do so.

Finally, I was assigned to the *New Orleans*, a cruiser that was at Pier 7, right across from Shop 11, where the big crane was stationed. I was to work on the shaft. So I walked over there and went aboard the *New Orleans*. Things were settled down a bit by then and the Japanese planes had already left. They were still bringing in the dead and wounded. I didn't work too long on the *New Orleans*, though, before there was another alert because there were Japanese submarines in the harbor and it was dangerous to be in the area. So I was sent back to the shop. A bunch of us stayed there all night.

I remember seeing the *Oglala* right in front of Shop 31. She was hit and over on her side. A lot of men were trapped in their ships, I was told. So many of the ships were not equipped to fight back. Many didn't have ammunition. It took time getting to the magazines and getting the ammunition out to fight back. I don't think we were ready, or prepared, to fight.

I remember later, the story went around that the Japanese embassy people entertained the admirals and navy officers at a big party, the night before the attack, to get them drunk so they would not be able to fight back the next morning. I don't know if that really happened, but that's what everyone was saying.

And we were supposed to be warned that morning. A radio message was sent warning us that the enemy was going to attack, but the officer in charge didn't pay any attention to it. A lot of mistakes were made that morning. I sure hope we learned from that experience and never let it happen like that again.

I didn't get home until Monday morning, then had to turn right around and go back on Monday afternoon. We were trying to help with the clean-up operation, taking care of so many damaged ships, to get them back in fighting form as soon as possible. We worked around the clock.

I remember, one of the carriers--I think it was the *Lexington*--came in for repairs a few days later. I worked on the net that was used to catch the airplanes when they landed on the deck.

And the junction at McCully and King Streets got bombed. That worried me, because my mother was living on Beretania, between Artesia and McCully, only about two blocks away from that bombing. I heard quite a few people got killed there, too. We were all tense and nervous. We expected to be invaded any day.

All they had to do was to come in with their ships and take us over. They could have easily done it, because we weren't that prepared to fight. All I can say is, the Lord was with us. He must have been. Because they never came back.

Joe worked at Pearl Harbor for thirty-one years. He made a name for himself in sports, breaking into local big time baseball as a short stop in the Hawaii Baseball League. During the war years, Joe played against All-American greats such as Joe DiMaggio and Pee Wee Reese. He played and coached a shop team in the Shipyard baseball league for years, winning three championships. He held many positions at Pearl Harbor, including that of shop planner, leadingman, and special leadingman. He retired in 1964. He and Vera had three children, two girls and a boy. Vera died in 1962. Joe, the grandfather of seven, and great-grandfather of two, lives in retirement in Kaneohe.

Richard M. Dolim

His grandparents came to Hawaii from Portugal in 1886 to work in the cane fields in Paia, Maui. His parents were born on Maui. His father managed the plantation stores there for years. "Ricky" was number six of seven children born to Joseph and Isabel Dolim. They were all born in Keahua. Ricky attended Maui Standard elementary school in Sprecklesville and graduated from Maui High School in 1936. He drove a truck for his dad's store for a period of time then set out to make his fortune in Honolulu. He worked as a relief driver for American Sanitary Laundry, getting the job through the efforts of his sister's brother-in-law, Reggie Rodrigues. He went to work at Pearl Harbor in 1939 as an apprentice. He lived with his sister, Olive, and her husband at 1515 Pualele Place, Wilhelmina Rise.

All of us guys had an opportunity, when we graduated from Maui High, to fill out an application for civil service apprenticeship jobs at Pearl Harbor. So we did, and then more or less forgot about it. Then in 1939, I got a letter from the 14th Naval District. They wanted to interview me for a job. I was in Maui then, so I had to catch a boat over to Honolulu--over and back on the same day. There were about two thousand of us that took the exam that day. I'm proud to say that I came in at two hundred ninth in the standings. And they called two hundred ten people.

The letter from Pearl Harbor offering me the job came and my dad brought it out to me at the work site. He said, "You're going to go and learn yourself a trade." In our family, we never said no to Papa. When he said go, we'd go. So I got on a boat that same night. My sister, Olive, picked me up at the dock. She and her husband, Nelson, had recently built a house.

I remember the first day at Pearl Harbor. I got my physical, and then they said to report to Building 6, Shop 81. I walked over there and the personnel door was closed. I opened it and took a step through that door and smelled all that foundry hydrocarbon, and fermented molasses (which was used to put a bond in the sand). I took one whiff of that stuff and I turned around and walked out. I said to myself, "I'm going back to Maui and tell Papa I didn't pass the physical."

Just then, Thornton C. Bunch, I later called him T.C., came walking across the street. He saw me step out of the shop and he said, "Oh, you're just the guy I'm looking for. You must be the new apprentice." He took the papers out of my hand and walked me into his office. I followed him in, all the while wondering how the hell I could get out of this thing. Obviously, I didn't get out of it. And I'm glad I didn't. That was the start of my career.

When I first started working at Pearl Harbor, I would ride in with Walter Souza. I think we paid $1.50 a week for the carpool. I only made $13 a week and I paid Nelson $5 a week to live at his house, so I didn't have much money in those days.

In order to work for the government in those days, you couldn't draw two government checks. I was already in the National Guard, in inactive service at the time. But shortly after I started work, they mobilized the guard. So I inquired right away to find out if I had to report. The guy that I talked to said, "If you didn't get a letter to report, you don't have to." Well, about nine days later, my cousin, Frank Dolim, who had joined the National Guard with me, was mobilized and he came looking for me. "Hey," he says, "the MPs are looking for you. You're supposed to be in camp with us." I told him I didn't get a letter. So, I called up T.C. Bunch and told him I was supposed to be mobilized with the National Guard. He told me to go out there the next day and that he will get with the commandant of the 14th Naval District and see if he could get me out.

So the next day, I borrowed my sister's car and drove out to Schofield. I reported in and was sent to take a physical exam. It took almost all day to get this physical. I stayed out there in Tent City that night, but because I still had my sister's car, I got this lieutenant friend of mine to take a leave to go back into town to return the car. Olive then drove me out to the Schofield gate at 4:30 the next morning and I hitched a ride back to Tent City.

I walked into the squad tent and reported to a buddy of mine, I said, "Froggy, give me my rifle and my uniform. I'm reporting for duty." He started to laugh. He showed me a letter that he had already received from Commander Rice of the 14th Naval District, saying, "Release this man. He's a vital employee of the navy at Pearl Harbor."

I said, "Well, what I gotta do to get out?"

"You gotta go take a physical," he said. Exasperated, I said, "But I just took a physical yesterday."

"Yeah," he said, "But to get out, you gotta take another one."

So he and I run around in a jeep, all over the base. I passed everything until I got to the dentist. He said, "I can't let you out. I got to fix your teeth first." I talked and talked to this lieutenant, trying to explain to him that my teeth were good enough to get me in the day before; so why shouldn't they be good enough to get me out today? That's typical army for you. Anyway, I was stupid. I should have let them fix my teeth for free.

Several months later I got my discharge, an honorable discharge. And on it, it read, "14 days service; 11 days AWOL." It seems they counted those days before I reported as absence without leave, even though I hadn't been notified. That, too, is typical army for you.

Later on, though, I was even the recipient of a medal. It came in a package from the Bureau of Ships. Because everybody that participated in the Guard from 1939 to December 7, 1941 was part of what was called the Great American Preparedness campaign. So I got a medal. Strange things have happened to me. So I was back at Shop 81 at Pearl Harbor.

Things started to pick up just prior to the war. We were working a lot of hours. At one time, we worked thirteen hours a day, six days a week. Skilled labor started coming in from the mainland. The shop went from about fifty employees to two hundred fifty employees prior to 1941. I was going to school for one week, learning the trade, and working in the shop for four weeks. School was eight hours a day. We had to accumulate so many hours of school and so many hours in the shop before we could graduate. T.C. was a metallurgical engineer and he was our trade theory instructor. He taught us good. I graduated before four years because I had all this overtime.

There were one hundred ten of us in the graduation class. We all had our pictures taken in a large group photo. It was taken by Tai Sing Loo, a short, little Chinaman with an elephant hat. He was the Pearl Harbor photographer, and quite a well known character.

On December seventh, we were asked to work with the clean-up crew. We were so busy, working so many hours. The shop would get all messed up, so they would send about thirty laborers in on Sundays.

Kwok Heen and I would go in and we were allowed to run the overhead cranes. I bummed a ride in with a guy that lived down the corner as Walter Souza wasn't going in that day. He dropped me off at Shop 81, Building 6 and he went on to his shop.

I got my clothes changed and started work at 7:45 a.m. I was working on the overhead crane in the foundry. I was on the crane when the first bomb went off. It shook like crazy. I hollered down to the lead man, "What the heck's going on?" I was in this overhead crane, about thirty feet off the floor. We had a big, wide-open door at the end of the shop and being that you're in the crane, you couldn't look up because you were up against the bulkhead. The crane was shaking and I hollered at Charlie, so he walked down to the big door and looked up.

He yelled back, "Ah, just maneuvers." We had been having a lot of that stuff the past year or so.

Just then, they must have hit the *Oklahoma* or *Arizona* or something, because boy, I'm telling you, the crane really shook. So I climbed out of the cab and came down the ladder. I wanted to see these maneuvers because they must have been really good.

**" *I ran down to the end of the shop . . . and
looked up. I couldn't believe my eyes.
These airplanes were going after the Cassin
and the Downes . . .* "**

I ran down to the end of the shop to the doors and looked up. I couldn't believe my eyes. These airplanes were going after the *Cassin* and the *Downes* and the *Pennsylvania*, and when one of them banked, I saw the big red moons on it. I just couldn't believe it. Then I saw another one bank and I could see the tracer bullets it was firing. It was real bullets. I hollered words that I can't use right now.

I ran the whole length of the shop yelling, "It's the real thing." Everybody ran behind me and we ran across the street, through the Pattern Shop, picking up some pattern makers working there. Right behind the shop was this big, old lumber pile--two by fours, two by twelves, stacked about three feet off the ground. We dove under there. We stayed there--under the wood pile--scared as hell.

From our vantage point under the pile, we could see more airplanes diving. Nobody was firing back at the planes at that point. Boy, were we scared. After a while, a truck full of marines came driving through that lumber yard and rounded us all out from under that wood pile. They handed each of us rifles, gas masks, and tin helmets. No ammunition. We questioned that and they said, "Don't worry. If they attack, we'll issue ammunition. You guys are going to have to help us defend this place."

DAMAGE IN DRYDOCK NO. 1 -- Japanese dive bombers attacked the battleship USS Pennsylvania (background), and the two destroyers USS Cassin and USS Downes (foreground), all in Drydock No. 1. The Pennsylvania was later repaired but the Cassin and Downes were finally abandoned after being refloated and removed from the drydock. (Official US Navy Photograph; War Depository Collection, University of Hawaii)

175

If you think we were scared before, having those rifles made it worse. I mean, I could fire the thing--I used to hunt a little bit. So we stayed there, with our empty weapons, for what seemed like an eternity. Finally, things calmed down a bit, the attack was over for the moment, and we were relieved from our post. So a bunch of us ventured to walk down to the 1010 Drydock and take a look at what happened. I'll never forget the sight. The *Arizona* was down, you could see just the superstructure, and it was really burning. The *West Virginia* was right along side the *Arizona* and it was going down. They were pumping water from it. The *Nevada* had pulled out and tried to make it to the Pearl Harbor gate--the entrance to get out--and it got nailed up against the West Loch, which was another island out there.

And then we saw the *Oklahoma*. We didn't know it was the *Oklahoma* until somebody told us. It was in the middle of the harbor and it was over on its side. We were only about two hundred yards from where the *Pennsylvania*, *Cassin* and the *Downes* were in drydock. The *Pennsylvania* didn't look like it was badly damaged, but the *Cassin* and the *Downes* were on fire. Behind there, they had a marineway, a track that runs down into the water. There, in that floating drydock was the *Shaw*, a four-stacker destroyer, and it was really burning. I mean they really blasted it. And that was a good sized marineway--it could handle a destroyer. The *Helena* and the *Honolulu* were tied up side by side on 1010 Drydock. *Helena* was on the outside and it was going down, they were pumping water from it. They hit the *Honolulu*, too, but mostly with bombs, because they couldn't get to it with torpedoes. It was havoc. We were all scared. We didn't know what to do.

We were ordered back to our shops to await further orders. A truck would come by and load a bunch of us guys on it. They trucked a lot of sand in and they dumped it on the docks. We were given shovels and they said, "Shovel." Because they couldn't put the fires out on the *Cassin* and *Downes* with water, they wanted us to shovel sand on them from the docks. You had to be pretty good to heave a shovel-full of sand from the dock and hit the boat. The best way to have put the fire out was to flood the drydock, but the *Pennsylvania* was also in there and they were repairing the four shafts on it, so they had pulled the propellers off and pulled the shafts out. That left four big cavities back there that they just couldn't plug up. Finally, the sand wasn't working and the fires became very dangerous, so they flooded the drydock and sunk the *Pennsylvania*, putting the fires out on the *Cassin* and *Downes*.

We were walking up and down that dock, trying to help. They were pulling bodies out of the water and laying them on 1010 Drydock, which was the longest dock in the world at one time. And, so help me, God, I remember four rows of bodies. I mean, they would cover them up with canvas, you know. Some of the guys, when they pulled them out, they would be missing an arm. It was terrible. I really hate talking about it. Even the memory of it gets to me still, today.

" **They were pulling bodies out of the water and laying them on 1010 Drydock. . . And, so help me God, I remember four rows of bodies.** "

One particular scene I will never forget. It's not easy to talk about it. I saw a sailor that was pinned up against the bulkhead by a boiler. A bomb exploded and blew this boiler off its mounting and pinned this sailor up against the bulkhead. It took three days to get him out of there. And, the boiler was hot. The stench was terrible. I became a pretty mature twenty-two year old after that.

A lot of Pearl Harbor workers had come into the yard during the attack. Word went out to them by radio that they were needed. A lot of them came in after the attack, but some of them came during the attack and got fired on when they were trying to come in the main gate. I think these airplanes were strafing Hickam Field and the gate to Pearl Harbor was located right at the end of their strafing run. So we had a lot of help later in the day, and they wanted us to get back in the shop and start working. So that's what we were doing that afternoon, working on rush jobs.

Marines would come by after it got dark and yell for us to put the lights out. When we'd try and argue and tell them that we have orders to get this part made in a big hurry, they'd click the bolt on the rifles, so we'd put the light out. It was impossible to work in the dark. But we couldn't leave, either, because they locked the gates. We were told that we couldn't leave the yard that night because we had to help the military defend the place.

So I had to spend the night in the shop. I had my rifle, without ammunition. Actually, I had it for two weeks, I think.

We had these big electric melting furnaces in the shop. They were built on pits, because they had to have a counter weight, so that when you tilted the furnace to drain the steel out, that counter weight would take it back into position. There was a lot of room down in those pits.

So, most of us in the shop spent the first night of the war down in those pits, scared as hell. There were a lot of us down there--big men, most of them older than me. They put up ack-ack guns right outside our shop. And a little later the ack-acks went off and we were sure that we were under attack again. They were shooting at planes. I mean, the guns would go off, and we would dive down into the lowest hole we could find in the pit. It was frightening. You felt so helpless.

Later we learned they were actually shooting at our own planes. There was a mix up--wrong signals or something. I think that night they shot down seven of our own planes.

We didn't sleep at all that night. The guys I worked with were a bunch of jokers. But nobody joked that night. We talked, but with what everybody had been through that day, it wasn't a joking matter. There were no phones available so no one could call home.

On Monday, we were up and at it again bright and early. We worked the whole day, doing our regular foundry work. That night, they still wouldn't let us go. So about midnight, T. C. Bunch, the master molder-- the guy that allowed Kwok Heen and I to run the overhead cranes--he got permission to drive us home. This was midnight of December the eighth. I had been at work straight through since 7:00 a.m. the day before.

We drove home in the blackout, with no lights. Fortunately, there was a moon out that night so we could see a little. He dropped me off on Waialae Avenue and I had to walk up the hill to Wilhelmina Rise. I got stopped a few times by MPs and I had to show them my ID. You'd think they'd give me a ride home, you know. But no, they'd say, "Okay, go ahead." And I had to keep walking up that hill.

When I got home, I knocked quietly on the door. Olive and Nelson were really worried. They didn't know what happened to me. Olive was real happy to see me. I told her what I had gone through. And, a few hours later, at 7:00 a.m., I was back at the yard at work again.

Later, I found out that the Japanese had planned another raid, but that was canceled because the carriers--the *Lexington* and the *Saratoga*--were not at Pearl Harbor. They were scheduled to be there, but were delayed because of bad weather. The Japanese admiral knew that they were in the area so he turned tail and headed back to Japan. The raid was to bomb the navy yard and the oil storage tanks that they used to refuel the ships. So the Japanese didn't come after those oil tanks--which was fortunate for the United States Navy, as well as Richard M. Dolim. If they had come back, there was no way we could have defended ourselves. They wanted to damage the yard so we couldn't repair the ships that were sunk there. Fortunately, they didn't. That probably held more importance in our turnaround, because Pearl Harbor was intact. If we had to initiate the turnaround from the west coast, it would have taken a hell of a lot longer.

The first major battle of the war was the Coral Sea, and we took a beating there. In Hawaii, we were afraid we were going to be attacked and invaded, until the battle of Midway in June, when we had some sort of feeling that we were on the offensive. I mean, those damned ships would come in to the yard for repairs and they were beat up something terrible. We'd say, "Boy, we're sure taking a beating in this war. We must be losing a hell of a lot of guys," you know. We never got much news. That was all classified information. Nobody knew about this big carrier getting hit and burning up out at sea. And then we saw it coming in. They put it right in the drydock, the same drydock that the *Pennsylvania* was in.

We saw the *USS Washington*, a brand new battlewagon, come in without a bow. I think it was one hundred and three feet of bow that was gone. The *Indiana* came in once with a hole right amidship that was, hell, you could have driven a 747 right through it--a huge hole. We put it back together again and it went out to sea.

Pearl Harbor built a drydock that at one time was the largest drydock in the world. We could put four cruisers abreast, two rows of them, and I think it was six destroyers abreast, and I can't remember whether it was three of four rows--pump the water out of that thing and there they are, high and dry on blocks, all of them. We built that in less than two years. Compare that with what they do today. Why, it took them twenty years to build that freeway from Honolulu to Pearl Harbor.

A lot of things happened during the war. We were working seven days a week, long hours. I mean we were busy. We worked like hell. We were a good foundry. We turned out the work. Shop 81--it was the best shipyard foundry, and certainly one of the best I ever worked in. I learned my trade in that Pearl Harbor apprenticeship, under old-timers from Honolulu Iron Works--the guys that built the sugar mills. They were all good mechanics.

I often thought that my life might have been different if the war hadn't come. It probably would have been different, too, if I had been allowed to go into the army and participate in a fighting war. If I would have come out alive, I would have had all the GI benefits. I could have gone back to college. Although I do get some GI benefits because of my fourteen-days service. I bought a house with a GI loan, and I have burial rights in a GI cemetery. But that's about it.

> **" I think that Pearl Harbor bombing experience and living in wartime conditions taught me to fight back. "**

I think that Pearl Harbor bombing experience and living in wartime conditions taught me to fight back. For instance, we had an accident in the foundry one time. A couple of guys got burned pretty bad. In fact, one guy lost his life. The damned foundry was burning and everybody ran. I grabbed a hose and I put out the fire. After working with it for a number of years, I learned not to be scared of fires. That's something I probably got out of going through the Pearl Harbor experience. I don't panic.

Another time, in 1969, we lived in Los Angeles in a canyon on the other side of a mountain, and suddenly that canyon was on fire. Two of my kids, Mike and Paul, were with me when we walked up to the hill and watched that fire come over the top of the mountain. It was quite a ways from us, yet. We figured it would probably take a couple of hours to get down to us. So I said, "Come on, kids, let's go home and get to work. We're not going to let this house burn."

We set the sprinklers up so that we could turn them on and wet down the house. Two of Mike's buddies joined us; they were up on the roof, keeping the roof wet with hoses and I was on the eaves with a hose. That fire came down inside of twenty-five minutes.

The police had come by a few times, making people evacuate the area.

When they came to us, I remember Mike telling the cop, "Get out of here. We're not scared of fire. We're going to save our house. It's not going to burn down."

The cop even broke our door in. He yelled, "Come on, you guys. You got to get out of here now." We finally convinced him that we weren't going, so he took off.

We had a big oak tree in the yard, and when the fire reached it, a big branch caught on fire. My son got out there with a bow saw and sawed the branch off and threw it over the hill. If that tree had caught on fire, it would have taken the house too. The fire went right past us, right over the house. We worked like dogs, but we saved the house.

When it was all over, there was so much water in the driveway. I went down there and I lay in that water, exhausted. The boys came all around me and I said, "We did it, boys!" And then I told them, "You know, I survived Pearl Harbor. And now I survived this fire. I think I'm going to live forever."

Pearl Harbor did it to me. When you got a problem, you gotta take care of it. You can't run.

Rick married Ethel Cambra in 1945. They had two children. Paula was born in 1946 and Michael in 1949. In 1952, the family moved to California where Rick was transferred to Mare Island, Vallejo. Rick and Ethel were divorced in 1961 and two years later Rick married Pauline Thomas. Pauline had two children, Susan and Paul, from a previous marriage. Rick worked for both government and private industry in metallurgy foundry work for forty-two years. He has four grandchildren and enjoys his retirement years hopping between Hawaii and southern California.

Air-Raid Shelters

*IT'S SAFE DOWN HERE -- Pictured here is a homemade air raid shelter in the yard of Mr. and Mrs. G. L. Gordon of Waikiki. While the photograph didn't identify the couple, it's pretty safe to assume they are the Gordons. Note the "V" for victory sign and the Morse code, dot-dot-dot-dash, for the letter V. (*Star Bulletin *Feb. 3, 1942; War Depository Collection, University of Hawaii)*

*HEADS DOWN! -- Open trenches were used in the early months of the war as a shelter from bomb and shrapnel debris. Here, students at McKinley High School react to the monitor's call to "lower your heads." (*Star Bulletin *March 4, 1942; War Depository Collection, University of Hawaii)*

William M. Borges

Bill Borges was born in Honolulu in 1908. His mother died when he was a young child and he was raised by relatives, often shunted from one to another. He attended school in Palama at the Kaiulani Elementary School, one of the oldest schools in the islands. He went to St. Louis College for his high school education and graduated in 1927. He went to work for the Matson Navigation Company. In 1939, at age 31, he married Violet Miranda, a Sacred Heart Academy graduate from Ewa. On December 7, 1941, Bill and Violet lived at 1511 Pualele Place, Palolo Heights.

I worked for the Matson Navigation Company, down at Pier 9, right next to the Aloha Tower. I did claims work for them—cargo claims for insurance. I worked there already twelve years when the war started.

That Sunday morning, December seventh, Violet woke me up very early saying that something was wrong, that she was frightened. I didn't pay attention to her at first.

All I had on my mind, as I usually did on Sunday mornings, was to go down to the Colonial Bakery on 9th Avenue in Kaimuki and buy doughnuts to have for breakfast.

We heard the noises of guns and bombs, but thought the army and the navy were conducting some kind of maneuvers again, you know. They did that a lot in those days. But I still didn't pay too much attention to it. I got in the car and drove down the hill to the bakery and bought my doughnuts. I didn't notice anybody running around in a panic, so I continued to think it was war games going on.

I got back home and had coffee and doughnuts. We turned on the radio. I couldn't believe what we were hearing. This wasn't possible. How could Japan come all the way over here and do this? This was impossible, I thought.

My cousin, Nelson Rodrigues, lived right next door. Violet ran over to tell them what was happening. His wife, Olive, said that Nelson was playing golf, down at Palolo Golf Course, with another neighbor and friend, Charlie Duck. She sounded frantic. Charlie's wife drove down to the golf course to get the guys, and to tell them what was happening. They were announcing on the radio that all Pearl Harbor workers should report to their work sites at the yard. Nelson was a Pearl Harbor worker.

Then we started hearing loud noises close by. We went up the hill across the street to the water tank, which was located right on the edge of the mountain, looking down into Palolo Valley. And we looked down and saw planes flying across the valley heading towards the ocean and until I saw the rising sun insignia on the planes, I really doubted that what I heard was true.

Then we saw this huge amount of smoke coming up from down near the Honolulu stadium. We thought that they must have dropped a bomb over there, or something. It finally hit me that this was the real thing, that we were really under attack. I was shocked.

" It finally hit me that this was the real thing, that we were really under attack. I was shocked. "

We stayed there for a while, taking in the sights, still numb from the shock of war. I later heard that the Japanese planes were throwing leaflets down to the civilians, telling them in crude wording and drawings, "You Yankees go to hell," and "Babe Ruth, you go to hell." Babe Ruth was our national hero at that time. I guess this was their way of getting us mad, see? While I never did see them dropping the pamphlets, I heard about it from others or read about it in the paper, I guess.

The fire and smoke from the Honolulu stadium turned out to be an apartment and store complex close by that was evidently bombed. I understand that many people were killed there, mostly Japanese.

Later on, I remember hearing that many of these casualties were really not from Japanese bombs, but were from our own shells, anti-aircraft shells, that the army was shooting up to the planes. They missed their targets and came back down on the civilian population and burned houses down. It was tragic, but that's war for you.

The night of December seventh was a restless one. We kept thinking that they were coming back. And, you know, they could have. I'm telling you, if they would have attacked and landed, they would have taken us over. I believe that. We seemed so unprepared, even though we had maneuvers going on for some time.

Then the rules and regulations started. We were cooped up in our houses, couldn't go out nights, and we were told that no lights could be seen at night. They were strict as hell. So we got black paper and covered the windows of our house so we could see at night without any light showing outside. We went down to the hardware store--building supply store—and they had a good supply of black paper. I don't think we ever ran out of it.

We just couldn't believe what was happening to us. The United States, the biggest, most powerful country, under attack? It didn't seem possible.

I thought of all the Japanese Americans living in the islands. We had a lot of them here. And, many of them had dual citizenship, you know. They were citizens of Japan, as well as the United States. Their parents were, in many cases, strong Buddhists, with strong ties to Japan. Particularly the father in the family. He loved his native country and he had a lot of influence on his wife and children.

I often wondered what would have happened if the Japanese had invaded the islands and taken over? I wondered what I would have done if I was Japanese. If it meant a matter of life or death, where would one's loyalty lie? But, thank God, they didn't come back. So we didn't have to face that problem of who would be loyal and who would be traitor. The true test never came.

" . . . thank God, they didn't come back. So we didn't have to face the problem of who would be loyal and who would be traitor. "

I went in to work on Monday. It was work as usual. But, shortly after that, we were taken over by the government. All of a sudden, we worked for the War Shipping Administration (WSA), that's what they called it. Matson ships were all taken over by the WSA for cargo and troops. There was no such thing as civilian pleasure cruises anymore. Passenger ships were converted to troop ships.

So we became government workers, although, we didn't really report directly to WSA bosses. We had the same bosses, we were just under control of the WSA. And we had to follow government regulations, which were much stricter than the commercial rules we were under. So I had the same job, doing about the same thing.

A story came out of the war that a Matson ship, the Monterey, went to the rescue of a Canadian ship that had been torpedoed and sunk by the Japanese. The Monterey, painted camouflage gray, saved a number of Canadian soldiers, picking them out of the ocean.

Nights were long and dark. In order to while away our time, Violet and I would go over to Nelson and Olive's house and play poker in their blacked out room. They usually had others there too. So that was our social life for most of the war.

I took the HRT bus to work. I left my car home. Gasoline was rationed, you know. And so was liquor. They would allow you to buy just so much a month. Butter, too, was hard to get.

Then a lot of people started to move out of here. They mobbed the shipping offices trying to get passage to the mainland. They thought that the Japanese were going to invade the islands and take over. I didn't ever think about moving. I had confidence in the United States.

But they were selling their houses and leaving Hawaii. I could have bought a house in Waikiki for $9,000. Now I think about it. Anyway, I wasn't going to move out of here.

Oh, and I remember there was censorship. When you pick up the telephone and it's hard to hear the person on the other end, you could tell that somebody is tapping your line. You get it? The voice is weak, not strong. That's how you can tell your line is being tapped. And it sure happened to me a lot.

And our money was stamped, I remember. We had to turn in all our paper money and they gave us bills that were stamped with a "Hawaii" on it. They didn't want the Japanese, if they invaded the islands, to get a hold of American money. So they stamped it with a big "Hawaii" on the back. That money became a collector's item following the war.

There wasn't a major change in my life due to the war. One thing that was curious, though. I was a member of the National Guard when war broke out. In two years, I went from a buck private to a staff sergeant. I used to do the payroll for the officers.

I think about it now, I might have had a very different life if the war hadn't started. They mustered a bunch of us out of the Guard when the war broke out because we owed the bank money. I built my house in 1939 when we got married, you know. I owed the bank about $2,800 from the house loan. I had joined the Guard in 1939 to make additional money. So the Guard said anybody that owed money to the bank had to get out. Something about they were going to have a moratorium on our loans and they didn't want to be involved. So I was mustered out, against my wishes.

I guess if I didn't get discharged, I might have made the military a career. I probably would have gone to college on the GI Bill, and I might have had a professional career. I don't know. I wouldn't have minded staying in the Guard, even during the war, you know. We used to train weekends. And every June, we went to Paukukalo, in Maui, for two weeks training.

So, as it was, the war didn't change things for me. I worked in the same office, doing the same job, for forty-six years.

Bill retired in 1974 as a claims agent, following a long career with Matson Navigation Company. Violet retired from the University of Hawaii in 1964. She served as supervisor of the stenographic pool and worked there for twenty-five years. She died in 1982. Bill and Violet had no children. Bill keeps in shape swimming a few times a week at the Elks Club in Waikiki. He has been an active member of the organization and has served on various committees. He enjoys cooking, gardening, and general home maintenance.

Gardens for Victory

CHURCH GARDEN -- To help alleviate the food shortage, community victory gardens sprouted up throughout Honolulu. Even the spacious lawns of the stately Central Union Church on Beretania Street were put to good use as a community garden in February 1942. (*War Depository Collection, University of Hawaii*)

Arthur J. Uchida

His grandfather was born in Japan and settled in Kona to grow coffee trees. His father, Charles Uchida, was born in Kona and his mother, Edith Takamura, was from Kauai. Charles and Edith took a trip to Japan and met aboard the ship. They were married in 1929 and had two children. Art, the second child, was born in 1932. His sister, Helen, is a year older. Art and his family lived in Alewa Heights, near Kamehameha School, at 2238 Aulii Street, when the war began. Art was in the fourth grade at St. Theresa's School.

My father was in the coffee business. My grandfather would send over coffee beans from Kona and my father would roast, grind, and pack coffee for sale to the cafes and restaurants in Honolulu. He also was a fisherman and had a small sampan, about a twenty-five footer, and loved to go out fishing on the weekends. He tied it up underneath the bridge at Kapalama Canal on King Street.

Once a week, usually on Fridays, the kids in the neighborhood would meet after school at my father's coffee shop and he'd walk us down to his boat. There was usually about ten of us and we'd all climb on the boat and we'd go out to the ocean for a ride. This was before the war. Those were really good fun times.

I remember I also had a bicycle boat that I kept in the canal underneath the bridge near my father's boat. It had two pontoons with a stand and a bicycle on it. The paddle wheel would push the boat and the bike handle would turn the rudder. I would play in the Kapalama Canal on that thing. I was only nine years old and I didn't know how to swim in those days. I remember once I was riding along and these kids--all bigger guys about fifteen or sixteen years old--would dive off the King Street bridge and hang on to the side of my bicycle boat. Once they rocked the boat so much that it flipped over and I just hung on under the water. They got scared and dove underneath and flipped it upright again. I was still on the boat, hanging on the handle bar. They said, "Please don't tell your father about this, or he won't take us out on his boat anymore." I kept quiet about it. I guess they appreciated that. I kept my word, and they still got to enjoy the Friday afternoon boat rides.

When the war started, the navy took my father's boat away. They just confiscated it and we never saw it again. They were taking all the sampans from the Japanese fishermen. There must have been hundreds of boats that were taken. What they did with them, no one knows. They might have used them for artillery practice, or something like that.

On Sunday morning, December 7, 1941, the family was up early preparing breakfast about seven o'clock. I would always play "soldier" in the yard and would raise my own flag on a pole next to the garage. It was only a white handkerchief, but it was my flag for the war games I would play. Neighborhood kids would come over and we had BB-guns. We would also make our own guns with cut wood. So I raised my flag that morning and played. It was waving in the morning breeze. Then, I was called in to have breakfast.

About eight o'clock or so, we started hearing all these explosions and noises going on. So we all ran outside to see what was happening and we could look right down at Pearl Harbor, about ten miles away, and see all this smoke coming up from the navy yard. My father said he thought it was just a practice exercise, so we went back inside to finish eating. Then the phone started ringing and the neighbors started shouting out that we were being attacked by Japanese planes and that we should turn on the radio.

They were announcing on the radio that they wanted people with trucks to come down to Pearl Harbor and help out as ambulance drivers. My father was part of the civil defense exercises, so he called his friend who was in it with him, and the two of them went down to Pearl Harbor to help out. He didn't come back until late that afternoon. His sweat shirt was just covered with blood from the people he picked up. And he was just knocked out--dazed and tired from what he experienced. He went into the room and went to sleep.

A short while later, about twelve marines with rifles came marching up our driveway. I got scared. I said to myself, "Oh my God, what's going on here? And my mother got hysterical. She just went crazy and ran inside to wake my father up. It was frightening seeing these guys coming to our house with rifles.

My father came out and said, "What's going on around here?" They said that they had a complaint that somebody was signaling to the Japanese planes with a flag. I said, "Oh my God, that's my flag. My white handkerchief." You know, we were the only Japanese people up at Alewa Heights at that time. It had been an exclusive neighborhood for the haoles[1] until we moved in. And we lived a half block away from a Japanese teahouse. Somebody must have panicked and thought my white handkerchief was some kind of a signal to the Japanese planes.

" They . . . had a complaint that somebody was signaling to the Japanese planes with a flag. I said, 'Oh my God, that's my flag. My white handkerchief.' "

I was hiding behind my father, scared to death. I thought they were going to grab me and take me away. So my father says, "If you guys don't trust us, come in the house and search around if you want." They could see that he was still wearing his Civil Defense arm band and had been through a lot with blood on his shirt, so they said they were sorry to bother us and went away.

We didn't realize what it would look like at that moment, but if they would have come into our house, they would have seen a picture of the emperor of Japan, a Japanese flag, a Samurai sword, all on display in the parlor there. A lot of Japanese homes were like that in those days. It was sort of a symbol to recognize their parents' homeland. And the emperor was really looked up to in those days. I don't know what would have happened to us, but they were picking up local Japanese that day for things like that.

After that, my father and his friend went back down to Pearl Harbor in his truck. We didn't see him again until the next morning.

My uncle--my mother's brother--and his wife came up to our house. My mother made them spend the night with us. They lived in Kalihi and my mother thought that was too dangerous a place to be in. We had a short wave radio and my uncle was trying to get it to work. He wanted to listen to announcements from Japan to see what they were saying about the attack.

It was very quiet and dark that night. We were all blacked out--no lights allowed at all. Nobody slept. Everyone was "up in the air"

---

[1]Hawaiian word meaning white person, Caucasian, formerly any foreigner.

thinking that an invasion was coming, or another attack or something. My mother was very protective of me, her only son. She kept an eye on me and for days I stayed in the house all day and night. My sister was so scared. I think I was too young to realize the danger we were in-- what was really going on.

About seven or eight in the evening, the shortwave broadcast started coming through from Japan. I didn't speak Japanese so I didn't know what they were saying. They listened to the radio until midnight or one o'clock in the morning. Of course, they couldn't make it too loud or the neighbors could hear it. They were huddled real close to the speaker in the dark. I guess they learned that the attack was a big success, from the Japanese viewpoint.

As time went on, all the Caucasian neighbors sold their homes and went back to the mainland. So, all around us all kinds of different people started moving in. There were Chinese people in front of us, a Portuguese guy moved in on the side of us and some Japanese people moved in the back. The neighborhood started to change drastically when most of the haoles moved out.

We had to carry gas masks and we had to go to bomb shelters whenever their was an air raid. I remember that the shelters were always dirty with spider webs and what-not. At St. Theresa's, when they would ring the alarm, everybody would have to go down into the shelter in the dark. There were spider webs all over the place and nobody wanted to go down there and sit on those dirty seats. But we had to. And I remember I used to carry all kinds of things in my gas mask bag--candy, gum, cookies, all that stuff. In the hot sun, the candy would melt and the cookies would crumble. It got so sticky and mucky, we'd have to clean it up.

My mother volunteered for the Red Cross and she knitted a lot of things for the men in the service. All these old Japanese ladies would get together and knit. They were given a quota to knit so many things before the next meeting--ten gloves, ten caps, and so on. They met at the Lanikila Recreation Center. My mother would knit until one, two o'clock in the morning in our blacked out room. She would knit sweaters, caps, mittens. She had to buy all the materials herself. You supplied your own materials and donated your work for the war effort. She worked very hard. My father continued his coffee business during the war.

When the war first started, President Roosevelt didn't accept Japanese

Americans into the service to fight for their country. So a group of them got together and formed the Varsity Victory Volunteers, the VVVs. They would build shacks, put up barbed wire, any kind of labor work. They would not give them rifles to use. The 100th Battalion, now, they were already in the service when the war broke out. There were a lot of Japanese in there so they formed their own outfit, all from Hawaii. They were a little older than the 442nd boys that came later.

My grandfather was all for Japan. He was born and raised there and was loyal to his country. After a while, though, when he saw these American Japanese boys joining the U.S. army, I think he realized that Japan did the wrong thing and what the American boys were doing was right. I think he backed America after that.

A lot of Japanese boys from the outer islands were volunteering for the army. When they would come in from Kona, my father's home town, they'd all come to our house because we had a pretty big house. My mother would be the cook and the servant for them. My father would be the tour guide. We treated them like kings. We fed them and showed them a good time. When they would go overseas, we would get pictures and letters from them. Our house was like a hotel most of the time.

When the 442nd Regimental Combat Team went over to Europe, they joined up with the 100th Battalion and formed one unit. General Mark Clark thought a lot of them. They fought a battle that was famous, under impossible odds. They saved a Texas battalion and lost a heck-of-a-lot of men in doing it. Just like a bunch of Buddha-heads,[2] they just charged up a hill like crazy guys and saved the Texans. I think they lost a lot more men than they saved. But they did it, and were commended for it. It was the Texas National Guard unit that was trapped there. I had two uncles who were in the 442nd. They came out without a scratch. They were lucky.

I still remember when my classmate at St. Theresa's, Alfredo Fernandez, his brothers, and some friends would go down to Pearl Harbor and shine shoes for the sailors. Alfredo and I were the youngest of the group, so we would just tag along. The older boys would shine the shoes and make money. And we used to go down to Makalapa Dump and pick up all this stuff they used to throw away. We'd find

---

[2]Slang term, used in Hawaii to refer to one of Japanese ancestry.

canteens, army belts, army blankets, pup tents, and stuff like that. They were throwing it away, I guess, to get rid of diseases or what-not. But it was still good stuff and we could use them for camping, and for Boy Scouts.

One day, we're carrying out all this stuff when we hear this jeep coming with soldiers shooting rifles up in the air to scare us. We grabbed our junk and took off into the cane fields nearby. Running through sugar cane fields, you get your face and hands all cut up from the sharp leaves. But, you either dropped the stuff and ran the other way, or kept the stuff and hid out in the cane fields for a little while. So that's what we did. The guards went away after a while and we came out and walked home.

So here I would come home with this big, huge, pile of things. It was junk to my mother, but it was my prize possessions to me. My mother would go crazy. "That stuff is full of germs," she'd say. So she'd put everything into boiling water and clean the stuff up like new. And I then had my special prizes--stuff to play army with for the rest of the war.

Those were the war years. I remember, at first, I was angry at Japan for doing what they did--my own homeland--me being Japanese and all that. But, of course, I was more American than Japanese. I'll never forget those war years.

Art graduated from St. Louis College (high school) in 1950. He went on to Honolulu Business College and to the University of Hawaii. He became a junior accountant. He married Amy Sakaguchi, a Roosevelt graduate, in 1953. He went to work for his father in the coffee business, then joined the Postal Service. He and Amy have three children, a daughter and two sons. Their daughter has given them two grandchildren. Art underwent heart surgery in 1985, but keeps fit serving as a mail carrier in the Hawaii Kai area. Art and Amy live in Aina Haina.

Charles F. Penhallow

His Hawaii heritage goes back to the missionary days in the 1820s when his great grandfather, a sea captain, arrived with his wife in Honolulu, bringing with them a group of missionaries. His grandfather was born in Honolulu in 1844. His father, born in 1877, was manager of the Wailuku Sugar Company from 1908 until 1932. Charles was born in Wailuku, Maui in 1912. He attended Maui Grammar School and graduated from Maui High School in 1929. He attended the University of Hawaii and graduated in mathematics and physics in 1933. He went to work full time at the Mutual Telephone Company on September 1, 1933. In 1941, he lived at a boarding house on Lanihuli Drive in Manoa Valley.

I held two jobs at that time. I would work at a regular job at the phone company during the day, handling land and property matters for the company. At five o'clock in the evening, I would go to another job for the phone company, which was in the transpacific telephone service. I was what they called a technical control operator. I had to listen to all long distance telephone calls that went through the telephone building. I worked from five until about seven o'clock on that second job.

On Saturday, December 6, 1941, Harrison Foss and I went for a drive out to Nanakuli and Makaha on the north shore. I had a movie camera with me and I took a picture of the sunset. Little did I realize at the time that the Japanese fleet was right over the horizon waiting to pounce on Honolulu.

We came back into Honolulu that evening and I stopped to buy gas at the Von Hamm Young service station next to the YWCA on Richard Street. I filled up the tank. Little did I know then, too, that the very next day gasoline restrictions would be going into effect. Harrison and I went to see "Mr. and Mrs. North," a play at Punahou School that evening. After the show, about 10:30, I went down to the main Post Office in town to get my mail. I was very much impressed by the fact that there were lines and lines of sailors at the armed forces YMCA waiting to get on the busses to go back to Pearl Harbor. Undoubtedly, a lot of those poor guys were blown up the next morning.

My second job included Sunday mornings and I would go in at six o'clock and open up the transpacific telephone service. So, that's where I was early on the morning of the seventh. The *Lurline* had left Honolulu the day before and was due in California on Wednesday. There was a call for the *Lurline*, that had been reserved from the previous day. We were supposed to contact the *Lurline* and put the call through. As it was, when the bombs started falling they imposed radio silence and that call never did get put through.

At about eight o'clock that morning, the "order wire" rang. The order wire is a telephone line between the telephone operator who actually handles long distance calls and the technical control operator, which was what I was. They would call down on the order wire if there were complaints that the connection wasn't clear enough and we would make adjustments. We had dials in front of us to make those adjustments.

And so Margie Choy, who was the long distance operator handling calls that morning, called down and said to me, "I'm going to let you in on a secret. They're sabotaging defense projects at Pearl Harbor. I can hear the explosions on the telephone." We could hear the explosions but had no idea it was an actual attack. We thought people had left time bombs when they went home on Saturday afternoon and the bombs were exploding. But we soon found out what the real story was.

A lot of calls went through early that morning before they imposed censorship on telephone calls. But, even after censorship was imposed, we could hear San Francisco talking on the air to Manila. We couldn't understand how they could have censored between us and San Francisco, but they didn't censor calls between San Francisco and Manila. That was corrected very soon.

Governor Poindexter called Washington D.C. and talked to President Roosevelt and I had to listen in on the call. The governor was requesting help. While this conversation was taking place, the chief censor came in and said, "You must have had it going out over the air on an uncoded signal because too many people are hearing that call." I explained to him that the equipment is fixed so that you either listen or you talk. You go out over one radio circuit for listening and another for talking. So unless a person had two receivers, he didn't hear both sides of the conversation. And, they went through a privacy device and the combination was changed every twenty seconds.

Every morning, when we started up, we would talk with the San

196

Francisco counterpart and we would synchronize the two devices that made these changes every twenty seconds so they would do it simultaneously. The person talking would actually hear a "chirp" when it was changing from one interval to the other. What it turned out to be was that everybody in Iolani Palace was listening to one side of that call between Roosevelt and Poindexter. I had nothing to do with giving it out. Anyway, the censor was upset and he wasn't too sure he was going to let me go scott free on that one.

During the attack, NBC in New York called Marion Mulroney, who was the owner of KGU radio station. I heard the conversation. NBC said, "Where are you stationed?" Mulroney answered, "I'm up on the roof of the Advertiser Building with a clear view of Pearl Harbor."

"Well, could you talk on a nation-wide network?"

"Yes," said Mulroney.

"Okay, start talking," came the response.

So he started talking a blue streak, explaining what he was witnessing from that roof-top vantage-point when all of a sudden an interruption comes from the San Francisco operator. "Interrupt, Honolulu," said the operator. "I'm talking to New York," said Mulroney. The telephone operator in San Francisco said, "The censors have disconnected this call. It cannot go through."

And so, Mulroney was giving a great description of all the black smoke he could see from Pearl Harbor and the bombs that were supposedly dropping on Honolulu when he was cut off. I don't think that story ever got in the newspapers or on the air.

Since I went to work at 5:30 that morning, I was free to go home at half-past twelve, but I was on call. My car was parked on Alakea Street, facing mauka[1] and we could hear explosions. These explosions were not due to Japanese bombs, we later found out. They were due to nervous American soldiers or sailors who were not fusing their anti-aircraft shells correctly and they would come down and explode in the city.

There was a Chinese man who was killed walking in front of the governor's mansion--Washington Place--and there was a picture in the newspaper of a big cavity in the ground there. He was just walking

---

[1]*Hawaiian word, a direction meaning toward the mountains.*

alone, there, and was killed instantly. The old Lewers and Cooke Building was hit by anti-aircraft shells that fell on it, causing some destruction to the building.

" These explosions were not due to Japanese bombs . . . (but) to nervous American soldiers or sailors who were not fusing their anti-aircraft shells correctly and they would . . . explode in the city. "

So I drove home to Mrs. Whitman's boarding house in Manoa and had something to eat. Mrs. Melda Whitman's boarding house had all kinds of people living there, including a bunch of old ladies who knew everything. They asked me, "So, Mr. Penhallow, what are you going to do after lunch?"

I said, "I'm subject to call so I'm going to go back to my bedroom and take a nap."

"How unpatriotic," they said. "Why aren't you out looking for parachutists like everybody else?" I don't know what I would have done to a parachutist if I found one. Run? I didn't have a gun.

The next morning I came into my office on the second floor and there was a neatly dressed sailor sitting there at my position with a 45 automatic on the table. And I thought, "How nice. The navy is providing me with somebody to protect me in case of sabotage." He told me that wasn't the story at all. "I'm here to shoot you in case you try anything." Maybe he was just giving me a line, but that's what he said. He became a good friend of mine later.

We got orders that day that everybody should be patriotic and see how much gasoline they could do without. I had a full tank from the day before, so I went the whole month of December without buying any gasoline. On January first, they said, "Alright, you've all proved how much you can do without gasoline, so you're frozen for that monthly allotment for the duration of the war."

I said, "Just a minute, now. That's too much of a sacrifice. I can't get by with **no** gasoline." They gave me ten gallons a month. I was using around sixty or seventy gallons, previously. Because they said you could always ask for more, I did, about two months later. I explained that I had three brothers, all in the service, and that I had a chance to see them for dinner one night at Ewa Plantation, so I requested an extra five gallons because my car only got about ten miles to the gallon.

They said, "Please sit down. You don't seem to understand there's a war going on. Everybody's making sacrifices and you want gasoline just for personal use? Application denied! You're very unpatriotic." So I used my ten gallons to go out there and then I had to park the car for another month before I could get gasoline again. I took the bus to work.

The bus company decided, at first, to be patriotic, too, and they cut down on fuel consumption, which was the wrong thing to do. They should have used unlimited supplies of fuel to operate their busses and keep people out of their cars. But they finally got the message and bus allotments were increased. But they couldn't get enough drivers and consequently, if you wanted to use the bus, you would often stand on the street corner for a long, long time. When the bus finally came, it was full of passengers--standing up--and the bus driver would ask you to take the next bus. Well, the next bus came an hour later and it was full, too.

Mrs. Whitman had a daughter-in-law who was a nurse stationed at Hickam Field. She told us her story about December seventh. She had to tend to the injured people, and worked hard around the clock. She was finally so exhausted that she decided that she had to take a nap. In the dark, she found something soft to rest her head against and fell off into a deep sleep. She rested very well. When she woke up, she found that the thing she was resting against was a bag full of body parts. This didn't bother her at all because she was a nurse. But on December ninth, which was my birthday, I was having dinner at the boarding house and this brave girl was there. A mouse ran across the floor and she let out a scream and jumped up on a chair and wrapped her skirt around her as if she didn't have a moment longer to live. I hurt her feelings by laughing at her antics. But, here she had been through all this peril of December seventh and slept on a bag of body parts and never thought anything about it, and she screamed in fear because a mouse ran across the floor.

Another thing the local people were doing during those early hours of the war, especially the old ladies at Mrs. Whitman's boarding house, was listening to the police calls on the radio. The two radio stations, KGMB and KGU were not really on the air that much in the beginning.

Anyway, they would hear the police say, "Go to such-and-such a street. There's a man up on an electric pole with a red and green lantern signaling to Japanese submarines at sea." When they tracked it down, it was an Hawaiian Electric man who was up on the pole, not with red and green lanterns, but with a red light (all you were allowed for light) repairing a transformer that was out of order. And these old ladies would get hysterical and pass the rumors on so that all sorts of subversive things were supposed to be taking place. Well, eventually the police department established codes so that the general public wouldn't know what they were referring to. Eventually these people stopped listening to the police calls.

The telephone company was having a big addition made to the building at that time and we had a Japanese outfit, all American citizens though, doing the construction work. There was a little bit of nervousness in the air at the Japanese workers. Would one of them be disloyal and maybe toss a bomb in there and blow us all up? It didn't happen, of course, but those were some of our apprehensions.

At times I slept there at the telephone building. While the construction was going on, there was scaffolding around that part of the building they were working on, where we were sleeping. Some of the locals didn't take the war very seriously and would climb out on the scaffolding, just being pranksters. The armed guards below would yell, "Halt." People in the building would yell down to the guards, "Shoot 'em, shoot 'em." That didn't go over very well with the soldiers who didn't know a Hawaiian sense of humor.

I didn't black out my room until much later. I would type letters in the dark, then read them over the next morning and make my corrections. I also listened to the radio. I could pick up Los Angeles stations after dark, stations KNX and KFI. I would hear Walter Winchell from time to time and that was my principal source of material for news. Our local stations were off the air quite a bit in the beginning. I think the feeling was that Japanese planes could use those stations as a guide coming in and find Pearl Harbor. I really don't think they needed it. I think they knew all the time where Pearl Harbor was.

We had to be off the streets by dark, but we still had quite a lot of social life. If we went visiting at somebody's house for dinner, we would take our pajamas and stay all night. So the curfew and blackout didn't curtail our social life much.

My sister-in-law lived down the street from Mrs. Whitman's boarding house and she had heard a rumor from a neighbor that made her very upset. The rumor was that on one particular night, all the people of Japanese ancestry in Manoa Valley were going to rise secretly and slit the throats of all the haoles[2] they could find. There wasn't a word of truth in it, of course, but she and her neighbor friends sat up all night in a blacked out room smoking one cigarette after another with no ventilation.

" If we went visiting at somebody's house for dinner, we would take our pajamas and stay all night. So the curfew and blackout didn't curtail our social life much. "

They wanted me to come over there and be their "safety person." I don't know what I would have done if there'd been any slitting of throats. I probably would just have contributed my throat. Anyway, they were all upset. The neighbor that started that rumor deserved to be given a swift kick for saying such a thing.

We had a lot of war workers living at the boarding house. Mrs. Whitman wasn't very happy with them because they were rough and ready people, you might say. One of them asked her one day, "What is your contribution to the war effort?" Mrs. Whitman replied, "My contribution is in allowing a bunch of bums like you to occupy my nice hotel." She was mad at them because they were dating the girls that waited on the tables. They were being nice to these girls, consequently, they got served first. The other people living there, especially the old ladies, didn't appreciate the favoritism that was being shown.

Two years later, after I moved from Mrs. Whitman's, I shared a house with some men who were officers in navy intelligence. They had access not only to gasoline, but could get in and out of Pearl Harbor to buy food at the commissary. Consequently, we had steaks when nobody else had steaks. We had roasts when nobody had roasts. And we had very cheap food. You went to the commissary with fifteen dollars in your pocket and you came back with enough groceries to fill the whole back seat of your car.

---

[2]*Hawaiian word meaning white person, Caucasian, formerly any foreigner.*

At the telephone company, there were many calls from the mainland coming through to Gen. Walter C. Short, who was our first military governor. General Short had a secret telephone that had a scrambler on it. It was installed before the war started by a man named Albert Akana. Being of part Oriental extraction, Albert was not about to go out on the streets at night, because he might be mistaken for the enemy and get shot. Anyway, the general's office called and said that the secret telephone wasn't working. He asked if someone would come right out and fix it. Albert took the call, thought about it for a few minutes, then said to the caller, "There's a little red button in front of the secret telephone. Is it lighted?"

"No, it's not lighted."

"Well, above the telephone, there's a pull cord that you can pull on, so pull it. Did the red light come on?"

"Oh, yes, it's on now. And the telephone works just fine now."

So Albert Akana saved a trip all the way out to Fort Shafter, or wherever the phone was located, and prevented the chance of getting shot at.

In order to get to the main building at Mrs. Whitman's--to the dining room to eat--I had to walk a short way on the public street. Once in a while, after curfew, I would cut through the yard of our neighbor, Dr. Morelock. One time I was out after curfew, cutting through Dr. Morelock's, when a warden came by and stopped me. "You're out after blackout," he said. "I'm going to have to give you a ticket." I explained to him that I was on private property and that I had the permission of the property owner to be there. I was fortunate that I talked my way out of it and he let me go. I was never given a ticket, but I understand from other people that they had to give a pint of blood for their fine. These were some of the so-called hardships of war.

We knew some submarine sailors that had special privileges and were able to get time off and stay at the Royal Hawaiian Hotel at twenty-five cents a night. The Royal Hawaiian was committed to submariners at that time. If you went swimming off Waikiki, you would see these sailors had hung their laundry out on the windows. This was not a very elegant thing to do to the "Pink Lady." I talked to some of these sailors and they were delighted with the Royal Hawaiian. "Boy," one sailor said, "this is the place for me. When I get out of the navy, I'm going to come back here and spend my honeymoon at the Royal Hawaiian Hotel." Of course, he didn't realize that when he did come back, it wouldn't be twenty-five cents a night anymore.

" . . . we all agreed that although we were always afraid for our lives . . . we would look back at these times as some of the happiest days of our lives. "

I continued to live at the boarding house until 1944. A few years earlier, however, the households were allowed to use what they called "blackout bulbs." They had been painted with a black material with just a little hole in the middle. They were twenty-five watt bulbs, so they only put out about six-and-a-half watts of light. You were allowed to have them with your windows open, as long as they couldn't be seen from the outside. You couldn't read, but you could at least see your way to the bathroom, if you had to, at night.

We would have conversations a lot. I remember one night we all agreed that although we were always afraid for our lives and expecting a Japanese invasion, the day would come when we would look back at these as some of the happiest days of our lives. We sure had a lot of parties and most of them had to be pau[3] by four o'clock in the afternoon so that we could be home before the curfew. And, there were those nights that we went prepared just to spend the night at our host's home. We did have some fun times, even under military law restrictions.

Charles Penhallow retired from the telephone company on December 31, 1977, following more than forty-four years of service. He has served as secretary for the Hawaii Chapter of the Independent Telephone Pioneer Association since 1979. He enjoys doing his own yard work and occasionally takes in a movie. He lives in Kahala.

---

[3]*Hawaiian word meaning through, over, the end.*

Schools Taken Over

Immediately after the attack, part of Farrington High School was transformed into an annex of Tripler. By noon, first aid workers had made up three hundred twenty-four beds, and by 4:30, Tripler had transferred its headquarters and some two hundred casualties there. At Kamehameha School for Boys, the infirmary and Iolani Hall were taken over, first as Provisional Hospital No. 1 and later as an annex to Tripler. In the fall of 1942, the Kamehameha School for Girls was moved to the boys' school campus and the entire girls' school thereafter was used as the army hospital, housing seven hundred fifty patients at a time. Punahou was "occupied" by the U. S. District Engineers. Two days later, the school trustees received a three-sentence letter informing them that the engineers had occupied the grounds for an indefinite period. At 2:00 a.m., December 8, St. Louis College received written confirmation that the army would take possession of the campus. The new hospital, with a capacity of five hundred patients, was originally known as Provisional Hospital No. 2, but after June, 1942, became the 147th General Hospital.

(Allen, Hawaii's War Years)

ST. LOUIS HOSPITAL — Temporary buildings used as hospital wards with elevated walkways and ramps transformed the St. Louis campus into an up-to-date army hospital. (Pacific Marianist Archives)

Antoinette Rodrigues Boucher

Her paternal grandparents arrived in Honolulu aboard the first ship to bring immigrants from Portugal to Hawaii in September 1878. Her parents were both born in Honolulu. The family lived at 1909 Liliha Street, in the Puunui district, a block below Judd Street. She was the last of five children and the only daughter. "Nettie" was born in September 1925. On December seventh, she was sixteen years old and a junior at Sacred Heart Academy in Kaimuki. She lived with her mother, who was widowed in 1936, and her brother, Rod, who was twenty-seven at the time.

I can remember Saturday night, December sixth. There was a party at the Frietas house on Keonaona Street. They were neighbors to my Aunt Carrie Brown. August Frietas was having a birthday party in the big rumpus room in the back of their house. It was fun. We left to come home about eleven o'clock and the last song they were playing when we left was "Sweet Georgia Brown." I've always connected that song as the last song we heard before we went home. I guess it represented-- although we didn't realize it then--the last of the happy experiences we would have for a long time.

I got up early on Sunday and caught the bus to go to the seven o'clock Mass at Our Lady of Peace cathedral on Fort Street. We were having a rehearsal for the junior class play at Sacred Hearts that morning and I was to meet Clotilde Almeida and her parents at Mass. It was traditional for the junior class to put on a play every year and Clo and I were in it. So we met at church. As was usual in those years, there were many servicemen in uniform at church on Sundays.

Near the end of Mass, we noticed some commotion going on. Ushers would go up to servicemen and whisper in their ears and they would bolt up and leave the church. We heard the droning planes overhead--it sounded like a lot of them--but we didn't think too much of it because we had been used to hearing maneuvers, or war games, going on. We were distracted, watching the servicemen leave, to the point that we didn't pay too much attention to what was going on at Mass.

The service was soon over and Clotilde, her parents, and I left the church and walked to the car in the parking lot. We could hear sirens as we got into the car. As we started off on Beretania Street, Mr. Almeida turned on the car radio to see what was happening and I guess that's when we heard Webley Edwards saying, "This is the real McCoy. We are under attack by Japanese planes. Please take cover. If you are on the street, go to your homes and stay off the streets."

Boy, I mean, it was a shock. We just couldn't believe it. I immediately thought that this must be another of those shows by Orson Welles, of "War of the Worlds" fame. But then I wondered why the radio station would schedule that kind of a program on Sunday morning? That kind of a dramatization was usually done on evening radio. Mr. Almeida said, "No, this must be the real thing. We've got to get home."

Ambulances and fire engines were zooming past us. I asked Mr. Almeida to drive me home, but since we were already well on the way to his place on Wilder Avenue, that's where we went. I was worried about my mother. She never did listen to the radio on Sundays and I knew she would be frightened by the noises.

We got to the Almeidas' house and I immediately phoned to tell my mother. She had apparently heard about it. Rod had already left in his car to drive servicemen down to Pearl Harbor, so Mother was alone and scared. I told the Almeidas that I had to go home. But they said that I couldn't leave--that we were told to stay off the streets. So they took my purse away from me to keep me there, thinking I couldn't get home without any money.

" I blurted out to the bus driver that I had to get home to my mother and that there was a war going on and I didn't have any money and, oh yes, I also needed a transfer. "

But I was stubborn, I guess. I just ran out of the house and down to the corner bus stop. The bus came by and stopped for me--I mean it was so normal to see the bus coming by. Some things were so normal while others were so unreal that it was hard to connect the two. It was like I was having a dream--a nightmare. I must have looked frantic, but I blurted out to the bus driver that I had to get home to my mother and that there was a war going on and I didn't have any money, and, oh yes,

I also needed a transfer. He waved me on and gave me the transfer. I was on the Punahou line and had to transfer to the Puunui line to get home. But, of course, the first bus that came by at the transfer point was the School Street bus, not Puunui--but I took it anyway, got off on Liliha Street, and ran all the way home up the hill.

My mother was relieved to see me. She was praying the rosary. I don't think she really understood the full impact of what was happening. She just prayed whenever there was a problem. We sort of sat there and wrung our hands. Our neighbors came over and they were panicked, too. Then, Buddy Edgar, the kid that lived next door, said that a bomb fell just up the street, and he was in our back yard picking up pieces of shrapnel for souvenirs. The bomb--or whatever it was--fell up on Judd Street, we learned later, and apparently someone was hurt or killed. Another one fell down near Kuakini Street, which was also close by. And, we were only about five miles away from Pearl Harbor, so it was scary. Anyway, we just sat around for the rest of the day and my mother must have said fifty rosaries.

Then, somebody from the Civil Defense came knocking on our door and said that we had to move out of the area--that we were too close to Pearl Harbor. We were living in what was considered unsafe territory. We were told that if we didn't have a place to go--away from town, preferably up in the hills--that we would be given shelter at a school in a safer location. Many people were reluctant to leave their homes, including our neighbors. But they wanted everybody out of there right away.

" So Mother and I packed a suitcase of clothes . . . and went up to my brother Reggie's house on Wilhelmina Rise. "

So Mother and I packed a suitcase of clothes and things and went up to my brother Reggie's house on Wilhelmina Rise. Reggie had been called away that morning--he was a laundry truck driver and a civil defense volunteer--so my sister-in-law, Rose, and her two sons, Larry and Billy, were home alone. I remember we all dragged mattresses into the living room and tried to sleep that night, next to one another. We had the radio on all night long. It would be off the air for a long time, then an announcement would come on, every once in a while, and we would all jump. There was only civil defense news on, telling you what to do.

I remember they reported that all entertainment events were cancelled and school was closed. No movies, no sports, and we were now under martial law. I don't know how much sleep anyone got that night. I know my mother was still saying the rosary and we were all praying with her. We were glued to the radio, waiting for the next bit of news. Of course we didn't realize it at that time, but we were going to stay there at my brother's for the next two months.

We hadn't heard anything about what happened to Reggie and we were worried. He had left early Sunday morning and it was now Monday morning and no word from him. It was also December the eighth, a holy day of obligation for Catholics. So we went down to St. Patrick's church in Kaimuki for Mass that morning and the church was packed. It was standing room only. It's amazing how you turn to God when you're in danger. The church was bulging with people.

People were warned against panic buying at the stores. They announced over the radio that there would be an inventory made of all food supplies and that there should be an ample supply for everybody, so people should not worry about it. But they panicked, anyway, and hoarded all the food they could get.

It was a few days before Reggie finally came home. I think it was Tuesday evening when he walked up that long walk in front of the house. His shirt was covered with dried blood and he walked like he was in a daze--like a zombie. He had picked up the dead and wounded at Hickam Field and transported them to hospitals. He went in and took a bath and then went to bed. I don't think he talked to any of us. Rose tried to get him to say something, but I guess he didn't want to talk about it.

As soon as we felt safe enough to travel on the bus, my mother and I went back home to take care of things. The weather was rainy, but she was worried about her plants, so we watered the plants. We emptied out the refrigerator, bringing the food we had back to Reggie's house. It kind of added to the larder because food was kind of hard to come by at that time.

I was immature for my age then, and I remember I would go out and climb trees, rough-house, and play games with my nephews. I was definitely a tomboy. Larry was nine, and Billy was six. Rose was also big on books--so we read a lot--and I would read aloud to the kids. And we colored. The days just dragged on. School was out for a long time.

I remember, that first week, I walked down to my high school, Sacred Hearts Academy, and they welcomed me in to roll bandages for the Red Cross. So, for two hours every afternoon, that's what I did. We didn't know when school was going to start again, but that kept me in touch and I was helping out, doing something for the war effort.

It was a very boring period--during those blacked out nights--not knowing what was going to happen or when school would start again. Rod kept us occupied with games that he would make up. I remember we'd try to guess the names of as many states as we could and write them down. But we mastered that one pretty quick, so we moved on to identifying the capitals of each state. That kept us going for a while. And, oh, we played Monopoly, too. Rod was home a good deal of the time at night and we would play Monopoly. In fact, we had Monopoly games going from one night to the next. We would just stop because we had to go to bed, then pick up where we left off again the next evening.

I would also go down to 8th Avenue and visit my cousins, Val and Mona Souza. We would play cards, Chinese checkers, and Monopoly there, too. And the three of us did a lot of bicycling during those days. I remember all three of us on one bike, coming down the 12th Street hill with no brakes. Val was on the seat, Mona on the back, and I rode on the handle bars. They didn't bother to tell me that we had no brakes, but I found out soon enough. We would also tie ropes to the mango trees in their back yard and play Tarzan, jumping from the tree to their garage, and down to the dirt driveway. That's how we amused ourselves.

When we moved back home to Liliha Street, I remember that we were told to turn off the pilot light in the water heater, under the house. The basement didn't have walls, just lattice work, and that tiny flame could be seen, I guess, by the wardens. Rod got tar paper and blacked out the windows with tape. Even though it was now February, cooler months in Hawaii, when you had the house all closed up for a few hours, it would get very warm. So about ten minutes out of every hour, we would put out all the lights and open up all the windows to let the air circulate. And I remember reading in bed under the covers with a flashlight, so the light couldn't be seen. Mother would come in and say, "You're going to ruin your eyes." But I did it anyway.

They started mentioning on the radio, right after the war started, that women and children should consider evacuating from the islands if they had a place to go on the mainland. People deluged the Matson Navigation Company offices looking for transportation to leave the islands. And the trip by boat would take twice as long, they said, since they had to avoid mines and submarines. They would only travel in armed convoys.

They also recommended that high school students work part-time so that adults could take on war-type jobs. Organizations actually came to the high schools and hired students. I guess workers were hard to get at that time. I worked for a while at the cathedral for Bishop James Sweeney. I also worked for Charles R. Frazier Company, where my brother, Rod, worked.

I did clerical work--working in the mornings from eight until eleven, and going to school from twelve until three-thirty in the afternoons. I did that for the rest of my junior year. I worked Saturdays after that. Although hours returned to normal during my senior year, we were missing at least ten members of our class who had gone to work for the government. It was good to see that my two best friends, Marjorie Todd and Gladys Trask, had also returned to school.

I can remember my senior prom, in June 1943, being held from two in the afternoon until five in the evening because of the curfew. It was held at Dreyer Manor, that big, old home right next door to the Honolulu Stadium that belonged to the St. Louis Alumnae Association. I went with Wilbert Martin, a Californian who was a few years older than me. He was renting a room at Aunt Carrie's house. So I got all dressed up in early afternoon to go to the dance. It had to either be held early, or forget it--no prom at all. So I went. We had an orchestra and everything. It was fun, though, because we had no social life at all during those days. No sports, no movies. Your only social activity was swimming.

Sacred Hearts Convent, a school just around the corner from us on Bates and Nuuanu, was converted into a hospital when the war started. They took the overflow patients from Tripler Army Hospital. I remember my aunt, Carrie Brown, walked over there and volunteered to work in the linen room. She would pass out the linens to be used for the beds. The patients there were the less serious casualties of the war.

When school started again, everything centered around patriotism. I remember we did things in the Girl Scouts for the war effort. Sister Julie Louise Thevenin was our faculty counselor at Sacred Hearts and she had us rolling bandages, learning first-aid and home nursing. We put on pageants on the four freedoms. I remember I represented the freedom of speech at that one--I can't imagine why. My friend, Marjorie Todd, was chosen Miss Liberty in the pageant. Even the songs of the times were centered on the war. I remember the songs "Praise the Lord and Pass the Ammunition" and "Let's Remember Pearl Harbor." The wartime slogan, "A slip of the lip will sink a ship" was also seen everywhere on posters and signs. The war really brought the country--and the Hawaiian islands, too--back together for a common cause.

As the war went on, Hawaii became the stopping point for rest and relaxation (R & R) for the servicemen. Private homes were turned into R & R places, such as Doris Duke Cromwell's home out at the foot of Diamond Head on Black Point. The Royal Hawaiian Hotel was also turned into an R & R spot for the guys from the submarine service.

OFF TO THE BALL -- Seventeen-year-old Nettie Rodrigues stops for a photograph on her way to the Sacred Heart Senior Prom in June 1943. Due to wartime curfew, the prom was held from two to five o'clock in the afternoon. Nettie proudly shows off her new white gown, purchased at the New York Dress Shop on Fort Street. (Photo courtesy of the Boucher family collection)

AIR RAID DRILL -- Students at Sacred Heart Academy in Kaimuki practice using their gas masks during one of the frequent air raid drills in the school's main shelter, below ground. Note the sand bags fill the window openings at ground level. Student at left, front (partially seen) is Nettie Rodrigues. (War Depository Collection, University of Hawaii)

I don't know how I was contacted--whether it was through school or what--but I was invited to join a group of young women who would visit the servicemen on R & R. I would be invited on a Sunday afternoon and we would be taken out to the Royal Hawaiian or to Doris Duke Cromwell's house and meet the guys. We would play ping pong, cards, swim, or dance to a juke-box. We were picked up at our doorstep in a military van and then taken right back home after the party. It was all very well chaperoned. They didn't want you to get involved with any of the servicemen. In fact, we only used first names. They could tell you their rank in the service and what their job was--within government regulations--but you had to stick to a first name basis only. So I met many young men that way. It was fun.

And we had a woman who was the organizer of these events who had the strangest name, I remember. We called her "Totsy" and she was responsible for coordinating the activities. If a guy wanted to send flowers or something to one of the girls, he had to do it through her. She would take the gift and see that the girl got it. I got a couple of bouquets of flowers that way, from servicemen I met at these R & R parties.

After having gone through close to a year with no social life at all, many of the girls were happy to be able to do something. I did that for about a year-and-a-half and met a lot of nice young men. I had a lot of fun doing it, and they fed us very well, too. Because it was hard for civilians to get good meat to eat--if they served steaks or lamb at these socials--I would bring the leftovers home to my mother. I always carried a bag with me in case I couldn't eat everything. I did that a lot.

But you always did wonder--when the servicemen got shipped out to fight in the war again--whether they were going to come back alive. So, in that respect, it was kind of a bitter-sweet experience.

As time went by, they relaxed the curfew so that we could stay out as late as ten o'clock. Then, towards the end of the war, I remember we didn't have to be in until midnight. That's when we were able to go down to the Souza's beach house in Punaluu. By this time, they had army bases all over the island and there was a big group camped just across the street from Mona and Val Souza's place. So I'd spend weekends down there with them and meet a lot of nice young men. I liked that very much.

As I look back on those years now, I try and only remember the good times. I'm still having a problem, however, stemming from Pearl Harbor.

Although I live in California now, I do visit the islands frequently. I really can't explain it, but I cannot visit the *Arizona* memorial. It gives me a funny feeling just thinking about all those lives that were lost out there that morning. It was so ghastly, I guess I've tried to put it out of my mind.

" ***I cannot visit the Arizona memorial. It gives me a funny feeling just thinking about all those lives that were lost out there.*** *"*

When my two youngest children were teenagers, we visited Honolulu and took them on the commercial tour of Pearl Harbor. This is the tour that doesn't actually stop and board the memorial--so in the last minute, I got up enough nerve to go. While the narration was interesting and well worth the experience, I really had a difficult time of it. It was hard for me. I still don't think I am ready to actually go out on the memorial over the *Arizona*.

Enough time has certainly passed that I ought to be able to handle it. I don't know why, but it's something I haven't been able to do. I guess I'm just going to have to work it out in time.

Nettie met a young lieutenant with the Army Corp of Engineers, Kenneth Boucher, and married him in May 1946 at the cathedral of Our Lady of Peace in Honolulu. She left the islands with her new husband and after a short stay in his native New Hampshire, the Bouchers made their home in Hayward and Castro Valley, California. They have four children and one grandchild: Jan Gibbs and son, Brandon, living in Utah; Gail Fiala of Orinda, California; Glen Boucher of Woodland Hills, California, and Sheri Flynn of Friday Harbor, Washington.

Nelson and Olive Rodrigues

Born in Honolulu in 1910, Nelson Rodrigues was the third of five children of Frank and Jessie Rodrigues. He graduated from McKinley High School in 1929, and went to work at Pearl Harbor. He married Olive Dolim in 1935. Olive, born in Keahua, Maui in 1912, was number three of seven children born to Joseph and Isabel Dolim. She graduated from Maui High School in 1929, and continued her education at the University of Hawaii, earning a degree in education in 1933. On December 7, 1941, Olive was twenty-nine years old and working in the secretarial office at the university. She and Nelson lived at 1515 Pualele Place in Wilhelmina Rise. Olive's younger brother, Ricky, was also living there temporarily.

Nelson: About 6:30 that morning, I went to play golf at the Palolo Golf Course. It was the regular monthly tournament, and my good friend Charlie Duck and I were part of a foursome. We teed off at 7:00 a.m. It was a beautiful day for golf. When we got to the fifth hole--I think it was--we were shocked to see a car come driving across the golf course, over the greens and around the traps. It was coming fast. We had never seen anything like that. The street into the golf course ends at the parking lot and the clubhouse, so he had to drive across the pathways and on to the course. I thought to myself, "Jesus, somebody's got to be drunk or something to drive on the golf course. Who is this crazy person?" When the car got closer, we saw it was Charlie's wife, Lucy. She looked frantic.

"The Japanese are attacking Pearl Harbor," she yelled, "and the radio said that all civilian employees should report to work." Charlie worked at Pearl Harbor, too, in fact he was a supervisor at that time. We still couldn't believe what she was telling us, but we jumped in the car and started for home. Up to that time, we did not hear explosions or anything, so she caught us completely by surprise.

When they dropped me off at home, I could see smoke coming from the area of Honolulu stadium. We were up high, with a good view of the city below. I jumped in my car, picked up my riders--Augustine

Dolim and a couple of other people--and dashed off to Pearl Harbor. When we got down near Damon Tract, we came to a stop. They were evacuating people who were living around there into the city and there was no way traffic could get through. We were all backed up. People were walking--cars, trucks, buses all coming one way against the traffic-- away from Pearl Harbor. So we were turned around and had to come back home. No sooner than I got home, the radio reported again, "The roads are now clear. All Pearl Harbor workers report to work."

So I got back in the car again. And, boy, I'm telling you, we were going sixty or seventy miles-an-hour and the cops were just waving us on. We were moving like a fire engine in an emergency. Traffic piled up just before we got to the gate. Suddenly, there were planes coming over our heads. They were flying low and they were strafing Hickam Field just before they got to us. And those bullets were flying down our way,

---

" Suddenly, there were planes coming over our heads. . . strafing Hickam Field. . . And those bullets were flying down our way . . . "

---

just before we got to the gate. And the marines at the gate were firing back at them, over our heads, the other way. Everybody in my car ducked down, but I had to drive out of there. Everybody was trying to get their cars out of the firing line, and I bumped another car in all the excitement. It was just a fender bender, and it didn't seem too important at the time, considering what we were going through. We just waved to each other and went on our way.

The marines wouldn't let us go through the gate so we had to park our cars in the housing area, next to the gate, and walk in. They were still bombing and shooting when we got there, but I think these were the last bunch to come over Pearl Harbor. We walked over to the sub base where we got on the ferry to take us to our machine shop on Ford Island.

I couldn't believe what I was seeing. There was fire burning on the water everywhere. The landing pier on Ford Island, where we had to go, was next to the *Oklahoma* on one side and the *California* on the other. The *Oklahoma* was already turned over, on its side. The hull was sticking up above the water. The *California* was going down at that time. It didn't tip over, it just went straight down to the bottom. We had to go around the burning oil and battleships to get to the dock. Smoke and fire was everywhere. We were in shock when we got off the ferry. By that time, around 9:30 I'd say, the damage was already done and the Japanese planes had all left.

We weren't allowed to go to the machine shop. They put us to work doing odd jobs. Some were loading machine gun belts in case they came back. Others carried the wounded and the dead sailors into the headquarters of the barracks and the cafeteria. There was no hospital on Ford Island, so they used these facilities as a first-aid station. I saw some dead and wounded sailors. They brought them in from the ships close by. There were quite a few dead in there.

I did go back to my shop and the destruction there was something else. Windows were shot up, bullet holes were everywhere, and shells from bullets were scattered all over the floor.

We were told that the navy was looking for a small Japanese submarine in the harbor--the two-man kamikaze type--that was in there looking for our aircraft carriers. And, none of the carriers were in the harbor that day. I don't know how come, but they weren't at Pearl Harbor that Sunday. I guess it was just luck, or they might have been sunk, too. The-mini sub was anchored alongside the hospital ship USS Solace--I found out later--because they knew they would be safe there. We wouldn't try to sink them if they were next to our hospital ship.

Anyway, because of the submarine alert, they wouldn't allow us to leave on the regular ferry. It was too big a target. So they shuttled us back to the shore on small motor launches, carrying about twenty people at a time. It was a slow process. But, we got back to the cars as it got dark. It got dark early in December, and we were told that we couldn't use our headlights, that we had to drive home in the dark. That was scary. It was very dark that night.

And we couldn't have lights at home. I remember we sat in the hall way where no windows were exposed, so we were able to turn on the light in there, sit on the floor, and talk. It was bad that night and we were under military law. I heard that early the next morning, someone had forgotten about black-out and turned on the light to find his shoes or something, and he got picked up and taken down to the provost marshal. It was very strict.

Early the next morning, we had to drive back to Pearl Harbor in the

pitch dark. I picked up my riders and we started off. It was so dark that
I couldn't see where I was going. I had a 1940 Buick that I had picked
up in Chicago in 1939 and it had a running-board. So these guys would
stand outside on the running board, hanging on, telling me when I was
getting too close to the side of the street and where the white line was
down the middle of the road. That's the way we got down to Pearl
Harbor that morning. And there were a number of head-on accidents
that morning, too.

When we got down close to Hickam Field and Pearl Harbor, we were
shocked to see tracer bullets firing up in the air. I thought, "Oh, no, not
again." It might have been foolish to put myself through that danger of
getting killed again, but we continued on. But we found out later that
we were shooting at our own planes. They were coming in from the
mainland and the nervous military fired at them, thinking they were the
enemy. I think they had to land at Molokai or Maui, or somewhere like
that. Guards were firing at everything that night. If something moved,
they'd shoot. They were so nervous.

Anyway, we went through the gate and went back to Ford Island. As
we passed by the *Oklahoma*, on its side, there was a group of people
working on the hull, cutting it open to save the sailors trapped in there.
I was told that they even had to get the plans from the damned factory,
so that they knew where the steam lines were. And it was three or four
days later when they were taking live sailors from the *Oklahoma*, through
the hole they cut. That was really something. And they say that some
of those guys that were saved were really off their heads. They had no
food, no light, no anything for all that time.

When we got to Ford Island, I thought we'd be repairing the airplanes
that morning, because our machine shop's job was to repair and maintain
the airplanes. But at that point, the wrecked airplanes were secondary
to preparing for our defense against invasion. So we were put to work
building stands for machine gun emplacements. Then, as days went on,
we started working on the planes. And a lot of them were damaged that
morning. Hickam Field had more plane damage, though, because their
planes were parked on the outside. Ours were in hangars.

Barbed wire was soon all over the island. The Japanese would have
had a hell of a time coming in if they wanted to. But, at that time, we
felt they would come back. They would invade. And we felt Hawaii
was going to be occupied. If the Japanese knew how badly we were hit,

they could have come right back and taken us over. We didn't have any defense against them. And, we didn't get any help from the mainland at all. I feel they were going to protect the West Coast and let Hawaii go. And that's no bull. They figured Hawaii was already lost. Hawaii would be sacrificed.

" . . . we didn't get any help from the mainland at all. . . they were going to protect the West Coast and let Hawaii go. . . Hawaii would be sacrificed. "

We had so many air-raid alerts where we had to stop work and get to the air-raid shelters. That happened quite often. Some of them were called just so that we would practice getting to the shelters. But some of the alerts, I know, were real. They knew there were airplanes approaching the islands. They saw it on the radar. But they didn't pay too much attention to radar that Sunday morning, and you see what happened? We weren't really prepared. And the planes that were destroyed, too--at Hickam, Wheeler Field, and Pearl Harbor--that was all because we were caught sleeping.

And I remember that radar was a top secret with the government. We had to work on radar systems, but when we did, we had marine guards-- two of them--standing by with their rifles. The fellow that was assigned to work on the radar couldn't write notes or anything. Everything was done by observation and with tools. There were no written notes, no drawings on paper, no blueprints, and no sketches. And the man working on it only knew he was making a particular part for it. He wasn't told anything more about it.

Shortly afterwards, they brought one of the Japanese planes into our hangar where our machine shop was and displayed it in a roped-off area. It had been shot down in the harbor. They laid out all the clothes and the belongings that the pilot had when he was shot down. He had American money on him. He had slacks and a colorful shirt--civilian clothes--so if he were forced to land, he would just blend right in. The display was open for Pearl Harbor workers who wanted to see it.

Some months later, when the *Oklahoma* was righted up and moved into the drydock, I went aboard to inspect it. We were looking for parts that could be salvaged. And, I tell you, the smell from the dead bodies was real bad. I could hardly stand it. We had to spend some time on the *Oklahoma*. It was a smell I will never forget.

Our lifestyle changed. Our entertainment was the card games we used to play at our house in the blacked-out room. In fact, our house became the headquarters for poker games. And we would let people sleep over after the game. They would sleep any place, on the floor, even out in the yard. They would stay until daylight--because they couldn't go out after curfew. My cousin, Val Souza, used to walk up from his house on 8th Avenue, and sneak home after the game in the dark. Whenever he would hear a car coming, he would jump behind a bush or wall, until the car passed by, then continue walking. If he was ever caught, he would be in big trouble.

As I look back on those times, I guess we did foolish things. In fact, I didn't have to report back to Pearl Harbor and put myself in that danger. We weren't the military. We didn't take any oaths to defend our country. But we were dedicated to the cause. It was strange, but we weren't afraid. And everybody felt the same way. You would give your life for America. In fact, I thought I belonged in the war. I tried my damndest to get into the army--I had nine years in the national guard and was a reserve army officer--but Pearl Harbor wouldn't release me. So I stayed at Pearl Harbor and did my part for the war effort. I'm glad I did.

Olive: We had heard, long before December seventh, that someday Japan would be at war with the United States. We didn't really take it seriously, though. The largest ethnic group of people in the islands at that time was Japanese, and we were all friendly neighbors. We couldn't imagine being at war with them.

I remember about a year or so before the Pearl Harbor attack, we had a practice blackout. We all cooperated. We lived on a steep dead-end street at the top of which was a huge water tank. The top was planted in grass, and by mounting the steps leading to the top, we had a beautiful view of Honolulu--from Diamond Head almost to Pearl Harbor. On the night of the practice blackout, we invited some friends to come to our house so we could all go up to the top of the water tank and watch the lights go out. It was a fantastic sight. At the appointed time, Honolulu suddenly went dark. We remarked at the time--thank goodness this isn't the real thing. Everything looked so spooky and eerie. Little did we know then that blackout would soon become a reality--a way of life.

On Saturday night, December sixth, I attended a Japanese wedding and reception with my friend, Marie Vare. A friend of hers was getting married and she wanted me to go with her, so I did. We sat through many speeches--all in Japanese--as we ate our wedding feast. It was a relaxed, joyful occasion, and everyone seemed to be having a good time. For those people who would question the loyalty of our local Japanese people--or dare to think that they knew beforehand that an attack was planned by their homeland--I ask: Would they be having a wedding feast at that time with so much hope, happiness, and in such a relaxed atmosphere? I used to argue with people about the loyalty of the nisei Japanese when I first came to the mainland in December 1944. They were loyal Americans. While perhaps a few oldtimers who had been born in Japan might have had mixed feelings about the war, I know for a fact that all of the Japanese I knew were American to the core.

I worked at the University of Hawaii, where so many of our students were young Japanese men. To prove their loyalty, they tried to join the U.S. army, but they were not allowed to. I guess the government felt that they would not make good soldiers if they had to fight against fellow Japanese. So they formed an all-Japanese working unit called the Varsity Victory Volunteers and they did manual labor. They dug trenches and built things--all the dirty work--so that the soldiers could concentrate on more important things. I was impressed by that. Later, when they could join the army, they volunteered in droves and formed the famed 100th infantry and the 442nd, and they did themselves proud fighting in Italy.

> " . . . all of the Japanese I knew were
> American to the core. . . Some of the
> Japanese boys that I knew from the
> university were killed. "

Some of the Japanese boys that I knew from the university were killed over there. And the important thing about it is--they didn't have to go. They could have sat the war out in Honolulu and let the other guys fight and get killed. So many of them gave their lives for their country.

Anyway, on the morning of December seventh, Nelson had left early to play golf with a friend, Charlie Duck. I usually go to church on Sundays, but on this particular morning, I decided not to go, as I was not feeling well. Perhaps it was something I ate at the wedding the previous night that didn't agree with me. Anyway, about eight o'clock, I heard this pounding at my door. I went to the door and it was Violet Borges, our neighbor, calling out to me. "Olive, Olive, put on your radio," she said, "the Japanese are attacking Pearl Harbor." I thought she must be crazy. But sure enough, I turned on the radio and the governor was telling the people to be calm, that we were being attacked by airplanes from Japan. He said to remain in our homes and to keep the radio on for further instructions. Then, shortly, they started calling for emergency assistance, and they announced that Pearl Harbor workers should report to their jobs.

Then the phone rang and a frantic Lucy Duck was telling me all about it and saying that she was going to drive to the golf course to pick up our husbands, and tell them they had to go down to Pearl Harbor immediately.

Nelson came home soon after that and I pleaded with him not to go. I remember saying, "What can you do?" But nothing I could say would stop him. This was exciting--high adventure! So he jumped in his car and was off. I ran outside to see if I could see anything happening, when a Japanese plane flew right over my head. I could see the rising sun insignia on its wings. Then, as I looked toward the Honolulu Stadium, I saw a whole section of stores go up in smoke. A bomb had fallen there. This was the closest I would come to falling bombs. And, as I looked off toward Pearl Harbor, past Honolulu harbor, I saw planes flying. There were many of them and they looked like they were engaging in dog-fights. And smoke was now coming up from here and there in the distance.

It just seemed a short time later when Nelson came back home, saying that the roads were blocked and they couldn't get through. Then the announcement came back on the radio that the roads were now clear and Pearl Harbor workers should try again to get down there. So, of course, Nelson took off again.

So I sat at home, worrying about his safety, and that of my younger brother, Ricky, who had gone to Pearl Harbor earlier that morning to work. I was just stunned, but I don't think I was really that afraid. It was more of a shock than fear.

Later, Marie and her husband, Al, and their two-year-old son arrived at our house. Marie was in shock. They lived out near Koko Head, practically on the beach. They slept in that Sunday morning and after breakfast, decided to go to Fort Shafter to visit a friend of theirs. As they were driving along the highway, they noticed many army trucks racing along, filled with soldiers. Things just didn't look natural to them, but they just dismissed it as army maneuvers. Al was an ex-army man. They drove along--a distance of perhaps twenty miles--passing all kinds of military vehicles. When they got to Fort Shafter, the guard at the gate shouted, "Where do you think you're going?" They answered, "To see the Cyrs." He said, "You won't find anyone at home because they're all in the air-raid shelters." Then he realized that they didn't know what was happening. "Good God, people, don't you know there's a war going on--the Japanese are attacking us?"

He told them to take to the hills. Since we lived on a hill, they came directly to our house. Marie and her family stayed with us for six weeks, until she and her son evacuated to Washington state where she had an uncle living there. She was pregnant with her second child and they were advising all pregnant women to leave the islands if they could.

Anyway, Marie and I sat by the radio that afternoon and waited for further instructions. Soon the word came that the water had been poisoned. We were told, "Don't drink any water without boiling it first." But, that was soon rescinded. Seems it was just a rumor.

Then we were told that we would have complete blackout that night and it would last until further notice. The islands were placed under military rule, and anyone breaking the law would have to answer to the provost marshal. I nailed army blankets over the windows in the kitchen and bathroom. We had a central hallway in our house--all the rooms opened out from this hall--and by closing all the doors, we could have the hall light on. This became our living room for weeks. We sat on the floor at night and read the paper. Then we would go into the dark living room and listen to the radio.

Nelson came home after dark and told me what he had gone through. I couldn't believe it. My brother Ricky still hadn't come home. We didn't know what happened to him. Nelson had to get up early again, the next morning, and report back to Pearl Harbor.

Just after he left--I guess it was about six a.m.--Marie and I were sitting in the living room, looking out at the dark city below. Suddenly we saw three large planes flying over Fort Ruger at the base of Diamond Head and bullets came flying up from the ground. We could see these tracer bullets light up the dark morning. We were panic-stricken. I said, "Marie, they're back, they're back." We were just scared as we could be. And Nelson had already gone back to Pearl Harbor. I thought to myself, "Oh no, another disaster at Pearl Harbor." Then, suddenly, the shooting stopped and the planes were still flying toward Pearl Harbor. We found out later that those were our own planes coming in from California-- coming to our aid. Good thing the ground fire didn't hit them. This was just one more example of poor communications.

Late that night Ricky came home. He was covered with soot from head to toe. He was just all black. He said, "I've been carrying the dead all day--bringing out the bodies. Smoke was everywhere, burning oil, ships sunk. You don't know how horrible it is down there. Just horrible."

Most people in Honolulu had no idea how much damage occurred at Pearl Harbor that morning. All information was shut off from the general public. They didn't want Japan to know what devastation they had caused. But because Nelson and Ricky were right there and saw what was taking place, we knew more than most people about what had happened.

" Most people in Honolulu had no idea how much damage occurred at Pearl Harbor that morning. "

Things got more and more hectic as time went on. Nelson began working nights and I worked days so we never had any time together. We couldn't do our food shopping--you had to be there at the stores when the food came in, or you were out of luck. So I arranged to work part-time at the University. I worked eight to noon, four days a week, and a full day on Wednesdays, I think it was, so I didn't have to come in at all on Saturdays.

We used to work half-a-day on Saturdays and, invariably, there would be an air raid alert on Saturdays, just before quitting time at noon. We would have to leave our offices and go into these big air raid shelters--they had shelters built all over the campus. They had mounded the tops over and planted morning glories over them. Anyway, it rained often in Manoa Valley and all the rain would go down into these trenches so that most of them had eight inches of water at the bottom.

I had a phobia about being in a shelter with dirt all above us--and if a bomb fell on us, we would be buried alive. So this friend of mine at work agreed with me that when we had an air raid alert, we would not go down into those bomb shelters. Instead, we would run down to the basement of the building--Hawaii Hall was where we worked--and we would stand between the student lockers. After all, they were steel, "so the bombs can't reach us here," we would say. We stayed there until we heard the "all clear." But this happened frequently on Saturdays and sometimes it was 12:30 or later before we were able to come out of the basement and leave the office for the day. And, of course, we didn't get paid extra for having to stay later. So I arranged my work hours so that I could be home on Saturdays.

From where we lived, we had a panoramic view of the ocean, from Koko Head to Honolulu Harbor, so we could see when there were ships coming in. On that day, we knew food would be delivered to the stores. So we would watch for the ships, then rush to the stores that afternoon to see what had come in.

I remember we didn't grow regular onions in Hawaii, brown onions. In fact, one time at the University of Hawaii cafeteria, someone had taken an onion and carved it into a beautiful rose. It was really pretty. It was sitting on top of the cash register next to a sign that read, "In case you have forgotten what an onion looks like." We had no onions for years. We had green onions--they would grow in Hawaii--but not the brown ones.

And I remember, too, that all our paper money was exchanged for bills that had the word "HAWAII" stamped across it. They did this in case we were invaded and the Japanese got hold of all this American money. In case that happened, the Hawaii money would not be honored at U.S. banks. So the Japanese would not be able to use the captured money.

225

THE HAWAII DOLLAR -- *In the event Hawaii was occupied by Japanese forces, the currency bearing the HAWAII overprint would identify captured American money and would not be considered legal tender on the mainland. All paper money was replaced with these special bills in July 1942 and about $200 million in old money was destroyed in a crematorium.(Photo courtesy of the Rodriggs family collection)*

R & R -- Civilians enjoyed Waikiki beach for wartime "rest and recreation," too. This 1944 snapshot pictures (in foreground, from left) Nelson and Olive Rodrigues and Nelson's sister, Nettie. The three went to the beach with Lt. Abel Dolim, on leave from the 8th Air Force in England. Dolim took the picture. (Courtesy Dolim family photo collection)

Saturday nights we would have our poker games at our house. We would close the windows so that we would be blacked out, and then we'd play poker. Of course, in those days, most everybody smoked.

" We stood in line . . . for just about
everything. But we didn't complain. We had
gone through much and survived. I guess
we were just glad to be alive. "

After a while, the smoke became unbearable. I would finally say, "Ye gods, everybody, this place is so thick with smoke you could cut it with a knife." So we would turn the lights out and open up the windows to air out the place. If you happened to be outside in the yard at that time, I'm sure you would think the place was on fire. Smoke would come pouring out the windows like Hernando's Hide-a-way. Then, after a short breather, we would close the windows, turn on the lights, and continue the game. That was our entertainment during the war years.

We stood in line, it seems, for just about everything. But we didn't complain. We had gone through much and survived. I guess we were just glad to be alive.

Nelson transferred from Pearl Harbor to the Alameda Naval Air Station in the San Francisco Bay Area and he and Olive left Hawaii in December 1944, nine months before the war ended. Following the war, Nelson and Olive went into business--a bar for about a year and a baby shop for about three years. In 1950, when the Korean war started, Nelson was asked to return to the Naval Air Station. He retired in 1965, following thirty total years of government service. Olive taught school in California, in the Hayward Unified School district, for twelve years and retired in 1967. They live, in retirement, in a mobile home park in Hayward, California.

Community Bomb Shelters

THEY'RE SPLINTER PROOF -- Over six hundred community bomb shelters were constructed undergound all around Oahu by the Office of Civilian Defense. This one, at Kalakaua Junior High School was built from wood designated as splinter proof. Upon completion, the shelter was covered with soil and planted with greenery. (Hawaii State Archives)

THEY'RE SMOKELESS, TOO -- An unidentified young woman reminds everyone that no smoking is permitted inside a community bomb shelter. This publicity photograph, which shows the starkness of the shelter, was taken at Kalakaua Junior High School. (Hawaii State Archives)

Esther Oyer Hoag

Her parents came to Hawaii from California to build the Kakaako Mission for the Atherton Estate in 1927. Irene and Alvin Oyer had three children, all born in Honolulu. Esther was born in 1929 and Ivan was born three-and-a-half years later. When the war broke out, little Paul was still in diapers and a little over a year old. The Oyer family lived at 1828 Young Street, at the corner of Young and Artesian. Esther, twelve at the time, was in the seventh grade at Robert Louis Stevenson School.

It was a Sunday morning, December 7, 1941, and we lived at what had been called Mission Church, which is now the Olivet Baptist Church. The front part of the church was our back wall. We had another family living in the back, and on Sundays, my father would take the cars out of our garage and put them on the street. He would then bring in some plants and make a nice little area for Sunday School for the children of the church. The adults would be in another part for services.

My father had training as a minister, but he wasn't one. He worked at Pearl Harbor at the time. He was an estimator in the planning department. He would estimate how much it would cost to fix the ships. My mother had been a part of the civil defense program in first aid training. We already had gallon jars of flour, rice, and beans--a month's worth--in storage in case an emergency occurred. You see, we expected something to happen, but the thought was that it would probably happen internally, through sabotage. Nobody believed we would be attacked from the outside.

In fact, I remember my father saying that we had this secret weapon that would prevent us from ever being attacked from the outside. "They can't get within miles of us without our finding out about it," he said. He was referring to radar, of course, but he never identified it at all because it was supposed to be a military secret.

That's the reason why the U.S. had all their airplanes parked together out on the fields at Hickam and Wheeler that morning--to guard against sabotage. The planes were in groups, surrounded with sandbags and guards so that they would be safe against sabotage. Of course, when the Japanese planes came in, they were prime targets all bunched together and most of them were destroyed in one fell swoop. The Japanese just mowed them down.

Anyway, that morning we heard the commotion and the sirens but didn't pay too much attention to them. We had the radio on and they were asking all firemen and policemen to report to duty immediately. The next thing, they were asking all people who worked at the navy yard and Hickam to report immediately. I ran out to tell my dad what they said and he said, "Oh, well, this is just a drill." We had just had Fleet Week the week before, and he said, "It's just a drill. Getting Sunday School ready is more important right now." He was putting a row of potted plants in the building.

When the announcer said, "This is the real McCoy," my folks misinterpreted it to mean "decoy," and were sure it was just a practice exercise. Then the radio mentioned the symbol of the rising sun could be seen on these planes. Webley Edwards was the radio announcer at the time. They didn't say Japan, they just said the symbol of the rising sun. I remember I grabbed a dictionary to look at the picture of the flags to find out who the rising sun was. That's when I saw that it was Japan. And we realized that this was the real thing.

My mother rushed over to the first aid station at Lunalilo School, a few blocks away, to await further instructions. That was her civil defense location. Later on, she told us that the school had caught on fire and the first case brought to the first aid station was an old Japanese woman. They brought her body over in a box, a victim of the bombing at McCully, which was just a block-and-a-half from where we lived.

Dad ran in to shower before taking off for Pearl Harbor. Just then the phone rang and it was someone from Pearl asking for Dad. I said, "He's in the shower." They said, "Tell him to come down here immediately." And he did. So there I was, left alone with my two brothers and not knowing where to turn.

We still had the radio on. Something I will never forget was when Webley Edwards, the radio announcer said, "...and now, ladies and gentlemen, your National Anthem. And you may **never** hear it again." I still get goose bumps thinking about it. It was the most beautiful music I had ever heard. We stood at attention. It was really a scratchy record, but it was the most beautiful I've ever heard. And, I cannot to this day

LUNALILO SCHOOL BURNS -- A half hour after the fire at King and McCully streets, the roof of nearby Lunalilo School burst into flames. It was believed that the fire was caused from sparks from the fires at King and McCully. First aid personnel were forced out of the school building and had to treat eighteen casualties under coconut trees. (*Star Bulletin* December 7, 1941; War Depository Collection, University of Hawaii)

DAMAGE AFTERMATH -- Lunalilo School suffered extensive damage to the library, roof, and several classrooms. This photo was taken six days later, December 13, 1941, and clearly shows the damage, which was estimated to cost $40,000 to repair at that time. (Board of Water Supply photograph; War Depository Collection, University of Hawaii)

sit down when the National Anthem is played. I even try to turn TV off before the channel goes off the air, because they play the Star Spangled Banner and I will get out of bed and stand at attention. The memory of that moment has never left me.

The lady that lived on the property in the back, Mrs. Mary Tyssowski, was a teacher at Lunalilo School. They had owned the church property at one time. She was a widow and lived there with her daughter, Ada, who was a few months older than me. She started hollering to us, "You kids come over here. Your place is nothing but termites. My place has a corrugated iron roof, it's much safer here." She was just hysterical.

So we ran over there and my brother looked up through the avocado trees and he said, "It's got a big orange ball on it." So he really did see the plane coming over us. I didn't.

My dad had come back home and said he couldn't get through to Pearl Harbor. He said that they had strafed the car in front of him and he knew there were several people killed. The phone rang and they were asking about him again. He talked to them and when he hung up, he said, "They told me to get there if I have to walk." So he left again. He left the car home and took public transportation. He caught the last train through to Pearl Harbor. They stopped running trains after that because it was too dangerous. Of course, I envisioned all kinds of things happening to him.

" . . . it looked like God had dropped all the red, yellow, and orange paint in the world on the sky. . . and I thought we were surrounded with flames. "

Mrs. Tyssowski decided that the car should be brought into the garage. And she was too nervous to do it. She wouldn't even go out in the yard. So she suggested that I go out there and drive our car in off the street. I had never driven a car before. When I went out to get into the car, a neighbor hollered to me, "Look, look, look." I looked up and the only way I can describe what I saw is that it looked like God had dropped all the red, yellow, and orange paint in the world on the sky. The whole sky was just brightly colored and I thought we were surrounded with flames.

So I dashed back in the house. Was I scared. I had no parents around; I had this woman who was hysterical; and I had two younger brothers for whom I was responsible. We found out later that the flames were from the bombing and fires at McCully and King, a block-and-a-half away.

Later on, Mrs. Tyssowski insisted that the car still had to be brought in off the street. There were no longer flames in the sky, so I went out there again. I was amazed at myself, because I drove that car in the garage and had no trouble with the clutch or anything. Of course, a few years later, when I was learning how to drive, the clutch was just awful.

We couldn't get a word out to our relatives all that day. You couldn't call the mainland. You couldn't get through on the phone. But we could make local calls. So I was sent over to our house, because Mrs. Tyssowski didn't have a phone. And nobody would dare go outside of the house except Esther. I was to call some people who were supposed to be preaching at the mission.

"BOMBING" DAMAGE — A block of stores and dwellings occupied by thirty-one families at King and McCully streets were destroyed by what was believed to be incendiary bombs. However, Honolulu Fire Department officials reached the conclusion that U.S. projectiles which missed their targets, fell on this civilian complex and started the blaze. (Board of Water Supply photograph; War Depository Collection, University of Hawaii)

Edwin and Mary Ellen Dozier were Southern Baptist missionaries from Japan who moved to Honolulu to work in the church, because they could no longer work in Japan. I was to call the Rev. Victor Koon, who was also a missionary, who worked in China. The Koons' son answered the phone and told me that they picked Edwin Dozier up to be a translator, since he spoke fluent Japanese. Our government was out picking up Japanese people who had been in Japan in recent years, or who had a lot to do with the Japanese public, such as Buddhist priests, etc. I remember Rev. Koon's wife got angry that Vic was telling me this. I guess it was supposed to be a secret. I could hear her saying, "Who are you talking to? Don't tell anybody about that."

At about two o'clock that afternoon, our neighbor, Bobby Soong, came by. He said that he saw my mother at Lunalilo School and he wanted to come by to tell us that she was all right. I said, "Well, why shouldn't she be all right?" He said, "Because we've been bombed out." It still hadn't hit me that we were all in grave danger at that time. He had a stretcher and he had someone else with him. "We're out looking for bodies," he told me. Then I really got scared.

It was getting late and we hadn't heard from my mother or father. Earlier that morning, Mother had put on some lunch in the oven and I turned it off before leaving our house. We didn't think about food, but we did have something there to eat if and when we felt like it. We were all frightened and uptight and Mrs. Tyssowski read the Psalms. We had the radio on all the time and they told us that we were not to burn any lights when it got dark. So we started preparing for the black out. We put up newspapers on the windows and hung blankets over them. We were afraid our electric lights would be too bright and show outside. So, we got out birthday candles. When one candle would burn down, we'd light another one. We went through a lot of candles that evening.

Mother finally came back, long after it got dark. She had been at the first-aid station at the school all that time. She came over to Mrs. Tyssowski's house, where she knew we would be. We had to blow out the candle to open the door and let her in. Then when we closed the door after her, we lit the candle again. It wasn't much light, but we were still scared that it could be seen from the outside.

Mrs. Tyssowski's daughter, Ada, was my age although she was more immature than I was. She went to bed and Ivan went to bed, and, of course, little Paul had been asleep for a while. Then we heard the whistle of something falling outside. It might have been an anti-aircraft shell, a bomb, or something, but we could hear that whistle coming our way. Then, we heard this tremendous thud. It shook the house. It was the most horrible sound. It happened about 9:30 that evening. Mother said, "A bomb." And we all fell to the floor, scared to death. Mrs. Tyssowski started praying again, out loud. We put out the candle and looked outside. We couldn't see a thing, and we were too frightened to walk outside.

" Then we heard the whistle of . . . an anti-aircraft shell, a bomb, or something . . . coming our way. Then we heard this tremendous thud. It shook the house. It was the most horrible sound. "

We found out later that it was a bomb, but it didn't explode. It was behind us, very close. There was a little lane next to us and it fell on the other side of that lane. The army came by to check it out. They thought it was an incendiary bomb. We were all too scared to go out and watch. I never did go over there. I was too frightened. But one neighbor told our neighbor what it was.

We were worried about Dad. He hadn't come home yet and it was very late. We all stayed together in the front room and tried to get some sleep. Mrs. Tyssowski had a strong short-wave radio and it was on all night, even though local radio stations had gone off the air. We heard faint Japanese talking over the radio and at first I thought that they had taken over the local radio station. It was frightening. Later on, though, Tokyo Rose would broadcast on that same short wave signal. Since there was no local radio going that night, we could have been listening to Radio Tokyo.

I don't know how much sleep we got that night, but we were up very early the next morning. Dad still wasn't home. We were in Mrs. Tyssowki's little kitchen, getting some breakfast, when we heard planes again. We just stood there, frozen. But it turned out that they were our own planes coming in. When there was no action, we realized that they were ours, coming in from the mainland.

Since Mom had to go back to the first-aid station, she said to tell Dad to come over to the school and see her when he got back. Mom left. We were still too scared to go outside. Then, the radio came back on. And it was President Roosevelt who was talking. He talked about the attacks at Pearl Harbor and the Philippines. About that time, Dad walked in. Was I happy to see him. It was the first time we knew he was alive. I told him that Mom wanted him to go over to the school as soon as he came home. He said, "I already did, now be quiet and let me hear what the President is saying." After that, he went over to our house and took a nap. Then he had to go back to Pearl Harbor.

The next day was Monday and we were able to send telegrams to the mainland, but you had to go downtown to Bishop Street, near the Young Hotel. So, that's where Esther was sent to send a telegram to her grandparents in California to notify them that the family was okay. I stood in line to take care of this. Then, after that, I got back at the end of the line to send another telegram to Mrs. Tyssowski's family. And all the time I was standing out in the street, in line, I was frightened.

They closed the banks right away, but in a couple of days, we were told that we could get three hundred dollars out of the bank. Mother wrote me a check and I went downtown again, this time to the Bank of Hawaii, to pull out our money. Then, of course, I had to go to Bishop Bank and get Mrs. Tyssowski's money out, too. I found out later that the three hundred dollars which I had in my wallet--which I was supposed to watch--was all the money my folks had in the world. That was their entire bank account. It was my responsibility and I was barely twelve years old. My birthday was the month before, November third.

I also was instructed to put together a suitcase packed with clothes and canned goods for my brothers and myself. Mother had said, in case we were invaded, "Figure a place to run, to be safe." I remember I picked the Manoa Falls area because there was a lot of greenery there so we could survive for a long time. You had to cross the stream seven times to get there. It was cool and damp with lush greenery. (It's where the bird park is now). I figured it would take the Japanese a while to get back up there and that maybe we could get lost in all that brush.

I told my mother, "Well, I'm going to Manoa Falls." And she said, "You keep your brothers together. You're responsible for them." She also told me, "If you never see us again, if something should happen to us, you and your brothers go to California. And if California is taken over," she said, "go to Lincoln, Nebraska, because we have relatives over there, too. And, those of us who survive this thing will meet there." I was twelve years old, going on thirty. Of course, we never had to evacuate, thank God. But little Esther grew up overnight because of that experience.

Dad was working twelve hours a day, seven days a week, and didn't have time to build a bomb shelter in our yard. So he hired someone to do it for us. My brother Ivan, Ada, and I collected the corrugated iron roofing from the burned out houses at the corner of King and McCully. We carried all we could, two kids on one end and one on the other. There were big holes through the roofing where shrapnel and shells had fallen. We made several trips and I remember our muscles would ache so much, carrying that stuff. But it might save our lives. That was the idea. So, we brought home the material that would become the roof of our new bomb shelter.

Mom went to the first-aid station every day, until sometime in February. That's when my dad said, "That's enough. We haven't had an emergency since December seventh and you should stay home with the kids."

When we went back to school, they wanted us to do something for the war effort. So I went to work in the afternoons for the civil defense at Kaahumanu School. I filed papers, and did whatever office work they wanted me to do. That only lasted two or three weeks, though. Then, an osteopath--a doctor friend of my mother--asked if I would help out at the Health Spot shoe store she was setting up. Her only employee, Robert, wanted to go into the service, and she needed someone to take his place. So I did, and I really felt important. I had made it possible for one person to go into the army. I worked there until after the war was over, after school and on Saturdays. I did the books, banking, and even learned to fit shoes. I eventually got paid twenty-five dollars a month for doing that. That was a lot of money in those days for a youngster.

The army had taken over half of Stevenson School. So we went half days, six days a week. My brother got the afternoon shift at Lincoln School and I went to Stevenson in the mornings. We stayed at Mrs. Tyssowski's house until the first of February. I'll never forget the first night we moved back into our house. That was Dad's birthday. (Dad always slept at our house, while we stayed over at Mrs. Tyssowski's. Her house was smaller and we felt cozier there).

So here we were, back in our large house, sitting at the kitchen table in the blacked out room, when we heard something hit the clothesline outside. We knew someone was coming. Dad said, "I'll turn out the lights. Esther, you get the door." I went through the darkness in the living room to the front door, and opened it. There was this huge figure in the doorway, a silhouette of a man with a helmet on, and this bayonet pointing at me. I threw my hands up and froze. I couldn't talk. I couldn't move. "Esther, this is Johnny," he said. He was a serviceman who came to the church services and was on patrol in the area. My father came to the door and let him in. We went back to the kitchen, closed the doors, and turned on the light. They said I was white as a sheet.

Then, shortly, they issued gas masks to everyone. I remember standing in line at Lunalilo School to get our gas masks. We had a "bunny mask" for little Paul. My dad was issued a different mask, with a hose down to the canister, like the military used. I remember we studied about the different gasses and what you would do and how you would tell if you smelled gas.

One time, at Stevenson school, we had to go in a room with our gas masks on to see if they leaked. They put tear gas in the room. You stayed in there for a while to see if your gas mask worked and then they made you take your mask off and walk out, so you could get a fear of the gas. I got a big whiff of it and I cried much longer than the rest of the kids. My eyes were so red and sore.

We often had air raid alerts. Whenever we had one, my job was to fill the sink and the bathtub with water, in case we needed the water for emergency use. Everybody else would rush down to the safety of the bomb shelter while Esther was still in the house, filling the tub. I remember one time I must have been extra scared, because when I went down into the shelter, my dad said, "Oh, the bathtub can't be full of water already."

"It's full," I said. "It can't hold any more water." So he let me stay down there. When the air raid was over and we all went back into the house, he called me into the bathroom. "Come here and bring a ruler," he said. I had an inch-and-a-half of water in the tub. You see, when we had an alert, everybody in the city filled their tubs, so the water flowed so slowly, you'd get just a trickle. I got the worst lecture you could imagine. I was told that I could have killed the whole family, because there wasn't enough water for us to live on, if we had to.

My job was also to change the water we had in the bomb shelter. We would put a little Clorox in it to purify it. And I would change it periodically, marking the date on the jar. We also had some food down there, and something to start a fire.

I remember we started a victory garden. We had always thought you couldn't raise any vegetables in Hawaii because of the insects. I remember, the only fresh vegetables we had before the war was lettuce from Manoa, because that was the only thing grown locally. Everything else came in by ship from the mainland. So people started growing things, because we didn't know if we would have any fresh foodstuffs shipped over to us. We planted things in part of our yard. We never did have too big a garden, because Mom and Dad were busy working. But that became our evening activity, after work. People went to work on their victory gardens in the evenings. That's when they found out that they could grow a lot of things in Hawaii. The hardest thing I had to learn was eating spinach fresh. I had never had anything but canned spinach. And I loved canned spinach.

There were community victory gardens all over town. The Central Union Church grounds was all victory gardens. You could go over there and stake out a plot and work your own garden for your family.

I used to visit our Japanese neighbors across the street. When I'd go over there, I can remember someone would always be combing "mama-san's" hair, putting this black stuff on it. Their daughter was in her early thirties and she was a school teacher. Her father had set up an insurance business in a garage at their residence. He was taken away on December seventh because he had recently been to Japan. He was gone for the entire war, interned in the mainland. Nobody in the family ever went into his insurance office. That just wasn't done.

When the war was over, he was coming back to Hawaii. So the kids, including his daughter, decided that while they had never been in dad's office, they would go in and clean up things for him--the four years of dust. They were shocked when they found a shortwave radio and other evidence that he was actually a spy for Japan. His daughter was so angry and hurt, she cried. She came over to my mother and said, "Mrs. Oyer, what do I do? I am an American and I hate people like that, but he is my father." My mother said, "The war is over and he is your father."

We had an army officer who came to our church. In fact, he taught a class at the church. His name was Lt. Rush McDonald. One day he called to say that he was shipping out. I answered the phone and he said, "I want you to know that I volunteered for a special mission. We have been told that it is very dangerous and that we might not make it back. But we're going to stop the Japanese fleet at Midway." He said that the Japanese were heading back to Hawaii and they had to be stopped at Midway. He was a pilot. We found out later that he shot down several zeroes, but he was killed. And I remember thinking, why would God take someone like Rush McDonald? He was such an outstanding young man. But, that's war, I guess.

I will never forget an incident that happened before the war. There was a lot of talk about the possibility of war with Japan. A Japanese friend of ours, Mae Nakaoka, said to my mother, "Mrs. Oyer, if Japan and America ever go to war, I'm going to be a person without a country." I was quite little then, but I was touched by that statement and I asked her why. "Because," she said, "America won't want me and I won't want Japan." And that was the plight of many Americans of Japanese ancestry during those years.

> " . . . she said, 'America won't want me and I won't want Japan.' And that was the plight of many Americans of Japanese ancestry during those years. "

The memories of those years will be with me as long as I live. In fact, the whistle sound made by anti-aircraft missiles, or bombs--or whatever they were--haunted me for years. I could not stand seeing a war movie--and didn't know why--until I discovered that it was the whistling sound of the projectiles that affected me. It would put me on edge and I couldn't sit through it. I would actually have to leave the room or theater, I was so upset.

Another thing living through the war years in Hawaii did for me--it made me more patriotic than ever. I can't talk about those years without feeling great pride in our country. And, I can't talk about it without getting goose-bumps.

I learned responsibility and accountability in just a few hours on December 7, 1941. And I grew up overnight. I just skipped over my teen years in a few short hours. I remember my mother mentioned that to me just before she died. She said, "One minute I had little Esther. Then, before I knew it, I had big Esther. Little Esther was gone forever."

Esther Oyer graduated from Roosevelt High School in 1947. She attended Westmont College in Santa Barbara, California, earning a BA in education in 1951. She later received a master's in Administration and Supervision from Greeley Colorado State College. She married Mitchell Hoag, an air force sergeant, in 1953. Mitch and Esther had two daughters, Martha and Carolyn. In 1955, they left Hawaii so Mitch could continue his education. Mitch was a teacher in the San Lorenzo (California) School District for twenty-five years. He died in 1989. Esther has worked for the Newark (California) Unified School District since 1964. She serves as a school principal and as coordinator of federal and state projects for the school district. Esther has two grandchildren, Carrie Lynn, and Christopher David Morrison.

Business (not) as Usual

Christmas shopping was dramatically curtailed in December 1941 as business hours were shortened to allow people sufficient time to get home before the blackout and curfew. The Christmas lights and holiday decorations that had already been hung in the downtown area were hurriedly removed. Sandbags, taped store windows, and community bomb shelters were a somber reminder that business was not as usual.

WINDOW-SHOPPING -- *Although a bit of a challenge, these women still were able to window-shop through the taped, plate glass windows in downtown Honolulu. The safety measure would prevent flying glass in the event of another attack. (**Star Bulletin** Jan. 2, 1942; War Depository Collection, University of Hawaii)*

Ted T. Tsukiyama

His parents both came to Hawaii from Japan. Ted, the fourth of five children, was born in Honolulu in 1920. The Tsukiyama family lived at 1042 17th Avenue, in Kaimuki. Ted attended Aliiolani Elementary School. He went to Roosevelt from the seventh grade on until graduation from high school in 1939. At the outset of the war, Ted was a junior at the University of Hawaii, living at home, and about a week away from his twenty-first birthday.

There was a junior class dance the night before at the University of Hawaii, so I came home late. I was sleeping it off on Sunday morning and I was awakened and disturbed by this constant rumbling of thunder. So I got up and went outside and the sky toward Pearl Harbor was very dark, black with smoke, punctuated by puffs of white aerial bursts. I thought to myself, "They're sure making this maneuver look real." We were used to maneuvers at that time, but I thought that this one sounded particularly intense. So we turned on the radio and that's when we heard the announcer screaming that we've been attacked by Japanese enemy planes and to take cover. "This is the real McCoy," he said, "get off the streets." Those words pierced me like a piece of shrapnel. I was numb. I heard, but I could not comprehend.

Not too long after that, I heard the announcer say, "All members of the University ROTC report to the campus immediately." So that's when I put on my uniform, took the family car, and rushed up to the university campus to the ROTC barracks. I was in the advanced program at that time. ROTC was normally taken for only two years. When you take ROTC in the junior and senior years, then you are working for a commission. So I was a non-commissioned officer in the ROTC, a first sergeant in Company B, 1st Battalion.

When I got there, many others were also reporting, all in uniform. The staff was grimly and feverishly inserting the firing pins into our Springfield rifles and issuing live ammunition. I think it was just five clips, but it was real live ammunition. We had never shot the rifles, actually. In fact, we were scheduled to get rifle and maneuvers instruction at Schofield the following summer.

I don't recall any registration or sign-ups, no swearing in nor any formalities. We were just members of an ROTC unit, responding to the call in defense of our country, as we were trained to do, just like any American soldier or sailor reporting to his battle station.

Our first mission, with rifles and real bullets, was to deploy in the woods across Manoa stream and repel the Japanese paratroopers who had reportedly landed on St. Louis Heights. We had a company of several hundred people. We were to prevent the enemy from advancing into the city. All the theory we had learned suddenly became the real thing. With pounding hearts we moved to the south end of the campus and scanned St. Louis Heights for the enemy. Dole Street was not there at that time. There were carnation farms at that location, just above the quarry. We went way back deep, across Cooke Field. To put it bluntly, we were scared witless! We didn't know what to expect. It was not beyond the realm of possibility that the enemy had landed and was invading the city. But as we thought of the sneak attack that morning, a wave of fury and anger swept over us. There was no doubt or indecision as we advanced. It was going to be "either them or us."

But, fortunately, the enemy never showed. This was just another of the many groundless rumors that spread across Hawaii that day. About noon, we got recalled and went back to ROTC headquarters.

This exercise lasted a couple of hours that morning. I remember having mixed feelings of tremendous excitement, anxiety and fear, particularly being one of Japanese ancestry. We couldn't help having this foreboding feeling of, "Gee, what's going to happen to us now? What's going to happen to our local Japanese, particularly people like our parents who were born in Japan?" I thought about a brother of mine, too. He was stuck in Japan when this thing happened. As it turned out, we never heard from him for four or five years.

For those first few hours, we had no official military status or standing, federal or territorial. We were just ROTC boys heeding our country's call to arms. That afternoon, however, martial law was declared, so the Governor commissioned the ROTC into the Hawaii Territorial Guard. So we were an active ROTC unit for only a few hours.

Significantly, though, as we found out later, the University of Hawaii

ROTC unit reporting to duty that morning and engaging in the "campaign of St. Louis Heights," was the first and only ROTC unit in the United States to enter active war service in World War II, and for which it now is honored with a battle streamer.

Little did we realize, then, that responding to the call to duty by the University ROTC regiment--comprised mostly of Japanese-Americans--would set into motion a chain of events during the course of World War II. These events would lead to a reopened opportunity for the American nisei to fight for his country. This ultimately would culminate--four years later--in the all-nisei 442nd Combat Team becoming the most decorated military unit of its size in the U. S. Army.

Anyway, we were now members of the Hawaii Territorial Guard, the HTG. They trucked us down to the National Guard Armory, where our state capitol stands today. We were issued those round tin helmets and gas masks and were immediately assigned to guard Iolani Palace, the Hawaiian Electric Company, Mutual Telephone, the Board of Water Supply, and other utility installations.

Our Company B was stationed in the Dole Cannery warehouse where we guarded the industrial factories, gasoline tanks, and Honolulu Harbor, armed only with puny Springfield rifles. Fortunately, no bombs dropped on the Iwilei area. The enemy never landed. The important thing was that we had responded to our country's call to arms. We were accepted. We were proud to be in uniform, serving our country in its dire hour of need.

" I'll never forget that night of December seventh. It was the longest, the darkest, and the wildest night that I can recall. "

But I'll never forget that night of December seventh. It was the longest, the darkest, and the wildest night that I can recall. We laid down on the Armory gymnasium floor, physically and emotionally exhausted, but sleep would not come. All kinds of emotions tumbled around inside us. It was terrifying. I remember the sounds of airplanes overhead. The machine gun on top of the Board of Water Supply building let loose with a barrage of bullets. It turned out to be our own planes, but that's what you did under those circumstances. You shot first

and asked questions later. Foremost was fear that the enemy would attack us again at any time. There were nerve-wracking sounds of occasional gun fire outside. The enemy was nowhere around, but a lot of dead dogs, pets and cattle were found on the island the next morning. Anything that moved was fired at in the dark. It was complete panic and fear. We didn't know what to expect.

A trigger-happy story also happened in our own outfit. We opened the HTG to "locals" and picked up some volunteers from downtown a short time later. They had no ROTC or military training at all. They were hurriedly sworn into action and taught how to carry out sentry duty—first to call, "Halt!" three times and then call, "Advance to be recognized." One of our brave officers made his rounds that night checking on his sentries. At one station, he was challenged with three rapid halts, followed by silence and the rattling of the bolt mechanism on the rifle. The officer yelled out, "All right, soldier, what do you do next?" And out of the darkness came this frightened Hawaiian voice quavering, "Dis goddam gun no can shoot!" But for the yet-to-be revealed mysteries of the safety lock, one of our young officers was spared for future service to his country.

There were eventually over five hundred of us in the HTG, eighty percent of which were of Japanese ancestry. There were three companies and they were dispersed all over Oahu. Some of them were even assigned as far out as Kahuku--out on the beaches. And now the loyalty of the Japanese in Hawaii became a big question mark. In fact, in his prelude to "Ambassador in Arms," a story of the famous 100th Battalion, Professor Thomas Murphy described the scene of two American soldiers sitting in a machine gun pit on the north shore of Oahu, one was Hawaiian and one was a local of Japanese ancestry. After a long silence, the Hawaiian finally blurted out the question almost every other non-Japanese in Hawaii had been burdened with. He asked, "Eh, if they come, who you going shoot? Dem or me?" To which the nisei soldier indignantly replied, "Who you think, stupid? Me just as good American as you!"

Our Hawaii Territorial Guard experience only lasted six weeks. After it became apparent that there would not be an immediate invasion by the Japanese, we were relieved from guarding the waterfront area and taken out to the Koko Head rifle range for rifle practice. That's when we first got to shoot the Springfields. We were camped out there in pup tents–

two to a tent. In the middle of the morning, when we were all asleep, we were awakened and assembled. It seemed that the War Department or the army had discovered, to its horror, that a bunch of Buddha-heads[1] in American uniforms were guarding Honolulu. We were awakened at three in the morning on January 19, 1942, and told by our commander that orders had been received that anybody who was of Japanese ancestry had to be discharged from the HTG immediately. In retrospect, I don't know why they had to do it so early in the morning--they could have waited until six or seven a.m. Anyway, just because our faces and names resembled that of the enemy, we were released. This was another totally unexpected surprise, almost beyond our comprehension. Those words were more devastating to us than if a bomb had exploded in our midst.

" . . . Just because our faces and names resembled that of the enemy, we were released. Those words were more devastating to us than if a bomb had exploded in our midst. "

Here we were born, raised, and educated as Americans. We were shocked that our country was ruthlessly attacked by Japan and we were proud that we were assigned to defend our country and that we were doing our share. Manpower was in dire need. Hawaii was the marshalling point for the defense effort. And yet, we weren't acceptable; we weren't considered useful. To have our own country, in its most extreme danger and time of need, reject and repudiate our services, was something more than we could take. The very bottom had dropped out of our lives.

But this was not all. Other Japanese Americans, already in uniform in the 298th Infantry, had their rifles taken away from them and were transferred to non-combat engineer units. The Draft Board reclassified all Japanese-Americans from 1-A draft status to 4-C (enemy alien) status so that we were precluded from military service. The president of a large Hawaiian utility company wrote a pamphlet entitled, "Shall the Japanese be Allowed to Dominate Hawaii?" and proposed that all Japanese be

---

[1]*Slang term, commonly used in Hawaii to refer to one of Japanese ancestry.*

moved to the island of Molokai. Secretary of the Navy Frank Knox pleaded with President Roosevelt for the wholesale evacuation of all Japanese from Hawaii, because "the military defense of Hawaii is now being carried out in the presence of a population predominantly with enemy sympathies and affiliations."

So we were demobilized out of the Territorial Guard. We packed up and they brought us back to the Armory. This was also a blow to the guys who stood side by side with us--people who we were brought up with--people we went to school with, who had no question about our loyalties or no qualms about serving with us. When we were dismissed, they all cried, the Hawaiians, the Chinese boys, the haoles.[2] It was a terrible, sad day. I remember our captain, Nolle Smith, one of the kamaaina[3] Black people, who had to give us the news out there that we had to be discharged, he cried too.

We had nothing to do but to go back to the University of Hawaii. But education became meaningless. Nothing made sense, when our nation was crying for war manpower and military servicemen, and yet we were deemed useless and unwanted. At that time, Japan was conquering country after country. It just seemed so out of place to be trying to study when the world outside seemed to be breaking apart. It was demoralizing and depressing being back in school.

In late January 1942, a group of us were sitting under a tree, feeling sorry for ourselves. That's when Hung Wai Ching, the secretary of the University YMCA came along and gave us a pep talk. He had been brought up in the slums around the Nuuanu YMCA, so he grew up with nisei kids. He also happened to be a member of the Morale Committee of our military governor, Gen. Delos Emmons. He said to us, "So you had a bum deal, what are you going to do about it? Are you going to sit on your butts and feel sorry for yourselves for the rest of the war? Are you going to lie down and be quitters?"

I remember him saying, "Don't you think there are other ways in which you can serve your country, especially when they are crying for manpower for defense?" Hung Wai opened our minds to other options to be of service to our country and to demonstrate our loyalty. We

[2]*Hawaiian word meaning white person, Caucasian, formerly any foreigner.*

[3]*Hawaiian word meaning native born.*

decided to offer ourselves as a non-combat labor battalion. A petition to the commanding general was drawn up and 169 of us signed it. It said:

> "We, the undersigned, were members of the Hawaii Territorial Guard until its recent inactivation. We joined the guard voluntarily with the hope that this was one way to serve our country in her time of need. We were deeply disappointed when we were told that our services in the guard were no longer needed. Hawaii is our home, the United States our country. We know but one loyalty and that is to the Stars and Stripes. We wish to do our part as loyal Americans in every way possible and we hereby offer ourselves for whatever service you may see fit to use us."

We had a great deal of doubt as to whether we might be accepted. Those were very critical, tense, and emotional times. But on February 25, 1942, Gen. Emmons accepted our petition. This group, mostly university ROTC boys discharged from the HTG and all niseis, were now accepted

VVVs READY TO WORK — Members of the Varsity Victory Volunteers, University of Hawaii students who are Americans of Japanese ancestry, assemble on the steps of Hawaii Hall for the send-off ceremonies in February 1942. The five students in the front row, as identified by Ted Tsukiyama, are (from left to right) Clarence Hamaishi, Robert Kadowaki, Yoshio Nakagawa, Harry Uehara, and Yugo Okubo. (Honolulu Advertiser; War Depository Collection, University of Hawaii)

as non-combat civilian laborers assigned to the 34th Engineers at Schofield. Because almost all of us came from the university, we were nicknamed the "Varsity Victory Volunteers," the VVV, and the name stuck. We were armed with hammers, saws, picks, shovels, and sledge hammers. We dug ammunition pits, built secondary roads on the Waianae range, culverts, warehouses, and portable field huts. One gang operated the stone quarry at Kolekole Pass. We did all those things that the engineers did, but we did it as civil service employees.

" . . . we were nicknamed the Varsity Victory Volunteers . . . armed with hammers, saws, picks, shovels, and sledge hammers. "

There was no rank. Former ROTC officers did manual labor like everyone else. We wore blue dungaree uniforms, lived in army barracks, and ate three square army chow meals per day. We got paid less than $90 per month. For eleven months, we performed labor battalion work as part of the 34th Combat Engineers at Schofield. We felt trusted, accepted, useful and productive. And we served as a positive example, to boost the morale of the Japanese population, while we could again serve our country in its time of peril and to prove our loyalty to America.

In fact, we were frequently asked to go out and speak before community groups. I remember being taken out one night, after blackout, to the Waipahu gymnasium to address a group. I spoke to the people about what we were accomplishing in the VVV. The guy that picked me up and guided me through the blackout was captain of the police contact division, in charge of intelligence and security. His name was John A. Burns, who later became our governor. After the war, when he ran for office, he got almost solid nisei vote because he was one of the few people who openly stuck up for the loyalty of the local Japanese.

Hung Wai Ching was very proud of his VVV boys. He bragged about how these boys gave up their education and other lucrative defense jobs to serve as lowly paid common laborers. He showed off his VVV boys every chance he got. One day in late December 1942, the quarry gang breaking rocks at Kolekole Pass saw Hung Wai Ching with some important looking brass. The Assistant Secretary of War, John J. McCloy, was touring Hawaii and Hung Wai Ching brought him out to inspect the

CARPENTER GANG -- A carpenter group of VVVs is shown building a portable field ice-box unit in 1942. Two volunteers identified by Ted Tsukiyama are Kenneth Kawate (center, facing camera) and Hideo Kuniyoshi (standing, at right). (Photo courtesy of Ted Tsukiyama)

ROAD GANG -- A group of VVVs repair a bridge culvert somewhere on Oahu in 1942. Nisei volunteers identified are (background, from left) Masaichi Sagawa, Raymond Nogawa, Ted Tsukiyama, Wilfred Mita, and Herbert Saito. In foreground, right, swinging the sledge hammer for the camera, is Sukeyoshi Kushi. Partly obscured behind horizontal beam, foreground, is Richard Zukemura. (Photo courtesy of Ted Tsukiyama)

251

work of the VVV. I don't know whether it was a coincidence or not, but just a few weeks later, in January 1943, the War Department announced the formation of an all-nisei combat team, changed the nisei's draft status from 4-C back to 1-A, and called for volunteers.

The VVV boys voted to disband so they could volunteer for the 442nd Combat Team. The "triple V" had served its purpose. It had stemmed and stopped the rising tide of hysteria, panic and prejudice against Hawaii's Japanese at the most strategic time, and had answered the big question of loyalty with bold, dramatic, and positive action, not mere words.

The 442nd carried on where the VVV left off. A call for 1,500 volunteers from Hawaii was made. Over 9,500 Japanese-Americans in Hawaii responded. The 100th Battalion had already been sent to the mainland and had finished a distinguished training record.

A lot of us were accepted into the 442nd. I was assigned to the artillery and sent to Camp Shelby, Mississippi, in April 1943. A few months later, around July, just before we went on final maneuvers, the army discovered that the best material for students at the military intelligence school was the nisei. Many of them had Japanese school training as children, as I did in Hawaii, and many of them were sent, by their parents, to schools in Japan before the war. A lot of them had better skills in speaking Japanese then they did in English. So many of the nisei were given higher priority then just infantry combat.

So military intelligence recruiters came down to Camp Shelby and about 200 of us were taken to the intelligence school that had been recently transferred from the San Francisco Presidio to Camp Savage in Minnesota. I had purposely flunked the test they gave me because I didn't want to leave my group, but they took me anyway. We were trained in military Japanese--very intensely day and night--for six months.

The six thousand niseis that went through the military intelligence school were assigned all over the Pacific area, from the Aleutian Islands all the way down to the Solomon Islands. We were the U.S. Army's secret weapon against the Japanese. For some reason, the Japanese figured that their language was difficult enough for Americans to understand, so a lot of their commands were not in code and could just be picked up verbatim.

Kazuo Yamane, a nisei, was working at the Pentagon later in the war. He was looking through a box of stuff that the navy discarded as having no military value. He found this big book that turned out to be the Imperial Army Ordnance Inventory manual. It listed the numbers of every type of Japanese weapon and the location where much of the Japanese ammunition was manufactured. Shortly after that, our B-29s were heading in that direction, dropping bombs on those factories. That's an example of the kind of intelligence that the niseis carried out.

Nisei interpreters and translators were assigned to forward units. They had to have a haole bodyguard for each nisei. It was risky work, you know. Because of his ancestry, a nisei could get mistaken for the enemy and shot by his own people. In fact, Sgt. Frank Hachiya, of Hood River, Oregon, volunteered to parachute behind enemy lines in the Philippines but as he made his way back to American lines, he was mistakenly shot by Americans as an enemy infiltrator. On his body they found a captured set of maps of complete Japanese defenses for Leyte. He was awarded the Distinguished Service Cross posthumously.

They sent me to the 10th Air Force in the China-Burma-India theater. We were assigned to the air force radio intelligence unit. As such, we monitored air-ground radio traffic. We were able to give our people information on the movements of aircraft. We were flown in to upper Burma in 1944 when the Japanese were being pushed down to lower Burma. We could hear the radio signals from Japanese fighter planes taking off from landing fields in lower Burma.

" The nisei intelligence translators were the eyes and ears of allied forces fighting the Japanese in the Pacific war. "

The nisei intelligence translators were the eyes and ears of allied forces fighting the Japanese in the Pacific war. They translated captured documents, intercepted and deciphered coded messages, deciphered and translated maps, battle plans, military orders, diaries and letters and interrogated captured Japanese prisoners.

In 1944, nisei interpreters translated the captured "Operation Z," a Japanese navy plan for the defense of the Marianas and the Philippines. When the American naval fleet steamed into the Marianas, our officers already knew exactly the number and location of Japanese ships and planes, resulting in a decisive American victory in the battle of the Philippine Sea and Leyte Gulf.

Nisei interpreters were instrumental in determining the location of Admiral Isoroku Yamamoto's whereabouts that led to the ambush of his airplane and his resulting death. Admiral Yamamoto, you will remember, was the architect of the bombing raid on Pearl Harbor.

During the war, over six thousand nisei served in the U.S. Military Intelligence Service (MIS) against the Japanese enemy. But little is known of their identity and exploits, because their services were ordered to be highly confidential and kept secret for years. After the war, the nisei MIS also served in the Japan occupation forces and the War Crimes Tribunals.

I have heard of critics who diminish the combat record of the 100/442nd by saying: "It's easy for the nisei to go fight against haole enemy in Italy and Germany, but would they be willing to go fight their own kind?" The answer to those sneers is that, unbeknownst to almost everyone outside the military in the Pacific war, there were over six thousand nisei, mostly volunteers, who willingly went over to fight "their own kind" without any qualms or hesitation whatever, and I am proud

THANK-YOU SPEECH — Col. William Sexton, Commanding Officer of the 34th Combat Engineer Regiment, gives a thank-you speech to assembled VVVs before the group disbanded to volunteer for the 442nd Combat Team in January 1943. Behind Col. Sexton, in background is the group's supervisor, Ralph Yempuku. The four VVV members shown to the right of the colonel are Hiroshi Kato, Richard Uyemura, Hiroshi Minami, and Akio Nishikawa, who was later killed in Europe with the 442nd. (Photo and identification courtesy of Ted Tsukiyama)

to be included as one of them. Unfortunately, there are many fellow Americans who have failed to understand the truism uttered by President Franklin D. Roosevelt when he opened up military service to the 442nd volunteers in 1943 when he said: "Americanism is not a matter of race or nationality. It's a matter of heart."

From December seventh on through the war, I was hardly ever at home. During the VVV days, we lived out at Schofield. So I had no feel for discrimination against Japanese Americans in the community. My father at one time was an officer with the Japanese Chamber of Commerce, but he wasn't taken away as many others were. He was a graduate of Keio University in Japan and he was invited by relatives to move here to Hawaii. He being educated, I suppose, gave him a bit more sophistication than the average guy that came over as a laborer. Another thing that might have shielded him from overt racism or discrimination was the fact that he was baptized a Christian in Japan. So when he came over here, he joined a Methodist Church congregation located on River Street. He was also an active leader with the YMCA.

I think he was well respected and probably many of the haole business leaders spoke up for him, if they were questioned by the FBI regarding his loyalties. So my father was not taken away, whereas many of the "big shot" Japanese who were community leaders found themselves rounded up immediately after Pearl Harbor and taken to Sand Island, then shipped on to the mainland to the camps.

I will not forget the anger and the fury I felt when we were attacked at Pearl Harbor that morning. We were oriented to believe that the Japanese soldier was a killing machine, extremely arrogant, proud of his country and his heritage, and not afraid to die in its defense. I vowed that if I ever met a Japanese soldier--not on the battlefield but under other circumstances--I would punch him in the mouth. I got that chance about three years later in Burma when I entered a prisoner stockade. When we walked into this compound, somebody yelled, "Attention." All these Japanese prisoners jumped up and bowed very meekly, like beaten dogs. They were simple, country youth, drafted by the military machine of Japan to fight a war they did not believe in and were unwilling to die for. This was so different from what we'd been told to expect. I didn't have the heart to punch or kick any of them.

When the 100th Battalion/442nd Combat Unit returned from the European battlefields, they were presented with a special presidential citation on the White House lawn, the only American unit to be so honored. Speaking for the whole nation, President Harry Truman rendered the final verdict on the loyalty of Americans of Japanese ancestry when he said: "You fought for the free nations of the world. You fought not only the enemy, but prejudice, and you won!"

General Douglas MacArthur stated: "Never in military history did any army know so much about the enemy prior to actual engagement," thanks to the nisei Military Intelligence Service. Gen. C. A. Willoughby stated: "The nisei saved a million lives and shortened the war by two years." Theirs was a ringing and undeniable response to the question: "Who you going shoot, me or them?"

The nisei soldier of World War II successfully won both battles he faced, defeating the Axis enemy and putting to rest the question of his loyalty to America. Yet, with the astounding worldwide economic success of Japan in the eighties--coupled with the 50th anniversary of Japan's attack on Pearl Harbor--there is a rising ferment of anti-Japanese prejudice rising up all over the United States again. Thus, it becomes vital to retell the story of the valorous record of the nisei soldier during World War II, to teach as well as to remind us all to distinguish between Americans of Japanese ancestry and those Japanese of Japan. Many Americans still need to learn that "Americanism is a matter of the heart."

Ted Tsukiyama was discharged in January 1946 and completed his final year of college at Indiana University in June 1947. He then went to Yale Law School, receiving his LLd in 1950. He married Fuku Yokoyama in 1951. They met in Washington D.C. while she was a nurse at Georgetown Hospital. They have three children. Sandra Ann was born in 1953; Paul in 1955; and Timothy in 1959. Ted worked with the city and county attorney's office for about five years; entered into a law practice with a firm for about ten years, then began his own law firm for the next twenty-three years. He specializes in labor-management arbitration and still practices from his downtown Honolulu offices, although he is slowly moving into a "retirement mode," trying to avoid the more stressful aspects of law practice. He and Fuku are grandparents of three.

Webley E. Edwards

*He was born in Corvallis, Oregon, in 1902. He graduated from Oregon State University and came over to Hawaii in 1928 to play semi-pro football with the Honolulu Town team. After an injury cut short his sports career, Edwards sold cars at Schuman Carriage, then returned to the mainland to work briefly for KNX radio in Hollywood, California. Within a year he was back in Hawaii as manager of radio station KGMB. He founded the long-running show, "Hawaii Calls," in 1935 and continued as its host until ill health intervened in 1972. On his early morning radio show on KGMB on Sunday, December 7, 1941, he announced, "This is not a maneuver, this is the real McCoy." His calm delivery was credited with leading the people of Hawaii through the confusion resulting from the shock of the surprise air attack. In the early days of the war, he became a Pacific correspondent for the Columbia Broadcasting System. Following are three radio scripts of his broadcasts, taken from the War Depository Collection at the University of Hawaii. His photograph is provided through the courtesy of the **Honolulu Star Bulletin**.*

KGMB Radio
Honolulu, Territory of Hawaii
Sunday, December 6, 1942

CBS "News Around the World"

By Webley Edwards

It was on a Sunday like this, 365 days ago, that this war started for America, right here at Pearl Harbor on the Island of Oahu in Hawaii. I had a sickening feeling in my stomach as I saw the great ships of our Pacific fleet bombed and torpedoed at their moorings. When it was all over the *Arizona* was sunk and destroyed; the *Oklahoma* was turned over, her keel up; the *California, Nevada,* and *West Virginia* were far down in the water. The *Pennsylvania,* the *Maryland,* and the *Tennessee* had been hit. The cruisers *Helena, Honolulu,* and *Raleigh* were damaged. Two destroyers, the *Cassin* and the *Downes,* were destroyed in a drydock. Another, the *Shaw,* seemed to be blown half away. The great old minelayer, *Oglala,* was down in the water. So was the old target ship, the *Utah.*

Two fleet task forces had been carrying out assignments at sea, and two Pacific fleet task forces were in the harbor after extensive operations at sea. Of the eighty-six ships in the harbor, nineteen were sunk or damaged. Both our army and navy forces on Oahu lost scores of planes.

All this had happened because we, as a nation, had thought Japan would play the game as an honorable nation. Dishonorably, the Japs threw a sneak punch. There was, of course, bewilderment, some confusion, and a lot of disillusionment. Ships stricken, planes crushed, airfields pockmarked with bombs. There was talk about our leaders.

Then all at once it didn't seem nearly so bad. Men worked as men had never worked before, and ships steamed out one by one to take their place with our fighting fleet. I'll never forget the thrill of seeing another battleship that had been on the bottom of Pearl Harbor going out through the Harbor narrows one bright morning, her flag proudly flying, her men lining her decks. She was going out to fight, and we had lumps in our throats.

Of those ships that were struck that reeling blow, only the *Arizona* is permanently and totally lost.

We have lost ships, but the enemy has lost far more. We have lost men, but the enemy has paid a price manyfold. At this minute our land and sea forces are busy in Guadalcanal and in New Guinea blasting out the foothold for our future drive toward Japan. Today, one year later, Pearl Harbor looks mighty sweet. The old harbor is bustling, noisy, busy, and men have the bright look of confidence in their faces.

This is Webley Edwards, at Pearl Harbor. We return you to CBS, in New York.

KGMB Radio, Honolulu
December 7, 1942
2:35 p.m., Hawaiian War Time

Mainland Cue: "Let's go over and chat with Web Edwards. Okay, Webley Edwards, go ahead from Pearl Harbor."

EDWARDS: Hello, Parks Johnson and Warren Hull, up there in Alameda. This is Pearl Harbor, the place where it happened one year ago today. With me here is Alexa Davidson, program traffic manager of station KGMB, Honolulu. Alexa, remember a year ago today?

DAVIDSON: How could I ever forget it?

EDWARDS: We were really jumping around about this time, weren't we?

DAVIDSON: Jumping is right. We were expecting to be bombed any second.

EDWARDS: Well, somehow they missed us.

DAVIDSON: I'll never forget you going on the air that morning and saying: "A lot of you people think this is a maneuver. This is no maneuver. This is the real McCoy!"

EDWARDS: I remember. I had to say something to convince them, and that was the first thing that popped into my head.

DAVIDSON: It did the trick, all right.

EDWARDS: Seemed to. I'll never forget you that morning. You had a smear of lipstick way up on your cheek. You didn't even know it.

DAVIDSON: Well, I couldn't help it if my hand was shaking.

EDWARDS: Come on, you weren't scared!

DAVIDSON: No, but I was pretty mad. I remember thinking how bombing doesn't scare you, it just makes you mad all over. Two days later, after I got a night of sleep, I woke up scared stiff, thinking back over that Sunday and what might have happened.

EDWARDS: Well, here's the question everybody always asks everybody. Where were you on the morning of the seventh, one year ago?

DAVIDSON: At my sister's house, out Pearl Harbor way, for the weekend. I'd been working pretty hard and she figured it would be good for me to get a quiet day of rest on Sunday.

EDWARDS: Nice place to spend a quiet Sunday, December 7, 1941, Pearl Harbor.

DAVIDSON: Well, I did get a good night's sleep on Saturday. In the morning I heard these terrific explosions, and I jumped up and ran to the window. It was a sight I'll never forget. Funny thing, I looked at my watch and saw it

259

was exactly 7:55.

EDWARDS: Good old radio training. Did you think it was a real attack?

DAVIDSON: Somehow I just <u>knew</u> it was. Maybe it was because we had been making plans at the radio station for several weeks, thinking that the Japs might attack - somewhere.

EDWARDS: What was it like?

DAVIDSON: The sky seemed to be filled with planes. Some of them came diving down with an awful screaming roar.

EDWARDS: So then?

DAVIDSON: I dressed and got the car. By this time the planes were all over. One almost hit the roof, it seemed to me.

EDWARDS: Any bullets around you?

DAVIDSON: Yes, bullets and shrapnel were hitting all around. Some shrapnel fell on the walk. But I finally got underway.

EDWARDS: What about the Jap plane that came down in flames on the way, right by the highway?

DAVIDSON: Gee, I was so used to seeing Jap planes fall by that time, I hardly -- well, I hardly had time to think about it.

EDWARDS: Uh-huh.

DAVIDSON: Where did <u>you</u> start from that morning?

EDWARDS: Uh-uh, I'm supposed to interview you.

DAVIDSON: Go on!

EDWARDS: Well, at the exact moment, I was in the kitchen, drinking a glass of grape juice. I honestly was. The explosion shook the dishes. I figured it was a bad accident somewhere, maybe to an ammunition dump. Just then, the phone rang. It was one of the boys at the station. "It's happened," he said, "the Japs are attacking." "No fooling?" I said. "No fooling, we've seen the Rising Sun on the wings of the planes," he said. I tried to put in a phone call to Paul White at CBS and couldn't get through. So I rushed to the radio station. I never drove a car so fast in my life. I got to the station just in time to see two Jap planes swooping down very low, but they evidently had already dropped their bombs.

DAVIDSON: I remember you arrived with your safety razor with you.

EDWARDS: Wasn't that crazy? Force of habit, I guess. I must have grabbed it on the way out of the house. But here, we're interviewing you. So you finally made the radio station.

DAVIDSON: Yeah, it seemed like the whole staff was piling in about that time. You could hear the explosions going off all over town. Some of them were pretty close, too.

EDWARDS: And I recall you did a great job, helping to summon officers and men, ambulance, medical workers, and so on. Fact is, you've been holding down a man's job ever since.

DAVIDSON: Somebody had to do it. I just happened to be there.

EDWARDS: You just happened to drive about ten miles through the blitz to be there! . . . Good luck, Alexa Davidson. We return you to Parks Johnson and Warren Hull in Alameda.

KGMB Radio
Honolulu, Territory of Hawaii
Sunday, December 5, 1943

CBS Broadcast "WE THE PEOPLE"

By Webley Edwards, interviewing Mrs. John Baird, Jack Doolittle

EDWARDS: This is Honolulu, Webley Edwards speaking, waiting to bring you We The People listeners the stories of two Americans who are putting teeth into the Allied proclamation announced in Cairo.

              Here are two war workers at Pearl Harbor who have been in this war since two years ago today. Mrs. John Baird, of Honolulu, for example, saw seven Jap planes shot down on December seventh, 1941. That right, Mrs. Baird?

BAIRD: Yes, and one came so close. We were living at Aiea

Plantation, just overlooking Pearl Harbor. We saw the whole thing, but we could hardly believe it was war until we saw the big bomb hit the *Arizona.* Jack, my husband, was wearing his new brown striped pajamas, standing out there with his shotgun trying to get a shot at a Jap. Then we started counting the Jap planes that were shot down, and we counted seven.

EDWARDS: And now you're on a war job, Mrs. Baird?

BAIRD: I'm not a welder, if that's what you mean, but I'm supervising about five hundred student war workers at their jobs.

EDWARDS: Now here is Jack Doolittle, who works at Pearl Harbor. Jack, what's your war job?

DOOLITTLE: I'm a machinist instructor at Pearl Harbor. We overhaul ships, repair them, reconstructing anything from a minesweep to a battleship. Our job is a lousy, dirty job. Sometimes I wonder how we can keep on doing the things we have to do. But somebody has to do it, and we're the guys. I think that most of us feel that we're really doing an important job in keeping ships of the Pacific fleet in battle trim.

EDWARDS: Are you related to the famous Jimmy Doolittle, the Tokyo bombing general?

DOOLITTLE: Yes, I'm a second cousin. The whole Doolittle clan is pretty proud of him, too.

EDWARDS: Jack, you were at Pearl Harbor on the morning of December seventh, right?

DOOLITTLE: Yes, I was in the navy yard when the Jap planes came over. Some guy came running up and said they needed somebody to help with the wounded, and I spent the rest of the time doing that.

EDWARDS: And what's the word from the Pearl Harbor war workers now, two years later?

DOOLITTLE: Just let 'em come again, that's all.

EDWARDS: Mrs. John Baird and Jack Doolittle are Pearl Harbor war workers who have been in this war from its first minute. They're representative of the fighting people who are backing up the fighting men out here on the Pacific Sea frontier. This is Webley Edwards, at Pearl Harbor, returning you to Milo Boulton, and We The People, in New York.

---

*Webley Edwards' coverage during the war included narrations describing Pacific naval engagements and island occupations, culminating in his live broadcast of the Japanese surrender aboard the USS Missouri in Tokyo Bay in 1945. His "Hawaii Calls" program of Hawaiian music became so popular that it spread to as many as six hundred radio stations throughout Canada, Europe, Japan, New Zealand, and Australia over its forty-year lifespan. Edwards became known as Hawaii's number one salesman, because of the promotion value to Hawaii tourism of his radio program. In 1952, he expanded his horizons to include Republican politics, winning election to the Territorial House of Representatives. He spent fourteen years in the Hawaii political arena, eventually moving up to the Senate. Among his many rightful claims to fame is an all-time standard of Hawaiian music, "Pearly Shells," which he composed with Leon Pober. Webley Edwards died on October 5, 1977. His ashes were scattered on the waters off Waikiki beach from where "Hawaii Calls" entertained millions of listeners with Hawaiian music. (**Star Bulletin** -- October 6, 1977)*

Wartime Waikiki

BARRICADES -- Barricades of barbed wire were strung on Waikiki Beach during the early hours of the war. They seemed no barrier to the bathers who merely circumvented them to enjoy the water. Note the Royal Hawaiian Hotel (center) and the former location of the Outrigger Canoe Club facility (right). (Photo courtesy of Outrigger Canoe Club and member Buddy Baptiste)

EQUIPMENT STORAGE -- Heavy army equipment of the U.S. Corps of Engineers was stored in Waikiki along the "mauka" shore (the mountain side) of the Ala Wai Canal. This photograph, taken in 1944, offers an unobstructed view of world famous Diamond Head. (Photo courtesy of Kenneth and Nettie Boucher)

Charles K. L. Davis

Charles Keonaona Laulani Davis was born in Honolulu in 1925. His father, Arthur Lewis Davis--originally from Nottinghamshire in England--came to Hawaii (via Chicago) as a medical officer for the U.S. Cavalry during the First World War, in 1915. He had become a U.S. citizen and was graduated from the College of Medicine at the University of Illinois. His mother, Rose Kaouinuiokalani Brown, was born in Waipio Peninsula in Waipahu. Charles' maternal grandfather, Charles Augustus Brown, came over to Hawaii from Massachusetts in 1877, to seek a warmer climate as a cure for his tuberculosis. He became a successful local banker and a frequent visitor to the Royal Palace to play cards and gamble with King David Kalakaua. His maternal grandmother, Malia Kaaumoa, was pure Hawaiian. The Davis family lived on the plantation in Waialua where Charles' father served as the plantation doctor.

I remember hearing the story about my grandfather Brown, who was a frequent guest at the old Royal Palace during the reign of King Kalakaua. My grandfather would always wear a Panama hat with a maile[1] lei around it. Queen Emma, the widow of King Kamehameha IV, would walk around the expansive lanai of the palace. She would know when my grandfather was there because she could smell the fragrant leaves of the maile. She would say, "Here comes Keonaona"--meaning my grandfather--with the sweet smell of maile. So when my parents were married, my father told my mother that when she had her first child--if it was a boy--he would be named Keonaona Laulani. That's how I got my name.

And another story I like to tell was how my parents met. After he got out of the army, my father became a member of the Board of Health and worked in Honolulu. He stayed at one of the cottages at the Courtland Hotel, which in those days was located on the corner of Wilder and Punahou. He was a doctor, but a wonderful musician, too.

My mother was staying with her chaperone, the owner of the hotel, Mrs. Hannah Palmer (we called her Aunt Hannah). One evening, Aunt

---

[1] *A native twining shrub with shiny, fragrant leaves, a favorite for decoration and leis.*

265

Hannah and my mother were sitting out on the little lanai after dinner, and it was a beautiful evening. The moon was bright. My mother heard this guitar playing--beautiful music coming from one of the cottages. She asked Aunt Hannah who was playing the music. Aunt Hannah said, "Oh, that's the Englishman, a young doctor with the Board of Health. He just moved into the cottage." My mother showed a little interest and thought she might like to meet him.

In those days, people used to picnic a lot. Because you had to be properly introduced and you had to have a chaperone, Aunt Hannah arranged for a picnic somewhere on the other side of the island. So Aunt Hannah's chauffeur loaded the car with picnic things and drove my mother and my father--and Aunt Hannah, of course--off to a wonderful picnic. That's how they met.

My father was also a piano player. He started me on the piano at two years old. I was great with two fingers. Later, when I was five or six, I would go to the movies in Waialua and if they were musicals, I would listen to the songs and I would come back home and pick out all the tunes on the piano--just by ear, you know. And it would come out pretty accurate. So, my folks started me in piano lessons at age six. Mrs. Butchard was my first piano teacher, down at the plantation. I took piano for eighteen years. I was going to go into concert piano, but the war changed all that.

I also took the pipe organ, and when I was in Waialua High School, I took the cello with Miss Whang. That only lasted a year, though, because the cello wore a hole in my mother's Oriental carpet and my mother was furious. She said, "You absolutely get that thing right back to the school and I don't want to hear you play it again."

When I was young, my mother and father always entertained. We had luaus and I'd always hear the musical groups and watch the hula dancers. We would all sing our family songs together.

I guess my first professional job--if you can call it that--was when I was fourteen or fifteen years old. I won an amateur program at the Young Hotel Roof Garden when Napua Stevens was the leading voice with Gigi Royce's orchestra. My prize was two silver dollars. It was marvelous--I'll never forget that. I kept the two silver dollars for a long time. Well, it more or less launched me on my professional career. I started getting paid for my work from then on. That was a year or two before the war started.

On Sunday morning, December seventh, we were at our house on the plantation. Dad was on the mainland at the time, so just the three of us were home at the time--my mother, my brother, and me. We were brought up Episcopalians, but we only had the Episcopal service in Haleiwa once a month. The visiting minister would come down from Honolulu and serve us communion in a store that they used as a temporary chapel. So, the rest of the time we would go to Liliuokalani Church. Mother loved the Hawaiian services at the Liliuokalani Church.

" We looked up and saw the planes come over, very low. You could see the red circles under the wings. "

So we all got in the car early that morning. I drove. As we were backing out of the yard, we saw this dirt "kick up" in the yard. They were strafing the area, but, of course, we didn't know what was going on. We looked up and saw the planes come over, very low. You could see the red circles under the wings. But we thought they were just having another mock battle. They had mock battles quite frequently then. The car radio was on and it was Webley Edwards--the Hawaii Calls announcer--saying, "Take cover, this is the real thing. The Japs are attacking Pearl Harbor."

My mother, in the back seat of the car, said--in no uncertain terms-- "We are going to church." So off to church we went. We were the first ones there. In fact, we were the **only** ones there. We had communion and went right back home.

We were back at home for just a short while when Maile O'Donnell and her husband, Raymond, called and invited us down to their home for the night. Maile was my mother's best friend. We had such a big place and it was kind of lonely without Papa around, so we went right on down to the O'Donnells' house.

Gordon Virgo was the welfare manager at the plantation, and that night, he organized a guard unit to patrol around the cane fields and watch for any Japanese invaders. He told the story about hearing noises in the cane fields. He called out, "Halt, who goes there?" He did that three times but the noise kept coming toward him, hidden among the cane. So Mr. Virgo fired his rifle. He killed one of the plantation cows.

So we spent the night of December seventh on the floor of the O'Donnells' living room, all together. We had the radio going all the time. We were frightened. We stayed with the O'Donnells for two days, I remember. Then we came back home.

Everybody in the neighborhood was talking about the minister of our Buddhist church in Waialua. It seems he was picked up by the FBI for having a shortwave set in the back of the church. I don't remember hearing anything about him again.

My father was on a train heading back to the West Coast from New York when the war broke out. He had priority to get back to the islands because he was a medical doctor. So he was home again shortly thereafter.

I was sixteen, and a sophomore at Iolani School when the war started. We didn't have school for quite some time, then we heard that Iolani was going to be closed. It was closed because so many of the men teachers were activated with the Territorial Guard. They shut it down temporarily. So I came back down to the country and went to Waialua High School because my folks wanted me closer to home during those years. When they reopened Iolani a few years later, I was already a senior at Waialua with only a year to go to graduation, so I stayed there. I graduated in 1943.

" . . . my war-time activities included playing piano for community singing parties. . . I also used to take movies to the different anti-aircraft batteries to entertain the troops. "

Some forty-five years later, however, Iolani gave diplomas to all those boys who would have graduated had the war not happened. They rounded up as many of us as they could and had a special presentation. So, now I hold diplomas from **two** high schools.

During my last year at Waialua High School, my war-time activities included playing the piano for community singing parties. I remember, I also used to take movies around to the different anti-aircraft batteries to entertain the troops. We were organized by our plantation welfare manager, Mr. Virgo, who also headed the USO troop down there. He was quite an organizer--a real leader--and he also had a beautiful bass voice, a wonderful singer. He would lead us in the community singing gatherings.

After graduation, as soon as I turned eighteen, I enlisted in the service. That was in 1943. They sent us to Schofield Barracks for basic training. We worked under Col. D'Eliscu, I remember, who had been in charge of the ROTC in Roosevelt High School. We had to go through jungle warfare with him. He was a terror! We worked like hell and it was terrible. But, I got through it.

I had my choice of duty after basic training and I chose the Air Force. I really wanted to fly. I passed the first part of the examination I took in Honolulu. Then we were all sent back to the replacement depot to await our orders. We were getting ready to ship out to the mainland for training. We even said our goodbyes at home, leaving our families all in tears. When we went back to the barracks, General Delos Emmons, Hawaii's military governor, posted a notice on the board for us. It contained all seventy-two of our names and it cancelled our orders to go to cadet training. It said that we could do more for the war effort overseas. So, although I did get into the Air Force, I never did get to fly.

I spent fifteen months in Hawaii then got shipped out to Saipan, and later, on to Okinawa. I became the head noncom[2] of the intelligence section, and I was only a buck sergeant. I had tech sergeants and staff sergeants working under my direction. It was an uncomfortable spot to be in, so when I had a chance to go to Washington D.C. with the historical personnel, I jumped at it. Our job was to write the war department history. I enjoyed it. We were in Baltimore, Maryland, and had contact with the Pentagon practically on a daily basis. I helped write the history of the war department. I felt like I was contributing something.

I got out of the service in 1946. As I look back on the war years, I guess my life was changed in many ways because of the war. First of all, I have two high school diplomas as a result of the war. How many people can say that? I had planned to be a concert pianist, originally, but I guess that was interrupted because of the war. And, of course, I did go to the University of Hawaii under the GI Bill. I'd say that really changed

---

[2]Slang term, abbreviation for non-commissioned officer.

my life, because from U of H, I got a scholarship to go to the Music Academy of the West in Santa Barbara. From there, I got another scholarship to Juilliard School of Music in New York to study voice—mainly concert and opera training. I have now spent most of my life in music--as a teacher and an entertainer. And I love it!

Charles K. L. Davis has become one of the foremost musicians in Hawaii. He has sung all over the world, including a performance in Russia, in 1959, with the Ed Sullivan Show. He has been featured in Los Angeles, Las Vegas, New York, Canada, Mexico, and, of course, in Hawaii. He is comfortable singing operatic arias, tunes from musical comedy, or Hawaiian music. He was the featured performer for years at Kemoo Farm Restaurant out in his old home territory, Wahiawa. A "people" person, Charles enjoys entertaining an audience in a personal way, accompanying himself on the piano. His recordings are widely distributed and his Hawaiian music is frequently heard on Hawaii radio. He is most often referred to as "Hawaii's Golden Voice."

Edward F. Galovic

The following short, eyewitness account, was printed on the second anniversary of the Pearl Harbor attack, in the December 7, 1943 edition of the **CHA-3 Pearl Harbor Banner.** *Edward Galovic was a Progressman in Shop 72. The article was headed: "Eyewitness Relates Enemy Attack on P.H." It is reproduced here by permission of the Commandant, Pearl Harbor Naval Ship Yard.*

I'll never forget Pearl Harbor because I was one of the unlucky persons to taste the baptism of fire. Then again, the reason may be because the doctors pronounced me dead.

I was at my shop about twenty minutes after the attack began and I noticed that ships in No. 1 drydock had already been hit and were burning furiously. They were two destroyers, the *Cassin* and the *Downes*. Five sailors were having a tough time trying to handle hundreds of feet of four-inch fire hose, so I dashed over and gave them a hand. It seemed like the *Pennsylvania* was firing her forward anti-aircraft guns directly over our heads and unless I'm very much mistaken, that's how I suffered a broken ear drum.

A little while later, the drydock just about exploded in my face. I was hauled back about two-hundred-and-fifty feet. When I picked myself up, I was facing the front entrance of my shop. As I straightened out, a stream of blood rushed from my throat. My hands sprang to my neck trying to find the pressure point, but it was so numb I couldn't feel a thing. I was beginning to get weak, so I ran for my shop. My knees were starting to buckle from under me and everything was turning black. I tried to run faster, but I could hardly pick up my feet. I just about reached the shop and collapsed.

The next day, the doctor told me I had a severed jugular vein and that it was necessary for him to cut it completely out. A piece of shrapnel caught me in the throat when a bomb and the warheads on the torpedoes had exploded. I sustained a paralyzed vocal cord on the right side and could hardly talk, but in the past two years, my voice has come along fine for a supposedly dead man. The doctor told me afterwards that I had lost four quarts of blood and was supposed to be dead.

Honolulu Wartime Scenes

TANK MANEUVERS -- Civilian automobiles cleared the way as army tanks rumbled along Beretania Street in an "attack" on opposing forces in this 1942 maneuver. Such scenes were commonplace in Honolulu during the war. (U.S. Army Signal Corp photo; War Depository Collection, University of Hawaii)

THE WASPs VOLUNTEER -- Civilian volunteers formed the Women's Ambulance Service Patrol (WASPs) to provide emergency ambulance services. The organization, unique to Hawaii, was formed in 1942 shortly after the sinking of the carrier USS Wasp. They operated under the jurisdiction of the Office of Civilian Defense. The members pictured are identified as Lila Tate, driver, Kay Hondo, "patient," and stretcher bearers Mercedes Holt (left) and Helen Medeiros. (**Star Bulletin** Nov. 20, 1943; War Depository Collection, University of Hawaii)

Charles S. Brown, M.D.

He was born in Honolulu in 1916. His father, Charles P. Brown, was born in San Francisco, California, but moved to Honolulu with his family as a child. His mother, Carrie Borges, was born in Honolulu. Charles attended Roosevelt High School, graduating in 1934. Following two years at the University of Hawaii, he went to Stanford University in California and earned a biochemistry degree in 1938. He then worked for the Hawaiian Trust Company for three years. With rumors of war and a draft system on the way, Charles joined the navy and received an ensign's commission in September 1941. His father had died while Charles was at Stanford. In December, 1941, he lived with his mother on Keonaona Street, just off Bates, in Nuuanu.

I had just gotten my commission and was sent down to Pearl Harbor to work in what they called the Issuing Department. It was a department of secret publications that contained decoding information that was used by ships and planes to communicate in codes. It was like a library, really. We issued these publications, giving military installations their quotas.

I was also the officer messenger. As such, I would carry secret mail-- picking it up and delivering it to ships and planes passing through. I was given a .45 pistol to carry with me, so I felt very important. But I didn't know how to fire it very well, as they only gave me one lesson with the gun.

I was always the first to go aboard the incoming Matson liners when they docked. I would go up to the master's room and collect the letters from a special place designated for keeping secret material. The captain didn't know what was in the letters and neither did I. They were deliverable to various offices in Pearl Harbor, usually the commandant of the naval district.

I also went to meet the Pan American clippers--the flying boats--that would come in from the Orient. They landed in the water near Pearl City and I used to go aboard them to a spot right under where the pilot sat--sort of a loft--and pick up and deliver packets containing secret messages.

One day I won't forget. It was in November 1941, I think, and I was sent aboard the Pan American clipper to send off a packet of secret material. The plane had come in from Japan. You could feel the undercurrent, at that time, of something that was going to happen. There was a lot of talk of war with Japan. But we thought if it were to happen, it probably would happen out in the Philippines. Certainly not here in Hawaii. Who could possibly imagine them coming all the way over here from Japan?

Anyway, I went aboard the clipper and one of the passengers who arrived on the plane was Saburo Kurusu, the Japanese envoy who was on his way to Washington D.C. to help smooth relations with the U.S. He was there with his wife who, interestingly enough, was an American. I believe they stayed the night in Honolulu and went on to Washington the next day. Of course, he played a part in an historic moment shortly thereafter when he and the Japanese ambassador met in Washington with Secretary of State Cordell Hull and presented a message of peace while-- at that very moment--planes were bombing Pearl Harbor.

I really feel that Kurusu went to Washington in all sincerity. I don't think his government kept him informed of what was going on--that an attack on Pearl Harbor was planned. He was just a scapegoat for his government at that time.

Sunday, December seventh, was my day off. Our office didn't work on Sundays. The first thing I heard were these loud booms and shots going off. I immediately knew something was wrong because the army and navy never held maneuvers on Sundays. But I didn't know what was going on.

My mother turned on the radio and that's when we knew what was happening. The radio announcer said that we were under attack and that this was the real thing, not a maneuver. So I hurriedly got dressed in my "whites," which was the uniform of the day, and jumped into my Chevy convertible and headed off to Pearl Harbor. I had the top down for better visibility and sped down the highway--what is now called the Nimitz highway. As I drove toward Pearl Harbor, I could see smoke mounting up into the sky, so I knew something big was going on.

When I got near the main gate to Pearl Harbor, I looked up and couldn't believe what I was seeing. These planes were just gliding down so low--they must have been only about fifty feet above me. I could see the big red sun painted on them. I could also see that they were torpedo planes. And the marines at the gate were busy shooting at them with their little rifles. I couldn't believe it. There were no big guns firing at the planes, just rifles--marines standing up firing away at the Japanese planes. Everything was so slipshod.

" I looked up and couldn't believe what I was seeing. These planes were just gliding down so low--they must have been only about fifty feet above me. I could see the big red sun painted on them. "

I got waved through the gate because, I am sure, I was in uniform. So I zipped through and drove over to the Administration Building. This was only about two blocks from where I could see this one ship that was quite bombed out. There was so much confusion--people running around hysterically. I could see the smoke and hear the racket going on--but there were trees and buildings obstructing the view--so I couldn't see the damage that was in progress at the docks and where the battleships were moored. I soon learned, of course.

I went into the building and reported to my station. Our responsibility, in case of emergency, was to stand by and protect the documents at all costs. So we waited there--about twelve of us in all-- including a few civilians. My boss, Lt. Cdr. Danford--I don't remember his first name--didn't show up until about noon. He lived in a cottage at the old Elk's club in Waikiki. He was a retired naval officer and was called back into the service. He had been retired because he injured his arm in an accident and it was almost useless. So he didn't come in until noon or so that day, but we had enough people there to carry out our assignment.

We really didn't have a good security system at that time. There was a great quantity of this secret material and there was no vault to keep it in. We couldn't leave our post and wander around. We just had to, theoretically, protect the documents. And that's where I stayed for forty-eight hours. We just stayed there and waited.

Everybody was worried. We didn't know where those planes came from. We didn't know if they were coming back in an hour or two. We wondered whether there were other ships out there--a task force, perhaps--that was planning to invade. We'd hear all these rumors about paratroopers landing here and there. We didn't know what was true and what was rumor.

I was concerned about my mother. I knew she would be worried and nervous about what was happening to me. But I couldn't get to a phone and call her. I knew, however, that she would be with her sister and brother-in-law, Clara and Fred Larson, who lived right across the street. I knew that my uncle and aunt would see that my mother was all right. And, sure enough, when I finally got home, that's where I found her.

As evening came, we just curled up on our desks and went to sleep, if sleep was possible at all under those circumstances. I remember being in the same clothes and sleeping on the desk--spending two nights there-- until I was released on Tuesday. We were fortunate, though, that we were close to the cafeteria. Somebody went over there and brought food back to us. So at least we had something to eat periodically. But, take my word for it, a desk doesn't make a very comfortable bed.

I recall that the blood bank was put to use immediately. It had gone into effect about a year before, in case of emergency. So they were prepared to take in blood donors right away. This doctor that I practiced with, Gilbert Halpern, told me that they had set up a medical system for civil defense, months before December seventh, and they were at a meeting that morning when the bombs started to drop. They were warned that if a disaster struck, they were going to have to set up their own first-aid and emergency stations--the military was not going to be able to help them. And that was the way it turned out. He reported to Fort Armstrong and helped with numbers of casualties that day.

" The thing that amazes me is why the Japanese didn't hit the big oil and fuel tanks when they bombed Pearl Harbor. "

The thing that amazes me is why the Japanese didn't hit the big oil and fuel tanks when they bombed Pearl Harbor. They were right there on the slopes above Pearl Harbor about a quarter-of-a-mile away, near the submarine base. My theory is that they had a set plan and they carried it out successfully. In my opinion, the Japanese people as a whole are excellent at following rules and plans set out for them. They do not initiate things as other nationalities might. For instance, I would think that an American or a German might spot those oil tanks and say, "Oh, that's a good target. Let's go get it." The Japanese followed orders and did what they were supposed to. And, if they knew just how successful that attack had been, they might have had troop transports close by and invaded. They surely would have taken over the islands.

Taking us over would have been easy for them to do that morning. We were totally unprepared. We even disregarded the radar warnings. And, every day--early in the mornings before dawn--they used to fly PBYs out and patrol the waters around the islands for a couple of hours, searching for ships. They may have thought those blips on the radar screens were those planes coming back, I don't know. But, whatever we were doing didn't work. The Japanese came in and surprised us.

In fact, I firmly believe that Washington knew more about the attack beforehand than they wanted to admit. There was a big investigation of Adm. Husband Kimmel and Gen. Walter Short, and they were relieved of their commands and found derelict in their duties. But I don't think they were given all the information that Washington had prior to the attack. I would place the blame right in Washington's lap. And I think the debate about who was really responsible for our lack of preparedness will go on for years to come in the history books.

" . . . one of the admirals looked at me and said, 'This, my son, is going to be the most important night of our lives. We'll either win or lose the war based on what's happening out there right now.' "

I was a courier and would carry messages, driving between one admiral and another on the same base. One evening, in early June, one of the admirals looked at me and said, "This, my son, is going to be the most important night of our lives. We'll either win or lose the war based on what's happening out there right now." He didn't tell me what's happening out there--but shortly after we heard that there was a major battle and a victory at Midway. And that became the turning point in the war for us. I'll never forget that conversation. Here, this troubled admiral was sharing his concerns with a little ensign. The following

June, I was shipped to the South Pacific, to New Caledonia. I worked under Adm. Robert Ghormley at first, then he was replaced by Adm. William Halsey.

There was an interesting thing I remember that happened ten or fifteen years before the Pearl Harbor attack. I used to go down to the Waianae area to visit my mother's oldest sister, Mary, and her husband, Ralph Turner. My uncle was a wise old man with a long beard. He raised animals--goats, turkeys, and such--but most of them became his pets. He told me one day that we would probably be invaded by the Japanese some day. When I asked him how he knew that, he said, "Because the Japanese are very curious people." He said that a few of them had been hanging around the area, asking questions of people. He said that one of them asked him, "What's in those mountains there?" pointing to Kolekole Pass in the Waianae range. "How do you get up there and back?" the Japanese man asked. My uncle told me that he answered, curtly, "I don't know and it's none of your business."

ENSIGN DOWN UNDER -- Ensign Charles Brown smiles for the camera, surrounded by the rugged terrain of New Caledonia, of the Melanesia island group in the South Pacific, in 1942. (Photo courtesy of Dr. Charles S. Brown)

The man said, "Never mind. Some day we're going to come over here and get this place." I'll never forget that little story. My uncle was an intelligent and inquisitive man, but he also was very idealistic. I remember he invented a pipe coupling that was used later on trains--only to have his patent stolen by one of his trusted friends. He predicted Pearl Harbor, but didn't live long enough to see his prediction come true.

Charles was discharged from the navy as a lieutenant commander in 1945. He returned to Stanford for a short stint to complete his pre-medicine training and then attended the University of Oregon Medical School. He practiced medicine, as an internist, in Waikiki and downtown Honolulu for thirty-five years, retiring in 1989. He left the islands to live in Nashville, Tennessee, at that time, and now enjoys his retirement years traveling the world.

Saint Louis Hospital

The U.S. Army commandeered the Saint Louis College campus for use as a general hospital on December 8, 1941. Acting under martial law authority, conversion began immediately and by December 17, the first patients were received at Provisional General Hospital No. 2. Because it was a real general hospital, it provided for all types of medical services. Construction of temporary wooden buildings began in April 1942 and continued until December 1944. On July 1, 1942, the 147th General Hospital officially superceded "Provisional No. 2." But for convenience sake, many army personnel referred to it simply as Saint Louis Hospital. The 2,500-bed hospital cared for 33,000 patients, including war casualties, dependents of servicemen, and veterans during the war. *(Pacific Marianist Archives)*

147th GENERAL HOSPITAL -- The red cross on the white field, displayed on the roof of the former school's administration building, identifies the 147th General Hospital, or St. Louis Hospital. The facility was under army jurisdiction from the early morning hours of December 8, 1941 until January 7, 1946. (Photo courtesy of Pacific Marianist Archives)

Dorothy R. Bright

Her father, Joseph Allen Rogers, came to Hawaii from Tennessee with the army at age fourteen, before the turn of the century. Her mother, Belinda Costa, was born in Hilo, Hawaii, but came to Honolulu when very young. Dorothy, born in Kakaako in 1918, was the oldest of five children. She attended Pohokaina School until the sixth grade. When she was fourteen, her father died and she had to work to help support the family. She went to work in 1932 for A. K. Magoon at the American Sanitary Laundry. At age sixteen, she married Hawaiian musician Simeon Bright. On December 7, 1941, Dorothy lived with her husband and seven-year-year old son, Simeon Jr., on Cooke Street near Kapiolani Blvd.

When we got married, Simeon was playing music all over Honolulu. He played the guitar, banjo, and ukulele. His sister, Hannah Bright, had the only jazz orchestra in Hawaii at the time. They were very popular in the 30s. Every weekend they played music at the nice places--the Elks Club, and the exclusive Pacific Club.

He finally got a job at City Hall as an accountant during the day, and at night he still played music. He joined up with Al Kealoha Perry and they were on "Hawaii Calls" for sixteen years. Simeon's first love was his music and he was good at it. But it was a rough life being a musician's wife. You had to turn your head and shut your ears to a lot of things.

On December seventh, I was up early and cooking breakfast when I started to hear all these noises. My husband just got up. He performed the night before at a club on Kalakaua and McCully. He had a little too much to drink the night before and mumbled that he was hungry. Our son had gone to spend the night with my brother-in-law and his wife on Young Street.

I looked out the window and saw smoke. I told my husband, "You know, something's wrong, this looks like the real thing." He said, "Ah, you're crazy." We were near the highway--Kapiolani Boulevard--and the cars were speeding by. So I turned on the radio to find out what was going on.

That's when I heard Web Edwards saying, "This is no joke. This is the real McCoy. Get off the streets. We're being bombed by the Rising Sun."

Dorothy R. Bright (continued)

They called for volunteers to report and, of course, my husband had to go to help. He met most of the musicians he worked with down at the Kakaako Fire Station. Of course, whenever you get a bunch of musicians together, no matter what was going on outside, they started to drink beer.

The first fire truck had already left to go down to Hickam Field to help put out the fires. The second truck was scheduled to leave shortly, and the musicians were supposed to be on that truck. But they missed the truck because they were in the kitchen enjoying their beer. As it happened, the second truckload of guys all got killed at Hickam. Every one of them.

That night, all the family came over to our house. Everything was blacked out. Two of my sisters-in-law came over with all their children, because their husbands were gone and they were scared. There were fourteen of us, all together in the living room. We just stayed there in the dark. Everybody was afraid. Nobody wanted to go into the bedrooms alone. Simeon was gone, too, still down at the fire station--still partying it up.

" I opened the refrigerator and--oh my God--I had a warden come running up to my door so fast, yelling, 'Turn off that light.' "

I remember I went into the kitchen to get some milk for the children. I opened the refrigerator and--oh my God--I had a warden come running up to my door so fast, yelling, "Turn off that light." He sounded mad. I couldn't believe that that little light could be seen outside. We didn't black out our house until the following week, so we had to be careful about things like that.

I remember we had a big baseball bat in the house. And we were afraid that the Japanese would come back. There was a lot of talk about them invading--landing at Kewalo Basin. If they ever did that, we would all be goners. Anyway, we heard some planes going overhead that night. I decided that I was going to be the one to hit that Japanese soldier when he came through our door. So I told everybody not to worry. I had the bat in my hand and walked over to the door--in the dark--ready to bop him one. At that moment, the door opened. We screamed. I was ready to swing that bat, when Simeon staggered in.

I know a lot of Japanese that were evacuated from the islands. A lot of them had to give up their land and everything they owned. That was a sad thing that happened to them. And a lot of people were leaving the islands to go to the mainland, where they thought it was safer. We could have bought a beautiful home for $5,000 if we wanted to. I could have gone off to the mainland, too, if I wanted to. But I felt, no--if it's going to happen, it's going to happen. I wanted to stay here no matter what happened.

I did not go to work the next morning. Things were so uncertain at that time. There were a lot of businesses that closed up that Monday. A lot of them. I remember that just before the war started, our American Sanitary Laundry delivery trucks were used as part of the civil defense program. So they were preparing for something to happen.

The laundry had a store in Waikiki, on Kalakaua at Saratoga. There was a very nice Japanese girl working there. Grace was her name, I remember. Anyway, just after the war started, the defense workers who lived in Waikiki used to bring their clothes there. They started giving Grace a bad time, just because she was Japanese. So Mr. Magoon asked me if I would go out and work at the Waikiki store. I did, and Grace was moved back to the main plant. I was working there in Waikiki all through the war years. The laundry was a close-knit family. All of the Magoons treated their employees well. And they made a lot of money in that business, as well as other businesses.

" Whenever any troops came to town, we would have to take care of them first. We would do their laundry and the civilians would have to wait--sometimes up to two or three weeks . . . "

Whenever any troops came to town, we would have to take care of them first. We would do their laundry and the civilians would have to wait--sometimes up to two or three weeks at a time. After we put out all of the troops' laundry, then we would do the civilians' laundry. And they really used to complain. There wasn't any such thing as washerettes in those days, you know, where you did your own laundry. It was just strictly a laundry. Anyway, I had to listen to a lot of complaints, but we had to take care of the troops first. That was our contribution to the war effort. We opened the store at seven in the morning and closed at five o'clock. We had to be closed before the blackout began so people could get home.

Oh, my Lord, Waikiki was beautiful in 1942. You could walk down the street on the sidewalk and look at the beach. You didn't have to go between hotels. It was beautiful in those days. Only the Royal Hawaiian and the Moana hotels were there. I remember the military took over those hotels for R & R for the troops.

My husband did volunteer work at the fire station, after hours, while working at City Hall during the day. There wasn't much time for music, at first. He only played on weekends, in the afternoons. Then, in the evenings, Simeon would drive a truck for the civil defense people. He would do deliveries from one base to the other for the military. There was no entertainment at night. As soon as it got dark--that was it-- curfew started. So all their music jobs were on Saturday and Sunday afternoons.

It was hard to get food, especially meats. There was a very popular meat market on King Street--the Metropolitan Meat Market. We used to go down there and stand in long lines--sometimes for hours--before we could buy any meats. And if you bought hamburger, you couldn't get any other kind of meat. In fact, I remember one day--after a long wait in line--I asked for a package of hot dogs. After I got my hot dogs, I said I also wanted some hamburger. I was told that I had already bought my supply of meat and couldn't have any more. I had to wait another three or four days before I could buy anything else. We had little cards that they would mark off. I learned not to buy hot dogs there again.

The military had their USO dances. They would announce on the radio that there was going to be a dance at Hickam and that any girl who wanted to go should go to the YWCA on Richard Street at a certain time. The military command cars would come by and pick up all these women and take them to the dance. Then, when the dance was over, the command cars would drive all of them straight to their homes--right to their front doors.

Simeon was Spanish-Hawaiian, born in Kakaako--two blocks from where I was born. We were neighbors. We fought as children--fought as kids growing up--I was part of his whole family growing up. He came from a family of fourteen kids. Both his father and his mother were reverends. They had a church on Cooke Street--a Hawaiian church--they called it "Ke Alaula Oka Malamalama."[1] His mother also played the organ for the services. It was Congregationalist, strictly Hawaiian. Everyone in his family spoke beautiful Hawaiian when they got together.

He loved his music. After the war, when the government gave back the hotels to the Matson Navigation Company, Simeon played music for the opening of the Royal Hawaiian. He played with Al Kealoha Perry and his orchestra. Winonah Love was the hula dancer with the group. She was a beautiful dancer. Anyway, that was a happy time, when the war was finally over.

The war years for me were mostly work. I had it kind of rough, at times, married to a musician. But I managed. I managed. And I think I did very well for myself.

Dorothy and Simeon had a second child, a daughter, born in 1949. Dorothy worked for the American Sanitary Laundry until it went out of business in the 50s, then went to Young Laundry, where she still works, part-time, today. The Brights have three grandchildren from their son, two boys and a girl. Their daughter, Mervina Sturgeon, is a school teacher living in Seattle, Washington, and she has two children, both girls. Simeon died in 1988. His guitar is Dorothy's prized possession.

---

[1]*Hawaiian words meaning "bright rays of the morning sun."*

Friend or Foe?

On several occasions following the attack, confusion reigned supreme as anxious gunners fired on friendly planes attempting a landing on Oahu. For example, at about 9:00 p.m. on December the seventh, six Wildcat fighters from the carrier *USS Enterprise* approached the islands and were greeted with a barrage of anti-aircraft fire. Four planes were shot down and three of the pilots were killed. The fourth parachuted to safety. Early the next morning, December the eighth, a group of bombers flew in from the mainland and received a similar welcome, but they landed safely.

OURS OR THEIRS? -- Nine-year-old Johnny Staszkow grabbed his Kodak Brownie and snapped this picture of a large group of airplanes flying over Kaimuki during the early hours of the war. (Photo courtesy of John G. Staszkow)

Richard Gossett

Richard Gossett was born in Topeka, Kansas in 1912. He majored in drama at Washburn University in Topeka and graduated in 1935. In 1937, after unsuccessful attempts to land a job in the theater or movie industry in Hollywood, Richard and a friend boarded the S.S. Lurline for Honolulu.

It happened one day in Los Angeles when we were searching for a job. We had the classified ads under our arms--it was still Depression times--and we were walking down the street when we passed the Matson Navigation Steamship offices. We looked at the pretty picture of the beaches, the hula girls, and the white ship. My friend, Kenny Griffith, pointed at the picture and said, "Let's go to Hawaii." I said, "Okay, let's do it." I sold my car to get enough money for the trip and we were off on the *Lurline*. It's pretty ridiculous, now that I think about it, but that poster attracted me to the place that would become my home.

When we got off the boat, we were pretty bewildered. We didn't know what to do or where we were going. A friend of my aunt lived in Honolulu, so I gave her a call. She picked us up and took us to Waikiki to find a place to stay. I think we had about $35 left between us at the time. But we found a place to stay on Uluniu Street--a little rooming house off of Kalakaua--for the magnificent sum of $27 a month, for both of us.

My grandfather, a retired Santa Fe official, had been to Honolulu some years before and had met the general manager of the Oahu Railway and Land Company (OR&L). So, before we left Los Angeles, he gave me a letter of introduction. So, Kenny and I immediately went down to the railroad offices and met Mr. Harry Denison, the general superintendent. The result of it was that they put us both to work a week after we arrived in Honolulu. I didn't even ask how much money I was going to make. I only wanted to know that I had a job. I became the cashier in the freight house and Kenny worked in the round house, because he had had a similar job back in Topeka. The pineapple season was just beginning and the railroad used to haul all the pineapple in those days. That's how my life began in Hawaii.

Mr. Ralph Warren, of the U.S. Engineers, was the government supervisor over the construction of Hickam housing, consisting of five-hundred-and-fifty units built just outside the main gate near the highway and opened in June 1941. My friend, Kenny, had been dating (and subsequently married) Mr. Warren's daughter, and through this connection another friend from Topeka, Dick Strawn, became the manager of the housing area. So I moved out to Hickam and shared a housing unit with Dick, which was a block away from the main gate of Pearl Harbor. That's where I was living when the war broke out.

I had become interested in the community theater in Honolulu, participating in plays from the time I arrived in Honolulu. Elroy Fullmer was the director at the time. He was a terrific director.

We had island-wide blackout rehearsals before the war began. I can remember one particular night, a blackout rehearsal was called right in the middle of the play. All the lights in the theater were turned off. We all found our way in the dark up to the roof on top of the theater to look out over the city and see if there were any lights showing. So we learned what we would have to do in case of an attack or an emergency during a show.

On Saturday, December sixth, Dick had gone off to the Royal Hawaiian Hotel for a party with a bunch of friends from Fort Kamehameha. I was in a play up at Punahou School. It was the final night of "Mr. and Mrs. North." As I recall, it only ran for a few performances. I was the stage manager, but I also had a part in the show. At the beginning of the play, a closet door was opened, and I was the "dead" man that fell forward out of the closet. That was the only part I had but I had to have make-up on. Anyway, that was our final performance of that show. Of course, we weren't aware that that would be the final performance of **any** show for a while.

We had a cast party, as was the custom following a closing night. It was held at the home of the Rev. John P. Erdman, which was located on a portion of the Central Union Church grounds, approximately where the administration building is now situated. He was the Conference Minister for the islands' Congregational churches and a past president of the Honolulu Community Theater. Mrs. Erdman was a daughter of B. F. Dillingham, from whose estate the church had purchased the property in 1920. Anyway, we had a good time and so I didn't get back to Hickam until two or three in the morning. Dick got home about the same time and since we both had had a bit to drink at our respective parties, sleep came quickly.

My very first recollection of December seventh was Dick shaking me and yelling, "Rich, Rich, get up, there's a big show going on out there." The walls of the house were just vibrating back and forth and there was an awful lot of racket--BOOM, BOOM, BOOM--going on outside. So I got up and stumbled out to the front yard and looked up in the sky. There were all these planes flying by. "Boy," I thought, "they sure are doing it up great today. They got the planes painted green with red spots on them. Must be the reds fighting the blues." They did that sort of thing for the military exercises.

" At that moment, another torpedo plane came by over the highway right by our house. . . I could see him looking out the cockpit as he headed for Pearl Harbor. "

Just then, one plane came right by us--practically out in the front of us--over the runway at Hickam and there was smoke coming out of the tail of the plane. Dick said, "Oh, the poor son-of-a-gun. Somebody put some live ammunition in by mistake and they shot this guy." We still had no idea what was going on at that time.

Then a fellow from down the street--a Hickam Field worker--came driving by in his car like a bat out of hell. He was yelling, "The Japs are here, the Japs are here." Dick turned to me and said, "What did he say?"

"I thought he said the Japs were here," I answered. That's when we thought about going into the house to turn on the radio. At that moment, another torpedo plane came by over the highway right by our house. He must have been only one hundred feet up. I could have shot him with a BB gun, he was that close. And I could see him looking out the cockpit as he headed right for Pearl Harbor.

It was hard for us to realize the impact of what was going on. We saw this huge cloud of smoke blowing over from Pearl Harbor, across Hickam Field. Our first reaction was that they were even putting up a smoke screen for the exercises. Little did we know that it was probably the *Arizona* burning up that caused all that smoke. In fact, we didn't find out until quite a while later where that smoke came from. And, you know, that ship was burning until Tuesday afternoon, two days later. It's amazing how long that ship burned.

So we went in the house and turned on the radio. Web Edwards was giving his now-famous speech. "Be calm, everybody, be calm," he said. "The Japs are here. This is the real thing." So I thought to myself, "Well, I still had some make-up on my face from the night before. I hadn't cleaned myself off very well, and since I don't know when I'm going to have a chance to bathe again, I think I'll take a shower." And I did-- while all this was going on outside. I got razzed about that for years. My roommate kept telling everybody, "Yeah, you know him, he goes in and takes a shower while the war is going on outside."

Anyway, I got dressed and went outside again when a squad of guys from the Hickam hospital came by in a truck. "Is that your car?" a corporal asked me. When I answered that it was, he said, "How about driving me back into the field? We don't have any water at the hospital. Its been bombed over there and I want to get some help for this squad to fill those big cooking pots with water for the hospital." So he sent his squad on to fill up the pots with water, and he jumped in my car.

I drove him back on to Hickam Field. That's the only time I ever drove sixty miles-per-hour in Hickam and had the MPs waving me on to go faster. I drove him over to the hospital. To this day, I have never been able to figure out why we had water at the house and the hospital didn't. Our main water line came from Hickam Field. I don't know how that happened.

After he lined up another squad to take care of matters, he had me drive him over by the main mess building. It had taken a direct hit, and he went inside looking for survivors or bodies. I didn't realize it, at the time, as I waited in the car. There were cars parked out in front of the building and one of them was on fire. I could have gone over there and thrown dirt on it, I guess, and put the fire out. It wasn't a very big fire. But I just sat there and watched it burn. I think I was still dazed from everything that was going on and a little groggy from lack of sleep. But at that point, taking everything that was happening into consideration, that car represented a material thing that just didn't matter anymore. So I sat there and watched it burn.

Then I drove the corporal back over to the hospital. By that time, they had bodies outside on the grass with sheets over them. It was so numbing, so unreal, you just couldn't believe what you were seeing.

" . . . they had bodies outside on the grass with sheets over them. It was so numbing, so unreal, you just couldn't believe what you were seeing. "

I went in the hospital and they had some food laid out for anybody that wanted to eat. Interestingly, there was also a bottle of scotch on the table there. Anybody who wanted or needed a swig of the whiskey could just help himself. And everybody needed it. I guess I thought that the bottle came from the officers' club. It was sometime later, when I was telling the story about the bottle of whiskey at the hospital, that I learned where it had come from. Gerald Corbett, who was at that time the purchasing agent for the city, and later a judge in Honolulu, told me, "I'm glad you enjoyed that booze. I got a voucher for that bottle and had it sent out there, paid for out of city and county funds." So I had a drink on the city on December seventh.

That afternoon, trucks from Theo. H. Davies Company showed up at the hospital. They were those old, low-bed trucks called Doanes. They had a chain drive on the wheels and hard tires and they were the Davies delivery trucks at that time. Anyway, these trucks were loaded with milk pails full of water. Evidently, somebody had gotten the word out that the water main was broken at Hickam, and they sent out all these pails of water for the hospital to use. Really amazing.

I continued to help out at the hospital where I could. I can recall going upstairs where the dormitory rooms were and seeing chips of concrete where the machine gun bullets had come through the walls of the hospital.

Because the plumbing didn't work, they dug ditches outside and put up canvas around them for temporary latrines. That was done almost immediately. Darkness came on us quickly that day. You didn't dare go outside after dark that night. The jittery military would shoot at anything that moved. So we stayed in the hospital and I ended up sleeping on the floor of the kitchen all night at Hickam Hospital.

The next day things calmed down a bit. A lot of the families had already been evacuated from Hickam. People moved into town, to safer locations, with relatives and friends. Some of the families of the Hickam workers stayed, though, as they didn't have any place to go. I saw the B-17s that came in from California during the attack and landed at Hickam. They were all shot up, but they made it in. I didn't see any of them coming in, though. I didn't see any of our planes at all during the attack. Of course, there weren't very many of them that got into the air. A few of the flyers from Wheeler Field went down to Haleiwa (where a few fighter planes had been parked, unbeknownst to the Japanese) and took off from there and did very well for themselves against Japanese planes. They shot down quite a few.

" I saw the B-17s that came in from California during the attack and landed at Hickam. They were all shot up, but they made it in. "

I finally went into town about noon, to my job at the railroad station. We all went home fairly early that day. My roommate Dick and I were talking about what had happened to us the day before. He told me that he was on the base, Hickam Field, along about 9:30 a.m. when the last Japanese plane–an observation plane--came over the base. He was at the service station at the time. Of course, at the time nobody knew it was an observation plane, so they reacted as if it was another raid. I asked Dick what he did. "Oh, I rolled under a gasoline truck that was parked nearby," he said. "Oh, that's real smart," I said. And we laughed. You do some stupid things when you're scared. Imagine being under a gasoline truck for protection from an air raid.

Everything was blacked out. At Hickam housing, everything was electric. We had all-electric stoves, hot-water heaters, just everything. And so to enforce the blackout, they would pull the main switch of the housing area at six o'clock at night. So just like that, we were out of power. Many's the evening we had a half-baked potato to eat, or something half-cooked when the electricity went off. It wasn't very long before we felt that that was "old hat" and we needed to do something about it. The grocery stores closed up real early too. I had to go into Rice's market--in town near where I worked--at noontime to try and buy something to cook that evening. They closed the store about 2:30 in the afternoon.

We had been invited a few times over to the Pereira family's house for dinner. He worked at Hickam, testing aircraft engines. She was a great cook. So one night Dick and I asked her if she would take us in as boarders. She said, "Well, if you don't mind eating what we have in the family, that's all right with me." She charged us fifty cents a meal. We had wonderful meals there at the Pereiras', and solved our shopping and cooking challenges.

The railroad was considered a vital wartime industry, so I wasn't drafted. Later, we were able to do theater work, too, to entertain the troops. Mrs. Walter Dillingham, (he was president of OR&L) was active in the women's groups that would entertain the troops. She came down to the railroad station one Saturday and I happened to be there. I was over by the dispatcher's office about noon, and he said that Mrs. Dillingham wanted a ride out to the Royal Hawaiian Hotel, which had been taken over by the navy as a rest and recreation area for submariners. Walter's car was there, so I said, "What the hell, I've got nothing else to do. I'll drive her out there."

So she got in the car and we started out for the Royal Hawaiian. I don't know who she thought I was, or anything, but she started to give me directions on how to get there as if I had just gotten off the boat. "Turn here, go this way," she'd say. When we got to the gate of the Royal, there was a guard there. She pulled out her pass and said, "Myself and chauffeur."

She was a great person--very civic minded. She was on the board of the community theater and I have to admit, if she lent her name to any cause, it was important to her. She attended board meetings and knew what was going on. She just didn't give money to have her name on a plaque or on the stationery. She was all right.

When we were doing plays, we all had passes to be out after curfew. I also had a pass because I worked for the railroad. So if I happened to be caught out visiting somebody in Waikiki after hours, I'd wait until the shift changed then just go down to Kau Kau Korner--where they had the cops stationed--and flash my railroad badge. "Okay, go along," they would say.

When the war first hit, everybody had to black out the house if you wanted any lights on, of course. The supply of electric fans at Liberty House went fast. By the time I got down there, they were all sold out. So I wrote my father back in Topeka and asked him to please get a fan for us. Remember now, this was in the middle of winter back there and all the fans for summer were packed away in storage. But my father managed to get a fan out of winter storage and sent it to me.

As civilian families moved out of Hickam, many housing units became available. So they were used as sort of barracks for the hundreds of mainland war workers that were coming to the islands. One night, in March 1942, I think, there was a plane that came over the city at about 2:00 a.m. and dropped a bomb on Mt. Tantalus. (After the war, it was learned that the bomb had been dropped by a Japanese float plane launched from a submarine. Well, of course, that created an air raid alert all over town, but not in Hickam. We could hear some sirens in the distance, but didn't pay any attention to it.

There were a whole bunch of new troops that just arrived in the area-- many of them were MPs. They put up barbed wire all around the housing area--God knows why--but they did a lot of foolish things during the war. And on the day before the Mt. Tantalus bombing, a whole bunch of new civilian recruits arrived from the mainland to work at Hickam. They had just moved in that afternoon. Huge trenches had been dug around the housing area to be used as bomb shelters, shortly after December seventh. There were no covers over them, just big ditches. Anyway, it had rained a lot that night and these MPs came around at 2:00 a.m. and pounded on all the doors, yelling, "Wake up, wake up, air raid, air raid, get out of there quickly and get into the bomb shelters." Dick and I looked at each other. No way were we going to run out and jump into those muddy trenches. The hell with it, we said. But you could hear all the doors slamming and all those poor rookies-- scared to death--running out to splash knee deep into all that muck. I'll never forget that.

The gas masks they issued became a damned nuisance. After a while, everybody started leaving them at home. But a very strange thing happened on or about the first of June, 1942. Everybody started carrying their masks again. Word of mouth got around that there was something big going on out at Midway. We would see B-17s come in to Hickam from the front lines with big holes in them, so we knew that the fighting was kind of close again. But, of course, after our victory at the battle of Midway, we felt pretty secure once again.

It was pretty deadly staying at home during blackout and curfew. Community theatre work helped to make the time much more exciting for me. After about a year, the army had set up an entertainment section headed by Capt. (later Major) Maurice Evans--a well-known Shakespearean actor--and located in temporary barracks behind Farrington Hall at the university. The theatre made an arrangement with the army that in return for entertaining the servicemen, they would build our scenery and transport it to the various camps all over the island. After a day's work at the railroad, I'd meet the rest of the cast downtown--all of whom had civilian jobs--and we would be transported to the military camp where we were to perform, and provided with a meal.

Each location provided the transportation. At the submarine base and Schofield, we rode in air-conditioned buses--which they rented from the Oahu Railway--but at other locations we rode in bumpy ten-wheel trucks. The quality of the food varied in inverse ratio to the distance from town-- at the sub base it was drinks and even steak. You didn't get steaks too often at that time, so that was pretty choice treatment. At Pupukea Pleasure Palace, which was located back in the hills above the north shore, it was pork and beans. Most of the performances were at night-- we were allowed to be out after curfew because we were performing for the military and they provided the official transportation.

After the curfew had been relaxed a bit, we would do two weeks of performances at Farrington Hall for civilians, then another two weeks solid out at Schofield with a different audience every night. Then we would go for four or five nights a week to different camps all over the island.

As I said, the military supplied our sets and moved them from camp to camp for us. There was one corporal, Bernie Gersten, who was assigned to us. (Bernie later became Joe Papp's assistant in New York.) It was his only job--to take care of the Honolulu Community Theater. We would also go over to Maui and to Hawaii to do one or two shows for the military over there, as well as weekend performances for the civilians. We would fly on those old DC-3s. All the windows would be blacked out, so you couldn't see a thing out of them. What a weird experience, coming in for a landing and not being able to see where you are going.

We used to do anywhere from seventy-five to ninety performances of the same show. It would go on for over a four or five month period. "Doughgirls" was one of the famous wartime comedies that we performed over a long period of time. If I had not been doing theater work during the war, it would have been very boring—especially in the first couple of years or so, when you couldn't go anywhere or do anything.

Those were unforgettable times. It taught you how precious life was. I will never forget sitting in that car at Hickam Field, watching the destruction around me. I watched as that car burned. The war had changed my outlook on material things, forever. I know I won't forget December the seventh, 1941. Those memories will be with me all the rest of my life.

Dick worked at Oahu Railway and Land Company until it closed down at the end of 1947, then continued on with the Oahu Transport Company, successor to OR&L. He did personnel and cost accounting work until his retirement in 1976. In 1965, Dick married a dear friend from school days in Topeka and they have been happily married ever since. He has one daughter who has followed in his theatrical footsteps, planning and organizing theme parties for conferences and conventions. His wife, Patricia, has two grown children and six grandchildren. In retirement, Dick continued theater work for the community theater. Also, he was cast in a 1962 movie with John Wayne--"In Harm's Way"--filmed in Hawaii. He has done many television commercials and appeared a number of times on "Hawaii Five-O." For about ten years, he has volunteered his time at the famous Central Union Church in Honolulu, printing the Sunday bulletins, the weekly newsletter, repairing and maintaining the carillon and hand bells, and doing other odd jobs around the grounds.

William Corlett

Bill Corlett was born in Oakland, California. He graduated from the University of California as an architect in June 1941. He was immediately employed by the U.S. Army Engineers and was sent to Honolulu aboard the Lurline to serve as an architectural draftsman.

We were headquartered on the top floor of the Alexander Young Hotel and our mission was the design of army installations. We designed buildings for the army, including the Fort DeRussy building in Waikiki. It was my first drafting experience and it was quite exciting.

I shared a nice studio apartment in Waikiki on Aloha Drive, and I was making $150 a month, quite a decent wage in those days. In October 1941, my parents came over to visit me and brought me a 1937 Ford roadster, a little green sports car with a rumble seat. Life was marvelous before the war started; we got off work at four o'clock, and I played golf every day at the Ala Wai golf course after work. We ate good dinners on Kalakaua Avenue every night for not more than a dollar; Kalakaua Avenue was full of little restaurants that served wonderful, inexpensive meals. And, there was always a Hawaiian holiday to celebrate--King Kamehameha Day, Lei Day, or queen so-and-so day.

We were having a ball, away from home for the first time, enjoying the glamour of the islands--the beautiful beaches--and we had all this money to spend! We didn't have a care in the world and could never have anticipated the changes we were about to experience.

On December seventh, I was living in a boarding house on Keeaumoku Street. There were about twelve of us living there, half boys and half girls. I heard on the radio that Pearl Harbor was being attacked and ran out in the front yard, just when a number of planes flew by. We could see the Japanese "sun" on the wings of the planes. We walked a little further up Makiki where we had a view of Pearl Harbor and could see the smoke rising from the yard and from Hickam Field. We were dumbfounded by the whole thing, there was mass confusion, but I don't think we were necessarily panicked by it. As I look back on it now, I remember being concerned about what my parents were thinking-- whether they feared that I was killed during the attack.

We went to work the next morning, I recall, and the office was in total turmoil. We were ordered to move all our files, major equipment, and drafting materials from our Alexander Young Hotel location to our new site. We heard that the orders were to take over the University of Hawaii, and as I understand it, there was a large caravan of trucks and equipment heading in the general direction of the university when they came upon the "Punahou College" campus. The lead truck driver, figuring that this must be the place, led the long caravan of trucks onto the Punahou school grounds and they took over the campus. I don't know when the error was finally discovered, but by that time it was too late. They dug bomb shelters, built a flat floor in the Alexander Hall Theater and tossed out the grand piano. The dormitories were taken over for the drafting rooms. So Punahou, not the University of Hawaii, became the new headquarters location for the U.S. Army Engineers.

" . . . I became a camouflage expert. . . one of my first assignments was to camouflage the famous Honolulu landmark, the Aloha tower. "

About that same time, there was a rumor that there was going to be a Japanese landing at Kewalo Basin. Remember, we were all civilians, not military, but they put many of us in army uniforms, issued us rifles, and hustled us down to Kewalo Basin. We were supposed to be a "show of strength" should the Japanese land. I never had a gun in my hand before. I don't think I ever had any ammunition in that rifle, but there we were, trying to give an impression of strength. The Japanese never did land, thank God.

A camouflage department was set up immediately by an army lieutenant, and since I had a fairly good drawing capability, I became a camouflage expert. Our charge was to camouflage gun emplacements, buildings, landmarks, and so forth. In fact, one of my first assignments was to camouflage the famous Honolulu landmark, the Aloha tower. I made drawings of it, mostly from photographs, and created zig-zags of different olive drab colors on it. At that point in time, the Aloha tower was perhaps the most famous landmark in Honolulu. In fact, the Aloha tower, the Royal Hawaiian Hotel and the Moana Hotel, were the three most publicized structures in Honolulu.

We confiscated all of the fish netting we could find amongst the fishermen. We also confiscated all of the pant pocket linings and old clothes we could get our hands on, since pant pocket linings are very strong and durable. We hired many of the local Orientals and fishermen

TOWER CAMOUFLAGED -- The stately Aloha Tower took on a wartime appearance as a result of the camouflage patterns designed by Bill Corlett. The entire dock area, pre-war site of ship arrivals and lei sellers, was off limits to most civilians. (Star Bulletin photo; courtesy of DeSoto Brown)

to rip this stuff up and tie it in knots on the fish netting. The pieces of clothes had been dipped in various greens and canvas colors.

We immediately had a problem. We could not get any of the workers to walk on the nets. That was sacrilegious to them, I guess. So we had to string the nets up for them to work overhead and they were happy. They worked all day long, stringing strips of clothes on the netting, tying them with string.

These camouflage nets were draped over many of the gun emplacements around the entrance to Pearl Harbor. I was out at many of them and would talk to the soldiers manning the guns. I remember asking some of them if they thought they could fire the guns if they had to. They thought maybe they could, but they didn't sound that confident. Some of the guns were test-fired, and, of course, the blast of the gun burned up all of the camouflage.

Another concern we had was our lack of air strength. Since the military didn't want to appear to be weak in that area, I was assigned to design some model P-40s and B-26s to resemble the real thing. I literally went down the street to a model airplane shop and bought the kits for the P-40 and B-26. I brought them back and systematically converted them into working drawings. They were constructed to full size with plywood frames. We put them on saw horses and wired them down so they wouldn't blow away. They were placed out on the runways at Hickam Field just to show that we had several airplanes. I was proud of the fact that they looked quite realistic. In fact, I enjoyed hearing the stories that on many occasions, guys would go out to gas up the planes and would drive up to one of these models because they were so realistic from a reasonable distance. Being off the ground, on saw horses, they cast a proper shadow. They were placed on the edge of the runways as if they were ready for action. There was fear that the Japanese would return for another attack soon and the military wanted to show air strength which was, in fact, not there.

When we first came to Hawaii, one of our initial jobs was the design of gasoline storage facilities. It was highly classified work, so we were all cleared to handle high-security projects. Anyway, drawings were made for a huge gasoline storage system to be buried in the middle of a baseball field located between Hickam Field and Pearl Harbor. We spent a lot of time on it. After it was designed, it was felt to be uneconomical to do, compared to the alternative of storing gasoline in the hillsides in tunnels, so the idea of burying the gasoline in this baseball field was abandoned, and so was the project. This was one of those projects generally known only amongst those of us on the staff with the army engineers.

Interestingly enough, when the Japanese attacked that morning, that baseball field was one of the targets selected by the bombers. There were large craters in the middle of the baseball field when they left, for they really bombed that "gasoline storage" area. The Japanese knew--or thought they knew--that this field was used to store gasoline. There obviously had to be some sabotage going on within our unit, or that target wouldn't have been so pinpointed. Somebody had to have taken those drawings out of our office.

" There obviously had to be some sabotage going on within our unit, or that target wouldn't have been so pinpointed. "

One day, I was called to come for an interview at the army headquarters at Fort Shafter. As I was on my way, I was petrified, wondering what they could want with me. Then I thought, "Oh boy, I've probably made such a great impression on them that they have a real high position in store for me. I was excited thinking about that possibility. As it turned out though, it seems that there was a very high-ranking general with the name of Corlett. As it is an unusual name, the only reason they wanted to talk to me was that they thought I might be a relative of General Corlett. So my dreams of grandeur all went up in smoke.

We were busy doing camouflage work. We painted the hell out of everything. In fact, I was flown around in a DC-3 a couple of times, just around the island, to look at the effectiveness of our work. The goal was to camouflage any formal lines that would be defined as a building--to break up the lines that would diffuse vision from above. You'd get up around eight or ten thousand feet or so and it was surprisingly effective.

Toward the end of 1942, although I was secure from the draft (being a civilian employee with the army engineers), I thought I should be in the service and went for a navy commission.

I was so naive that I remember telling the recruiter, with a straight face, "I think I'd like to start out as a lieutenant junior grade." The guy looked at me without batting an eye and said, "Oh, okay, I'll be sure and put that down," although there was no way in the world I would be anything more than an ensign, if I got a commission at all! I had to survive the "90-day wonder" training--they called it at that time--before I could earn a commission and the right to be an ensign.

So in November 1942, I was sent by ship to the mainland--to Tucson, Arizona, for training. We were issued uniforms and boarded the ship in Honolulu. I left my car in the care of Mary McElrath, a girl from my hometown (and my fiance) whom I met in Honolulu. It took us about eight days to reach California by ship, zig-zagging all the way because there was apparently a submarine threat between the islands and the mainland.

I was assigned to duty aboard ship on the upper deck, where all the life boats were rigged. In an emergency, they would swing out and drop down for use in case we had to abandon ship. There were no railings there and it was pitch dark at nights. To this day, I don't know how I didn't walk off that ship. I would have to observe the horizon, check the ship for lights, then go up and yell, "All clear on the starboard, sir," and salute; and I really didn't even know how to salute properly at that point.

I finished school in Tucson and shortly after, told Mary to sell my car and join me in Oakland to get married. I got two weeks' leave. After a short stint in Oklahoma, we were sent to Pensacola, Florida, where I was the Public Works officer. Then we were sent to Washington D.C. where I was trained as a photographic interpreter. Mary was with me in Washington and she worked for the Red Cross there.

I was later shipped over to Guam, and Mary went home to stay with my father temporarily (my mother had died in the interim) and I was on Guam at the time of the dropping of the atomic bombs. After which, I was stationed in Japan, living at the Imperial Hotel in Tokyo for three months. Among the first Americans in Japan after the war, I worked on the strategic bombing survey.

As I think about our short stay in Hawaii during the war, life went on somewhat as usual. While it's true that the war disrupted our paradise and the horror of Pearl Harbor hung over all, we still enjoyed a social life. I preferred to work one of the night shifts, because then I was free to go to the beach during the day--threading my way through the barbed wire--and surfing at Waikiki. If you went to a party--it was kind of exciting in a way--because you couldn't go home after the blackout and curfew, so you stayed all night. In later years, we often talked about how naive we were at the time; everything was totally proper.

> " While it's true that the war disrupted our paradise and the horror of Pearl Harbor hung over all, we still enjoyed a social life. "

Recalling the first few days of the war, while we were appalled and shocked that Pearl Harbor happened, I don't ever remember feeling that the Japanese would return. I looked at it as not only a "sneak" attack but a "freak" attack. It was a foolhardy, maniacal thing for the Japanese to do. While it certainly was a tragic disruption in many normal lives, we were sure that the United States would prevail.

Following his discharge, Bill went to work at his father's architectural firm and after a few years, opened his own organization in San Francisco. He and Mary have two daughters. Bill worked at his own architectural business for twenty-seven years. Among his many successful projects, Bill states that his "claim to fame" includes the design for all of the buildings for the 1960 Olympics at Squaw Valley, California. He also specialized in school construction--including, ironically, the American School in Japan. Bill retired in 1979. He keeps active playing golf twice a week and tennis two or three times a week. He also serves on many boards of directors in his community and particularly enjoys painting and sculpturing. He and Mary have three grandchildren.

Gas Masks: The Latest Fashion

SAY CHEESE -- Isabel C. Rego, administrative assistant in the office of Civil Defense, demonstrates the latest fashion in head gear, the gas mask. She is modeling the typical canister-type mask that was used by most civilians in Hawaii. She is shown sitting on the entry step to the underground community bomb shelter in Honolulu. (Photo courtesy of Carmen Rego Amadio)

NUMBER, PLEASE -- In a demonstration that must obviously make work difficult, U.S. Engineers department phone operator Mabel Thomas demonstrates the use of another type of gas mask. This version was used by telephone operators in vital industries in the event of gas attack. (**Star Bulletin** June 2, 1942; War Depository Collection, University of Hawaii)

Mary McElrath Corlett

Mary was born in Oakland, California. Following graduation from the University of California in 1941, she and a friend sailed to Honolulu aboard the Matsonia. She had always wanted to visit Hawaii and had never lived away from home before. She found a boarding house in San Souci, near Diamond Head, and got a job at McInerny's in downtown Honolulu. She was secretary to Paul Leong, the store's credit manager and accountant. On December 7, 1941, she was twenty-three and enjoying an exciting life in paradise.

That morning, I'd say it was eight o'clock exactly, I heard a terrific explosion. I didn't know what it was, but it was frightening. Later, we figured that the Japanese might have dropped a bomb nearby, as there was a cable station somewhere close, but we never did see any planes fly directly overhead. Our house was just below Diamond Head.

I switched on the radio right away and I must have heard the first announcements: "The islands are under attack. All police officers report to your stations at once." I ran to tell the other people in the boarding house--there must have been fifteen of us living there--and they just laughed at me. They had a big night the night before, dancing at the Royal Hawaiian Hotel, and they weren't quite recovered from that, and they shrugged it off as maneuvers--an idea widely accepted at first in Honolulu.

We had a big living room that went all the way out to the water. From there, we could look toward Pearl Harbor and I remember seeing clouds of black smoke there in the distance; and I could see one of the ships that I think was trying to escape, being hit by planes. Later in the morning, a Japanese plane emblazoned with the Rising Sun emblem, and all alone, flew closely around Diamond Head.

The radio would come on every once in a while, saying, "Okay, okay, everybody be calm. Now, we'll play the Star Spangled Banner." While we couldn't hear the sounds of the explosions from that distance, we could see the planes and that everything was burning at Pearl Harbor.

We weren't really frightened, just in a state of shock. Maybe that was because I had been in Europe on a student tour when war broke out in

1939. I had quite a time trying to escape from Europe then. So this experience may not have seemed so fearful to me after going through that.

Numerous Japanese servants throughout Honolulu did not show up that morning to serve breakfast, so many local Japanese knew in advance that this was going to happen. Otherwise, they would have been there before the attack started, at eight o'clock. No matter what people say, there had to be a number of local Japanese aware of the attack plans.

We were told to stay indoors, and there was complete blackout and curfew that night. We all congregated together in the living room and that's where we spent the night--supporting one another.

On Monday, I went to work at McInerny's as usual. Everyone was frantic about what had happened. Many knew people at Pearl Harbor and there was much concern for the safety of their friends. And, of course, everybody had their individual stories to tell. One of my friends, and a fellow-employee at McInerny's, lived out at Hickam Field. Claire O'Callahan's husband worked for the army engineers and they had housing out there on the base. When the bombs starting dropping all around their house, they jumped in their car and evacuated the area. So there wasn't too much work done that Monday, and people weren't shopping, either.

Rumors ran wild. I was told that a certain advertisement that appeared in the newspaper the day before the Pearl Harbor attack was a coded signal to the local Japanese people so that they would know the attack was on. It was a listing of silks for sale and supposedly told, through a code, what ships were in the harbor that day. I don't remember what the codes were, but I clipped out the ad and sent it to my parents in California with a letter, explaining what I had heard about the ad. I had no idea what I was getting myself into by doing that.

One morning my boss came by my desk and said, "I don't want to worry you unnecessarily, but the FBI wants to see you over at the Alexander Young Hotel right away." So I went over there, and I must admit I was pretty nervous, wondering what this could be all about.

When I entered this huge room, there were three uniformed men sitting at the far end of the room. They started grilling me and were pretty antagonistic. My mail had been censored and they wanted to know where I heard about the newspaper ad being a code? They asked

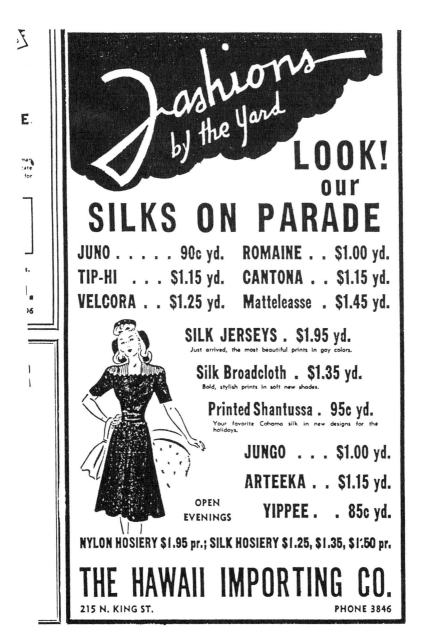

Fashions by the Yard

LOOK!
our
SILKS ON PARADE

JUNO . . . . . 90c yd.	ROMAINE . . $1.00 yd.
TIP-HI . . . $1.15 yd.	CANTONA . . $1.15 yd.
VELCORA . . $1.25 yd.	Matteleasse . $1.45 yd.

SILK JERSEYS . $1.95 yd.
Just arrived, the most beautiful prints in gay colors.

Silk Broadcloth . $1.35 yd.
Bold, stylish prints in soft new shades.

Printed Shantussa . 95c yd.
Your favorite Cohama silk in new designs for the holidays.

JUNGO . . . $1.00 yd.

ARTEEKA . . $1.15 yd.

OPEN
EVENINGS

YIPPEE . . 85c yd.

NYLON HOSIERY $1.95 pr.; SILK HOSIERY $1.25, $1.35, $1.50 pr.

THE HAWAII IMPORTING CO.
215 N. KING ST.   PHONE 3846

RUMOR SUBJECT -- This advertisement appeared in Honolulu newspapers before December 7, 1941, and was the subject of rumors that spread throughout Honolulu. It was reported to contain hidden messages that would warn local Japanese of the attack. The sub-headline, "by the yard," allegedly referred to the Navy Yard at Pearl Harbor. The word "parade" in the headline was loosely translated as "air raid" (if you dropped the P and used your imagination). Also, the design in the upper left corner supposedly depicted a cloud of smoke. (Newsclip courtesy of DeSoto Brown collection) me what I was doing spreading rumors? I didn't know the answers to their questions, having heard about the ad from lots of people, since the story was really going around town. I was being royally chastised for spreading rumors.

And, they asked the same questions over and over, calling me a rumor monger. I was afraid that they would ship me back to California, but after an hour of grilling--it seemed like three--they sent me back to work with a warning.

I met Bill Corlett through my friend and fellow worker at McInerny's, Claire O'Callahan. Her husband worked with Bill. We met, on a blind date, but not with each other. Anyway, Bill left the islands in November 1942 to attend a navy school, and left his precious car in my care. We had a big rain and floods at that time. I was living in Kahala and the water and mud flooded the inside of the car. Since weather was another subject you never mentioned in letters, I said nothing about it to Bill. I learned my lesson and didn't want another meeting with the FBI.

I left McInerny and went to work at Central Union Church in mid-1942, as secretary to the minister at the church. I stayed there until early 1943, when I was able to get transportation back to California to marry Bill Corlett in April. The trip by boat was long and rough. My exciting adventure in "paradise" didn't last long because of the war tragedy, so I was happy to be back home again and looked forward to being reunited with family, friends, and especially Bill.

Mary McElrath married Bill Corlett on April 3, 1943. They had two daughters, Cameron, born in 1947, and Amanda, born in 1948. The Corletts make Berkeley, California their home, but enjoy frequent trips back to "paradise," where they met. They have three grandchildren, two boys and a girl.

Joseph Gordon Hauoli Dowson, Sr.

Joe Dowson's father, Charles Phillip Dowson, Sr., was half Japanese, English, Scottish and Irish, and was born in Yokohama, Japan. Joe's grandfather had been commissioned by the Emperor of Japan to build subways and bridges in Yokohama and Tokyo at about the turn of the century. His grandfather attended Waseda University in Japan and later moved to Hawaii to become the chief engineer at the Ewa Plantation in about 1910. Joe's father, Charles Dowson, graduated from McKinley High School in Honolulu, then attended Waseda University in Japan. He then continued his studies at Northwestern University in Illinois and at the University of Iowa, becoming a dentist. He came back to Hawaii and married Marguerite Kapuina Evans, a school teacher. Marguerite was Chinese, English, Hawaiian, Cherokee, and French. They moved to Maui where Charles Dowson set up his dental practice with an office in Kahului. They lived in lower Paia. Joe was born in Puunene, Maui, in 1924. He was Charles and Marguerite's third child.

I remember when I was young, my father was one of only two dentists on Maui. Doctor Ting was the other one. In the Haiku Plantation, the Filipino laborers loved gold teeth. So my father made a fortune on gold teeth in those days. So we had a chauffeur who drove a Packard touring car. And we also had a washwoman, a cook, and a maid. And we lived in the biggest house in Paia. Life was good in those days.

We all went to Kanoa School. I guess my best three years in Kanoa School was the first grade. I just couldn't get out of first grade. My mother kept flunking me. She was the principal.

When I was about six years old, my mother got sick. Funny, but, cancer was considered like leprosy in those days, so they told me she died of a busted appendix. We lived upstairs in this big two-story house. My mother came and visited me on the night she died. She came in and kissed me and said, "Goodbye. I'm leaving you for a while." I was quite sad.

My father came in the next day and told me that Mother died. I told him that she visited me the night before and he just smiled. I told my sister and brother about it and they thought that I was full of beans. Nobody believed me. But it happened.

She was at Peters Funeral parlor in Maui. Everybody came by. My grandfather, who was the son of Sir Charles Phillip Dowson, an English Lord, even came over for the funeral. It was sad, everybody was crying. But I couldn't cry. I don't know why, I just couldn't cry. I didn't know what to do. They shipped the body over to Honolulu and she was buried in the family plot at Nuuanu Cemetery.

Usually a mother holds the whole family together. When a mother dies, the whole family is destroyed. That's what happened to us. My father went off and married another woman. It was disastrous. We lost our land, my mother's jewelry, and everything. My father was so depressed. We got shunted off to relatives to live. I went with my Japanese grandmother. We lived in Kaimuki on Koko Head Avenue and she sent me to Japanese school at Aliiolani School.

In Japanese School, we read about the Russo-Japanese War and how the Japanese conquered the Russians and drove them out. And there was this young Japanese teacher, I still remember his face. He was in perfect physical condition. His hair was cut just so. He would come in and make us all stand up, perfectly straight. We'd sing the Japanese national anthem, salute the Japanese flag. He ruled us with a bamboo stick. If we didn't do it right, we'd get whacked.

I later thought he must have been a spy. He reminded me of a Japanese army lieutenant and I always imagined him in uniform, even though he didn't wear one. He was mysterious and kept to himself. He was not the normal Japanese teacher you would get. I knew something was wrong with him. About a year before Pearl Harbor, he disappeared. Probably went back to Japan.

I still speak fluent Japanese, in fact I can speak seven languages. But in those days, particularly after the war began, a lot of my Japanese friends changed their names to Chinese names.[1] If anybody asked me if I was Japanese, I would tell them that I had some Japanese in me.

We had fun living in Kaimuki before the war. I remember we played rubber gun fights with all these kids. I invented the first canon, you

---

[1]*During the first year of the war, about 2,400 persons of Japanese descent in the territory filed petitions to change their names. (Allen, Hawaii's War Years)*

know. I'd put a whole inner tube on a stick, with a clothes pin and, as they charged, I'd pull the pin, and they'd all fall down. We played on top of the reservoir in back of the fire station. We knew that area by heart. I grew up with Albert Evenson, now a lawyer; and Dickie Given, who has an art shop on Bishop Street; Stennett Bell of Bell Furniture; Phillip O'Toole and Abe Aiona.

" . . . after the war began, a lot of my
Japanese friends changed their names to
Chinese names. "

We knew all the firemen at the fire station. I spent most of my time over there, sliding down those poles. I would watch them play blackjack and poker all day, too. It was quite a scene watching those firemen lose their pants.

I went to Robert Louis Stevenson Junior High School, then on to Roosevelt High School.

My father moved to Molokai to open a dental office there. In 1941, I was a senior at Roosevelt and my brother was at the University of Hawaii, playing football. I quit Roosevelt to go to Molokai and visit my father. I attended Molokai High for a couple of months there. We lived in King Kalakaua's old home in Kaunakakai. What an elegant home. It had a rambling porch. But it was old. It even had an outside privy. It was so old you almost had to cook outside. It was real authentic. The only thing I didn't like about that home was the outside privy. Later, they destroyed it. They didn't know the value of an historic place like that, I guess.

Anyway, on December seventh, I was in Molokai. My father had gone down to Honolulu on the boat to watch my brother play football. They were scheduled to play San Jose State College.[2] Many of the players became policemen when war broke out. They couldn't go back to California, they were stranded because of the war. All transportation closed down.

---

[2]Members of the San Jose State College and Willamette University football teams, in the islands for post-season games, became volunteer policemen and handled other defense jobs, many for the duration of the war.

We heard the radio station from Honolulu, Webley Edwards, saying, "This is the real thing. This is not a maneuver." Everybody was standing around outside, looking around in the sky. The Judge family--their son Kauka Judge, and his son were officers, and they formed a militia patrol. They had people running all over the place--running into each other. Nobody knew their left foot from their right. It was more dangerous with them than with the enemy, you know. It was complete panic.

Anyway, Charlie McCoriston, who was the unofficial mayor of Molokai--he ran the movie house and some other things on the island-- was the colonel in charge of the local Hawaiian Territorial Guard. They knew I had ROTC training at Roosevelt, so they gave me a group of men to train. These were big Hawaiians, an ethnic mixture of everything, half of them didn't know how to use a gun. We had old Springfields. I taught them how to put bullets in them. Then they started shooting street lamps out.

I took a group down to Momomi Beach to guard the beach that night for the invasion of the Japanese. This beach is famous on Molokai. We figured this is where the enemy would land. It's where the canoes take off. You sat and waited for the Japanese. You dug a semi-trench around you and you sat there with your gun all night. After dark, you heard the centipedes. They would come out because they would look for a warm spot. That place was famous for centipedes. In the morning, you would get up in these little dips, and the centipedes would try and crawl up on you--about twenty at a time. It was frightening. I couldn't stand centipedes. The worst enemy wasn't the Japanese. It was those damned centipedes.

The Hawaiians on Molokai were something else. We would pull up with the truck to pick up a Hawaiian from his house to take him to his post on the beach. He'd say, "Eh. We go fight the Japanese, yeh? Okay, 'at's right, I get rifle and be right there." We would wait, then yell, "You ready, yet?" He'd say, "No. One more minute." After some time, we go up to the door to look for him, and there he is in bed with his wife. He looks at us. "This gotta be my last one, bruddah," he says, "that's natural, huh? One more minute." His wife is crying when he comes out, and we leave for the beach.

Colonel McCoriston placed a bunch of us at a post. It was a crucial intersection, the Houlehua junction, where people were going to Houlehua and Maunaloa and down to Kaunakakai. With me at that post

I had the Inoka brothers--the fearsome Inoka brothers. They were sharp-shooters. Also with us was a comedian named Jiggs Leslie. He was a famous local entertainer. He would keep us entertained all night, playing the ukulele. We'd stop any car that would go by. If there were any lights showing, the Inoka brothers would shoot them out. They were crazy. It was a hell of a situation. They'd patrol the town of Kaunakakai and any lights that were on, they'd tell them to turn it off otherwise, "We'll turn them off for you." They'd shoot the street lamps. They were having a ball, but they sure caused a lot of damage.

" With me at that post I had the Inoka brothers . . . If there were any lights showing, the Inoka brothers would shoot them out. They were crazy. "

We actually saw a submarine come up out at Kaunakakai and shoot at the Shell gasoline tanks. They missed. So then we got the orders to paint the tanks black. We painted those big silver tanks black, even at night.

We waited and waited for the invasion of the Japanese. We were sure, once, that we saw a carrier off Lanai. But I don't think so, because their carriers were way off by that time. It could have been our carrier, coming in.

During the day, they thought they saw parachutes coming in. That night, hundreds of guys went out on the pineapple fields looking for them. It was nothing. People were going crazy. The only people that got hurt on the outside islands were the people shooting at each other.

Every time there was a rumor that they were landing on the east side of the island, we'd all rush to that area. And there we'd find a fisherman, coming in with a lamp, trying to pull up his crab nets.

A couple of days later, I jumped a pineapple barge and came back to Honolulu. I found things so sad here. They were running the Japanese down. Because my father was born in Japan, they gave us black badges to wear to go into a military post. You were Japanese, even if you were only half or one-quarter. My father might still have had Japanese citizenship. He never took time out to get American citizenship. I don't know if he was too lazy or what, but he didn't bother about such details. He was considered a Japanese alien, even though he was so pro-American. He just loved America.

" My father . . . never took time out to get American citizenship. . . He was considered a Japanese alien, even though he was so pro-American. He just loved America. "

My brother was scheduled to go to Annapolis, nominated by Hawaii representative and future governor, Samuel Wilder King. And he was turned down because of his Japanese ancestry. It was sad. My sister was in charge of a group of ladies at the University of Hawaii--it was a patrol group. She dropped out. She wasn't accepted because she was one-quarter Japanese. We got really ostracized because we were part Japanese. We were what they called a "third rate" citizen.

I got a job at Pearl Harbor. That's where I had to wear the black badge. It meant I could only go in certain areas. I worked for a salvage company and I was what you called a "tool diver." I worked with divers who were cleaning up the mess of sunken ships at Pearl Harbor. I would dive down in about twenty feet of water, holding my breath for two minutes, and bring tools and stuff to them. I did it part-time. It was good money.

It was really something down there. They were salvaging, to see how bad the ships were--whether they were salvagable--or whether they should leave them as tombs. When they had lights on, you could see in the thick port holes, a whole room full of guys lying around, floating--and they'd say to leave it as an entombment.

The guys that had the red badges, they handled ammunition and everything. They could go anywhere, any military area. We had to be stopped and questioned. The civil service wouldn't hire you if you had Japanese blood. But I got so insulted by that black badge that I got this picture of Gargantua, the gorilla that had acid thrown in his face. He was really ugly. I put that picture in place of mine on the badge. But I really got insulted when they took one look at that picture and let me in. I guess I really did look like Gargantua.

We were still in school, now, and working. School was out for a couple of months. The navy moved into Roosevelt High School and made it into a barracks. They considered anything you did for defense as equivalent for school credit, so we were later given what they called a wartime diploma.

So school opened up again. All of the guys got hired at the first-aid station. They closed all the Japanese schools and they became first-aid stations. They paid the high school seniors to man these stations. We'd sleep there overnight. It was a wonderful job. You'd go to school during the day but stay there at night, and you were trained in first aid. In case of any disaster, we were supposed to have everything ready. The Red Cross instructed us.

To get around town in those days was the hardest thing, because of the curfew and blackout. And it was hard to get gas, because it was rationed. Another job I had, I was in charge of a USED (the engineers) gas station at Kalakaua and Beretania Streets. A Samoan guy and I handled the job--he was the day shift guy and I was on the night shift. I had a lot of friends in school because I had that job. We used to fill up all the football players' cars. I was the most popular guy in school because of that. That was a rotten thing to do, but what the hell, I never got caught. We had no big crimes in those days. We might have siphoned gas and stole hubcaps, but never anything serious.

There was a guy named Bruce Cameron. He was related to the Baldwins of Maui. He really had a system to fool the army and the patrols. He went out and bought a hearse. He put on a black coat and hat and he would drive that hearse anywhere at night, after curfew and blackout. He had a casket in the back and he'd go through all of the road blocks. And half the time the back of the hearse would be full of all of us guys, and we'd go all over town. We had a ball. God, it was funny. Bruce Cameron, he was so crazy. He would walk into a party in Manoa and they'd run out of booze. He'd say, "I'll get some." And he'd go down the street to another party, steal their booze, and bring it back. And booze was hard to get in those days, you know. It was rationed. But Cameron got around.

You couldn't get the mainland standard brands, so local companies started putting out Five Island Gin and Diamond Head whiskey. You had to stand in line to get this stuff once a week. I never drank, but if I got my hands on any bottles, I'd sell them. We did anything to make money in those days.

They had a strict curfew and we'd have parties up at Alewa Heights on weekends after football games. We used to get gas from Mayor Petrie's house. He lived up there. What the hang, he had his own private gas. We made good with his daughter and she would give us gasoline.

Oh, I remember, one night we were swimming in Dr. Hanchett's pool and people complained. So the cops came and chased us up the hill. We were completely nude, holding our clothes in our hands, running up the road. They told me, "Joe, jump over the hedge." And I jumped right over a three-foot hedge. But what they didn't tell me was that there was a twenty-foot drop down on the other side. The cops came up, shined the flashlight over, I'm lying there, they said, "Oh, he's had it. Forget it." We had good fun in those days. Now it's all coming back to me.

At Roosevelt, I was on the '43 championship football team. It was the greatest. They still talk about it. We beat everybody, even St. Louis. Why we had a powerful team was the fact that Iolani High School was completely dismantled during the war. They didn't have a school. So all the players from Iolani came to Roosevelt. So we had all the good players. Spike Cordeiro, Augie Rieman, George Hong, who is now president of the Waialae Country Club. We always have a reunion. In fact, we recently buried one or our teammates, Stanley "Mousy" Alama. That team was the greatest.

I became a policeman after the war, and stayed there for twenty-nine years. There were still policemen from San Jose State football team on the force after the war. Many of them stayed on because they loved Hawaii.

I had a very strange life growing up. I lived with my grandmother, then from one aunt to an uncle, to an aunt, to an uncle. I was like an unwanted child. It was a sad situation. I guess I was a rascal. And, I guess the war years helped to make life more exciting for me. I will always remember those years.

Joe married Christine Kananiolele Aki in 1948. They had four children. Joe earned a degree in philosophy from the University of Hawaii after taking courses for ten years, part-time. He returned to take art courses and is now a most distinguished landscape artist. He has painted throughout the United States, Canada, and Europe, but is best known for his island scenes. His paintings are part of private collections throughout the world, including the collections of Loni Anderson, Jack Lord, Pat Morita, Shirley Jones, Burt Reynolds, and U.S. Senators Dan Inouye and Spark Matsunaga. He retired as a special investigator in the office of the Chief of Police and Internal Affairs in 1976. A daughter is also an illustrator, and has done all the extinct birds for the Bishop Museum in Honolulu. Joe's oldest son is a Honolulu Police Field Sergeant in Wahiawa. His youngest daughter is a chef and his other son is an F-15 fighter pilot with the Hawaii Air Guard. Joe and Christine have six grandchildren. Joe continues his art and works as a legal investigator for a Honolulu law firm. Joe and Christine live in Mililani.

Evacuation: Get Out of Town

DOWNTOWN EVACUATION -- With a grin at the camera from an unidentified sergeant, civilians and military personnel (not on duty) evacuated the downtown business district in fifteen minutes in air-raid alert and evacuation exercises. Here, a Manoa-destined bus loads passengers in front of the Alexander Young Hotel on Bishop Street. Note the blacked-out head lamp. (**Star Bulletin** Nov. 5, 1943; War Depository Collection, University of Hawaii)

AN EMPTY STREET -- Normally bustling with shoppers and business people, Fort Street in downtown Honolulu was suddenly emptied. Evacuation exercises, staged during the middle of busy work-days, were conducted a number of times during the war by the army and the Office of Civil Defense. (**Star Bulletin** Nov. 5, 1943; War Depository Collection, University of Hawaii)

Abel L. Dolim

His father, Augustine Dolim, was born in Kapakalua, Maui. He worked for the sugar plantation there, helping his father to cut and haul fire wood from kiawe trees. He married Mary Mendonca, who came to the islands from Portugal when she was two years old. Augustine and Mary had two children, born in Honolulu. Abel was born in 1922 and Henry was born in 1923. The Dolim family lived in Kaimuki at 811 7th Avenue. Augustine worked at Pearl Harbor. Abe attended Lunalilo School to the sixth grade, then went to St. Louis from the seventh grade through high school, graduating in 1940. He was nineteen, living at home, and was working for the Hawaiian Pineapple Company as a machinist on December 7, 1941.

My father had a 30-foot boat--a cabin cruiser that we called a "hapa-haole"[1] sampan--and he went fishing every Sunday. The boat was built at the Matsumoto Boat Works down on Kapiolani, near Pier 2, and was launched in 1940. My father would get up very early Sunday mornings and first go to the six o'clock Mass at the cathedral on Fort Street. By 7:00 a.m., he was usually leaving Kewalo Basin and heading out to sea. He often fished off Pearl Harbor, outside the three-mile limit. They always had a destroyer patrolling the area, and if you were caught inside the three-mile-limit, you'd get a citation.

I went with him often and we'd fish way out where it was pretty deep. We'd often fish out at Barber's Point, trolling all the way down there and back. And we'd deep-fish, too, as far down as two thousand feet. In fact, we caught fish that nobody could identify--black devils with sharp teeth--like prehistoric monsters. I really enjoyed going fishing with my old man. He was a cracker-jack fisherman. On December 7, 1941, however, for some reason I didn't go out with him.

That morning, I got up early, dressed, and went to the seven o'clock Mass at St. Patrick's. It was about eight o'clock, I'd say, when I got back home. Our house was a two-story home, on the high side of the street. We had a front porch that looked down toward Pearl Harbor. Going up

---

[1]*A Hawaiian word meaning a person part white and part Hawaiian.*

the steps to the porch, for some reason I turned around and looked out. I saw these white puffs over Pearl Harbor and I thought, "What the heck's the navy doing having gun practice on Sunday?" I was really surprised at that, so I went in and turned on the radio. Then I was really puzzled because KGMB was not on the air at that time. I purposely left the radio on.

A few minutes later a very excited announcer came on and he said, "We are under sporadic attack by unknown airplanes." I'll never forget he said "sporadic." Then he really got excited and I realized that something important had happened--that something was very wrong.

Anyhow, my dad was on his boat, out of Kewalo Basin, before the attack, and heading for open sea when he came upon the destroyer *USS Ward* patrolling out there. He watched in amazement as he saw an airplane drop a bomb near the *Ward*.[2] When he saw the explosion it

TORA TORA TORA – Pictured are three Nakajima torpedo bombers going into Pearl Harbor for the kill. (Tora Tora Tora were the Japanese code words meaning the "surprise" was successful). This photo, taken by one of the Japanese flyers, was given to Abel Dolim by a Japanese historian. These are the type of airplanes--on their way back to the carriers--that Dolim saw above his house on December the seventh. (Abel L. Dolim photo collection)

[2]*The airplane, in fact, was an American PBY which joined the Ward in dropping depth charges, sinking a Japanese two-man submarine outside the Pearl Harbor entrance. The Ward was credited with firing the first U.S. shot in World War II, before the attacking planes arrived at Pearl Harbor.*

produced, he turned right around and headed back to shore. He came back home and that's about the time they were calling all Pearl Harbor workers to report to their shops, so he immediately got in his car and took off.

I watched the whole thing from my front porch. I remember seeing formations of aircraft. I was quite an aviation buff and built a lot of models when I was a kid. In fact, that's all I could think of--flying! So I saw these high-level bombers--torpedo-type Nakajimas--about a dozen of them flying right over our house, heading north at about eight thousand feet, I'd say.

---

*" So I saw these high level bombers--
torpedo-type Nakajimas--about a dozen of
them flying right over our house . . . "*

My dad came home late that evening and told us what he had gone through down there. And, of course, that night Pearl Harbor was lit up like a carousel again. What a fantastic amount of anti-aircraft fire filled the night sky. We were sure the Japanese had come back for another attack. It turned out that they were firing at our own navy aircraft--the planes trying to come in from our carriers, I think.

Then the next morning, I got up real early and I saw three B-18 bombers heading east, over toward Fort Ruger. And they were flying low--maybe three thousand feet. The guns at Fort Ruger opened up on them in broad daylight. I knew what B-18s looked like because I built a model of that airplane, but here we were shooting at our own planes again. I don't think any got shot down.

For the first few days at Pearl Harbor, my father was making stretchers for moving the wounded. He was a joiner in his regular job there. He specialized in doing concrete forms--the heavy work. Then he got very busy working overtime. The U.S. Coast Guard commandeered his fishing boat immediately.

Then there was a radical change in our lifestyles. There was blackout every night. You had your curfew. Before the attack, I used to spend a lot of my time at the beaches, hiking in the mountains, and fishing with my father. You couldn't do anything like that anymore. There was nothing to do. In fact, it got so bad, I couldn't wait to get away from the islands.

At the Hawaiian Pineapple Company, we went on a six-day, ten-hour-a-day shift. We did a lot of work for the navy and the army. A great deal of the machinery was brought up from the sunken ships and we reconditioned them. I remember that we had to work on electric motors–great big electric motors. We had an electric shop that would bake them and dry them out. We would straighten out a bent shaft, and we made parts for gun equipment. Some of the motors we were working on were used to raise and lower the five-inch naval guns.

Then they put me on a lathe making parts from micarta rods for intercommunication sets for naval vessels. They were very difficult to machine--the damned things kept cracking all the time. So the foreman and I worked out a way to use flat-fluted drills with an air nozzle to cool the piece as you worked on it and, by gosh, it worked. I was on that job a couple of months. I must have made hundreds of those darn things.

You went to work, you came home, hit the sack, and started all over again the next morning. For a nineteen-year-old kid, you know, that could be a real bore.

It turned out that the fact that my dad had his boat taken away from him was a real break for me. They offered him an appointment in the coast guard temporary reserves. He declined the appointment but said that he would recommend that I go in his place. I jumped at the chance.

So in January 1942, I began taking classes at night, studying charts, maps, Morse code, and navigation. We were taught by a young ensign who had been one of the sailors on the famous sailing vessel, the *Yankee*. He was excellent on navigation. We learned simple types of navigation like pilotage dead reckoning (time and distance checkpoints), and celestial navigation (checking your courses by using the stars). It was very interesting and I really enjoyed it.

Then they started taking young men for the air cadet program. They dropped the requirements of two years of college to just a high school education to qualify. As soon as that happened, the first chance I had, I went in and applied. I already had a cousin, Henry P. Dolim, who graduated from the flying school in Texas and was a lieutenant on active duty in Panama at the time the war began. So I wanted to get in too.

There were eighteen of us that took the written examination in March

1942. Only five of us passed. Of the five of us that then took the physical examination, only three of us passed--all Kaimuki boys–Tom Foley, Bob Duncan, and myself. Bob became a fighter pilot. He was an instructor all through the war. He even did some ferrying of aircraft to Alaska for the Russians. We wrote to each other all through the war. He later became a pilot for Hawaiian Air Lines. Tom Foley got posted to the 15th Air Force as a gunner, and I became a navigator. Only three of us made it out of the eighteen candidates.

So I was called to active duty as an aviation cadet in August 1942 and we were shipped to the mainland following a short stay at Hickam. We were on the old *Matsonia* liner, built in 1910. It was a six-ship convey and it took us ten days to get to San Francisco, zig-zagging all the way at about eight knots. We had daily emergency drills and anti-aircraft gunnery practice and because we were cadets, we got to do all the dirty work on the ship. Cleaning the latrines and sweeping the scuppers was a real come-down for guys that were looking forward to flying.

My brother, Henry, was eighteen and he wanted to beat the draft. So he joined the air force in 1942. They assigned him to the 11th Bomb Group which shipped out right away without giving him any training. They took off for the support of the Guadalcanal campaign. He was a bookkeeper for the Honolulu Iron Works when he joined up, so naturally they made him a baker in his squadron. And he enjoyed it. Even now, every once in a while when we get together, I'll sing him that old army song:

> "Oh, the biscuits in the army, they say are mighty fine.
> One fell off the table, and killed a friend of mine.
> Oh, I don't want no more cf army life.
> Gee, Mom, I want to go home."

It's a little ditty that goes on and on. Anyway, he became a pretty good baker. Still can bake a pretty good apple pie.

So anyway, this navigation that I learned from the coast guard ensign helped me to get the highest score in navigation. I didn't realize it then, but my coordination and dexterity weren't too good. I failed those tests. I qualified for pilot training, but barely. I did most of my training at Mather Field, near Sacramento, California, then they shipped me up to Washington state to join a bomber group. Within a week, we all got shipped to Florida for aircrew training and from there they shipped us out to England. Some of the guys went to Italy.

All my life all I ever wanted to do was fly. When I got assigned to a bomber group, I thought that was a big deal. And the B-17 was quite an airplane in those days. I was literally on top of the world. I was a navigator, flying bombing missions over France and Germany.

I will never forget one hairy experience I had in June 1944. It was the day after D-day, the allied invasion of Europe. We flew a mission over France to bomb the railroad bridge over the Loire River at Nantes. The object was to keep the Germans from moving tanks up to the invasion area. We hit the target and headed home. It got dark as late as ten o'clock that time of year. When we got to the channel, the weather was bad. We had to knock down from twenty thousand feet to about eight thousand. It got dark, so we couldn't fly in formation anymore. So everybody split and we were on our own.

It turned out there were German "intruders" waiting for us right off of the base area. They were "working" the bombers that got back ahead of us, shooting them down in their landing pattern. They were twin-engine German fighters--ME 410s--and they had 40mm cannons on them. Those shells, an inch-and-three-quarters in diameter, could really punch a big hole in you.

FLYING FORTRESS CREW – Abel Dolim (left) poses with crew of B-17G bomber at Bury St. Edmunds, England, in December 1944. Abel served as navigator. Next to Abe is pilot Ed Reed; ground crew chief Dominic Pacific; bombardier H. Keith Cearley; co-pilot Raymond Rosbury; and ball turret gunner Jack Ewers. (Abel L. Dolim photo collection)

Anyway, we saw fires on the ground below us. Turned out that they were the bombers that had been shot down by the Germans. We were told to detour over to Ireland for half an hour to evade the enemy aircraft. So we did. Then we headed back for our base and they had already left to return to Germany because they only had so much fuel.

> " . . . we saw fires on the ground below us.
> Turned out that they were the bombers that
> had been shot down by the Germans. "

But it was pitch black, one o'clock in the morning, and we were running out of fuel. It was my job to get us back to that base--and I hit that sucker right on the money. What a great feeling. We flew right over that base. They had no lights on, of course, everything was blacked out. We

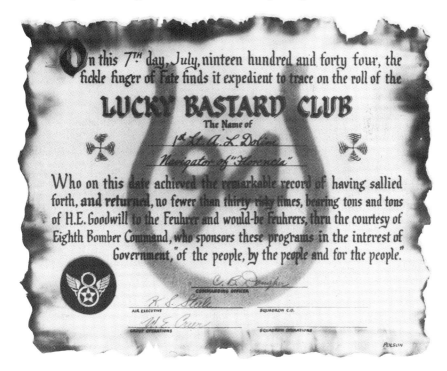

On this 7th day, July, nineteen hundred and forty four, the fickle finger of Fate finds it expedient to trace on the roll of the

LUCKY BASTARD CLUB

The Name of

1st Lt. A. L. Dolim

Navigator of "Florencia"

Who on this date achieved the remarkable record of having sallied forth, and returned, no fewer than thirty-odd times, bearing tons and tons of H.E. Goodwill to the Feuhrer and would-be Feuhrers, thru the courtesy of Eighth Bomber Command, who sponsors these programs in the interest of Government, "of the people, by the people and for the people."

THIRTY FLIGHTS AWARD – The 8th Bomber Command presented this "Lucky Bastard Club" certificate to Abel Dolim for thirty bombing raids over France and Germany. Dolim went on to complete fifty-one missions over enemy territory--including seven flights over Berlin--more than anybody in his bomb group. (Abel L. Dolim photo collection)

331

had an identification code to determine friend or foe--that changed every day. As soon as we were identified, they turned the landing lights on for us and we came in and landed. Our engines quit before we got back to our squadron area. We were pretty proud. We were only one of a few bombers that made it back to the base that night. The rest of them were scattered all over England, or shot down.

I flew fifty-one missions--twenty-seven on my first tour and twenty-four on my second. I flew seven missions to Berlin--more than anybody in my bomb group--that was because they were short on navigators and I would go up with different crews. I was very lucky. As a matter of fact, I've been lucky all my life. Some people say they don't believe in luck. I say, bull! I believe in luck. I wouldn't have made it through fifty-one bombing missions if I didn't have a lot of luck.

In 1946, Abe married Mary Frances Nuzum, who was from St. Petersburg, Florida. He met her when he was stationed at Drew Field, an air force base nearby. He was discharged in 1947 and settled in Oakland. Abe and Mary adopted two children, Patricia Ann in 1949 and Robert in 1951. Abe worked for the American Can Company in Oakland until 1951 when he was recalled to active duty during the Korean war. He became a real estate broker in 1966 and branched out into the construction business in 1972. He retired in 1982. He is still active in real estate and in building. He is a pilot and has a Cherokee 180 that he keeps at the Livermore Airport. He and Mary frequently fly up to visit their daughter in Lincoln, California. The Dolims have three grandsons.

Irene R. Chilton

She was born Margaret Irene Rego on June 3, 1908 in Wailuku, Maui. Irene was the sixth of eleven children born to Joseph and Mary Rego. She attended St. Anthony's School and Maui High School. After a year at Phillips Commercial School in Honolulu, Irene returned to Maui and worked in the Alexander House Settlement kindergarten program. In 1929, Irene married Clive Chilton, from Honolulu. Clive, a 1924 St. Louis graduate, worked for the Inter-Island Steamship Navigation Co. Their son, Colin, was born in 1930 and five years later a daughter, Anise, was born. On December seventh, the Chiltons lived at 912 5th Ave. in Kaimuki.

On that Saturday night, December the sixth, I will never forget that Ann was so sick. She was six years old at the time and in the first grade at Sacred Hearts Academy. She had something like the intestinal flu and we were all up most of the night with her. So, early the next morning, I went to Mass at St. Patrick's church. Colin would help out as an altar boy at Sacred Hearts Academy (he went there from the first through the third grades). He was eleven and a sixth grade student at St. Louis at the time. So, he was serving at the 7:30 Mass at Sacred Hearts. Clive was washing all of Ann's bedding and messy clothes from the night before. Ann, of course, was sound asleep.

I came home and started to cook breakfast, when we heard rumbling sounds in the distance. It got louder, and Clive said, "That sounds like Ford Island blowing up." I asked where that was and he said it was where they keep ammunition and explosives. Then many planes started flying overhead. It was different from what we experienced before. It was strange.

Clive climbed up on our roof while these planes flew by. They looked close enough to knock him off the roof. "Get down," I yelled. He said, "I don't know where they came from, but they're not our planes." I was frightened. Something seemed very wrong. I yelled at him again and he got off the roof. Just then, a neighbor came running over, screaming at the top of her voice that we should turn on our radio, that something terrible was happening. We did, and that's when we found out that they were bombing Pearl Harbor.

"Get off the streets. Everybody off the streets," the announcer said. "Oh my God," I told Clive, "Colin must be walking back from church about now." So Clive ran up to the corner and sure enough, here came Colin, slowly walking home. When Colin heard what was happening, that eleven-year-old paced back and forth with his rosary beads in his hands.

Our house just shook from an explosion which sounded very close. I said to myself, "Oh, no, the next one will fall on us, I'm sure." We were all scared to death. Later, we heard that a bomb fell down at Moilili, which is not that far away from where we lived. So that was the big explosion we heard.

That's when I decided I wanted to go over to Mama's house--she only lived around the corner from us. Clive didn't like it, because we were supposed to stay off the streets, but we all walked over to my folks' house on Kaimuki Avenue. I thought, "If we're going to die, we're going to die all together."

We got to the house and I told them what was happening. My brothers Bob and Joe were at home. Papa turned on the radio and we listened for more information and instructions, the rest of the day. Others of the family came to the house. We stayed there all day.

That afternoon, there were a group of military buses parked along Kaimuki Avenue. They were crowded with people. We didn't know it then, but they were the military dependents that had been evacuated from the bases. I don't know where they were going or why they were parked there. The Red Cross people came by that afternoon, asking for donations to help feed and house, I guess, the displaced people. Papa gave them five dollars. I said, "Papa, you should give them more than that." But he said that that was enough.

Colin was friendly with the boy who lived across the street from us-- Ralph Berry was his name. They were a navy family. Colin saw Ralph get into the bus that morning and that was the last we saw of the Berry family. I suppose they were shipped out of Honolulu right away.

We spent the day and evening there and Mama wanted us to spend the night. Clive didn't want to stay because he didn't want to leave our house unattended. So he went back home, and Colin went with him. Bob and Joe came home after midnight with a couple of nurses--friends of theirs--who had worked all day at Tripler Hospital, tending to the

Pearl Harbor casualties. So Bob and Joe gave up their bedroom for the nurses. I don't know where they met them, but I suppose they were also being evacuated away from the military bases and had no place to stay.

The whole day's events started to sink in on me, and with the little sleep I had gotten the night before, I just collapsed on the sofa. Ann was sleeping on the floor. In fact, there were quite a few of us Regos there on the floor that night, I can't remember who all stayed.

Early in the morning, planes started flying over again, but they were our planes this time. I remember there were lots of them coming in. We didn't realize that they were ours at first, so you kept waiting for something to happen. The nurses had brought their little dog with them and Papa was annoyed because when he got up, he stepped on the dog's droppings. As he went to put the dog out, he muttered under his breath, "First, the bombs; then, all these people; and now, dog doo," only he didn't say "doo." Mama felt she had to get up and cook breakfast for the whole gang. I told her, "No, you don't have to fix breakfast for everybody." Everybody was so tired that they wanted to sleep in, anyway. Ann and I walked back home that morning.

When I saw some of the pictures of the destruction and devastation at Pearl Harbor, I was shocked. I was just horrified. I guess I saw the pictures in the paper or somewhere, I don't remember. I really didn't believe all the horror stories that we were hearing about what happened that morning. I thought that people were just exaggerating, you know.

" When I saw some of the pictures of the destruction and devastation at Pearl Harbor, I was shocked. I was just horrified. "

We blacked out the kitchen windows with blackout paper. It was miserable being in there for any length of time. Clive was such a heavy smoker--a chain smoker--and before long, the children and I would get sick in that stuffy kitchen. There was no air, just smoke. I remember once, just after the war started, Clive went outside to smoke and when he lit his cigarette, this crazy, trigger-happy national guard fellow shot at him. He didn't hit Clive, thank God, but that scared me half to death. Clive should have known better than to do that during the blackout. Those guys would patrol the streets and if they saw any light, they would go crazy. What a terrifying experience.

Well, I couldn't sleep nights, and as time went on, I became very ill. I was frightened all the time. And the kids were sick with bad colds. I went to see Dr. Gaspar, our family doctor. Louis Gaspar was more than a doctor, he was really a friend. He told me that the military governor was encouraging women and children to leave Hawaii and go to the mainland. He told me that he was even sending his parents to the mainland. Dr. Gaspar said that these were very difficult times for everybody in Hawaii and that somebody like me was a nuisance around here at times like this. Since I had a sister in California, he recommended that I take the children and leave the islands as soon as possible. He would make that recommendation, he said, for medical reasons.

Clive and I talked about it for a long while. At first, he didn't like the idea of me leaving. He even talked to Dr. Gaspar about it. The doctor convinced him that I was a very, very frightened person and that leaving the islands was the best thing for me and for the children. Then Clive was all for it. He was concerned for our safety, too. I guess he felt--as everybody did then--that there was an invasion on the way. Even though he couldn't leave at the same time we did, Clive said that he would do what he could to leave, too, and join us in California a little later.

So we went down to the steamship offices and stood in the long lines. It looked like everybody was trying to leave the islands. The steamship office people wanted to be sure that we had a place to go to in California, and so I gave them information on my sister, Dora Bauman. If I'm not mistaken, I think they even called Dora to see if it would be okay for us to come live with her. So we got our passes and had to wait for our time to leave.

Right after the attack, I noticed that our regular milkman, a Japanese man named Frank, never came around to deliver milk anymore. He worked for Hind Clark Dairy and we became friends. He had two adorable little girls. Then one day, he came to our door. I was so happy to see him, I gave him a big hug and he cried like a baby. He said he felt so badly about the attack and he thought that we wouldn't accept him because he was Japanese--that we no longer could be friends. I've never seen a man cry so hard like that man did. A week later, we invited him and his family over for Christmas dinner. The dairy was doing a promotion for new customers just before the attack and they were taking pictures of children as a premium for having milk delivered. We had a photo taken of little Ann. Anyway, when he came to dinner that evening, he had taken the photo and had it enlarged, colored, and framed for hanging. I was so pleased. In fact, it is still one of my prized possessions today. What a beautiful person he was. The Japanese attack was just devastating to him.

" He said he felt so badly about the attack and he thought that we wouldn't accept him because he was Japanese--that we no longer could be friends. "

Well, it was now January and we were waiting for word about when we would leave the islands. That was a very difficult decision for me to make. I had never travelled anywhere, except between Maui and Honolulu. I had never been out on my own. I was now thirty-three with two children who were going to need me--to depend on me. I was leaving my husband, my home, my family and Hawaii, the only place I knew on earth. I was more scared than ever.

My next-door neighbor, when she came to say goodbye, told me, "You know? You're awfully brave to leave." I said, "You call this being brave? I think **you're** braver for staying here." Then I said what I had been thinking all along. "You are all going to be killed. They're going to come back and bomb this place again. And this time, they'll get everybody." And that's exactly how I felt. Sure, I was afraid. But there were a lot of other people leaving, too, and I tried to tell myself over and over that I was doing the right thing--that the children and I would be better off on the mainland.

Ann didn't want to leave. When the time finally came, she cried and cried. She didn't want to leave because she loved her dad so much. The day arrived when we had to say our goodbyes. It was February 18, a Wednesday. We went to Clive's mother's house and to Mama and Papa's. We said our goodbyes and took a taxi to an army pier where the ship was docked. But as we drove away from Papa's house, I looked back and saw Mama and Papa sitting on the front porch, waving. I'll never forget that scene. That's the last time I saw Papa.

We got to the gate and they wouldn't let Clive or the taxi driver in. We had to walk in from the gate. So we said our goodbyes to him. I

337

didn't realize it then, but it would be a year-and-a-half until we saw him again. Ann was crying. When he kissed her goodbye, she said, "Will you promise me something, Daddy?" He said, "Sure." She asked, "Will you promise me you'll go to church for me?" He hadn't been going to church with us. He would get up early every Sunday, but would work in the yard or something. But he went to church after that. As far as I know, he kept his promise and never missed Mass on Sundays from that day on.

So we went aboard the ship--the *USS Garfield*. Ann and I stayed in one room with another woman, but Colin wasn't allowed to be with us. He had to stay with some men in another stateroom. That bothered me terribly. But they came by to meet me and said that they would take good care of Colin. So I felt better about it. Then we sat around for two days before the ship finally left the islands. That was long, boring and frustrating--not knowing when you're going to finally leave. We couldn't even notify Clive that we were still there. Clive wrote later and said that he would walk the beaches at Waikiki looking for the convoy of ships hoping to see the one we were on. We left Honolulu on February 20, 1942. I remember, because two days later, on Washington's Birthday, we hit rough weather that I will never forget. It was so rough, nobody could go out on deck and they had to tie down furniture and everything.

And, Ann cried every day for her daddy. She just cried and cried. The steward came by and told her that on that big ship in front of us, the *Aquatania*, there were hundreds of children who didn't have their fathers **or** their mothers. He said they were orphans from the Orient who were being evacuated. He then invited her to go around the ship with him when he rang the dinner bell, calling the passengers to the two dinner seatings. She was quite thrilled and happy to do that. There were nine ships in that convoy and it took us nine days to get to San Francisco. We arrived on Sunday, March first.

When we got off the ship, the Red Cross woman said that we were now on our own. That was a shock to me. We were on the pier and Ann and Colin were having some hot chocolate while I tried to call Dora in Sacramento. I could just see the children sitting there, watching me, as if to say, "Come on, do something. Don't you know what you're supposed to do?" I didn't. All of a sudden I felt the pressure of being depended upon. Then up walked Mrs. Williams. She was a guardian angel who came down to help me do the right thing. She introduced herself as being with the Red Cross, on her day off. She brought her mother down to see the convoy of ships come in and wanted to know if she could help us. She helped me call Dora, showed me where to catch the ferry to Oakland and told me what train to catch on the other side. She took us to send a wire to Clive. She bought comic books and candy for the children and since we had all afternoon before we had to catch the ferry, she drove us all around San Francisco and showed us the sights. She was a lovely, lovely woman. Clive wrote her a nice letter, later, thanking her for being so nice to his family.

So we caught the ferry, and found the train for Sacramento on Track 16. Mrs. Williams had handled all of that for us, including buying the tickets and everything. So my sister, Dora and her husband, Bob, were waiting for us when we arrived in Sacramento that evening. Our lives in California had now begun.

The following month, I think it was, I had to send a wire to Honolulu, so I went to downtown Sacramento on the bus. All of a sudden, there was a terrific traffic jam. We all came to a stop. Then, we saw a bunch of buses coming by--in kind of a convoy--and I noticed that they were filled with Japanese people. They were being taken away. Of course, I didn't know where they were going at that time. I couldn't believe the faces of these poor people looking back at us. They looked so sad. I was absolutely horrified. I couldn't help myself, I started to cry. Bus after bus of Japanese civilians being taken away, God knows where. That made a terrible impression on me. But, you know, there were many people in Sacramento who didn't feel as I did about what happened to those Japanese people. I just think it was a hideous thing our government did.

" Bus after bus of Japanese civilians being taken away, God knows where. . . I just think it was a hideous thing our government did. "

The kids were enrolled in Hagenwood School in Del Paso Heights, Sacramento. When the school year was over, we moved to San Leandro with my other sister, Rose, and her two sons, Larry and Bill, who had just evacuated from Honolulu. All four of our children were enrolled at St. Mary's School in San Leandro for the fall term in 1942.

Ann still missed her daddy terribly. At school one day, she was telling her classmate, Arlene Long, how much she missed her dad. Arlene said, "You're lucky you **have** a father. I wish I did. My dad was killed on the *Arizona* at Pearl Harbor." So Ann realized that there were others who were worse off than she was.

Clive managed to leave Hawaii by getting a job with the War Department in San Francisco in September 1943. We bought a house of our own in San Leandro, on Arroyo Street, and were once again a whole family.

Looking back on those days, I'd say the biggest effect the war had on my life was the evacuation to California. I had never thought of leaving the islands. I might never have moved from there had Pearl Harbor not happened.

The move did affect my children. I know that Ann was so miserable-- for over a year-and-a-half--until her father was able to join us again. And Colin would never say much. He kept things to himself. He was sure that his father and I had separated--that we were going to get a divorce. It wasn't until years later that I learned this, but that is what he told his high school classmates. He just assumed that.

And, I guess the thing I'll never forget was that scene of my mother and father sitting on their front porch as we drove away. I wrote often to my father over the next ten years, but I never saw him again. He died in 1951.

Clive worked for Del Monte as a personnel manager for many years. He retired in 1970, and died in 1986. Colin passed away in 1984, leaving three children. Ann married Wendel Marsh, of New York, and they live in Hollywood, Florida. The Marshes had four children, the oldest died in 1979. Irene still lives in the little house they purchased in San Leandro in 1943. She is very active at St. Leander's church and keeps herself busy with walks, reading, and cheering for the Oakland Athletics.

Harold S. Edwards

His father, George Edwards, and mother, Bessie Rego, were both born on Maui. Harold, the fourth of six children, was born in Wailuku, Maui in 1919. He attended St. Anthony's School from the first through the eighth grades. In 1933, his father sent him to Honolulu to attend St. Louis College (high school) where he boarded with his relatives, Millie and John Baptist. He graduated from St. Louis in 1937. He worked for a few financial companies before joining the Territorial Auditor's office in 1939 as a bookkeeping machine operator. On December 7, 1941, Harold lived with his sister, Cyrilla King and her husband, at 1401-L Makiki Street.

Some of the best years of my life were the first two years of high school. I lived at my Aunt Millie's home on Wilhelmina Rise and shared a room with my cousin, Adrian. We were about the same age and both freshmen at St. Louis. We did everything together and got along so well--I don't recall that we ever had an argument. It was good family living with the Baptists.

My relatives were good to me--a Maui country boy attending school in the big city. I also lived for two years with my mother's sister and her husband, Helen and Manuel Freitas, on Lusitana Street. Later, after I started working, my sister Cyrilla and her husband, Eugene "Bud" King, allowed me to share their home on Makiki Street, right across from Pawaa Park.

I was working for the Security Loan Corporation in 1939 when the auditor of the Territory of Hawaii, James Reid, came to the office. He suggested that I apply for a position in his office through the Civil Service Commission. Civil Service was just coming into existence at that time. So, I was one of approximately seven hundred people that took the very first Civil Service examination in Hawaii. It was given at the McKinley High School auditorium. It was sort of nerve-wracking, but it didn't seem that difficult. Anyway, I did very well and in October 1939 started my new job, increasing my salary from $60 to $91 a month.

By 1941, I was making $165 a month in the auditor's office. I was fortunate in being in the right place at the right time. Whenever a vacancy occurred, I'd take the exam, pass, and get promoted. I was also keeping the books for the Farm Loan Board of Hawaii on the side, earning an additional $40 a month. I did this job on weekends and off-hours, and that was what I was doing on Sunday, December 7, 1941.

That morning I got up early and went to the six o'clock Mass at the Fort Street Cathedral of our Lady of Peace. After Mass, I went to the Eagle Cafe, right next door, and had breakfast. Then I walked over to the Territorial Building on Punchbowl Street.

I worked on the mezzanine, where the Farm Loan offices were. We made loans to homesteaders. I was working on the books there when one of the janitors came by--some of them did the cleaning of the offices on Sundays because we worked half-days on Saturdays. She said, excitedly, "Oh, Mr. Edwards, Pearl Harbor is being attacked and they sunk a lot of ships down there." I said, "Sarah, you had too much to drink last night."

"Oh, no, no, honestly," she said, "I just heard it on the radio." She had been working on the fourth floor in the Radio Commission of Hawaii office, and she had the radio on up there.

I ran into Jack Bal, one of the senior accountants, and told him what Sarah had said. "Let's go up to the roof and see what we can see," he said. So we took the elevator up to the fifth floor—to the Public Works offices--then from there we went up the stairwell to the roof.

Boy, we could see lots of planes, fire and smoke. We had a clear view toward Pearl Harbor and saw the planes diving at their targets. It was hard to believe. We were watching an historic event, the attack actually taking place. I don't know how long we were frozen there, speechless, when we felt a concussion, an explosion, which came from the dock area near the Honolulu Iron Works.[1] I mean the place really shook. "Oh, boy, Harold," Jack shouted, "Let's get the hell out of here." So we dashed down the stairs. We were both really shook up.

After a while, a lot of our office employees started showing up. Remember, this was the location of the territorial treasury--the vaults were right there. Then guards starting arriving. I don't know who they represented or where they came from, but I guess they were there to

---

[1] *An errant anti-aircraft shell landed on Channel Street, next to the Honolulu Iron Works, destroying a parked car.*

guard the "treasures." I don't know what they could have done had there been an invasion. I'd be afraid to think what would have happened if the Japanese had come in that day. There couldn't have been very much resistance because the military bases really didn't have many combat troops.

" I don't know how long we were frozen there, speechless, when we felt . . . an explosion, which came from the dock area near the Honolulu Iron Works. "

A lot of people kept coming in to the office. Some of us were asked to stay there that night and to watch for fires, lights, or anything suspicious. They asked for volunteers, so I stayed. Jack went home to be with his family that night. I called my sister and told her not to expect me.

We had the radio going and heard all the rumors about parachutists landing on St. Louis Heights. We were in the basement, where two telephone operators were working at the switchboard. There were all kinds of telephone calls coming in.

I spent some time back on the rooftop that night, with another territorial employee--I can't recall who. We were up there for a couple of hours until about midnight. We never saw a light; we never saw a fire; or anything suspicious. Everything was completely blacked out. It was quiet and really spooky. Everybody was waiting for something to happen. We went down to the basement again and they brought out blankets for anyone who wanted to try to sleep. I don't think anyone slept. We just sat around, mostly in shocked silence.

Everything slowed down the next morning. Only the most urgent things were taken care of. I went home by bus about noon that Monday. Cyrilla said that Bud was ducking shells down at Pearl Harbor, Sunday morning, running all over the base. Bud was working down there that day and he had some frightening stories to tell later, when he returned home. In fact, a little later, during the war, we would hear from him about ships coming in for repairs with big holes in them.

The office was disrupted completely that week. Some of us worked part-time with the Civil Defense people. I remember I worked several days up at the territorial offices in Iolani Palace--in the senate chambers-- answering telephones. I returned to my job half-days, and worked at the palace half days for a while.

For the next few months, we lived a very different life. I had my work, but after work, there wasn't much to do. The moment it got a little dark, that's it, no lights. We blacked out the house so we could read after dark. We listened to the radio. Then, when things got stuffy in the blacked-out rooms, we would turn off the lights, open up the doors and windows, and sit out on the front porch and play the ukulele in the dark. That's about it.

Anyway, shortly after Pearl Harbor, I received "Greetings from the President of the United States." I got my notice to report to the army and did so on February 7, 1942. I reported to the railway station down at Iwilei, the OR & L, and was off to Schofield Barracks for basic training. I remember I went in on the same day my uncle did. Bob Rego--he was my uncle but only a year older than I--was drafted at the same time and caught that same train on February seventh.

They rushed us through six weeks of training--chemical warfare, firing range--then they assigned us to regular army units. I was transferred to Fort Armstrong, which was the headquarters location for the Finance Division. I felt good about that, because it looked as if my experience in finance and bookkeeping would be utilized.

Instead, I ended up in the 16th Quartermaster Truck Company. The first morning, we got up, lined up outside, then were marched down to the motor pool. There were huge two-and-a-half-ton trucks lined up there. The sergeant asked me, "What kind of a truck can you drive?" I said, "I've never driven a truck before. In fact, I've never even been in a truck like that."

"Okay, that's all right," said the sergeant. He called another staff sergeant over and said, "Take this man out and give him some driving lessons." And he did. What an experience. Those things were something to drive, let me tell you. The springs were so stiff, your back would take a beating driving them. And I couldn't have been more than 110 pounds then. They gave me a driver's license.

I hauled rations, supplies and different types of cargo from piers to warehouses. I had to chuckle as I drove the truck on my first trip to the warehouse. I really chuckled all the way, saying to myself, "Look at me, a bookkeeper driving a truck." My experience was certainly not being used. But I figured, oh well, that's the army for you. I took it with a grain of salt.

" I had to chuckle as I drove the truck on my first trip to the warehouse. . . a bookkeeper driving a truck. My experience was certainly not being used. "

One evening, the NCO in charge of quarters was in the office when I passed by. I asked if I could go in and use the typewriter--I wanted to send home some letters. "Sure," he said, so I went in and started to type my letters. The company clerk happened to come by. He was one of

THE ARMY WAY -- Private Harold Edwards, one-hundred-ten-pound bookkeeper, becomes a truck driver. This photo was taken at Fort Armstrong in early 1942. (Photo courtesy of Harold Edwards)

those old career army fellows who got stuck in the office and who would "hunt and peck" with two fingers on the typewriter. He was anxious to get out of that job. So the next morning he told the first sergeant, "I think I found you a new clerk." So I was sent in to see the captain, and he asked me if I would like to work in the office. I said, "Yes, sir," and happily, my truck driving career came to an end.

After a while, I got to be the regular secretary to different officers. Whenever one of the trucks would get into an accident, we would go out and investigate the accident. I'd carry a portable typewriter with me. I would take the people's statement down in shorthand, then type it out on the portable. For a while, there, I was also a special courts martial reporter. We handled such cases as drinking, fighting and major disciplinary problems.

Shortly after that, our whole unit was moved just outside of Fort Shafter, up on Middle Street. I worked there as secretary to Maj. Armin L. Grahlfs--a nice guy--he later made Lt. Colonel. I got itchy feet about then--I wanted to try something different--so I put in for Quartermaster Officer's Training School. I passed the board but there were no vacancies at that time, so I put in for aviation cadet training and was sent to Hickam Field to take the tests.

SERGEANT EDWARDS -- Sergeant Harold Edwards finishes a report at his desk at Fort Francis E. Warren, Wyoming, in July 1944. Note the hometown newspaper sent to him from a "work buddy" at home. (Photo courtesy of Harold Edwards)

One of the tests they put you through was the pressure chamber that simulated conditions at an altitude of twenty-eight thousand feet. You had an oxygen mask on, then when the pressure got up to twenty-eight thousand feet, they'd tell you to take off your mask and write your name, rank, and serial number, until you just about passed out. One guy had a bad tooth cavity and the pain he experienced in that pressure tank was so severe they had to let him out. I passed the tests successfully and on Christmas Eve, 1943, I was on my way to Keesler Field in Biloxi, Mississippi.

I was given pre-aviation cadet training, but before we were through, they curtailed the program and reassigned us to different branches of the service. It was determined at that time, April 1944, our losses suffered in the air war over Europe were not as great as earlier anticipated, that a curtailment of the program was necessary. I was sent to Camp Shelby, Mississippi, to await reassignment. It was here where the 442nd Regimental Infantry Combat Team was in training.

While waiting around for reassignment to another base, we were given passes to go throughout the camp. I enjoyed visiting with some of the 442 guys--Toshi Anzai, from Maui, a supply sergeant at the time who later became a state senator from Maui. Another friend I met was Henry Doi, from Hilo. In fact, we corresponded all the time he was in Italy. I also saw a former office worker from the auditor's office, Robert Miyata. I really enjoyed seeing them. This was just a few weeks before they were shipped out.

I received my orders to report to Fort Francis E. Warren in Cheyenne, Wyoming, and was assigned to the headquarters company. I worked in the status and inspection division as an examiner of administrative and service records from units preparing for overseas assignment. Our duties changed when hostilities ended in Europe and our entire division was converted into a separation center. We were responsible for discharging thousands of troops who had returned from the European theater of operations.

I was discharged on November 1, 1945 with the rank of master sergeant. Came back to Hawaii on the *Lurline*. She still was a troop ship--she hadn't been refurbished yet--but I didn't mind. It was nice to get home. My mother was so happy to see me and my brothers. All four of us were in the service--Vernon and Walter in the merchant marine, and Arthur and I in the army.

I don't regret one day that I spent in the service. I can always say that I'm very proud of my record. I never got to see any combat, but am content that I did the very best I could. My job was available for me when I returned, and I was happy to hear that it paid $200 more a month in January 1946 than when I left in 1942. I had been gone almost four years.

> *" I don't regret one day that I spent in the service. . . I never got to see any combat, but am content that I did the very best I could. "*

One thing about the war I shall never forget, though. That scene from the roof of the Territorial Building was just unbelievable. I couldn't believe what I was seeing--Pearl Harbor being attacked. My skin literally turned to goose flesh when I witnessed that. And, you know, I get that same goose flesh when I talk about it today, fifty years later.

Harold worked for the Territory--later the "State" of Hawaii--until his retirement in 1972, due to a heart problem. He married Hazel Barnett in 1962 and they have one son, James, born in 1964. Hazel has two children from a previous marriage, so the Edwards family has grown to include three children, five grandchildren, and six great-grandchildren.

Celia R. Illum

Born in Wailuku, Maui, in 1916, "Cis"
was the tenth of eleven children born to
Joseph and Mary Rego of Maui. She
attended St. Anthony's school and Maui
High School, then went to Phillips
Commercial business school in Honolulu.
While in Honolulu, she met Frank Illum, a
sailor from Idaho. Cis returned to Maui
and worked as a secretary at the Alexander
House Settlement. Frank followed her to
Maui, proposed, and they were married a
month later. A few years before the Pearl
Harbor attack, they lived in an apartment
at Circle Lane, in Honolulu. Frank was
transferred for a brief period of time, and
he and Cis lived in Washington state.
Frank earned his commission as an ensign and he and Cis were transferred
back to Honolulu. Their daughter, also named Celia, was born in August
1941. On December the seventh, they had a little house next to Fort Ruger,
at the foot of Diamond Head.

Some weeks before the attack, I remember there was a newspaper headline that read, "Enemy May Attack Over the Weekend." That really bothered me. Frank was an ensign on a ship, the *USS Oglala*. The weekend before the attack, Frank took me to Pearl Harbor to have dinner with the officers on his ship. It was the first time I had ever been on a ship for dinner. It was very enjoyable. After dinner, we went over to the *USS Arizona*--which was docked just across the way--to watch the boxing matches they were holding that evening. I had a good time, but something kept bothering me.

Finally, thinking about that newspaper article, I said what was on my mind. "My goodness, Frank," I said, "this is terrible--all of these ships docked out here in one place. Suppose that article is true and those lousy old Japs are on their way over here? They could have a field day out here with all those ships lined up."

"Oh, no, no, that could never happen," he boasted. "They could never get into this fort. We'd know miles out before they could get near Pearl Harbor," he said, sounding so sure of himself. And, you know, he had that overbearing attitude that so many of the military brass had at that time. They maintained that the Japanese could never penetrate our territory.

That morning of the seventh, I was working in our little house. Baby Celia was four months old and she was sleeping in the carriage. Frank was home for the weekend and was laying in the sun with his shirt off. Anyway, some time a little after eight o'clock, his partner, also a naval officer, came driving up hurriedly in his car. He looked anxious and he asked for Frank. "He's over there, on the porch, taking a sun bath," I said. He turned up his car radio, "Listen," he said, "I want you two to hear this." Frank jumped up at the news, his face was pale white. He ran into the house to get his clothes. I was stunned, listening to the report about the attack on Pearl Harbor.

Frank came rushing out of the house carrying his uniform to change in the car. He jumped in the car and my face turned white, too. "You mean to say that you're going to leave us here, and there's shooting going on?" We were right next to Fort Ruger, a likely target, and by that time I could see smoke in the air--a lot of black smoke--down toward Pearl Harbor. I was frightened for myself and for little Celia. Just before they drove off, he turned to look at me and his face was white as a sheet. "You knew that the navy came first," he said. "You knew that when you married me." His partner felt sorry for me. He leaned over and said, "Take the baby and everything you need and go down to your mother's. It's safer there."

They sped off down the road and I was left there, in shock. I couldn't believe what was happening to me. Just as they drove out of sight, my sister, Rose Rodrigues and her husband, Reggie, came driving up. Their boys Larry and Billy were in the back of the car. They didn't seem to know what was happening and I yelled to them to come in the house, that the Japs were bombing Pearl Harbor and they should get off the street. I had the radio turned on in the house by then and they listened, too, in disbelief.

Rose was always the organizer, and she reacted immediately and told me to gather up the things for the baby--diapers, milk, food--and pack a suitcase of my clothes. "You follow us over to Mama's," she said. "You don't know how long you'll have to be there, so you'd better be prepared. Besides, it's safer for both you and the baby at Mama's," she said. "Frank will know where you will be. If he can get away, he'll come for you there." Rose was so reassuring. I felt a little better and started to pack the things.

So everybody was at my mother's place. People were coming and going all day. There were even a couple of the nurses from the hospital who spent the night there with us. They were just worn out from hours of attending to the wounded and dying.

I had a bunch of diapers that I had taken out of my washing machine at home, so I had to hang them out to dry. The bombing was still going on, but I went outside and hung the diapers. My father came out, saw me, and smiled. "Good, good, keep your head," he said. "Keep doing things that you do every day." He complimented me for being calm. "I have to," I told him, "I have a baby to take care of."

---

*" So everybody was at my mother's place.
People were coming and going all day.
There were even a couple of the nurses from
the hospital . . . there with us. "*

A little later, my sister Lou called. She was frightened. She was alone at an apartment on Circle Lane, down near town. "Please come get me," she pleaded. I immediately volunteered to do it. My father got mad. "Nothing doing," he said. "Your brother will pick up his sister." My brother, Joe, was not too excited about picking up his sister. But Papa was the boss in the family, particularly in his own home. So Joe did pick up Lou and brought her over, however reluctantly.

Joe had belonged to the Businessmen's Military Training Corps, and had been training for this kind of an emergency. That Sunday night, he was out patrolling a few blocks around the neighborhood, looking for blackout violators and things. He didn't stay out there too long when he came back home. He said that it was dangerous out there. "Guys can't see in the dark and they don't care who they're shooting at," he said. My father told him not to go back out again. He was afraid Joe might get shot.

Frank came to the house about nine o'clock that night. He knew that Celia and I would be at Mama's house. He told us what had happened. He said he drove up to his ship just as she was going down. He lost all his personal belongings on the *Oglala*, but thank God he wasn't on it when it went down. He said, "We got out there and my ship was sinking. White caps were floating in the water and blood was everywhere."

He said, "They were getting it all around me. Arms and legs were flying all around me. Skin would just burst right off bodies, right in front of me, and I came out of it without a scratch. Nothing happened to me." I remember later telling him that that wasn't true. He might not have realized it then, but something did happen to him that morning. His mind was really affected by that experience.

He also told us the story of trying to get ammunition to fire back at the planes. "We wanted to at least try and shoot some of them," he said, "but nobody had the key and we couldn't open that damned door to the ammunition. It was a mess--the biggest mess you ever saw," he said.

THE OGLALA IS DOWN -- *The USS Oglala, minelayer and flagship of Rear Admiral William Furlong, rolled over and sank along 1010 Dock. The venerable old ship, unarmored, was damaged when a torpedo passed beneath it and detonated against the USS Helena, moored next to the Oglala. She was eventually repaired and rejoined the fleet in February 1944. (Official US Navy Photograph; War Depository Collection, University of Hawaii)*

We stayed at Mama's overnight, with all the relatives. People were sleeping all over the floor. Frank, Celia, and I drove back home the next day. Frank thought it would be safe enough for us. Frank painted all our windows black so that I would have light at night for the baby. Then he had to go back to the base. I didn't see him for about a week. They were very busy down there, trying to put the pieces together.

When he came back, he was in a pick-up truck. There was a navy man on a machine gun that was mounted on the back of the truck. He had to stay out there and be on guard all the time Frank was in the house. "We're on alert," Frank said. "I can only stay for a little while." I said, "Gee, tell that guy to relax. I'll give him a cup of coffee or something." But everything had to be done the navy way.

I had gone down to donate blood when they first announced that blood was needed. I went right down to Queen's Hospital and gave a pint of blood. Frank was not too happy about that. "I'm fighting this war," he said, "so you don't have to." That upset me. "I think you have the wrong idea, Frank," I said. "Before this war is over, every one of us is going to have to do something." And I really believed that.

I shopped at the navy commissary, and I could get food that wasn't available in the stores in town. And food was much cheaper there. So I bought food for the whole family. Frank didn't like that idea, either.

I would visit my father's house frequently, driving back and forth. I don't think I was really frightened about everything that was going on. Uppermost in my mind at the time was the baby. Celia kept me pretty busy. This was particularly true because I had lost our first child, a little girl, who was born premature. She only lived one month. That was in 1940. So I didn't want anything to happen to Celia. Whenever there was an air-raid alarm at my father's house, we would run next door to the bomb shelter that belonged to the Japanese neighbors. They were aliens, and they would offer us something to eat when we would go over there. They were very nice people, but I thought it was curious that they had their bombshelter built before December 7, 1941.

Frank came home one day and told me that Celia and I had to leave Hawaii. I couldn't believe what he was telling me. "You're going to have to leave right away," he said. "I don't want to leave," I shouted. "This is my home, I was born here. My whole family is here," I said. He was adamant about it. "You have to. It doesn't matter where you were born. The navy is reponsible for you and the baby and they think it is safer for you both to leave Hawaii and go to the mainland. And I do, too," he added.

I was shocked. The navy was responsible for us because we had spent a short time on the mainland and we were actually transferred **back** to Honolulu. So I was treated as if I was originally from the mainland.

" Frank came home one day and told me that Celia and I had to leave Hawaii. I couldn't believe what he was telling me. "

So Celia and I were scheduled to leave on one of the first convoys from the islands. Frank took us down to the pier, to the ship we were going to board. He had on his officer's uniform, but they wouldn't let him go aboard the ship with us. He had to leave us at the gangplank. I remember telling him, "My God, Frank, if they can't trust you, who **can** they trust?"

There were military families aboard, including so many babies and little toddlers. It was a crowded, rough, trip and most of the babies got seasick. Celia got so sick, it even developed into pneumonia later.

We couldn't notify anyone that we were coming, but Frank had told me that the Red Cross would help us when we arrived in San Francisco. He told me to ask them to call his aunt, who lived there. So when we arrived, the Red Cross was very helpful to us. They brought me a sweater, something I didn't have. Gee, it was cold when we got in, and I didn't have anything warm to wear.

Frank's aunt came down to pick us up. She was warned not to tell anyone she was going to do that. She called the doctor for Celia, and we stayed with her a couple of days.

I was fortunate that my car was shipped up by the navy, so I had a car to use. Frank had told me to drive to Ogden, Utah, to be with his folks. He was sure it would be safe there. He said, "I don't know how long it will be, it could take quite a while before I can join you. As soon as I can, I'll come," he had said. So before I knew it, here I was, driving all the way to Ogden with a six-month-old baby. I was young then and didn't know fear. I guess I was pretty brave.

So we stayed with his folks in Ogden and I got a job at the Naval

Supply Center there. I did secretarial work first for the contractors that built the center, then I was asked to work for the new commanding officer at the center. Frank came up a year later and got me to transfer to the Naval Supply Center in Oakland, where he had been transferred. I worked as a purchasing agent and was quite successful in it, but the stress was terrible and Frank and I were beginning to have problems.

Shortly afterwards, we split up and I got out of the "rat race" of purchasing and got a civil service job as a chauffeur, driving officers around to different bases. It was a fun job and we got to wear uniforms, we looked like the navy women, the WAVEs. We had a pinochle game going all day long, and they were a nice bunch of people.

When I look back on those years now, I can't help but feel a resentment that I had to lose my home in Honolulu. We had bought that little house with some help from my father. And, overnight, the navy said that we had to leave the islands. I don't know what would have happened if the Japanese hadn't bombed Pearl Harbor. Who knows, I might have still been living there.

But that morning was nothing but sheer stupidity on the part of our military. They were just bumbling. They were running around all over the place and they didn't know what they were doing. No one seemed to be concerned at all about that newspaper headline that I read. And we were caught redhanded by the Japs. So many of our men were killed and so many others suffered from battle fatigue as a result of that attack. Frank may not have realized it, but I know that he suffered, too. God help us if something like that should ever happen again.

Cis got into the real estate business in California following the war. She officially retired from that business in 1983. In the meantime, she has worked in various businesses on her own. She ran a restaurant, owned and operated a couple of mobile home parks, she owned and ran three motels, a hot dog stand, many rental houses and apartment houses, and even worked as a mobile ice cream vendor. Cis lives in Pinole, California. Celia is a teacher and lives in San Francisco.

355

Gas Attack Alarm

SIMPLE, BUT EFFECTIVE -- An automotive brake drum and a steel bar comprise the gas alarm system in Honolulu during the early days of the war. About fifteen hundred of these "alarms" were hung on utility poles--about one thousand feet apart—throughout the well-populated districts of Honolulu. Pictured in this 1942 photo is Marjorie Carter of Waikiki. Note the prosecution warning for unauthorized use, "by order of the Military Governor." (Hawaii State Archives)

Chester Carsten

He was born in Camino, in the lumber country of northern California, in 1920. He attended El Dorado County High School in Placerville, graduating in 1938. After two years at Sacramento Junior College, "Chet" Carsten entered San Jose State College, majoring in physical education. In December 1941, his senior year, he was a fullback on the college football team. On December seventh, the team was in Honolulu for two post-season games.

San Jose State had been going to Hawaii for two or three years to play benefit games, so we were scheduled to go again in 1941 and were all excited about it. In November, about two weeks before we were to leave, coach Ben Winkleman called us all together and told us that the trip had been cancelled because there were problems between Japan and the U.S. They considered the trip too dangerous. That was very disappointing to all of us. But then, shortly after that, they gave us notice that we **could** go--the game was on again as scheduled. So, we left on the *Lurline* on Wednesday, November 26, 1941, and after a stop-over in Los Angeles, arrived in Honolulu on Wednesday, December third.

They had been on alert in Honolulu at that time, so consequently--all the way over on the *Lurline*--guys were making jokes about spotting periscopes in the water. Little did we know that though we thought of it as a big joke then, there **were** Japanese submarines in the ocean not too far from where we were travelling.

We were scheduled to play the University of Hawaii on Wednesday night, December tenth, and Willamette University (from Oregon) on Saturday the thirteenth. The Willamette team was on the same ship with us, so we got to know some of them and had a great time. The games were scheduled to raise funds for the widows and orphans of the police and fire departments in Honolulu. So we received a royal welcome and escorts by the Honolulu Police Department when we arrived.

Willamette played the University of Hawaii on Saturday night, December the sixth, and we had a big party on the university campus that night. The chain of events that followed overtook my memory of that game, so I really can't recall the score, or even who won. But we were there as a team and saw the game. But I can recall the party we had at the university after the game--with refreshments and dancing--and, although we were told that we had to be in no later than 1:00 a.m., some of us didn't show up until much later that morning.

I remember that Fred Lindsay--another fullback, we called him "Bulldog" Lindsay—and I showed up at the front of the Moana Hotel in Waikiki about three or four o'clock in the morning. There, standing on the front porch was coach Winkleman, waiting to catch the late arrivals. He didn't see us, so we did a quick reverse and went around the back to the servants' entrance and up the service elevator, sneaking into our room. He never found out that we were out after hours. As it eventually turned out, though, if we had stayed out all night it wouldn't have made any difference anyway. We would never get to play those scheduled games.

A trip around the island and a picnic was scheduled for Sunday, December the seventh. So, we had to get up early to have breakfast in the dining room. The picnic food had been placed outside the hotel, along Kalakaua Avenue, waiting for the arrival of the two buses and the girls from the university who were going to accompany us. There were lots of good things packed and ready to go--including fried chicken, cakes, and 10-gallon thermoses of pineapple juice.

When we were in the dining room, we could see a ship going out the channel, near Honolulu harbor, and it was doing all kinds of capers. As they were having a lot of maneuvers down there, we thought nothing of it. We finished our breakfast and went out front, along Kalakaua Avenue. Dick Hubbel, a sergeant in the Honolulu police force--who was a graduate of San Jose State--hurriedly drove up and jumped out of his car. He was supposed to give us a police escort around the island. He approached us and said, "The trip is off, the Japs are bombing Pearl Harbor." That was the first we knew about what was happening.

So a bunch of us dashed up to the roof of the Moana to see what was going on. We could see smoke coming up from the harbor, and we did see planes diving in to attack. Army trucks started moving up and down the streets of Waikiki in a big rush, and it looked as if nobody really knew where they were going or what they were to do. We just stood around and watched everything that was going on.

So, after a while, I suggested that we couldn't let all that wonderful food go to waste. "Why don't we take some of this food and go down by that big outdoor pool and have a picnic?" I proposed. So, a bunch of us walked down to the Natatorium in Kapiolani Park--sat around enjoying our picnic lunch--and talked about what was going to happen with us. Along toward afternoon, barbed wire was strung up along the beach and a few 50-caliber machine guns were put in place.

We knew that we could stay in the Moana Hotel for a while, anyway, because we were scheduled to leave on the fifteenth or thereabout to go back to California. We knew that the *Lurline* had already gone back to San Francisco, as it left the day of the bombing, so we were too late to get out of Honolulu on it. We didn't know what to do. I had come over with about $40 in my pocket and had already spent most of it buying aloha shirts and things.

---

*" . . . I suggested that we go down to the
police station and volunteer our services to
do police duty. "*

It got to be late afternoon and we were still standing around talking. We really didn't know which way to run. So, I suggested that we go down to the police station and volunteer our services to do police duty. I felt sure they could use our help. Anyway, for myself, I wanted to get hold of something that I could shoot, just in case I needed to. So about ten of us jumped on the electric trolley and went downtown to the police station. We were welcomed, and assigned gas masks, helmets, arm bands, and riot guns. Some of us were assigned to patrols with regular police officers and others went out to stand guard at the various utility buildings. I was to accompany a Korean officer on foot patrol beginning at midnight. So I went back to the hotel for a short nap.

No sooner had I started to doze when this fifty-caliber machine gun just started a-rapping away. I said to myself, "Oh, brother, here it comes." All it turned out to be, though, was a little dory that broke loose from its moorings right off from the Moana beach. That machine gun sunk that little boat so fast. Those guys were real edgy out there, waiting for the Japanese to send in the troops. Nobody knew what was going to happen.

HONOLULU STAR-BULLETIN, MONDAY, DECEMBER 8, 1941

Grid Games, Sport Events Are Canceled

All remaining football games on the local schedule, and all other sports listed for the Honolulu stadium, have been called off for an indefinite period, Theodore (Pump) Searle, manager of the stadium, announced today.

Mr. Searle also said the University of Hawaii has opstponed indefinitely the opening oft he senior ASUH basketball league.

The junior ASUH basketball games have also been canceled.

Other events postponed are the swimming meet scheduled for Punahou pool the evening of December 19, and the wrestling match at the Civic auditorium Wednesday night.

Al Karasick, manager of the Civic auditorium, has offered the use of the auditorium as a dormitory or for any other purpose.

San Jose Players Special Policemen

All members of the San Jose football team, scheduled to meet the University of Hawaii in the police benefit football game Saturday, today volunteered their services as emergency police officers.

The offer has been accepted by Police Chief W. A. Gabrielson.

FROM FOOTBALL TO FOOT-PATROL -- *The San Jose State football team was in Honolulu for benefit games with the University of Hawaii and Willamette University (from Oregon). They were stranded in the islands following the Pearl Harbor bombing and volunteered for police duty, many of them shown in a drill above. Some remained throughout and after the war, making Hawaii their home. (Star Bulletin; War Depository Collection, University of Hawaii)*

360

Anyway, I went out with the Korean officer at midnight and boy, was it black out. Believe me, when they said blackout, they meant blackout. It was dark. We came upon a small bar on River Street and the pinball machine "tilt" light was glowing in the dark. That Korean was pretty wild. He blasted that little light out. Then we heard some shooting taking place off in the distance and he took off running toward the noise. I didn't. I stayed there and waited for him to come back. Shootings were taking place all over the place for no rhyme nor reason. Everybody was on edge. There were rumors that the Japanese were landing on the other side of the island. There were rumors that paratroopers were landing in the mountains. We heard that somebody's goat got loose and was mowed down in a cross-burst of machine gun fire.

Along about four or five o'clock in the morning, we heard all these airplanes coming over. We were down near River Street and Aala Park. All of a sudden, the sky lit up with tracer bullets. Guns were firing from the Fort Shafter area, and from all over. The sky was just full of tracers. There's a stone wall along River Street there, and that's where we dove to take cover. We hid down low, alongside that wall, waiting for bombs to drop. I thought that this was it. I imagined that everything was about to happen. But those planes just flew right over and continued going. I'm sure they were our own, not enemy planes. But we never did hear a word about what happened to them. I don't know whether they landed at Hickam or not.

The next night, I was assigned to a prowl car with three other men. We drove around town with no headlights on at all. Gunnar Eke was the name of the shore patrolman from the navy who was with us. I'll never forget that name as it was quite unusual. Also with us were a civilian policeman, Sing Chang, and an army MP. I was the volunteer in the group. We came upon the Studebaker dealership near Queen's Hospital. It was strange, but all of a sudden, the large neon sign--the Studebaker script--lit up behind the big plate glass window. It must have been on timers or something, I don't know. So Gunner Eke took his 30.06 and he blew that sign away, and the window along with it. There was another Studebaker sign on the roof of the building. They told me to shoot that one out. I was using buck shot and the same type of gun I had at home, so I felt at ease with it. I blasted away and took care of that one. That was the kind of shooting that was going on all around the city those first few nights.

One night, I was patrolling with a police officer who was on the call box near North King and Dillingham streets when these huge army ten-wheeler trucks came barreling down the street in the dark. They couldn't see that there were median strips, islands, in the middle of the road separating the two-way traffic. They came speeding down the street heading in Ewa direction, when all of a sudden we saw this mass of sparks flying all over the place. They went skidding off in the distance and the whole undercarriage of that truck was left right there on the road, on that island. It was scary hearing all that racket and just seeing shadows, and then the bright fire of sparks showering all over the place. So we ran down the road to see if we could give him a hand and here comes another one hitting that island again and doing the same thing. It was not safe being out there in the dark, let me tell you. That night, we called the MPs to come out and take care of that situation. They were out there right away that night, and the following day the dividers were being removed.

Martial law was declared and strict rules were immediately imposed. We heard reports of people lighting a match after dark and getting a $200 fine. People had to be off the streets by six o'clock in the evening. The military courts were rough on the civilians. I had some experiences with the military courts and I can say, in no uncertain terms, that you were assumed guilty until you could prove your innocence. It was as simple as that--just the direct opposite of civilian law. But that's the way it was. I picked up a lot of civilians out after the curfew, and we had to take them in to the police station. If they didn't have an ID with an authorization to be out after blackout, we'd take them in. They would be detained until such time that they were cleared.

We were volunteer policemen for about a week when we were offered a job, provided we could pass the tests. About eight of us accepted the offer and we were sent to police school for eight hours during the day, then we'd go out on patrol for eight hours at night. At school, we learned firearms and a minimal amount of law, and we had to learn their police codes. Believe me, we were sent out on the streets not knowing very much about police work. We knew just enough to keep out of trouble. But it was good to be on a payroll, as we had to leave the Moana Hotel and had moved in with a gentleman we met on the ship coming over. He even loaned us $200 to help us out. He was a steel salesman named Stanley Cronin. He and his wife were very good to us.

We were issued our uniforms, our .38s, and we were all set to work for money when word came that we could return to the mainland on the next ship. We were given all of two hours' notice to board ship if we wanted to. This was about three weeks after the attack. Seven of us decided to stay.

We were on the foot patrol, downtown during the nights, and in school during the day. Some of the team members--Paul Tognetti and Don Allen were two of them--were sent out on "accident prevention," riding around in those brown and white highway patrol cars outside the city limits. Paul ended up marrying an island girl and made Hawaii his permanent home. Kenny Stanger was placed on dispatch--manning the radio. Another member of the team, Bill Donnelly, died on the operating table from a burst appendix within the first year we were there. Jack Lercari and I were on the regular patrol.

OFFICER CARSTEN -- Wearing badge number 333, Officer Chet Carsten poses for his formal police photograph after being accepted into the force in December 1941. (Courtesy Chet Carsten photo collection)

It didn't take me long to make that decision to stay. All I had in the way of experience to that point was that I had a job piling lumber in a saw mill; I had gone to school; and I played a little football and baseball. I didn't really have any skills and I figured that I could get some good experience as a police officer. I thought with that experience, I would have a good chance to get into the military police force. The army had a great, well-trained, MP unit, which was housed in the same building as the Police Department. Also, I was engaged to a girl back home, and I thought I could get her to come over to the islands and marry me. So, I passed up the chance to board that ship.

Captain John Burns was my captain for nearly two years after that. He was the head of the vice squad and I was transferred there. I was a haole[1] and I could pass as a defense worker over from the mainland. They put me on undercover jobs at Punahou School and at the old Kamehameha School, to find out who was running the gambling games and selling the bootleg liquor. Gambling was a violation of the territorial law. U. S. Engineers were headquartered at Punahou and Naval Air Construction, if I remember the name correctly, was headquartered at old Kam School.

" They put me on undercover jobs at Punahou School and at the old Kamehameha School, to find out who was running the gambling games and selling the bootleg liquor. "

My girlfriend, Vernice Woldit, was working out at Mather Field in Sacramento at that time. She arranged a transfer to another military job in Honolulu and came over. I received a telegram from her: "Wire me $180. See you soon." She arrived and I called Capt. Burns. I said, "Captain, I'd like to take a couple of days off." He asked why and I told him, to get married. "Oh, okay, go ahead," he said. Vernice and I were married on Tuesday, May 19, 1942, and we got a little studio apartment in Waikiki. After my two days off, though, I couldn't stay with my bride for the next eighteen days, because I was back on the undercover detail.

---

[1]*Hawaiian word meaning Caucasian, white person.*

I posed as a war worker just over from the mainland and got a job as a carpenter with the U.S. Engineers at Punahou. Even the police bulletin reported that I had left the force to work for the engineers. Before my wife came over, I had a roommate, and he thought I had quit the force, too. I lived right there in the dormitory with some unsavory characters. Many of them had "rap sheets" a mile long, and they were running gambling games and selling bootleg liquor. I had to buy the stuff for $30 a bottle and mark it for evidence. I didn't relish the nights, living in the same room with these guys. If they ever found out that I was a cop, that would have been really bad for me. I took part in the gambling, too. Chief William Gabrielson had told me that if I lost any money gambling, the department would replace it. And if I won, he said, I could keep the winnings. It sounded like a good deal, but wouldn't you know, I didn't really win anything.

Then came the night the police decided to raid the place. There were about forty guys in there playing poker, black jack, craps, and so on. It was really interesting. They never had the slightest idea that I was an undercover cop. When the police came in, they were wearing denims, aloha shirts, and people didn't pay too much attention to them. They were milling around the big room. Then I saw Sergeant Chester Dodds head over to the table where I was. I felt my face turn beet red. I got my back up against a corner and Dodds threw his badge down on the poker table and shouted at all of us, "You're under arrest for gambling." As people started to react, this one guy says to me, under his breath, "Hey, Slim, you get that light over there near the window and I'll get the one near the door, and we'll jump out the window. Those gooks won't shoot." I said, "Don't fool yourself." I didn't want to have any part of that. I started putting the pool balls in my pockets as I didn't want those guys to start throwing them. It was getting pretty tense in there.

Since I knew who was running the games, who was cutting the pots, and who was selling the liquor, Sergeant Dodds nodded to me to "finger" them. They didn't want to take in the ordinary gambler, the poor sucker who was losing it all. So we walked around the room and I would nonchalantly nod toward one guy and they'd come and load him in the wagon, then another, and so on. I tried to be so discreet about it. They took me away in one of the police cars, too, and let everybody else go.

I was separated from the others, taken up a back stairway and brought into the vice squad office. I'm sitting there with Captain Burns when they bring in the ringleader of the gang. He looks at me, and Burns says, "I want you to meet Sergeant Carsten." The guy's eyeballs bulged out wide. He never had the slightest idea. He lunged toward me and Capt. Burns grabbed him by the collar and sat him back down. Boy, he was a bad penny and I guess I was his downfall. He went to jail for three or four months and then got out. The day he got out, he was drunk on the street, and of all people, I arrested him and he got locked up again. Later, I didn't even know that he was out of jail, and I arrested him again, this time for sleeping in a bomb shelter, which was illegal to do. After that, they shipped him out of Hawaii. He was from the mainland and he had a real long "rap sheet" on everything imaginable. His purpose for being in the islands was not really to work, but to make some easy money.

In one other undercover job, I almost got discovered. It was out in the old Kam School building, now the Bishop Museum. I overheard one of the ringleaders ask, "Hey, any of you guys know who that tall fellow in the blue shirt is over there?" looking in my direction. One guy said, "I don't know but he sure looks like the guy that threw his badge on the table at Punahou." He had made a connection there and I was on the spot. After eighteen days, I called Capt. Burns and said, "You guys better raid this place tonight, or I'm not going to be here tomorrow." It was getting rather hairy.

" . . . I called Capt. Burns and said, 'You guys better raid this place tonight, or I'm not going to be here tomorrow.' "

I was happy to get out of that undercover work. That element could get rough. They were completely the mainland element--no local people were involved in it at all. But, I'd have to stay with them and work with them, and sleep at night in the same dorms with nothing to protect myself. Six or eight guys sleeping there in one room, half of them drunk and raising cane.

Then I was put on the prostitution detail for a couple of years. While prostitution was actually against the territorial law, it was controlled and allowed to operate. And, under martial law, it went pretty well because the gals were watched closely. They would be regularly checked at the clinic at Palama Settlement and if there was anything suspicious, they weren't allowed to work.

There were many restrictions on the prostitutes. They couldn't go to public beaches, they couldn't go to bowling lanes. They were literally told what they couldn't do. There were even some areas where they couldn't live. And, believe me, many of them had the money so that they could have bought their way into any area. They were told that they couldn't have a man in the house past 5:00 p.m. So, we had daytime prostitution in Honolulu during the war. There must have been sixteen or more houses on River Street, Hotel Street, near Aala Park, and we had records on all of them. Also, the FBI was always checking up for violations of the Mann Act--white slavery--transporting these gals across boundaries for prostitution. So we worked closely with the FBI.

We kept having those air-raid drills. It could be two o'clock in the morning and the sirens would go off. I would get up from a sound sleep, get dressed in my uniform and head for the station. Invariably, half way there, the all-clear would sound. All off-duty officers had to do that--to report as soon as the sirens went off. I don't know how many times I went through that routine. We didn't mind that it wasn't the real thing, though. We were always hoping it was just a dry run or a false alarm.

In my estimation, the Japanese people were the most well-behaved of the ethnic groups in Honolulu during the war. They were always under scrutiny, especially the aliens. They had to prove their loyalty like no

---

"... the Japanese people were the most well-behaved ... They were always under scrutiny ... They had to prove their loyalty like no other group did. "

---

other group did. The old mama-sans and papa-sans, they were real good to me. They would throw a beef steak on the grill for me, they'd cook up a storm. A particular couple, the Watanabes, were so thoughtful to me and to my family. I've never forgotten that. There was a Japanese officer who worked on the vice squad when I was there. His name was Earl Kubo. He had a wife and two or three kids. When they asked for volunteers from the Japanese community to join up with the 442nd, he volunteered. He told me, "Chet, the only reason why I'm going, is so that my kids will one day be able to say that I was an American." He fought in Italy.

Then, there were the local bums, I used to call them the "blalahs." These are the guys who would fake a fight in a back alley just to get a cop in there, then beat the living daylights out of him, take his revolver, and put him in the hospital. And some of them were only sixteen years old, but they were big. Kids mature fast over there. And, they were tough. A lot of cops really got hurt in those situations. We worked alone, you know, and you could get yourself into some bad scrapes like that.

We had considerable trouble with servicemen, too. In fact, I had a situation when I was at Queen's Hospital, in emergency, with a couple of soldiers. One of them had a badly bleeding hand. He said he got into a fight and put his fist through a plate-glass window. I had to do a report on him. While he was being treated, for some reason, I didn't believe him. So I followed his blood drops back up the street to a little house. The glass was broken out of the front door. I shined a flashlight inside, and a little kid, a couple of years old, was on the bed just terrified. His mother was in the back bedroom. She had been beaten up something terrible. Those two guys had forced themselves on her and beaten her up. I took them in and they were arrested and court-martialed, results of which I do not know.

Even though while on the vice squad I covered all of Honolulu, later when on prowl car duty, my beat was basically the Kalihi area. But I had to be available for calls in other parts of the city as well. There was a beef one day down on Hotel Street that I swear--for three solid blocks--you could see nothing but khaki and white. And they were all mixing it up. The bars could only serve drinks for four hours, from noon to four o'clock. And, they were only allowed to serve two drinks per customer. So these servicemen would go from bar to bar to get their two drinks in each place. Many of the bars were air conditioned, too, so it was cool in there. At four o'clock, they would all have to come out in the heat, all at the same time. Oh, geez, that would be the worst time of day to be on duty. It was a bear.

So, anyway, this one day, there were, I'd say, forty thousand servicemen in town, many of them near Hotel Street. And it seemed like every one of them was in a fight. They loaded up these guys in every patrol wagon they could get, Shore Patrol, Military Police, civil police. Every policeman, MP and SP available was called in on that one. And when it was all over, nobody really knew what the fight was all about.

I used to have a police beat out by the Palama Fire Department. I was lucky that I took a deep tan. I went spear fishing a lot and got quite dark. And I could hold my own with pidgin English, so many of the locals took me for Portuguese, I guess, or a local boy, anyway. I'd be on the call box and one of these big old kanaka[2] firemen would come by. There weren't too many fires in those days, so the firemen would play volleyball and cook luaus in the back yard for parties for their friends and relatives. "Eh, bull," this guy said, "kaukau[3] twelve o'clock." So, I'd go over there at noon and they would have this roast pig, poi, lomi salmon, yams, and man, I'd have a feast with those firemen. I loved all that stuff.

I enjoyed special duty after a few years on the force. After work, I would be hired to do special duty at Kewalo Inn. I would just stand by and see that everything was all right. They wanted a uniformed officer there to serve as a bouncer if anything happened. I got $5 an hour doing that--more than I was making at the police department. Don McDermid and his orchestra would be playing there and Alfred Apaka--eventually one of the best-known entertainers from the islands--was the featured vocalist. I really enjoyed that. The woman that sold leis at the door would always give me flowers to take home to my wife. And, occasionally, I'd give Alfred Apaka a ride home to his place in Pauoa Valley. I got to know him quite well. That was good duty, and profitable, as well.

I was doing well in the police department and I think I probably would have stayed, but after talking with Capt. Burns, he said that most of the senior officers were fairly young men. It would have been a long while before I would advance, so I made the decision to leave in 1945, just before the war was over. I was offered a job with the Kauai Medical Service Association (HMSA) and spent a year there before deciding to continue my education and become a coach, my life-long ambition.

---

[2]*Hawaiian word meaning person, man, but used as a term for someone with Hawaiian ancestry.*

[3]*Hawaiian term, slang, commonly used as meaning food or dinner.*

Vernice and I loved living in the islands. Two of our daughters were born there, one in Honolulu, and one in Kauai. I'm sure we would still be there if I hadn't decided to finish my schooling and go into physical education. We lived just off the Ala Wai Canal, on Tusitala Court. We would take a dip at Kuhio beach in the moonlight. Somebody was always playing Hawaiian music on the beach. It was so beautiful.

We had some police officers who would take out their musical instruments when they got off duty and sit around and play the most beautiful music--right there in the squad room. They all seemed to have such beautiful voices. One of them was Sterling Mossman, who was a dispatcher at the time I was on the force. He became a famous entertainer. I have some of his records.

Those were some of the best times my wife and I have had. We'll never forget the early years of our marriage in beautiful Waikiki. And, of course, my job there gave me some special privileges as well as some special challenges. The attack on Pearl Harbor changed my life, drastically, in just a few hours. You know, I sometimes think about it--I wonder how our football team would have done had the bombs not cancelled those games?

Chet and his family went to San Jose where Chet earned his degree in physical education in 1947. He taught a year at San Jose High School, serving as coach of the baseball team and assistant coach of the football team. He taught elementary school for three years in Placerville, California, then realized his life's dream, returning to his old high school as athletic director and coach. He coached varsity football, baseball and basketball at El Dorado County High School in Placerville. In 1958, Chet entered the insurance field and is still active in the business. He and Vernice had six children, five girls and then finally, a boy. They have fifteen grandchildren and two great-grandchildren. The Carstens are busy during the summers when their Sacramento home is filled with visiting grandchildren.

John G. Staszkow

His father was born in Paahao on the big island and his mother was born in Honolulu. His grandparents had come to Hawaii from Portugal and Austria. John was born in Honolulu in 1932. He attended Aliiolani School from the first through third grades. In September 1941, John began the fourth grade at St. Louis College. At the time of the attack, John, an only child, lived with his parents at 1014 3rd Avenue, Kaimuki. He was nine.

Weeks, perhaps even months prior to December seventh, I remember my dad going to meetings at Pearl Harbor that were briefings on the world situation and the possible war with Japan. He was a quarterman, an electrician at Shop 51 at Pearl Harbor. I don't know whether these meetings were run by the civil defense or the military intelligence, but I know they were preparing for something to happen.

I remember it was on Thursday, December 4, 1941, that my dad came home from work and told my mom and I that war with Japan was imminent. They didn't know when, but they knew the Japanese were coming. I didn't understand what I was hearing. "Why would the Japanese want to do this to us?" I asked. His answer was direct, but just as difficult for me to understand. "It has to be," he said. I asked further, "What do you mean, it has to be?" He just repeated himself, this time more adamantly, "It just has to be." There was no other explanation and it left me confused and frightened.

Sunday morning, December the seventh, I was at the 7:00 o'clock Mass at St. Patrick's church with my grandmother, Pauline Marques. We heard planes going over and it sounded like there were a lot of them. We thought that was unusual. Then, sometime a little later, we began hearing explosions and loud noises. Everyone seemed to be calm at church. The Mass ended quickly and everyone was told to leave the church. We weren't told why.

My grandmother and I left the church and walked over to my uncle Manuel Staszkow's house, about five or six blocks up on Palolo Avenue.

My uncle Manuel was my father's brother and he was in the merchant marine. I don't recall if he was there at that time, or if he had already been called down to help. Anyway, the adults were all milling about, talking about Pearl Harbor being attacked. I was outside with a couple of neighbor boys.

We decided that we wanted to see what was going on down at Pearl Harbor, so we climbed up the side of the hillside behind the house. It was actually the St. Louis Heights area. When we got up as high as we could climb, on the Palolo Valley side of the mountain, we could see smoke and fires coming from the Pearl Harbor area. We were just curious kids, and had to see what was going on. I guess the adults thought we were outside playing and hadn't given a thought to where we were. It was exciting, in a scary way.

Then, we couldn't believe what we were seeing. This airplane came down into Palolo Valley heading makai,[1] going towards Waikiki. It was low, almost at eye level from where we were standing. "Oh, boy," yelled one of the kids. "Here comes the U. S. Air Force to the rescue." And he started jumping up and down and waving at the plane. We joined him, then after a few seconds into this celebration, it began to dawn on us that maybe it's **not** a U. S. aircraft. And, so help me, he banked as if to turn toward Pearl Harbor. He couldn't have been more than five hundred feet up when he passed by us. We could see the pilot clearly. He had this white cloth around his forehead. We really could see him. I couldn't

---

" *We could see the pilot clearly. He had this white cloth around his forehead. . . Then it sunk in. This was . . . a Japanese aircraft.* *"*

---

estimate the distance, maybe a quarter of a mile away from us when he banked. Then it sunk in. This was really a Japanese aircraft. He banked as if to turn, then straightened out and flew straight forward. Was it a salute to three crazy kids, waving and jumping up and down? I really don't know.

I do know, however, that that scene scared the hell out of us. We

---

[1]*Hawaiian word, a direction, toward the ocean.*

372

scrambled down the hill as fast as we could run. We rushed back to my uncle's house, panting, out of breath, but very excited about our close encounter with the enemy. All the grown-ups were still inside the house, unaware of our little adventure. And, we didn't tell them, either.

In the meantime, my dad had been called down to Pearl Harbor and my mother was left alone at home, worried about the two of us. Later that afternoon, my dad came home from Pearl Harbor in the afternoon and he and Mom drove over to Uncle Manuel's to pick me up.

My father was just exhausted. He said that some of the cars were being strafed trying to get into Pearl Harbor and he could see the results of it. He went to his shop and there was some damage there, but it was only superficial. The drydocks were close to his shop and they were damaged, too, but not destroyed. He said they spent their time trying to clean things up as much as possible. Most of the guys down there spent their time that day fighting fires.

That night was blackout. It was dark and eerie that night. Early the next morning--it must have been about dawn--these three airplanes were flying over our house at about the time anti-aircraft batteries started firing at them. They were twin-engine planes, I remember, and one of them looked as if it got hit. There was smoke coming from one wing. I didn't know whether they were ours or Japanese. I suspect they were ours. Anyway, Mom and I were scared as hell. Dad had already left for Pearl Harbor and we were alone. We ran downstairs to our basement to seek shelter. We thought for sure that the Japanese were back and that we were going to be bombed again. It was a frightening feeling.

We had a full basement down there. A short while later, Dad and I filled up sand bags--I don't know how many, but it seemed like hundreds--and made a bomb shelter in the basement. We lined the outside of the basement with sand bags. That's where we went every time the air-raid alarm went off. And that happened a lot.

Our neighbors across the street were Japanese. He was a dentist. His parents had come from Japan to live in retirement with their son in Hawaii. They had a little cottage in the back. His father, I think, was retired from the Japanese military--I don't know whether it was the army or the navy. Anyway, they used to shoot arrows against a straw target down the side driveway of their house. Archery was practiced with a certain ritual that they would go through. Us neighbor kids would gather the arrows from the target and bring them back. They used fabulous control and discipline when shooting those arrows. It was just incredible. They would have many family gatherings and would show movies in their living room. I remember seeing my first movie cartoon, Felix the Cat, at the neighbor's house.

Anyway, the old man had a powerful telescope out on the front porch. I remember looking through it. It was big--about two feet long--and very powerful. When I looked through it, I could see the ships down near Pearl Harbor. There were no buildings in the way at that time and you could see directly down to the navy yard. I recall seeing the three large cranes in the shipyard--I would guess we were about seven miles away--and I could see them very clearly.

But, Pearl Harbor was located so that anybody could see what was going on at any time from any of the hills and mountains around it, so it was ludicrous to think that anyone with a telescope was a spy. But, within twenty-four hours of the attack, the old man **and** his wife were gone. We never saw them again. I remember asking the kids about their grandparents and I got no answer. They just disappeared. I imagine, the fact that he was a retired military from Japan and considered an enemy alien, they were probably sent to the mainland to the internment camps. I don't know. I only know I never saw them again.

" . . . it was ludicrous to think that anyone with a telescope was a spy. But, within twenty-four hours of the attack, the old man and his wife were gone. We never saw them again. "

Our bathroom was the only room in our house that was blacked out. I remember when we went back to school, I would do my homework on the toilet bowl. Since St. Louis was taken over by the army for a hospital, we went to St. Patrick's to school for half a day, in the mornings. The St. Patrick students used the same rooms in the afternoon. I remember Brother Sam was our teacher, Brother Sam Gressock.

Dad was away most of the time, working at Pearl Harbor. They worked long hours, trying to rebuild the fleet. Those first few months were filled with fear. We always knew that there was the possibility that the Japanese would come back again. I guess that was a fearful time for me too, as a child. With my dad gone most of the time, I guess I felt that I was the man of the house.

Then, a slew of new residents started coming to Hawaii from the mainland to work at Pearl Harbor, getting the islands on a war-time footing. They repaired the damaged and sunken ships and got them out to sea again in record time. This was really the beginning of the population explosion in Hawaii. Many of those mainland workers stayed in the islands after the war.

I remember my father talking about the chain of events that led to our final victory in the war. First of all, he said, we were so fortunate that the Japanese didn't destroy the shipyard and the fuel tanks all around it. Secondly, he would say, the ships that were sunk were in shallow water. There were only a few that never did get repaired, and those that did were fitted with more up-to-date equipment and armament. The third thing that helped us to turn the war around was the fact that our aircraft carriers were not in the harbor that Sunday morning. It might have just been a fluke that they were still out at sea, but it was very fortunate for us.

In June 1942, my father worked solidly over a period of time. He didn't come home. We found out later that that was during the battle of Midway. By the grace of God, too, we won that battle. We caught all the Japanese carriers with their bombs and everything on the decks. And we found them before they found us. We lucked out, again. If it had been the other way around, they just might have invaded Hawaii, encouraged by their success. So I guess it was "touch and go" for a while there.

I remember I was so excited to be going to St. Louis in the fourth grade in September 1941. The campus was up on a hill and the high school students would be going there, too, though the high school buildings were on the other side of the campus. Anyway, I felt like it was "big time." Because of the Pearl Harbor attack, though, I was denied those four years on the St. Louis campus when the school was turned into an army hospital. I guess in a way, that changed my life. We returned to the campus in early 1946, when the army returned it to the brothers.

I have often thought about those wartime events, particularly December the seventh. It's amazing how the world changed between the time my grandmother and I entered the church and when we came out.

A calm, normal, Sunday morning was transformed immediately into frenzied activities of death and destruction. In that one hour, the whole world changed.

And, I guess the thing I shall never forget about that wartime experience was the scene up on the hillside--cheering and waving at what we thought was an American airplane--only to see that pilot and feel the frightening reality that we were waving to the enemy. It's been fifty years now and I still shudder just thinking about it.

John graduated from St. Louis College (high school) in 1950 and attended the University of Hawaii for a short time. He went to work at Aloha Airlines in 1951 and married a stewardess, Lani Case, in December 1954. In November 1958, John joined Canadian Pacific Airlines, now Canadian Airlines International, and has been there ever since. He and Lani had three children: Robin, born in 1955; Dawn in 1956; and Brian in 1959. John and Lani were divorced in 1983 and John transferred to the San Francisco airport as a passenger agent with Canadian Airlines. He has three grandchildren, who live in Everett, Washington, with Robin and her husband. Besides work, John spends his time in nature hikes, keeping fit by walking the hills of San Carlos, Redwood City, and Palo Alto, in the San Francisco bay area. He lives in San Carlos with his widowed mother.

Rodney L. Rodriggs

He was born Oliver Rodrigues on July 7, 1914, the fourth of five children born to Frank and Jessie Rodrigues. As he was primarily known as "Rod," he dropped the use of Oliver and later anglicized the spelling of his surname. Rod attended Kauluwela School, Central Grammar School (English Standard), Lincoln Junior High School, McKinley High School for the first two years, then was transferred to the newly organized Roosevelt High School for his junior and senior years. Rod became a member of the first class to graduate from Roosevelt in 1932. He worked at McInerny's Shoe Store from 1933 to 1939. After a summer speaking tour on the mainland for the Honolulu Junior Chamber of Commerce, Rod worked for a short time for Manufacturer's Shoe Store. In 1939, Rod went to work for the Quinn Company, owned by Charles R. Frazier Co., selling advertising and novelty items. He lived at the home he was born in, at 1909 Liliha Street.

I was at my brother Nelson's house the night of December 6, 1941. We were playing poker, I remember, in the basement. Al Vare and Larry Ponza were there, too. I left there about 3:00 a.m., and drove home and went to bed.

I had the front bedroom, along Liliha Street, and I was awakened by explosions and bombs going off. "Jesus Christ," I yelled, "what the hell's happening? Maneuvers on a Sunday? What's the matter with those papayas?"

My mother turned on the radio. We had one of those big Atwater-Kent radios. "All military personnel, report to your bases at once," the announcer was saying. Then we heard what was happening. Pearl Harbor was under attack. We turned to both stations--KGMB and KGU-- and we heard the same type of message.

I heard them announce that all navy personnel should report to their bases immediately. I had a navy pass on my car because I sold merchandise at the ships' service store there at the sub base. So I jumped into my 1940 Plymouth convertible and headed off to taxi sailors to Pearl Harbor. Our neighbor, Buddy Edgar, joined me. I drove over to Bates and Nuuanu where there was a Japanese hotel where sailors used to stay.

We picked up a couple there, who were waiting for transportation to Pearl, then stopped at the old Senator Hotel on Fort Street and picked up a few more. We dashed down to Pearl Harbor--Buddy and I and four sailors--speeding as fast as that Plymouth would take us. We zipped through the gate to the sub base and dropped them off. They would catch the jitney boats to take them to their ships. We saw the *Oglala* being hit. It was on 1010 Dock, not far from the sub base. It was hit by a bomb or torpedo, or something, and was in trouble. We then went back into town for another run.

We loaded the car up again and when we got back to the gate at Pearl Harbor, there were planes strafing overhead. We could see the "fried egg" on the wings and, as they passed over us, we shook our fists at them. I don't know how it happened then, but I guess one of their bullets ricocheted off the roadway and blew a hole through my felt hat. It was just a little hole and I didn't even know when it happened because I didn't feel a thing at the time. I discovered it later. There was mass confusion by this time at Pearl Harbor. Everybody seemed to be running around without knowing what to do. I really believe that if the Japanese had sent in troops that morning, they could have taken over the islands. Nobody knew what they were supposed to do.

I drove back to town and since there were no other sailors looking for a ride, I went back home. My sister, Nettie, was there with my mother and neighbors started coming over. My brother's wife, Rose, called, and she was all maka'u.[1] She asked me to come over and pick up her and her sons, Larry and Billy, and take them to their house on Wilhelmina Rise. They were at her parents' house in Kaimuki. My brother, Reggie, had been gone all day--he was a civil defense ambulance driver--and she didn't know when he would be back home. I also got a call from "Rusty" Frazier, my boss, who asked me to take care of the business, as he was called by Governor Joseph Poindexter to help activate the Hawaii Territorial Guard. He was a major in the guard. He said he would be at the armory on Hotel Street for a while, so I could reach him there if need be.

About that time, the Coast Guard cutter *Itasca*, I think it was called, was firing at the second wave of attacking planes. One of the shells from the *Itasca* missed its target and fell at Liliha and Kuakini Streets. Another

[1]*Hawaiian word meaning frightened or afraid.*

378

one fell just a few blocks from us, at Liliha and Judd Streets. As a result, they were asking everybody to vacate the Liliha area. So, I took my mother and sister up to Rose's house on Wilhelmina Rise and that's where we all spent the first night of the war.

We all slept in the darkened living room, right on the floor, with the police radio band going all night long. Reggie didn't come home that night and we hadn't heard from him.

Governor Poindexter came on the radio and said that he had appointed Gen. Walter C. Short as acting military governor of Hawaii and that we were under martial law. They announced that the two radio stations were going to go off the air for several days. That's when everyone started to tune in to the police radio frequency. They also announced that anyone who had a shortwave radio had to turn them in. They had a Portuguese woman--who could speak Japanese--come on the radio and give the same order to the Japanese-speaking population. I had a shortwave radio, so I took mine down to a place at King and Liliha Streets and turned it in, the next day. I don't know what happened to it, but I never saw it again.

On Monday morning, I went to work as usual. I stopped by to talk to Rusty Frazier at the armory and he told me that they were assigned to guard and protect the coast line and had a gun emplacement at the Waialae Golf Course, where they thought the Japanese would be trying to land. The Territorial Guard was made up primarily of Americans of Japanese ancestry, and Rusty was one of their strongest supporters at a time when there were a lot of military who doubted their loyalty.

On Tuesday evening I went back up to my brother's house, and that's when he finally came home. He was hysterical. He said that he had never seen anything like that in his life. He was in shock and crying. He had been down at Hickam Field on Sunday, I believe, and his American Sanitary Laundry truck was converted to an ambulance, and he was picking up badly injured servicemen and taking them to Tripler Hospital. He had somebody working with him, but he was the driver. He wouldn't say much about it--he was so upset. Since he was home, I didn't sleep there any longer. I decided to go back to my house on Liliha Street. It didn't seem, at that point, that the Japanese had an invasion in mind.

Then, the houses of prostitution, which were allowed to operate under martial law, were closed, along with the bars, for a short period of time.

Later, they opened up the houses between 8:00 a.m. and 4:00 p.m., and you never saw such lines in the middle of the day downtown. I did a lot of good-will business with the houses and knew many of the owners--the ladies who ran them. In fact, two of them were registered nurses and volunteered their time at Tripler Hospital on December seventh, and stayed there for several days, helping out.

The girls were tightly controlled and carefully watched. They were required to take a smear test weekly and the Wassermann test monthly to be sure that they had no venereal diseases. If they showed positive, they were shipped right back to the mainland, where they came from. The guys were also encouraged to take precautions. Each patron was offered a condom at no charge. There were prophylactic stations all over town, run by the army at no charge for the services.

The girls were called "sporting" girls, and they listed their occupation as "entertainer." They even filed their earnings with the Internal Revenue Service and paid taxes. I remember they charged $3.00 for the haoles.[2] They gave the locals a break, only $2.50 for kamaainas.[3]

Our advertising business increased tremendously during the war. We incorporated the business and the name was changed to The Quinn Company, Ltd. We took over the Quinn Company Building at Beretania and Punchbowl. Rusty was president and I was vice president. We branched out into novelty souvenirs, and Rusty Frazier thought I should go to California to get more lines to sell. So I did. In fact, I took four trips during the war, from 1942 to 1944. There was no trouble getting up to California during wartime, but getting back to Honolulu was a real problem.

I struck up a good acquaintanceship with Lawrence Campus, of the L. W. Campus Dairies, of Kailua. They would call on various dairies in California and buy bulls and springers--a cow that was almost ready to drop a calf. So, I would go to California, call on the companies that we represented, then I would come back to Honolulu as a cattle tender, feeding the cows for the Campus Dairies. They would have about a hundred cows and bulls in stalls on deck. There would be one cattle tender for about ten animals.

---

[2]*Hawaiian word meaning Caucasian, white person.*

[3]*Hawaiian word for native-born.*

On one trip, we had seventeen calves drop on board ship on the way over to Hawaii. And seven of them were breech births--the calves were dropping feet first and you had to turn them around during the birthing process. We had one guy who had veterinary experience from the dairy, but we all had to do the job ourselves to save the stock. There was a lot of alfalfa and straw on the deck and we would have to clean the stalls out during the morning and pile the mess up along the rail of the ship. You couldn't throw anything overboard during the day, because we were in submarine-infested waters and if a Japanese sub spotted the debris, they would be able to follow us. So we tossed the stuff over after dark, at night.

The ships zig-zagged all the way over. I remember sailing on the *Mauna Wili*, the *Mauna Kai*, and the *Mauna Lani*. I was paid twenty-five cents by Matson Navigation Company for being a cattle tender on each trip. That's not twenty-five cents an hour, or a day, but for the whole trip. But, I got the transportation out of it and was able to get back to the islands.

In December, 1943, I was on one of my trips as a cattle tender and we were scheduled to join a big convoy of ships. The convoy was all lined up outside the Golden Gate when the fog came in so thick you couldn't see anything but your own ship. So we stayed there overnight. The next morning, you still couldn't see anything. They sent blimps out to line us up once more--I believe there were four rows of ships. They herded us in place and at five in the afternoon, when we finally were ready to start, the fog came in thick as can be, again. Finally, they did the same thing the next day, and we were on our way.

Our ship could normally travel at eighteen to twenty knots. But, wouldn't you know, the speed of the convoy is governed by the speed of the slowest ship. And this little lumber ship, the *Lumber Lady*, could only go seven knots, top speed. We left California on December tenth. We finally passed by Koko Head on Oahu on Christmas Eve, December twenty-fourth. We were so happy to finally see land, then these planes flew over us and informed us by radio that we couldn't get into Honolulu Harbor because another convoy hadn't been able to get out yet. So we had to circle all around the island for another day. We got in on Christmas day.

I got to know Lawrence Campus real well. I remember when he was asked to try the artificial insemination process rather than having to ship those bulls down from California. His response was: "No. Who know bettah den de bull when de cow want it?" We would be in San Francisco at the same time and he would always have guests out to dinner and he was well known as a generous tipper. One evening, at the Copacabana club on Powell Street, when we were seated at our table, the band leader announced on the microphone, "Ladies and gentlemen, we are privileged to have as our guests at the Copa this evening, Mr. Lawrence Campus, the biggest bull shipper in Hawaii." Then, he added, "and his secretary, Mr. Rod Rodriggs, the second biggest bull shipper in Hawaii."

Those were interesting times in Hawaii. I don't know how things would have been different had Pearl Harbor not happened. I imagine the mainland travel would have been much easier to arrange, and perhaps the business would have flourished even more than it did. I still think about the morning of December seventh. I have often wondered what happened to those sailors that we dropped off in the middle of the bombs and torpedoes. Did all of them survive? I certainly hope so.

In 1945, after the war, Rod came to California to introduce the Ka Lae Company's line of aloha shirts and gift line of monkey pod wood, including the one-piece ukulele made of monkey pod. He sold to such stores as Macy's in New York, Marshall Field in Chicago, the Emporium in San Francisco, and many other major organizations in the U. S. In 1949, he married Gertrude Scruggs. Rod and "Trudy" welcomed a daughter, Diane, in 1953. Rod worked in laundry supplies, the shoe business, and set up coin laundries over the years. He retired in 1980. Diane married her high school sweetheart, Dennis Gerrity. She is a graduate from San Jose State and Dennis graduated from Santa Clara University and U.C.S.F. School of Dentisty. Diane and Dennis have three sons, Christopher, Kyle, and Jeffrey. Rod enjoys reading and swimming in his back yard pool. He and Trudy enjoy taking an occasional trip back to Hawaii, but his favorite retirement activity is being with his three grandsons. Rod and Trudy live in retirement in Sunnyvale, California.

Adrian and Roselyn Baptist

Adrian Baptist was born in 1919 in Kahului, Maui. He was the fourth of five children born to Millie and John Baptist. He attended St. Anthony's School for four years and was ten when the family moved to Honolulu. He attended Waialae and Liliuokalani schools through the eighth grade then went to St. Louis for his high school years, graduating in 1937. He had a dance band, Adrian's Collegians, and played for dances at night while working at Honolulu Laundry during the days. In 1939, he went to work at the Hawaiian Plumbing & Sheet Metal Company. In February 1941, he married Roselyn De Silva. Roselyn was born in Honolulu in 1922, the fifth of six children born to William and Virginia De Silva. She attended St. Anthony's in Kalihi Kai, and Kalakaua Junior High School to the eighth grade. She worked at Dole cannery and at the Hawaiian Printing Company. On December 7, 1941, Adrian and Roselyn lived at the corner of 21st and Kaimuki avenues.

Adrian: After high school, I played tenor sax and made good money for those Depression days--four or five dollars a night--playing down at the Armory. I had a seven-piece band and we were pretty good. Whenever there was competition among the bands, we would always come out among the top--usually second place.

In 1939, I worked at Hawaiian Plumbing and Sheet Metal and started my trade as a sheet metal worker. We worked forty-four hours a week, including four hours on Saturday. Roselyn and I got engaged on Christmas 1940, and we were married on February 22, 1941. That's when my music career ended because being married didn't mix well with the life of a musician. But my boss down at the plant gave me a raise when I told him I was getting married. He increased my wages from 50-cents an hour to 60-cents an hour. I had additional responsibilities, a wife, right?

My father-in-law was a cement man. Since I didn't know much about cement, he planned to help me pour cement on Sunday, December seventh. We were going to put it in the back of my garage where we planned to put our laundry trays. So I was going to pick him up after Mass. So, we went to the seven o'clock Mass at St. Patrick's that morning. After Mass, when we started for home, we began hearing a lot of noise--much commotion. Nobody ever believed that the Japanese would try to attack us. They were too weak and we were much too strong for anything like that to happen.

Anyway, we listened to the radio and learned that we were under attack. I got a call from work and was told to report down there immediately. So, I drove Roselyn over to my mom's house and then drove down to the plant, which was near Kewalo Basin. As I was going down Kapiolani Boulevard, there was a big explosion nearby that really shook me up. I thought sure it was a bomb, you know. I found out later that it was our own shells that fell at McCully and King Streets, in the Moilili area.

I have never been able to figure out why they called me down to the plant. When I got there, everybody was in an uproar. They didn't know what they should do. We just stuck around and waited for orders on what to do. Finally, we were let go and I went back to my mother's house at Wilhelmina Rise. I really didn't feel scared up to that point. Even the explosion from McCully didn't frighten me too much. But, after I got back to my mother's house--everyone there was frightened--then I began to think about what had happened and what could happen. And the worst thing we could do, we did--that was listening to the radio. The radio was just frightening people all the more by spreading the rumors about the water being poisoned and the paratroopers who were supposed to have landed in the mountains.

My sister, Violet, and her husband, Leonard Fry, came over with their two girls, Gaynelle and Damienne. Leonard brought his gun with him. So, we had a gun in the house, anyway. We didn't know if the Japanese were on their way back or what, so at least we had one gun in the house. My brother, Herbert, was also there with his wife, Lillian, and their daughter, Arlette. Lillian was about five-months pregnant.

And we stayed there at Mom's one whole week. Everybody went to work from there and came back there in the evening. I guess we all felt safer together. We all slept in the living room on the floor--my folks had a big living room. My sister, Mildred, was still living at home at that time, so she had a bedroom of her own. The rest of us congregated together.

Right after the war started, Hawaiian Plumbing and Sheet Metal was taken over by the U.S. Engineers. They just walked right in and said, "We're taking you over." And that was it. They took over all the sheet metal companies and moved in all of their junk. We became U.S. Engineers Mill 17, I think it was. So, overnight, we all became civil service employees in a military mill.

" Right after the war started, Hawaiian Plumbing and Sheet Metal was taken over by the U.S. Engineers. They just walked right in and said, 'We're taking you over.' "

They were putting up barracks everywhere on the island at that time. They were mobilizing to defend against the invasion they thought sure was coming. Anyway, our main job for many months was fabricating those "piss" troughs for the barracks. That's what we did, we made urinal troughs--hundreds and hundreds of them. And they weren't made to last, either, just light sheet metal--not stainless steel or anything like that. They didn't want to waste money. So that was my contribution to the war effort for those first few months.

Then, we were assigned to a top secret project. It seems that there was a big, underground base up at Kunia in the Waialae Range of mountains. They must have had it going for some time before the war, but nobody knew about it. We were never to discuss anything about it. We had to have special passes. I was never allowed to drive up to it. We would be picked up in trucks and transported to the site. We installed all the ventilation sheet metal for the underground air conditioning. It went three stories underground and it contained a number of rooms where the brass made decisions about the war. I remember one very large room with conference tables and maps and charts all around. It was an elaborate place. They wouldn't let you go in that room unless you had some work to do in there. We had two shifts going at Kunia. We were on that job a good six months, I think. And, I finally felt that I was really doing something for the war effort. Sure was better than constructing piss troughs.

I never drank in my life until the war started. Even when I was playing music, I never took a drop of liquor. But when the war started and we had blackout and curfew, I learned to drink. That was at my brother Herbert's place. We would walk two blocks to his house and play cribbage. My uncle, Leonard Rego, would come over and play cribbage with us, too. That was long before he opened Leonard's Bakery in Kapahulu. Anyway, since I didn't like the taste of whiskey, they would put my whiskey in root beer so I couldn't taste the liquor. There was nothing much you could do for entertainment, since blackout was from 6:00 p.m. to 6:00 a.m. So we would walk to Herbert's for our wartime entertainment.

In 1943, I transferred to Pearl Harbor. I always wanted to work down there and, since I had been made a civil service employee when the Engineers took over our company, it was easier to get a transfer to Pearl Harbor. So I worked at Shop 17, the sheet metal shop in the shipyard.

AT DAY'S END -- Pearl Harbor Navy Yard war workers rush to catch the train, the bus, or to join their private car pools at the end of a hard day's work. (Official U.S. Navy Photograph; War Depository Collection, University of Hawaii)

We were over eight hundred employees in that one shop. Everybody was just on top of one another. We did ship repair work, but at times there was a lot of sitting around, waiting, until your list of materials was filled so that you could get to work.

Gas rationing was always a problem, so we had car pools to go to work. Pearl Harbor was a busy place during the war.

As I look back on those years now, I really believe that the Japanese could have taken us over that day--perhaps with only five hundred troops. I don't think the Japanese thought that it would be that easy. But, if that would have happened, it would have been a very different war. And we might not have survived to tell our stories.

Roselyn: Those early days of the war were frightening. I remember when I first heard the radio announce the attack. I was so worried about what was going to happen to us. I couldn't help but think that we were just married earlier that year, and what was going to become of us? I was so scared. Mom Baptist called and said, "All of you come up and stay with us. If anything happens, we'll all go together." I'll never forget that.

When the first bombs started to drop, our friend Richard Rego called to tell us about it. He was actually standing on the roof of his mother-in-law's house, watching the planes go over.

So, anyway, we went over to Mom's house and were all together to give each other support. We were told to stay indoors and not to leave the house. We would look out the window of her house on Wilhelmina Rise and whenever we would see anybody outside, Mom would say, "He's not supposed to be walking on that street. He's supposed to be indoors." She would worry about anybody walking around outside, even in the daylight.

When Leonard came over with his gun, we felt a little safer. He said he was there to defend the household from the Japanese invaders. But even with that protection, we didn't sleep much at night. We were always worrying about what was going to happen. And, I guess we all felt that the Japanese were going to come back.

Mom had a lot of canned goods in the house, so we would put everything together and feed the whole gang without too much trouble. We would eat and rest in shifts. The women didn't go out at all, at first.

The men took off for work during the days and the women supported one another and the children at the house.

I remember Mom was so afraid that the big water tank up on Wilhelmina Rise would be hit by a bomb and would flood everything below and we would all drown. She was so upset. I would tell her, "Now don't get upset, Mom, just pray that everything will be all right." And we did a lot of praying. We stayed there a week and then finally went back home.

I remember my mother phoned with terrible news. I grew up in the Kalihi Valley area, and one of my mom's friends who lived up in Kalihi Uka was killed on December seventh. Her whole family of four was wiped out when a bomb or a shell dropped on them when they were outside washing their car. They were a Portuguese family and lived near the Holy Ghost church. It was tragic. My mom was so upset, telling me about it.

> " . . . one of my mom's friends who lived up in Kalihi Uka was killed . . . Her whole family of four was wiped out . . . "

We blacked out the house so that we could have lights on at night. Then, shortly after that, I got pregnant. I was so sick, and the closed-in rooms, without air, made everything worse. We'd have to open up all the windows when we went to bed, to get some air in the house. Even the smell of coffee would make me sick. When Adrian got up in the morning, he would have to close the bedroom door before making the coffee so I wouldn't get sick.

Then I got worse. At about five months into my pregnancy, I was rushed to the hospital. This was at night, after dark and after curfew. We were told by the staff at Queen's Hospital that we had an emergency priority and that if we were stopped by the military, we should tell them to call the hospital and verify our emergency. Luckily, we weren't stopped at all. I was in the hospital for three days and almost lost the baby. After that, I had to be off my feet for the rest of the pregnancy. I would get around by crawling on the floor--it was that bad. I'm sure the stress of the war, and the blackout and everything, made it hard on me. Our daughter, Verda, was born on Sunday, September 26, 1942.

Many times during the war, I remember, Adrian had to work long hours or at night on the swing shift, and I was home alone with the baby. I was scared stiff, so frightened. I will never forget those war years in Honolulu. I think the thing that helped us the most was our faith. Somehow, we knew that God would protect us.

After the war, the Hawaiian Plumbing and Sheet Metal company was turned back to private industry again, and Adrian returned to the company after working for two years at Pearl Harbor. He later became a foreman. A second child, son Roy, was born in Honolulu in 1947. In 1951, the Baptist family moved to California and Adrian worked at the Alameda Naval Air Station. Verda married Gordon McMullen, an air force staff sergeant, in 1969. In 1973, Adrian retired from the naval air station, intending to return to private industry, when he was struck with a serious health problem. Although he must watch his health carefully, Adrian is able to keep busy around the house adding rooms, building cabinets, painting, and helping his daughter and son-in-law in their household projects. In February 1991, the Baptists celebrated their fiftieth anniversary, surrounded by their many relatives and friends.

Removing the Reminders of War

COLLECTING GAS MASKS -- A call to turn in gas masks was made in June 1945. Many masks were never returned as some people kept them for souvenirs or for spear fishing. Boy Scouts, helping in the collection, are Paul Lee, Richard Emerson, and Frederick Kawamoto. (**Star Bulletin** *Jul. 26, 1945; War Depository Collection, University of Hawaii*)

BURNING BOMB SHELTERS -- The bomb shelter at Lincoln School is set afire by the Office of Civilian Defense in May 1945. Burning the shelters collapsed the structure, destroying the termite-ridden lumber, and making the job of leveling the site much easier. (**Star Bulletin** May 5, 1945; War Depository Collection, University of Hawaii)

Alfred Hideo Goya

Al's father, Gashin Goya, came to Hawaii from Okinawa when in his mid-teens, about 1911. Al's grandfather had already come to the islands to work in the cane fields in Ewa. After a short stay on the Ewa plantation, his father moved to Paia, Maui, and worked for the sugar plantation. Many Okinawan families settled there. Gashin married Kame Tamanaha on Maui. They had seven children, six girls and one boy. Four were born on Maui and the rest on Oahu. Al was the second child, born in 1925. Gashin became an independent pineapple grower in Kula. In 1932, the family moved to Oahu to seek better working opportunities during the Depression. At the outbreak of war, the Goya family lived on a ten-acre farm in Haleiwa. Al was fifteen and a freshman at Waialua High School.

We moved to Oahu because my mother had a brother living over here. My father found a place in a camp where there were about a dozen homes near Kemoo Farm in Wahiawa. A few years later, he moved to Haleiwa where he leased a ten-acre farm. As an independent farmer he planted beans, corn, tomatoes, cabbage and all types of vegetables. By the time the war started, my father had some laborers working for him. And, during the peak years, he hired many Japanese ladies to harvest the crops. The truckers used to come to our farm and pick up the vegetables to sell to the markets. We also had chickens, pigs, and other animals. So, although we were a family of seven kids, there was always plenty of food on the table. We never did starve.

The property next to us was called Fresh Air Camp. It was like a park. The Palama Settlement people used to come there and camp during the summers. On the other side of the camp there was another place they called Section Camp. That was where the people lived who maintained and repaired the railroad tracks. A lot of the railroad crew laborers lived there, close to the section of railroad that they worked on. The Asato family lived near us on another farm. There was always a lot of people around. All the kids used to get together and play sports. And the ocean was just five minutes away. The Schofield officers used to have a beach club nearby, where they would go for recreation. We would play football, baseball, basketball, and we would swim almost every day. The years of my youth were good ones.

On December seventh, we didn't know what was going on because we were far away from the attack. There might have been planes flying over, but I don't remember seeing them at all. In fact, no one out there seemed to know what was going on until one of the neighbor girls--she was older than me--told us what happened to her. She was in Honolulu and early in the morning, she caught a taxi to bring her home. She said that the road was all blocked off at Pearl Harbor and she saw all the smoke and destruction when they passed by the harbor. It might have been after the planes left, I don't know. I know the adults were shocked and concerned, but it didn't mean too much to us kids.

But the realization that war had come to Hawaii hit us right after that when my father told us that we had to move away from the farm immediately. He was told by the military that we had to leave the place because it was too close to the sea coast. They had to put barbed wire all around there to protect the coast from the invasion that was supposed to come. The navy was taking it over, and we had to move off our farm right away, with no place to go. The Asato family had to leave their place, too.

My father went to the plantation office and they said that there were some vacant homes at a camp called Pump Three down near Haleiwa. It was the place where they processed all the water and pumped it for use by the plantation and for the community in the area. There was a vacant house there. So we moved there temporarily, for a couple of years.

But my father lost his farm and his business at Haleiwa. A few weeks after we were chased off the farm, the military allowed my father to go back down there to finish off his crops. I don't know how comfortable he was doing that, because he couldn't speak good English and he had to go through sentries and fences to get there. And he had to be out by a certain time every day because of the curfew and blackout. So they let him work the rest of his crops for a short while, but he still lost a lot because we were chased out of that farm by the navy.

They closed the Japanese school down when the war started. All the kids in our community were sent to the Japanese school before the war. That was what the parents wanted--that their children learn the language and keep their Japanese heritage. I didn't learn too much in Japanese school. To me, it seemed more like going to a babysitter. I can speak a little Japanese, but they spoke pidgin mostly, you know--a little Japanese, a little Hawaiian, and English all mixed up. But I remember they stressed discipline at Japanese school. If you got out of line, the teacher would make you stand in front of the class for one hour--with your arms straight out–holding erasers or chalk. Your arms got very sore, so you behaved after that. When I started playing sports in high school, I didn't have time to go to Japanese school. So when the war started they shut the school down. The timing was just right for me.

> " All the kids in our community were sent to
> the Japanese School before the war. That
> was what the parents wanted--that their
> children learn the language and keep their
> Japanese heritage. "

We had bomb shelters at Pump Three. In fact, we had a big community bomb shelter there. But when the siren would ring for an air-raid warning, we would all run to that community shelter and we couldn't all fit into it. Really. About one-fourth of the people could not get in the shelter.

The government was stressing the need for victory gardens at that time, so my father went into it in a big way. He leased about ten or twenty acres near Pump Three and grew mostly tomatoes. He hired some people to help him pick tomatoes each time the crop was ready. The family also pitched in.

Meanwhile, I started playing varsity baseball in my freshman year. The following year, I played football as a lineman, at one hundred forty five pounds. The backfield was filled with lots of talent. We took the rural championship, and I made the all-star team. In my senior year, I played running back. I also played baseball and basketball.

During my junior year, the school told everybody that we could get school credits if we went to work in war-type jobs. They needed a lot of help, and there was no manpower available. So I went to work at Schofield in a defense-type of job. I was a carpenter's helper and I got school credit for doing it. We blacked out the windows at the Schofield Hospital and we built barricades on the sides of the hospital for bomb and shrapnel prevention. We made columns of forms and filled them with sand bags to cover the sides of the hospital, to protect them. I remember when I was working out there, I saw some of the damage from the attack. Wheeler Field was all busted up. And I saw a couple of Japanese planes that had crashed, still in the pineapple fields outside Schofield.

A lot of guys left high school and went to work at that time. Some of the guys, I remember, went to work on a tunnel, digging a secret place underground. I was one of the fortunate guys from my class that went back to school in the senior year. A lot of them ended up working for the government and they didn't graduate because the money was too good. They are invited for class reunions, though, as it wasn't their fault that the war caused them to drop out of school. But I wanted a diploma, so I went back and finished up my high school education.

After a few years at Pump Three, my father bought a place down in Haleiwa and changed his profession. He bought a truck and started peddling fish. He also opened a fish market on Paala Road. He would go to town every morning at four or five o'clock and be there for the fish auction--buy whatever he had to buy--bring them back home and stock up his store and truck. Then he would go out to all the plantation camps all the way to Kahuku, and sell fish. And he would sell other things, too, like sausages, luncheon meat, eggs, tofu, whatever. And he would sell fish for sashimi. And he learned how to cut the fish for sashimi, which took some talent to do. He prepared special fish displays decorated with vegetable carvings for weddings and special parties. Kemoo Farm used to hire him to cut fish for sashimi and he used to do the same thing out at Seaview Inn in Haleiwa when they had big parties out there. You had to know just how to cut it, you know. My father was a hard worker and a very talented man.

I graduated from Waialua High School in 1944 and went to work at Wheeler Field as a storekeeper in the tools shop. I didn't go to college at that time, because everything was so unsettled due to the war. I was classified 4-F because of a perforated ear drum, so I didn't go into the service, either, like a lot of my friends. Being in a small place like Haleiwa, the draft board had to make its quota every month, so I thought I would get in. They would give the 4-F guys another exam when they needed to make their quota. Some of the guys were accepted into the service, but not me.

I wish I could have gone. If I had gone into the service, I might have continued my education when I got out. That's one of my biggest regrets.

I didn't find out until much later that some Japanese people were picked up and taken to relocation camps. I remember a man in Haleiwa--he just left one day and we didn't see him again. It never dawned on me what could have happened to him. It was long after that that I found out that he was taken to the camps.

Right after the war, my father put in a claim with the government for the loss of the farm. We lost our home, the farm house and whatever else we had there. So he put in a claim with the government for about $20,000 and asked some lawyers to help him with it. Nothing happened. After many years, I inquired about that claim. After waiting more time, we were told that somewhere along the line all the records were lost.

My father was bitter about that. He was bitter about losing the farm in the first place. I think he never did get anything for it, because he was still a Japanese citizen. If he was a U.S. citizen, he probably would have gotten something. But, in later years, he went to night school to become a citizen and to learn to speak some English. And he did it. When he died at ninety, a few years ago, he was an American citizen and proud of it. And he was still going to night school, learning to speak and write English.

My story is mostly about my father and the kind of a man he was. When he came to Hawaii in his mid-teens, he already must have had some personal goals for himself. He was always achieving something. He was a very positive man. He bounced right back and succeeded after things were bad. He lost the farm and started another career when he saw it was the thing to do. Everything he accomplished he did on his own. And, during his whole life--he worked hard--but mostly he only worked for himself. He always taught us to work hard. He also taught us the importance of a close family. Whatever successes my children and I have had, we owe it all to my father and the example he has given us.

My three children attended college. My eldest son, Kenneth, is an attorney. My second son, David, is a CPA and executive vice president at a tour company. My daughter, Suzanne, is self-employed. I have six grandchildren.

The war changed my life a lot. I would probably have gone on to college if it wasn't for the uncertainty of the war. I often thought that if

I had gone on, I probably would have taken up agriculture. Because of the war, I missed out on some of my high school activities, because I did war work and missed a lot of school.

I regret very much that we didn't have a school yearbook (paper shortage during the war). It would be nice if I could look through the annual and see the activities we had in our school years, as others do. I would like to show my children and grandchildren pictures of me as an all-around athlete and an achiever at Waialua High School. But, I think I was very fortunate. I had my sports to keep me busy and to keep me out of trouble. It was a good life when I was young, even during the rough times of the war years.

Al continued to play sports following graduation from high school. He played baseball with the Waialua and Wahiawa teams in the AJA League, and in the Hawaii Senior League with the Wanderers team. He played football in the Alumni League for the Leialums, which were graduates from Leilehua and Waialua high schools, augmented by local boys who were army all-stars stationed at Schofield Barracks. He played for a number of years on championship teams, with exhibition games on the mainland against university teams such as Portland, San Jose, Fresno, Loyola, etc. Al was also an active member in the community. He is a past member of the Wahiawa Jaycees, and organized the first Pop Warner football team in Wahiawa. He is also a past member of the Wahiawa Lions Club, organizing the first Pony Baseball League in Wahiawa. He was a backfield coach for the Leilehua High School football team in 1951 and 1952. Al did government work at Wheeler Field and Schofield Barracks, then worked for Meadow Gold Dairy for nineteen years before taking an early retirement. He worked at Wahiawa Distributors with Leo Rodby for a while, then joined a transportation company, Island Movers, Inc. as a sales representative. Al and his wife, Betty, live in Wahiawa. He works part time for Island Movers. He also helps care for his mother, along with his sisters. He enjoys golf, working in his yard, traveling, and most importantly, his grandchildren.

My Story -- Lawrence R. Rodriggs

His great-grandfather came to Hawaii from Portugal in 1878. His grandfather and father were both Honolulu-born. His mother was a Maui girl from Wailuku. Reggie Rodrigues went to Maui to court Rose Rego and they were married in October 1930. Larry was born in December 1932 and the family moved to Honolulu in 1933 where Reggie thought there was a better chance to seek employment during the Depression years. A second son, William, was born in Honolulu in 1936. In the late thirties, the family lived on 6th Avenue in Kaimuki where Larry attended Sacred Hearts Academy from the first through third grades. In the fall of 1941, at age eight, Larry entered the fourth grade at St. Louis. On December the seventh, the family lived at 1318 Wilhelmina Rise.

My father would listen to the radio every workday morning. Billy and I would be in bed, cat-napping, before the final call would come from Mom to get ready for school. Radio station KGU scheduled the morning news at 7:00 a.m, sponsored by the Shell Oil Company. Dad would be in the bathroom, shaving, and the news would start with words I've never forgotten.

> "Shell breaks the news!"
>
> (Sound effect of wireless telegraphy)
>
> "The Shell Oil Company and all island Shell dealers bring you news of the world from United Press and news in the islands from the editorial rooms of the Honolulu Advertiser."
>
> (Sound effect fades as newscaster begins reading the news)

It was a routine that we went through every weekday morning. We would then get up and get ready for school and breakfast. We would all leave in the car together. Bill and I were dropped off at Sacred Hearts and St. Louis, Mom at Kodak Hawaii on Kapiolani Boulevard and Dad would go on to the American Sanitary Laundry, where he was a delivery truck driver.

After school, Gladys Tamashiro, a teenager, would come to our house to be there when Bill and I got home. Bill took a school taxi and I usually walked. Gladys was more than a babysitter or a housekeeper. She was a friend, a playmate. She taught us to sing a few little songs in Japanese. We memorized the words by rote but never really understood what we were singing. It was fun, though, and we were proud of our "mastery" of another language.

I was "big stuff." I attended St. Louis, up on the hill in Kaimuki. We had to walk up the oval roadway to get to the school buildings. Even though the grade school was located in Henry Hall--on the right side of the campus--we would walk up the entry road on the **left** side, along with the high school students, and we felt pretty important. And, we wore white dress shirts, ties, and khaki pants. It's amazing how clothes can bolster one's ego, particularly at eight or nine years of age. It was exciting attending this all-boys school, conducted by the Marianist brothers. Brother Sam was our teacher. He was firm, but he seemed fair. I liked him.

On Sunday morning, December seventh, we were on our way to church at St. Patrick's. As we walked down our front yard to the garage--which was a carport near the road--we looked up and saw what looked like hundreds of planes going overhead, flying in a westerly direction. My father made a comment about maneuvers starting earlier than usual, and we drove down to my Aunt Cis' house, near Fort Ruger.

She seemed hysterical when we got there. She was standing on her front porch, yelling for us to come into her house for safety. She said something about Pearl Harbor being bombed by the Japanese and that my Uncle Frank, who was a naval officer, had already left to go down there. It all sounded so strange to me, but the reaction of my father and mother told me that something was terribly wrong.

Things happened rather rapidly, in my memory, from that moment on, but I recall speeding on to my Grandmother Rego's house on Kaimuki Avenue where many of our relatives were gathering. All were excited and worried. My father drove off in a hurry. I was not aware, at that time, that he was on his way to an experience that would affect him for the rest of his life.

That evening we were back home, and things were very different. My Grandmother Rodrigues was there, as was Nettie, my father's sister, and Uncle Rod, my father's brother. It got dark very early and Dad wasn't home. We didn't have any lights on, and we were warned by the adults not to touch the light switches. Mattresses were dragged into the living room and we all sat around on the floor. The radio was on, broadcasting police calls, with a blanket draped over it so that the tuner light couldn't be seen.

Grandma wanted everybody to pray with her. She held a flashlight under a blanket and read from a prayer book, reciting the Litany of the Blessed Virgin. We all were to respond, "Pray for us," to her readings. Litany prayers could be very monotonous to youngsters, particularly when the prayer leader spoke in a monotone. Although I didn't mind praying, I could think of other prayers I would have preferred. Nettie, at age sixteen, didn't seem too excited about participating, either.

" Grandma wanted everybody to pray with her. . . We all were to respond, 'Pray for us,' to her readings. "

Anyway, Grandma went on and on, "Queen of angels," and we dutifully answered, "pray for us." "Queen of all saints," etc. Toward the end of the litany, which took time when read slowly, Grandma said, "Queen of the most holy rosary," and we promptly answered, "Pray for us." Then, instead of Queen of Peace, she said, "Cream" of Peace. That was about all Nettie, Bill and I could take. We immediately snickered and snorted, holding back the laugh. Only Mom responded, "Pray for us," without a break in the cadence. Then we broke out in loud guffaws, much to the disgust of my poor grandmother. She was tired, worried, and very angry at us for being so disrespectful.

One other "Grandma story" I will never forget from those early days of the war involved another praying incident. Again, we were sitting or lying around on our mattresses on the floor, in the dark. Grandma was leading us in praying the rosary. She would begin reciting the first part of "Hail Mary" and we would complete the last few lines of the prayer in unison. She started, "Hail Mary, full of grace, the Lord is with thee. Blessed art thou among women and . . ." Instead of continuing with "blessed is the fruit of thy womb, Jesus," Grandma uttered a muffled sound, and then there was complete silence. It was very dark and we couldn't even see shadows in the room, but we could hear rustling of blankets and heavy breathing coming from Grandma's direction. Then, in a meek tone of voice, we heard, "I lost my teeth." Immediate howls of laughter came from our side of the room. It continued as we crawled around on all fours, searching between mattresses on the floor for Grandma's false teeth.

The forty-eight hours following the attack are rather blurred in my memory. Routines were all screwed up, though, I do remember. There was no school, of course, and Mom didn't go in to work. There was no Shell news in the morning--no radio, either, other than police calls--and Dad still wasn't home. It was fun sleeping on the floor and having Nettie around. I knew that Mom and Grandma were somber because we hadn't even heard from Dad, but I don't believe I realized that he could be in any danger.

Dad had been involved with a civil defense program, called the Major Disaster Council, for many months and would practice with them on Saturdays. I don't think I knew the purpose of the meetings, and Dad usually wouldn't talk about it anyway. But, we were used to him being gone on weekends, because he usually played golf. I found out later that his laundry panel truck was one of many that were designated

> " *Dad had been involved with . . . the Major Disaster Council. . . his laundry panel truck was one of many that were designated 'ambulances' in the event of an emergency.* "

"ambulances" in the event of an emergency. They fabricated metal frames that were inserted into the back of the truck so that as many as six patients, on litters, could be transported. He "lived" in that truck for the first two days of the war, operating out of Hickam Air Field. Not much more is known about his experiences at that time, as he would never talk about it. One event is very clear in my memory, however. Dad came home on Tuesday afternoon, fifty-six hours after he left at 8:30 on Sunday morning. He was just a shadow of himself. His shoulders drooped and he seemed dazed and in shock. His white shirt was all stained with dark, dried blood. Mom shrieked when she saw him walk up the long sidewalk in front of our house. Dad didn't say anything. He just shuddered, sobbed, and disappeared in his bedroom.

As days went by, Dad returned to work and things got back to some semblance of normalcy, if that was possible with martial law, blackout, and curfew. Dad seemed to sleep a lot, even on weekends. And when Bill and I would slam the door, he would let out a yelp and jump a mile. We thought that was funny, at first, and would giggle. After seeing the look of terror on his face when that happened a few times, we did our best to keep the noise level down when he was around.

School was out for a long period of time. Grandma Rodrigues and Nettie were still with us, so Mom went back to work at Kodak Hawaii, which had been taken over by the navy. Nettie often walked down to Sacred Hearts to help out, rolling bandages for the Red Cross, and there wasn't too much for Bill and me to do. So, when the Kaimuki theater opened again, we would go to see an afternoon show. Of course, there were no evening shows. No nighttime activities were allowed at all, and the military was strict about enforcing curfew regulations.

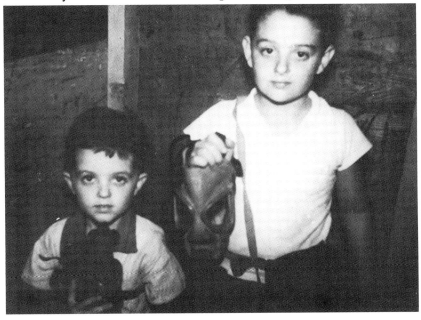

WE'RE READY! -- Author Larry Rodriggs (right, age nine), and his brother Bill, seven, display their gas masks in a drill, underground, in the family bomb shelter. (Photo courtesy of the Rodrigues family)

One day, after we got out of the theater, a large number of army tanks came rumbling up Waialae Avenue. We held our ears tightly as the deafening roar passed by. I could feel my heart pounding as Bill and I ran back home, frightened by that display of military power.

Like most people, we dutifully built a bomb shelter in our yard. It was small, with two benches facing each other, with room on each bench for two large adults. We entered through a hatch-like door and walked down about four steps underground to the wooden floor. There was a pipe vent, I recall, that helped with the ventilation, but it always seemed hot and musty down there. We would run down whenever there was an air-raid warning, and that happened frequently.

It was exciting getting our gas masks. I remember going through the "testing" routine with the mask, placing my chin in the mask first, then wrapping the head straps around the top of my head and pulling them tight. Then I would place my hand over the bottom of the canister, covering the air intake, and try to breathe. If I felt the suction around my face and couldn't breathe, then I knew that I had placed it on properly. While it was fun to practice with, it was hell to carry around everywhere I went. It was carried in a canvas bag--olive drab in color--with a shoulder strap that you'd sling across your shoulders. It was rather heavy for children to lug around. But we were instructed to carry it everywhere--even to the bathroom.

Christmas 1941 was eventful only because everything was changed. No family gatherings for evening dinners, no pine tree in our living room. We got our holiday trees from the mainland each year. But in 1941, Christmas trees were not considered a necessary item for the war effort. The only trees in Honolulu were those that arrived before December seventh, so we decorated a coconut branch. It wasn't the same. It was just a further reminder that this was wartime. Even Christmas had changed. And, my birthday was two days after Christmas. Mom would always make my day a special event, so that I wouldn't feel deprived by having a "Christmas" birthday. I remember nothing about my ninth birthday on December 27, 1941.

St. Louis School was turned over to the army and became a hospital. We were told that we would have to go to St. Patrick's School and share the classrooms there on half-day sessions. I was disappointed that we

WAR IS SERIOUS (?) BUSINESS -- Rose Rodrigues, mother of the author, provided a lighter moment for the camera during the early days of the war. Kodak Hawaii, where she worked as secretary and stenographer, was taken over by the U.S. Navy to handle the censorship and V-mail programs. She wears the cap of the commander in charge. (Photo courtesy of the Rodrigues family)

wouldn't be going back to that beautiful campus up on Kalaepohaku.[1] It was exciting, though, to know that we would finally be going back to school. This was now in late January, seven weeks after the attack.

Because Nettie and Grandma went back to their house on Liliha Street, we needed Gladys Tamashiro to come back to be with us after school. We hadn't heard from her at all since the war started and, since they didn't have a phone, Dad suggested we drive over to her place and ask her to return.

The Tamashiros lived on a chicken ranch in Kuliouou. We drove down the red dirt lane to their little house. Gladys came running out to greet us. We were so happy to see her. Her parents, though, were prostrate on the ground, face down in the dirt, sobbing and jabbering in Japanese. Gladys told us that her parents were so ashamed of what Japan did that they didn't feel worthy enough for us to see their faces. They were asking for our forgiveness, as if they had anything to do with what had happened. I never saw anything like that before in my life and was really touched by it. Anyway, we were able to get Gladys to come back and be with us after school, again.

I don't know exactly when it began, but I often had the same nightmare, early in the war years. I can recall it so vividly.

> It seems we were under attack and Dad had already left for Hickam. To get a better view of the action, I climbed up on our garage roof to see Pearl Harbor off in the distance. I remember some terrific explosions in the area and Mom yelling at me from the front porch to get down off the garage. Then, out of nowhere came this Japanese Zero right over the garage, so low that I could see the face of the pilot clearly. He was in trouble as fire and smoke poured from the plane. The deafening roar frightened me, and I heard Mom screaming in the background as the plane just about knocked me off the garage, then crashed on the hill above. I jumped off in fear and rolled a number of times along the ground.

For many years, that same scene haunted me. In fact, at some point in my life, I imagined the nightmare actually happened. A plane did crash in the mountains, not too far from where we were, and a friend gave me a piece of the wing as a souvenir. I took it to school to share

---

[1]Hawaiian word, the name of the hill on which the St. Louis campus was built, translated as "the peaceful rock."

with my classmates. I think having that souvenir supported my imagination, helping my subconscious to verify that the garage incident actually happened.

In 1942, many people were evacuated to the mainland. I heard my folks talking about that possibility but I didn't take it too seriously. Then, one evening, Bill and I were told that we were going to California, as soon as we could make the arrangements. But Dad couldn't go because they needed every able-bodied man to remain in the islands in case they needed to be defended again.

Toward the end of the school year, we were told that we should be ready to leave when the call came. I remember Mom came to my classroom one day and brought Billy with her. Because she worked at Kodak, she had access to film. It was difficult to get film in Honolulu during the war. Anyway, she came to school to take a picture of my class for our scrapbook, as we didn't know if we would ever be back in Hawaii. As it happened, we did finish out the school year before the call came to leave.

It wasn't easy leaving Dad, home, relatives, and classmates to go to "the mainland," a place I knew nothing about. But we did, in early summer 1942.

FOURTH GRADE -- Class 4B of St. Louis looks at the "birdie" in this May 1942 photo. As their campus became an army hospital, the class shared the room at St. Patrick's School, attending the morning session. Author Larry Rodrigues is in front, left, sitting next to his younger brother, Bill, who was visiting the classroom. (Photo courtesy of the Rodrigues family)

We were on a very large transport, the *USS Grant*, I believe it was called. We were the lead ship in a convoy of eleven vessels. Navy destroyers patrolled our flanks and rear. We were the only armed transport. It was a very rough trip and many people were seasick. We had a small, cramped room, way below deck. Each morning, at four o'clock, we were awakened by an alarm and ordered to report to our life boat stations with our life vests on. As it was very dark in the ship-- blackout was strictly enforced--we had to grope our way, bumping into other passengers, up the many flights of stairs to the main deck.

I felt responsible for my mother and little brother. So, during the daytime, when I was certain no one was looking, I carved notches in the wooden railings, marking the way to our lifeboat station. So it was a game I played at four in the morning, guiding my family through the dark and crowded stairwells, until we finally reached our appointed spot. I was proud of the accomplishment.

Then we would sit on the deck, or in the lifeboat, wrapped up in blankets, until the "all clear" alarm sounded at 7:00 a.m. The theory was that if a submarine attacked, it would normally be during those early morning hours. Bill had no trouble going back to sleep in Mom's lap. I would sit in the cold air and let my imagination go wild. One morning, we got the scare of our lives when a submarine was actually discovered. The ship came alive, with navy men running here and there, when the alarm sounded "general quarters." It was just light enough to see, and those destroyer escorts were circling around and dropping depth charges. It was exciting, but nothing untoward occurred.

> *" . . . we got the scare of our lives when a submarine was actually discovered. The ship came alive with navy men running here and there . . . "*

Each afternoon, they would bring out Japanese prisoners of war to walk the decks down near the bow. We could see them from the deck above--a sorry looking lot they were. Their heads were shaven and they were chained, one to the other. On one occasion, as they were getting their exercise, one of them got loose and jumped overboard. I didn't actually see it happen, but the ship came alive with the "man overboard" emergency. Ships in the entire convoy came to a complete stop and the destroyers circled around again, among the various ships of the convoy. After not too long a period of time, the "all clear" sounded and we learned that the prisoner had been picked up. I was impressed by the alertness and effectiveness of the emergency procedures. It took us nine days to reach California.

In San Francisco, we were met by my dad's Aunt Emily and Uncle Tony. They brought with them Aunt Irene and her two children, Colin and Ann, who had evacuated from Honolulu earlier in the year. We all stayed together for a number of months in San Leandro, until the dads could get away from the islands and join us. Bill and I were enrolled in St. Mary's school at St. Leander's parish in San Leandro. I was in the fifth grade and Bill in the second.

I was somewhat of a celebrity in school, having come from the "Pearl Harbor action." It was amazing how so many of my classmates in California felt that Honolulu was nothing more than a village of thatched huts with girls wandering around in grass skirts and bare tops. Initially, I don't think I did much to discourage their opinions. In fact, I remember rather embellishing it. I particularly remember one of my classmates in the fifth grade, Benjamin Long, who was originally from Guam. His father went down with the *Arizona* on December 7, 1941, and I learned to be thankful that while my father was in the area, too, during the attack, he was still alive--even though he couldn't be with us.

He was able to join us in California, though, in 1943. So we were a family once again, only this time in California. Both Mom and Dad worked in defense jobs in a supply depot nearby.

In 1944, my Grandpa Rego, who was now living in Waikiki, became ill and Mom started talking about moving back to the islands. In fact, many kamaainas[2] were returning to Hawaii about that time, since the likelihood of an another attack or an invasion seemed remote.

We sailed back in early 1945 aboard the *SS Phillippa*, but this time we were all together, so it was much more pleasurable. And we were returning to the land of our birth. My dad was usually the life of any party, and often entertained with his ukulele, singing and dancing. He led the community-sing program on the *Phillippa* every evening and even

---

[2]*Hawaiian word for native-born.*

though the trip took eleven days, it went rather quickly.

We lived at Grandma Rego's house in Waikiki, on Prince Edward Street near Kaiulani. The Fullard-Leo family lived right next door to us on the corner. Ainsley was a few years older than me, in high school at Punahou, but we got to be friends. I enrolled in the last few months of my seventh grade at St. Augustine's School in Waikiki.

In spite of the thousands of people wearing khaki and whites that were everywhere in Waikiki, it was very pleasant there. I do remember, however, climbing up on that big banyan tree at Kuhio Beach Park to watch the local boys and the sailors fight over the girls. And we played pee-wee golf often at the little course on Kalakaua, right off of Kaiulani. Of course, we spent every afternoon after school at the beach, swimming and surfing. The Moana Hotel had little white cottages across Kalakaua from the hotel entrance, and we also enjoyed swinging on the banyan tree in the middle of the beautifully-groomed grounds. Waikiki was a wonderful place to live as a kid in those days.

I delivered the **Honolulu Advertiser**--getting up before dawn each morning--riding my bicycle all around Waikiki on my route. It was

THE WAR IS OVER! — *Sailors and civilians whoop it up on VJ Day, August 14, 1945, the day Japan surrendered. This photograph was taken by twelve-year-old Larry Rodrigues with his Kodak Brownie camera on Kalakaua and Uluniu in Waikiki.* (Photo courtesy of the Rodrigues family)

a hand-me-down bike I got from my father's cousin, Charlie Brown, and was over twenty-five years old, but I painted it to look like new.

I will never forget August 14, 1945. At long last, the war was really over. People went wild in Waikiki. I ran down in front of the drug store at Kalakaua and Uluniu to watch the parade of revelers go by. People just jumped on passing cars and waved and screamed at everyone watching them. There was a lot of kissing around me as local girls ran up to servicemen and wrapped their arms around them. The war with Japan was finally over, bringing World War II to a close.

I may have been just a child during those war years, but those memories--good and bad--will be with me until I die. I only wish I'd tried a little harder to get my father's story. I might have pried it out of him. It would have been the best story in this book.

Larry graduated from St. Augustine's eighth grade class in June 1946 and returned to St. Louis for his high school years, graduating in 1950. After a brief stay in Los Angeles at Woodbury College, he returned to the islands and joined the Naval Reserve, working at Pearl Harbor in the Industrial Relations Office. He lived at home in Waimanalo at the time. He completed eight years in the reserves, including active duty, and attended San Jose State in California, where he received a degree in Public Relations in 1958. He worked for Blue Cross of California in public relations for over thirty years. In 1959, Larry married Betty Jean Nigro, an education major at San Jose. Prior to their marriage, Larry anglicized the spelling of his name, changing it from Rodrigues to Rodriggs. They have two sons, Steven Lawrence, born in 1962, and Michael Allen, born in 1964. Jean teaches school in the Newark Unified School District. In 1986, Steven married Mary Ann Burke (whose father, John, was a seventh-grade classmate of Larry's in San Leandro in 1944). Steve is a graduate of Santa Clara University and an engineer at Lockheed. Michael, also an engineering graduate of Santa Clara, works for NASA in Houston, Texas. Larry and Jean's first grandchild, Patrick Steven Rodriggs, was born in January 1990. Grandchild number two is expected in January 1992.

List of Illustrations

Index

417

About the Author

Lawrence R. Rodriggs is a third generation-born Hawaiian of Portuguese ancestry. This book is dedicated to his father, a truck driver in Honolulu for the American Sanitary Laundry, who would never talk about his experiences as a civil defense volunteer at Hickam Field on December 7, 1941. "Larry" Rodriggs is a 1950 graduate of St. Louis College (high school) in Honolulu. He worked two years at Pearl Harbor and following a short stint of duty with the Naval Reserve, attended San Jose State University, earning a degree in Public Relations in 1958. Following graduation, he worked for Blue Cross of California, retiring in 1989 after more than thirty years of service. He has served as president of the Advertising and Marketing Association (Oakland, California) and the Public Relations Society of America (Oakland Chapter). Larry started this book in 1988, then taught public relations and advertising courses at the University of Pacific in Stockton, California, for the 1989-1990 school year. In 1990, he began working full-time on researching, interviewing, and writing this book. He is married and lives in Newark, California. He owns his own writing, editing and publishing business, Communications Concepts.